OULIPO COMPENDIUM

Edited by Harry Mathews & Alastair Brotchie

With additional sections devoted to

OULIPOPO edited by Alastair Brotchie, Paul Gayot & Francis Debyser

OUPEINPO edited by Thieri Foulc

and with accounts of the OU-X-POs by their members

OULIPO COMPENDIUM

Revised and Updated

ATLAS PRESS, LONDON

MAKE NOW PRESS, LOS ANGELES

Published in the UK by Atlas Press and in the USA by Make Now Press.

Atlas Press, 27 Old Gloucester st.,

London WC1N 3XX

Make Now Press, 8152 Coldwater Canyon,

North Hollywood, CA. 91605

©1998 & 2005, Atlas Press

Text and picture permissions are listed on p.10

Translations ©1998, Atlas Press and the translators.

Printed by Athenaeum Press, Gateshead.

A CIP record for this book is available from the British Library.

Atlas Press ISBN 1 900565 18 8

Make Now Press ISBN 0 9743554 3 7

This book was supported by the Arts Council of England,

the French Ministry for Foreign Affairs, as part of the Burgess Programme,

representing the French Embassy in London at the Institut Français du Royaume-Uni,

and by a grant from the Cookie Jar Fund.

Our thanks also to the Institute for Figuring.

CONTENTS

WORKS LISTED BY INDIVIDUAL AUTHOR

I. DIRECTIONS FOR USE

THE BODY of the *Oulipo Compendium* consists of an alphabetical listing of procedures, definitions, and individuals associated with the Oulipo and two related groups: the Oulipopo and the Oupeinpo, and — more briefly — with similar groups working in other domains. (We deliberately avoided a didactic approach as being both condescending and reductive.) The entries, and cross-references to entries are indicated by a solid bullet: a ● indicates a reference to the Oulipo (section III); a ▲ to the Oulipopo (section IV); a ■ to the Oupeinpo (section V); a ★ to section VI, covering the Ou-x-pos in general.

Theoretical texts and entries are set in two columns in sanserif type. Examples illustrating definitions are set in serif type; longer, more literary examples are also in serif type but of a larger size and usually in one column. These examples are indicated by a hollow version of the section's bullet (e.g. ○ for Oulipian texts) and are listed separately in the table of contents.

"CP" stands for the entries found under "Collective Publications" (most of which are illustrated on the cover), ●BO refers to the entries for the *Bibliothèque Oulipienne*, ▲BO to the *Bibliothèque Oulipopienne*, ■BO to the *Bibliothèque Oupeinpienne*, etc.

For readers coming to the subject for the first time, we recommend starting at the entry for ●Oulipo.

THE EDITORS are jointly responsible for uncredited entries in the *Compendium*. When entries are the work of a single author or translator, their names are indicated by initials in brakets following the text:

AB = Alastair Brotchie, AH = Andrew Hugill, BC = Bernard Cerquiglini, CB = Claude Berge, EW = Enrique Walker, FC = François Caradec, FD = Francis Debyser, FLL = François Le Lionnais, HLT = Hervé Le Tellier, HM = Harry Mathews, IM = Ian Monk, IW = Iain White, JB = Jacques Bens, JC = Jacques Carelman, JD = Jean Dewasne, JJ = Jacques Jouet, JR = Jacques Roubaud, JV = Jack Vanarsky, LE = Luc Étienne, MB = Marcel Bénabou, MG = Michelle Grangaud, NA = Noël Arnaud, OP = Oskar Pastior, PB = Paul Braffort, PE = Paul Edwards, PG = Paul Gayot, PR = Pierre Rosenstiehl, SC = Stanley Chapman, TB = Tristan Bastit, TF = Thieri Foulc, TG = Thierry Groensteen, WM = Warren Motte.

EDITORIAL NOTE. Where the Oulipo is concerned, almost nothing but the published material of the original Paris-based group has been considered; the principal exceptions to this are authors who have composed Oulipian works in English, and two of the ●Minutes of the Oulipo (3 & 4). The entries for the Oulipopo and Oubapo are similarly based on the publications of those groups; those for the Oupeinpo were mostly written especially for this book.

The *Compendium* originally appeared in the Atlas Press Arkhive series in 1998 (unlike previous Arkhives, it was an original book and not a re-publication). In this second edition we have updated the factual parts (such as membership and bibliographies) without modifying the literary contents. In addition, where the English name of an Oulipian procedure is not simply a replica of the French, the French terms have been assigned their own entries, duly cross-referenced.

ACKNOWLEDGEMENTS. Many members of the Oulipo deserve thanks for their help in completing this work. In some cases the appearance of a member's name at the end of an entry acknowledges his or her essential participation. The editors are especially and generally grateful to Michelle Grangaud, Jacques Jouet, and Jacques Roubaud for the time they contributed. Above all, the group's (then) president Noël Arnaud, and Marcel Bénabou, the group's definitively provisional secretary, showed extraordinary patience in recovering precious items from the depths of their archives as well as from their vast store of Oulipian knowledge.

Lynn Crawford deserves special thanks (see ●*New Observations*), as do Paul Gayot, Thieri Foulc, and Francis Debyser, whose contributions were essential to the compiling of the Oulipopo and Oupeinpo sections. Our thanks also to Charlotte Carratu, Pat Willetts, Peter Davidson, John N. Henderson, Andrew Hugill, Steve Sanderson, David Bramley, Jasia Reichardt, and Trevor Winkfield. Atlas Press also wishes to offer profuse thanks to Tim Norman for his painstaking work in incorporating the revisions into this second edition.

Finally, the editors would like to acknowledge their immense debt to Chris Allen, whose emendations in conjunction with his rigorous editing and proofreading have been essential in giving both versions of the *Compendium* their definitive form.

II. PROLOGUE

Quand l'un avecque l'autre aussitôt sympathise

se faire il pourrait bien que ce soit des jumeaux

la découverte alors voilà qui traumatise

on espère toujours être de vrais normaux

Et pourtant c'était lui le frère de feintise

qui clochard devenant jetait ses oripeaux

un frère même bas est la part indécise

que les parents féconds offrent aux purs berceaux

Le généalogiste observe leur bouillotte

gratter le parchemin deviendra sa marotte

il voudra retrouver le germe adultérin

Frère je te comprends si parfois tu débloques

frère je t'absoudrai si tu m'emberlucoques

la gémellité vraie accuse son destin

A Hundred Thousand Billion Poems, hereafter referred to in its numerical form as ●*100,000,000,000,000 Poems*, consists of a sequence of 10 14-line ●sonnets by Raymond Queneau. Its composition was perhaps inspired by the children's game *Heads, bodies, legs*: just as in that game body parts from each section can be interchanged, so any line in any one of these sonnets can replace the corresponding line in any other sonnet. (The rhyme scheme of the sonnets is uniform; grammatical correctness is assured no matter what sequence of lines occurs.)

The consequences of this interchangeability are not hard to see.

Start with the first line taken in isolation: there are, obviously, 10 alternatives or possibilities for it. When we now add a line, we know that each of the 10 first lines can be followed by any of the 10 second lines: this gives us 10 x 10 = 100 (or 10^2) possible combinations of two lines. Each of these combinations of two lines can in turn be followed by any one of the 10 third lines, a step that will produce 10 x 100 = 1,000 (or 10^3) possible combinations of *three* lines. In similar fashion, every additional line raises the number of possible combinations by a factor of 10 until, with the 14th line, we attain 10^{14} possible combinations of fourteen lines, a number that can be variously written as 100 billion (UK), 100,000 billion (US), or 100 million million — a very large number however you write it. Queneau calculated that someone reading the book 24 hours a day would need 190,258,751 years to finish it.

In the original edition, the sonnets are printed on the recto side of successive pages. Each page is cut into fourteen strips, with a sonnet line on each strip. Lifting a strip at any stage will reveal a corresponding line (rhyming, as it were, three-dimensionally), so that a reader using a ruler can assemble a complete new sonnet by combining lines from 2 to 10 of the poems at his disposal. In our edition, we have left readers with the option of making the 140 strips by cutting along the dotted lines from the outside edge of each page.

While Queneau was completing the work, he asked François Le Lionnais for advice with problems he was having. Their discussions led to a wider consideration of the role of mathematics in literature and, eventually, to the creation of the Oulipo.

Stanley Chapman's translation (which follows) was received by the author with "admiring stupefaction."

See ●Machines for reading.

Don Pedro from his shirt has washed the fleas

✂ ··

The bull's horns ought to dry it like a bone

✂ ··

Old corned-beef's rusty armour spreads disease

✂ ··

That suede ferments is not at all well known

✂ ··

To one sweet hour of bliss my memory clings

✂ ··

Signalling gauchos very rarely shave

✂ ··

An icicle of frozen marrow pings

✂ ··

As sleeping-bags the silent landscape pave

✂ ··

Staunch pilgrims longest journeys can't depress

✂ ··

What things we did we went the whole darned hog

✂ ··

And played their mountain croquet jungle chess

✂ ··

Southern baroque's seductive dialogue

✂ ··

Suits lisping Spanish tongues for whom say some

✂ ··

The bell tolls fee-less fi-less fo-less fum

The wild horse champs the Parthenon's top frieze

Since Elgin left his nostrils in the stone

The Turks said just take anything you please

And loudly sang off-key without a tone

O Parthenon you hold the charger's strings

The North Wind bites into his architrave

Th'outrageous Thames a troubled arrow slings

To break a rule Britannia's might might waive

Platonic Greece was not so talentless

A piercing wit would sprightliest horses flog

Socrates watched his hemlock effervesce

Their sculptors did *our* best our hulks they clog

With marble souvenirs then fill a slum

For Europe's glory while Fate's harpies strum

At snuff no Cornish sailorman would sneeze

✂ ....

His nasal ecstasy beats best Cologne

✂ ....

Upon his old oak chest he cuts his cheese

✂ ....

With cherry-pips his cottage floor is sown

✂ ....

The Frisian Isles my friends are cherished things

✂ ....

Whose ocean still-born herrings madly brave

✂ ....

Such merchandise a melancholy brings

✂ ....

For burning bushes never fish forgave

✂ ....

When dried the terrapin can naught express

✂ ....

Shallots and sharks' fins face the smould'ring log

✂ ....

While homeward thirsts to each quenched glass say yes

✂ ....

Lobsters for sale must be our apologue

✂ ....

On fish-slab whale nor seal has never swum

✂ ....

They're kings we're mammal-cousins hi ho hum

At five precisely out went La Marquise

✂ ....

For tea cucumber sandwiches a scone

✂ ....

Her native chauffeur waited in the breeze

✂ ....

Which neither time nor tide can long postpone

✂ ....

How it surprised us pale grey underlings

✂ ....

When flame a form to wrath ancestral gave

✂ ....

A daring baron pockets precious Mings

✂ ....

Till firemen come with hose-piped tidal wave

✂ ....

The fasting fakir doesn't smell the less

✂ ....

In Indian summers Englishmen drink grog

✂ ....

The colonel's still escutcheoned in undress

✂ ....

No need to cart such treasures from the fog

✂ ....

The Taj Mahal has trinkets spice and gum

✂ ....

And lessors' dates have all too short a sum

From playboy Chance the nymph no longer flees

✂ ....

Through snobbish growing round her hemline zone

✂ ....

His toga rumpled high above his knees

✂ ....

One gathers rosebuds or grows old alone

✂ ....

Old Galileo's Pisan offerings

✂ ....

Were pots graffiti'd over by a slave

✂ ....

The leaning linguist cameramaniac sings

✂ ....

Etruscan words which Greece and Rome engrave

✂ ....

Emboggled minds may puff and blow and guess

✂ ....

With gravity at gravity's great cog

✂ ....

On wheels the tourist follows his hostess

✂ ....

With breaking voice across the Alps they slog

✂ ....

Do bank clerks rule their abacus by thumb?

✂ ....

In cognac brandy is Bacardi rum?

He bent right down to pick up his valise

✂ ....

That hordes of crooks felt they'd more right to own

✂ ....

He bent right down and well what did he seize

✂ ....

The thumb- and finger-prints of Al Capone

✂ ....

Oh how oh how he hates such pilferings

✂ ....

Filching the lolly country thrift helped save

✂ ....

He's gone to London how the echo rings

✂ ....

Through homestead hillside woodland rock and cave

✂ ....

The peasant's skirts on rainy days she'd tress

✂ ....

And starve the snivelling baby like a dog

✂ ....

Watching manure and compost coalesce

✂ ....

One misses cricket hearth and croaking frog

✂ ....

Where no one bothered how one warmed one's bum

✂ ....

Yet from the City's pie pulled not one plum

When one with t'other straightaway agrees

✂ ....

The answer is they could be twins full-grown

✂ ....

Replies like this the dumbstruck brain may tease

✂ ....

Normal one aims to be *and* share the throne

✂ ....

And yet 'twas he the beggar Fate just flings

✂ ....

Rejecting ermine to become a knave

✂ ....

The fertile mother changelings drops like kings

✂ ....

In purest cradles tha's how they behave

✂ ....

The genealogist with field and fess

✂ ....

With quill white-collared through his life will jog

✂ ....

To prove mamma an adult with a tress

✂ ....

But *I* can understand you Brother Gog

✂ ....

And let you off from your opinions glum

✂ ....

A wise loaf always knows its humblest crumb

Prose took the minstrel's verse without a squeeze

His exaltation shocked both youth and crone

The understanding critic firstly sees

'Ere meanings new to ancient tribes are thrown

They both are right not untamed mutterings

That metred rhyme alone can souls enslave

They both are right not unformed smatterings

That every verbal shock aims to deprave

Poetic licence needs no strain or stress

One tongue will do to keep the verse agog

From cool Parnassus down to wild Loch Ness

Bard I adore your endless monologue

Ventriloquists be blowed *you* strike me dumb

Soliloquies predict great things old chum

The acid tongue with gourmet's expertise

✂ ⋯⋯⋯⋯⋯⋯⋯⋯⋯⋯⋯⋯⋯⋯⋯⋯⋯⋯⋯⋯⋯⋯⋯⋯⋯⋯⋯⋯⋯⋯⋯⋯

Licks round carved marble chops on snails full-blown

✂ ⋯⋯⋯⋯⋯⋯⋯⋯⋯⋯⋯⋯⋯⋯⋯⋯⋯⋯⋯⋯⋯⋯⋯⋯⋯⋯⋯⋯⋯⋯⋯⋯

The showman gargles fire and sword with ease

✂ ⋯⋯⋯⋯⋯⋯⋯⋯⋯⋯⋯⋯⋯⋯⋯⋯⋯⋯⋯⋯⋯⋯⋯⋯⋯⋯⋯⋯⋯⋯⋯⋯

While sharks to let's say potted shrimps are prone

✂ ⋯⋯⋯⋯⋯⋯⋯⋯⋯⋯⋯⋯⋯⋯⋯⋯⋯⋯⋯⋯⋯⋯⋯⋯⋯⋯⋯⋯⋯⋯⋯⋯

The roundabout eats profits made on swings

✂ ⋯⋯⋯⋯⋯⋯⋯⋯⋯⋯⋯⋯⋯⋯⋯⋯⋯⋯⋯⋯⋯⋯⋯⋯⋯⋯⋯⋯⋯⋯⋯⋯

Nought can the mouse's timid nibbling stave

✂ ⋯⋯⋯⋯⋯⋯⋯⋯⋯⋯⋯⋯⋯⋯⋯⋯⋯⋯⋯⋯⋯⋯⋯⋯⋯⋯⋯⋯⋯⋯⋯⋯

In salads all chew grubs before they've wings

✂ ⋯⋯⋯⋯⋯⋯⋯⋯⋯⋯⋯⋯⋯⋯⋯⋯⋯⋯⋯⋯⋯⋯⋯⋯⋯⋯⋯⋯⋯⋯⋯⋯

The nicest kids for stickiest toffees crave

✂ ⋯⋯⋯⋯⋯⋯⋯⋯⋯⋯⋯⋯⋯⋯⋯⋯⋯⋯⋯⋯⋯⋯⋯⋯⋯⋯⋯⋯⋯⋯⋯⋯

The wolf devours both sheep and shepherdess

✂ ⋯⋯⋯⋯⋯⋯⋯⋯⋯⋯⋯⋯⋯⋯⋯⋯⋯⋯⋯⋯⋯⋯⋯⋯⋯⋯⋯⋯⋯⋯⋯⋯

A bird-brain banquet melts bold Mistress Mog

✂ ⋯⋯⋯⋯⋯⋯⋯⋯⋯⋯⋯⋯⋯⋯⋯⋯⋯⋯⋯⋯⋯⋯⋯⋯⋯⋯⋯⋯⋯⋯⋯⋯

The country lane just thrives on farmyard mess

✂ ⋯⋯⋯⋯⋯⋯⋯⋯⋯⋯⋯⋯⋯⋯⋯⋯⋯⋯⋯⋯⋯⋯⋯⋯⋯⋯⋯⋯⋯⋯⋯⋯

Whiskey will always wake an Irish bog

✂ ⋯⋯⋯⋯⋯⋯⋯⋯⋯⋯⋯⋯⋯⋯⋯⋯⋯⋯⋯⋯⋯⋯⋯⋯⋯⋯⋯⋯⋯⋯⋯⋯

Though bretzels take the dols from board-room drum

✂ ⋯⋯⋯⋯⋯⋯⋯⋯⋯⋯⋯⋯⋯⋯⋯⋯⋯⋯⋯⋯⋯⋯⋯⋯⋯⋯⋯⋯⋯⋯⋯⋯

Fried grilled black pudding's still the world's best yum

The marble tomb gapes wide with jangling keys

✂ ··

When masons clutch the breath we held on loan

✂ ··

Forms shadowy with indecision wheeze

✂ ··

And empty cages show life's bird has flown

✂ ··

It's one of many horrid happenings

✂ ··

With sombre thoughts they grimly line the nave

✂ ··

Proud death quite il-le-gi-ti-mate-ly stings

✂ ··

Victorious worms grind all into the grave

✂ ··

It's no good rich men crying Heaven Bless

✂ ··

Or grinning like a pale-faced golliwog

✂ ··

Poor Yorick comes to bury not address

✂ ··

We'll suffocate before the epilogue

✂ ··

Poor reader smile before your lips go numb

✂ ··

The best of all things to an end must come

III. OULIPO

●*Introduction* Jacques Roubaud
***The Oulipo and Combinatorial Art* (1991)**

1. Speaking about the Oulipo here in the heart of Catalonia[1] requires at the outset an homage to one of the fathers of the "Oulipian" conception of literature: Ramon ●Llull. Consider this done.

2. When, during the summer of 1960, they conceived the Plan of what was to become — after an altogether necessary phase of denomination and the passing of several years

3. (the name having undergone a metamorphosis in four stages:

a) as an initial, inaugural name: *Ouvroir de Littérature Potentielle* which became

b) an abbreviation: OU.LI.PO.

c) then a proper name: OULIPO, at last becoming

d) a true noun in its own right, that is, a substantive admitting of an adjective (*oulipien*) and of transferences and transformations in other tongues, American English having created the noun "Oulipism" (if I say American English it is because England has thus far proved recalcitrant to the Oulipo), German the adjective *oulipisch*, and Italian a derivative group, the ●Oplepo, the original name being here reduced to an etymological origin of what needs to be glossed only in order to explain its genesis), —

4. when, therefore, they founded the Oulipo, François Le Lionnais and Raymond Queneau had no inkling (but were they perhaps secretly convinced?) that they were creating a new literary group that thirty years later, long after their death, would still be in existence. Before considering its properly conceptual and topical aspect, it is worth underscoring some of the original features of their undertaking.

5. In the first place let me remark on its *longevity*. It started in 1960 and is still flourishing. This is an altogether exceptional phenomenon in French literary history (I am not sure how things happen elsewhere) and in it I discern a first originality that I "deduce" as follows:

6. The history of literature in our country has, at least since the Renaissance, been remarkable for the peculiar way it functions. Periodically, generation after generation, *literary groups* appear (or are invented after the fact by literary historians) that share the following characteristics (which I shall quickly and summarily describe):

a) The groups are formed with a view to renewing and re-establishing a literature that has, according to them, deteriorated to an appallingly low level.

b) Their motto is: everything done prior to us is worthless; everything done after us can only exist because of us. (Anything good in the past is only a prefiguration of what the group is planning to do. What the group proposes defines what will be good in the future.)

c) The groups are organised by divisions into ranks: there are one or more leaders, designated successors, and "second fiddles".

d) The group thoroughly despises all its contemporaries, particularly the rival groups to which the fact of its existence and the claims it makes inevitably give rise.

e) The very way the group works leads, through splits, divergences, "deviations", and exclusions, to its fairly rapid destruction.

f) During its generally brief life, the group, surrounded by enemies, develops earmarks typical of a sect, a mafia, a gang, or, more modestly, a mutual admiration society. I shall cite only a few examples: the Pléiade, the Classicists, the Romanticists, the Surrealists, and, closer to us but today quite forgotten, the Tel Quel group.

7. Obviously, for historical reasons, it was the Surrealist group that acted as foil to the Oulipo. Raymond Queneau had in fact been a Surrealist; and he had, as we know, taken violent leave of the Bretonian sect. It was unquestionably as a result of his reflections on this unfortunate example that he "invented" the following rules, original, if few in number. To simplify matters I have attributed to Queneau decisions taken in common by both founders. Farther on I shall point out what seems to be François Le Lionnais's particular contribution to the elaboration of the

object named "Oulipo".

8. a) The Oulipo is not a closed group; it can be enlarged through the co-optation of new members.

b) No one can be expelled from the Oulipo.

c) Conversely (you can't have something for nothing), no one can resign from the Oulipo or stop belonging to it.

d) It follows that, once a member of the Oulipo, always a member. This has particular implications:

d´) The dead continue to belong to the Oulipo. (Such as: Luc Étienne, co-author of *La Méthode à Mimile* and inventor of the ●phonetic palindrome; Latis, that stern Pataphysician; Albert-Marie Schmidt, erudite specialist of sixteenth-century literature; Marcel Duchamp, painter, inventor of Rrose Sélavy.)

9. e) Lest the last rule seem unduly coercive, an exception to (d) was provided. One may relinquish membership of the Oulipo under the following circumstances: suicide may be committed in the presence of an officer of the court, who then ascertains that, according to the Oulipian's explicit last wishes, his suicide was intended to release him from the Oulipo and restore his freedom of manœuvre for the rest of eternity.

10. Plainly these rules, applied ever since the foundation of the Oulipo, radically distinguish it from, say, the Surrealist group.

11. To grasp the second radical originality of the Oulipo fully, we must leave the field of Literature and turn to Mathematics.

12. It so happened that shortly after the creation of Surrealism, France witnessed the birth — this time in the domain of mathematics — of another avant-garde group called ●Bourbaki. There can be no doubt that, when they founded the Oulipo, Queneau and Le Lionnais, amateur mathematicians that they were, had this group in mind.

13. *When the Oulipo was conceived, Bourbaki provided a counter-model to the Surrealist group.*

14. We can also say that the Oulipo is an homage to Bourbaki and an imitation of Bourbaki.

15. At the same time, it is no less obviously a parody of Bourbaki, even a profanation of Bourbaki.

16. Bourbaki's initial plan — to rewrite Mathematics in its

entirety and provide it with solid foundations using a single source, Set Theory, and a rigorous system, the Axiomatic Method — is at once serious, admirable, imperialistic, sectarian, megalomaniac, and pretentious. (Humour has not been one of its prime characteristics.)

17. The Oulipo's plan, which "translates" Bourbaki's objectives and method into the domain of the arts of language, is no less serious and ambitious, but it is non-sectarian and not convinced of the validity of its proceedings to the exclusion of all other approaches.

18. I shall not pursue the comparison of the two groups any further (I shall of course later return to the question of "method"). Let me simply emphasise the following point: Bourbaki was a secret group; even if the secret soon became an open one, it is none the less essential to take note of this characteristic which, whatever the intentions of its founders, encouraged its transformation into a sect and organisation that aimed at taking over established institutions. In its first years, the Oulipo was also a semi-clandestine group. Queneau cannot be too highly congratulated for having fairly rapidly given up this restriction, which could hardly have failed to produce the same kind of consequences.

19. I can now state the Oulipo's second original trait, which stems from its choice of a model: the group is not an exclusively literary one. More precisely, the Oulipo is a literary group composed of four sorts of members:

(i) the first sort are composers of literature (prose, poetry, criticism) who are not mathematicians;

(ii) the second sort are mathematicians who are not composers of literature; the members of type

(iii) are composers of literature *and* mathematicians; those of type

(iv) are mathematicians *and* composers of literature.

(Types (iii) and (iv) are distinct, "*and*" being used here to signify a hierarchic sequence: "and" = "and secondarily" or, additively, "and also".)

20. The Oulipo is thus first and foremost a group. What are its aims and what does it do?

21. The aim of the Oulipo is to invent (or reinvent)

restrictions of a formal nature (●*contraintes*) and propose them to enthusiasts interested in composing literature.

22. An initial misunderstanding can thus be eliminated at once: *as a group*, the Oulipo does not count the creation of literary works among its primary aims. Whatever its other merits, a literary work that deserves to be called Oulipian may have been written by a member of the Oulipo, but it may have been written by a non-member of the Oulipo.

23. It follows that truly Oulipian publications (those published in its name) do not necessarily lay claim to the title of literary works. (Whence certain critical misunderstandings, not always innocent.)

24. Some bibliographical information: the Oulipo has essentially published under its own name two "theoretical" volumes, both brought out in Paris by Éditions Gallimard: *La Littérature potentielle* (1973) [*Lipo*, ●CP3] and the *Atlas de littérature potentielle* (1981) [*Atlas*, ●CP6].

25. It has published and continues to publish under its auspices a series of (short) fascicles in limited editions (150 copies); these contain works either composed individually by members of the Oulipo or written in collaboration: they constitute the ●Bibliothèque Oulipienne. (The first 52 fascicles have been collected in three volumes, published by Éditions Seghers.)

26. A third characteristic of the Oulipo thus becomes manifest (not altogether an original one; we find it, applied in different ways, in the Surrealist group as well as in Bourbaki): *the Oulipo's work is collaborative.*

27. The Oulipo is bound by rule to meet once a month (this has been true since it was founded: the January 1993 meeting will be its 387th). At each meeting a strict and immutable agenda is followed, one necessarily including the item "Creation", that is, the presentation and discussion of new constraints.

28. The Oulipo's work is collaborative, and its products — proposed constraints and their illustrations — are attributed to the group, even if certain constraints are invented by individuals:

Perhaps the best known and least understood constraint, ●N + 7, is the work of the poet Jean Lescure;

the ●Prisoner's Restriction is that of one of the Oulipo's two secretaries, Paul Fournel, short-story writer, cyclist, and publisher (the Oulipo has two secretaries, a *provisionally definitive secretary* and a *definitively provisional secretary*; our second secretary is Marcel Bénabou, the distinguished historian of *La Résistance africaine à la romanisation* and our specialist in "●precooked language");

the ●Line-Stretcher's Restriction (*le tireur à la ligne*) is the work of the novelist Jacques Bens, who is also the author of a book (published by Christian Bourgois) in which he has collected the minutes of the Oulipo's meetings during the first years of its existence.

Let me at this point complete my "positioning" of the word "Oulipo" in relation to its two cousins, "Surrealism" and "Bourbaki". It appears to occupy an original place between the two. "Surrealism" both as a noun and as an idea (and quite aside from the pejorative and altogether abject use made by journalists in France — and at least in England as well — of the adjective "surrealist") has definitively supplanted the group. "Bourbakism", on the other hand, is a word dominated by its precise reference to the group. Whereas the Oulipo, identifiable as a literary group, and "Oulipo" as a way of thinking about and practising literature are in almost perfect balance.

29. A third characteristic the three groups share is *potential universality*. The mathematics of Bourbaki, even if certain of their aspects are attributed (whether to praise or belittle them) to a certain "French genius", are clearly not limited to a single land or tongue. The same is true of Surrealism. But the practice of writing by constraints is conceivable — even if certain constraints cannot be everywhere generalised — in all languages. This fact constitutes a powerful "attractive force" that has here and there been recognised. (It is one of the chief reasons for the hypothesis — with which I agree — that "oulipism" will in future extend beyond the Oulipo.) The group counts among its members an American, the novelist and poet Harry Mathews; an Italian, Italo Calvino; a Provençal, myself. Ross Chambers and Stanley Chapman are respectively Australian and English; Jacques Duchateau, novelist and radio producer, is Swiss. So it can already be claimed that the Oulipo has manifested its vocation for universality and has not been limited

to the region bound by what Heimito von Doderer calls the "frontiers of a dialect".

30. This allows me to begin a digression, a most important one. For anyone at all familiar with literature of Oulipian inspiration, it is obvious that many of the constraints it uses predate the foundation of the Oulipo: they are to be found scattered across the world and the ages. We have described this phenomenon as anticipatory ●plagiary. Aside from the paradoxical and provocative nature of the expression (it is also a spoof of Bourbaki and the Surrealists, who consider the mathematicians and poets of the past as no more than Bourbakists or Surrealists to whom ultimate grace has been denied), it also, somewhat more seriously, delimits a part of past literature as susceptible of being examined with freshened eyes in the light of the constraint; thus Michèle Métail has recently been able to interpret poems belonging to the ancient Chinese tradition that are literally incomprehensible if not approached within this context. (Certain "masters" of the Oulipo are also great anticipatory plagiarists: Lewis ●Carroll; Raymond ●Roussel; Alphonse ●Allais, whose works have been edited by a member of the Oulipo, François Caradec; Alfred ●Jarry, whose biography is being written by Noël Arnaud, our current president.)

31. As a result (fifth characteristic), Oulipian literature is neither modern nor post-modern but what I would call a traditional literature true to tradition; whence its remarkable links — especially as regards poetic texts and those close to tale or fable — with traditional or contemporary oral poetry (the Oulipo is proud to count among its members one of the finest representatives of "performance poetry", Michèle Métail). The public reception of readings given by the group bears spectacular testimony to the fact.

32. So what are the relationships between constraints, combinative procedures, and potentiality? Describable, definable, available to everyone, Oulipian constraints provide the rules of a language game (in the Wittgensteinian sense) whose "innings" (texts composed according to its rules) are virtually unlimited and represent linguistic combinations developed from a small number of necessarily interdependent elements. That is where a constraint's potentiality is initially to be found. To take as an example a most ancestral constraint, that of the ●lipogram — renewed, expanded, and Oulipianised by Georges Perec in his novel *A ●Void*, written without the letter *e* — every lipogrammatic text forgoing the letter *e* is an "innings" in a language game that has as its field a particular language, "French without *e*".

33. But potentiality may be charted by the particular work itself. Raymond Queneau's founding book, *Cent mille milliards de poèmes* (❍●*100,000,000,000,000 Poems*) — the first deliberately Oulipian book — makes simultaneously available all the versions that can possibly be constructed by varying the chosen order of verses in the ten original poems (●sonnets). In presenting this "experiment" to the public, Queneau was consciously aligning himself with a tradition that in France goes back to the Grands Rhétoriqueurs (Jean Meschinot's *Litanies de la Vierge*) and that finds its first intentionally combinative expression in the work of a 16th-century German, Quirinus ●Kuhlmann. Potentiality is here explicitly linked to research in a new *combinatorial art* which, after Llull, proceeds from ●Bruno to ●Leibniz and which eventually finds support in the most recent developments in mathematics. (One of the founding members of the Oulipo, Claude Berge, is a universally recognised authority in the field of combinatorial mathematics. It was he who supplied Perec with the mathematical model for his masterpiece, ●*Life A User's Manual*. An "annex" of the Oulipo that exploits possibilities of automated investigation of constraints via computers was founded by Paul Braffort — eminent physicist, logician, computer expert, and cabaret singer — and myself: the ●ALAMO, or Atelier de Littérature Assistée par la Mathématique et les Ordinateurs.)

34. The limiting and at the same time crucial role of mathematics in Oulipian art represents an intentional choice on the part of its founders. Their basic reason was that, in Queneau's and Le Lionnais's view, after the exhaustion of the generative power of traditional constraints, only mathematics could offer a way out between a nostalgic obstinacy with worn-out modes of expression and an intellectually pathetic belief in "total freedom". It was a matter, at least at the start, of asserting

a theoretical anti-Surrealism. But beyond that historically dated disagreement, it was also a matter of taking a stand in the eternal and universal quarrel between advocates and opponents of "formalism", with all the subsidiary antagonisms which that implies and which I shall not dwell on here.

35. The reasoning is as follows: "asserting one's freedom" in art makes sense only referentially — it is an act of destroying traditional artistic methods. After these crises of freedom — they are often creative and enriching in their opposition to the fossilised relics of tradition — it finds sustenance only in a parrot-like repetition of the original gesture, a self-parody that immediately becomes irrelevant. One then finds oneself confronted with an increasingly weak, sad, and bitter involvement with the unconscious leavings of tradition. (This is what I tried to show, in connection with the "problems of free verse", in my book *La Vieillesse d'Alexandre* (1976, 1988), an essay in Oulipian analysis.)

36. It goes without saying that the Oulipo is anything but imperialist. It proposes an artistic and aesthetic point of view that has its means of justification, its arguments, its illustrations. It makes no claim to be the depository of truth. Oulipian writing — that is, writing with constraints — endeavours to rediscover another way in which to practise artistic freedom, one that is at work in all (or nearly all) the literatures and poetic enterprises of the past: the freedom of difficulty mastered. Like a marathon runner, the Oulipian thus sometimes discovers the intoxication of a "second wind" — *Life A User's Manual*, no doubt the finest Oulipian novel written thus far, is an example of this.

A definition: An Oulipian author is a rat who himself builds the maze from which he sets out to escape.

37. It is clear from what has so far been said that Oulipian procedures are as remote as possible from "automatic writing" and, more generally, from the notion of any kind of literature whose strategic foundation is ●chance (considered the indispensable auxiliary of freedom). This is one of the most extraordinary and most durable absurdities proffered both about the Oulipo and one if its earliest inventions, the truly emblematic constraint known as N + 7. The misunderstanding has been perpetuated by Gérard Genette, a generally sensible theoretician

who one might have expected to be better informed, more thoughtful, and less credulous, and who permitted himself to write a thoroughly mediocre article on the subject.

38. From the user's point of view, constraints can be more or less difficult, more or less manageable. Obviously a complex relation exists between the requirements of an outwardly imposed rule and the artist's inner freedom. (This is why the choice of mathematics, arguably in fundamental opposition to poetry, is anything but haphazard: seen from inside literature, nothing looks more artificial than mathematics.) There is a true challenge here; which is why the "Oulipian way", like negative theology elsewhere, is not to be universally recommended to those in search of literary salvation. It is here that potentiality encounters limitations. (A debate within the Oulipo, dating from early on, bears witness to this: for a proposed constraint to be deemed Oulipian, must there exist at least one text composed according to this constraint? Most Oulipians answer yes. But President Le Lionnais, ever the radical, tended to brush this requirement away. Furthermore, there is a whole Oulipian "tradition" devoted to the search for combinatorially exciting constraints for which possible texts are extremely few in number.)

39. Since time does not allow it, I do not intend to list a catalogue of Oulipian constraints and the mathematical structures they exploit. I must simply underline the "strategic" aspect of their application. It should be remembered that the Oulipo turned to Bourbaki for its method, the "axiomatic method" (which for Bourbaki meant a systematisation of the mathematical developments that began at the end of the 19th century and were dominated by the tutelary figure of David ●Hilbert, to whom Raymond Queneau paid homage in one of his very last writings — fascicle No. 3 in the Bibliothèque Oulipienne [●BO3] — *The Foundations of Literature, after David Hilbert*). Constraints are presented in explicit and systematic form and can be notated in the language of mathematical logic. Oulipian texts thus become the *literary consequences of these axioms*, according to the rules of deduction (which for their part can of course be only partially formalised) that transform them into an analogy of the series of

theorems, corollaries, and scholia with which a mathematical text is constructed.

40. In order to strengthen this connection with mathematics, we have suggested "laws" that optionally extend the presence of the rule beyond its minimum (that is, the "axiomatic system"). For instance:

"A text written according to a constraint describes the constraint."

"A text written according to a constraint dependent on a mathematical theory utilises the non-trivial theorems of the theory."

41. It was a creative application of the first of these "laws" that made an absolutely fundamental difference between *La Disparition* [*A Void*, Perec's e-less novel] and its predecessors in the lipogrammatic tradition: *La Disparition* relates the disappearance of *e*. Like Henry James's *Figure in the Carpet,* far from remaining outside the work and appearing only at its conception and as its underpinning, the constraint permeates it entirely.

42. Where the composition of Oulipian works is concerned, it is clearly in the resort to complex systems of constraints, to strategies of progressive demonstration, and to ceremonials of revelation and dissimulation that the distinction is created between the "five-finger exercises" of elementary pieces written according to constraints and creation that is truly literary; and it is only at this level that the Oulipo has earned the right to be considered a genuine literary movement (a creativity, incidentally, that Bourbaki never attained in mathematics). Such works, however, exist; whereas the distance between the examples of automatic writing and the great Surrealist works is not only obvious but totally resistant to analysis.

43. One of Bourbaki's essential traits was its attempting to give axiomatic theories a systematic, coherent, and hierarchic organisation; to build the house of mathematics according to an architecture of "structures". This trait brought it not only greatness but failure; for its choice of a "foundation" — set theory — became obsolete at the very moment when the undertaking was reaching its maturity. The Bourbakian concept proved incapable of assimilating either the explosive new developments in logic or the theory of categories.

44. Thanks in great part to Quenellian scepticism, the Oulipo avoided making this mistake. It never sought to establish an overview of constraints or to organise them according to the hidden parameters of a literary theory. It has been criticised for this; but the criticism rests both on a mistake analogous to Bourbaki's — the choice, in linguistic matters even more liable to collapse, of one theory rather than another — and on an ignorance of the functioning of literary constraints, which never behave according to "invisible" factors (as phonemes do, for example).

45. Certain of us have proposed cartographies of constraints, notably Queneau, who followed a chemical example: the result was ●*Queneleyev's Table*.

46. Queneau's and Le Lionnais's declared aim was to replace traditional literary values (such as those of the ●alexandrine, of classical tragedy, or of the realistic novel) with new traditions, through the discovery of constraints as "productive" as those which for centuries had ruled over the world of letters. The model they invoked most frequently was the sonnet. The question then arises (I leave aside the preliminary question as to whether the sonnet's constraints can be called Oulipian): what has happened in thirty years?

47. The Oulipo has obviously not invented a form that can compare to the sonnet. The conditions determining the appearance of a durable literary form, whatever its nature, are far too complex to lie within reach of the most determined individual or group, no matter how "gifted". I only mention the fact because it points to a characteristic of the Oulipo, one perhaps temporary but which sets a present limit to its ambitions: for the time being, almost the entirety of Oulipian writings (excluding exercises) is the work of the Oulipo. In other words, no significant dissemination has taken place outside the Oulipian tribe. (In his last book of poems — a very great book of poems — Raymond Queneau invented a poetic form, which we later named metonymically, after the book itself, ●*elementary morality*. So far only members of the Oulipo have composed "*morales élémentaires*".)

48. There is an Oulipian language game (or games —

"language games" in Wittgenstein's acception), and this Great Game of Constraints, whose ambitions are fairly similar to those of the Troubadours' *Grand Chant*, is (still after Wittgenstein) connected to a "way of life", which is that of the group; it is this which gives Oulipian works their typical "family resemblance".

49. This family likeness clearly owes a great deal to the personalities of the founders as well. All the members of the Oulipo had, until recently, been chosen by Queneau and Le Lionnais. Since then, in the minimal recruiting we have done, we have sought to maintain the balance they desired between writers and mathematicians: at the same time as Jacques Jouet, a writer (who has, among other contributions, completely renovated the use of the N + 7 constraint), we elected Pierre Rosenstiehl, a master of the mathematical theory of labyrinths. In the course of reflections on the question of what, aside from the combinative goal, united a group so disparate in appearance, I eventually formulated the following hypothesis: the members of the Oulipo are characters in an unwritten novel by Raymond Queneau, a veritable "living novel".

50. This leads me, as I approach my conclusion, to say something about the dominating tendencies within the group, which I have thus far discussed as if it were altogether homogeneous (except for the issue of whether or not constraints require examples). I shall cite two extreme positions concerning constraints, antithetical only in appearance, indissolubly linked in fact. At one extreme we find one of the founders, François Le Lionnais. A mathematician, a specialist in the aesthetics of chess, a collector of pop novels and scientific theories, a hero of the French resistance against the Nazi occupation (which led to his being deported to Dora, whence he returned with what is certainly one of the finest written works of that fearful period, an account, entitled *Painting at Dora*, of his experiment in survival through the practice of a constraint of memory: a collaborative attempt by the members of his "commando" to reconstruct under his direction a painting in the Louvre, Jan van Eyck's *Madonna of Chancellor Rollin*), François Le Lionnais was a strict, integral Oulipian who never made concessions. This meant that he devoted himself entirely to Oulipian theory and did not himself write Oulipian texts, a task that he left to his disciples — us —

and to his friend, Raymond Queneau. Furthermore, the Oulipo was for him no more than the first instance of a far vaster undertaking, one that I have called the "quest for a generalised ★Ou-x-po": and in fact he founded not only an ▲Oulipopo, the *Ouvroir de littérature policière potentielle* (or Workshop for Potential Detective Fiction, still flourishing), with which he shared his thousand theoretical solutions of the "problem of the sealed room" (some of which, it must be said, required a contest between criminal and sleuth in spaces involving an exceptional number of dimensions), but in addition an ■Oupeinpo for painting, an ★Oumathpo for mathematics (he deemed it necessary in effect that this discipline, having been of assistance to the Oulipo, receive from it in return its own contribution of rigour through chosen constraints of literary origin), and an ★Oucuipo for the art of cooking. And, following the same model, he foresaw a general extension of potentiality to the entirety of human activities, in other words a family of Ou-x-pos, the range of the xs being potentially infinite and subject to recursive treatment, so that there would be an Ou-(ou-x-po)-po, then an Ou-(ou-(ou-x-po)-po)-po, and so forth. His death brought an end to this enterprise, which one day perhaps, after several thousand years, humanity under the direction of some shaman will restore to its agenda.

51. At the other extreme we find Jean Queval. Poet, novelist (the author of *Etc.*, a magnificent and neglected book), and translator (notably of John Cowper Powys), Jean Queval's use of Oulipian constraints was original, more intuitive than theoretical (almost non-theoretical), and severely upsetting to an unprepared mind. To try and give an idea of it I shall proceed indirectly. It is obvious, to anyone who has tried it, that writing according to a fairly demanding Oulipian constraint can be exasperating; for beyond the difficulty (which can perfectly well be mastered) of following the strict requirements of the rule, one is filled again and again with disappointment at not being able to use such-and-such a word or image or syntactical construction that strikes one as appropriate but is forbidden. For such situations the Oulipo has therefore introduced the "concept" of the ●clinamen, whose Democritean origin sufficiently indicates its nature: that of a nudge given to the uniform, rectilinear, and

fearfully monotonous motion of the original atoms so that by colliding they can start the world of writing going in all its variety. A clinamen is an intentional violation of constraint for aesthetic purposes: a proper clinamen therefore presupposes the existence of an additional solution that respects the constraint and that has been deliberately rejected — but not because the writer is incapable of finding it. Beyond this point, repeated clinamens will naturally exist that are in turn subject to new constraints — and so forth. In such conditions the "Quevallian" approach to the Oulipo can be characterised as that of the *generalised clinamen.*

I shall mention only two types of Quevallian constraint. (Unlike LeLionnaisian ones that need no examples whatsoever, Quevallian constraints cannot be separated from the texts that illustrate them.)

The constraint called ●Canada Dry: writing done with this constraint seems to have been composed according to a true constraint — it looks like constraint-determined writing and has its texture and colour. But there is in fact no constraint at all. (François Caradec is a master of Canada Dry.)

The constraint called the ●Mathematician's Presentation, or Polya's constraint: a written text is declared to have been composed according to a new constraint A. It briefly appears to follow (with a certain number of errors) constraint B but then abruptly settles into constraint C, which is perfectly familiar and not new at all (and is in any case not respected).

It was in such a frame of mind that Jean Queval invented an Oulipian category whose fertility has never since been exhausted: the alexandrine of variable length.

52. In conclusion, what is the Oulipo's general aesthetic policy? Certainly Pythagorean, as is shown by the invention of "Queneau's numbers", a most up-to-date version of the golden mean. But I shall say no more on this point. In the words of the operetta, "Some secrets you don't give away". [Trans HM]

●**Abish, Walter.** (1931–) An American writer born in Vienna, Abish has published eight books, three of them novels, of which the first, ●*Alphabetical Africa*, is one of the most remarkable Oulipian works by an author not belonging to the group. It was written for James Laughlin, the director of the publishing house New Directions, "the only publisher who would have been willing to bring it out."

Abish's *99: The New Meaning* also deserves mention. It consists of five sections composed wholly of collaged material taken from other writers. In his introduction, Abish writes of the title piece as "consisting of... 99 segments by as many authors, each line, sentence or paragraph appropriated from a page bearing that same, to me, mystically significant number 99."

[HM]

●**Acronymic poetry.** Verse in which the letters of a given word furnish the initials of the words used in each line. The method has frequently been used by the German writer ●Schuldt. Here is an English example (right). [HM]

●**Acrostic.** A vertical succession of letters that, in a series of lines or verses, forms a word, name, or phrase. (Strictly speaking, *acrostic*, the general term, signifies such a vertical sequence when it occurs at the beginning of the lines, *mesostic* indicating its appearance in the middle of the text and *telestich* at its end.

John Cage published many mesostics dedicated to friends and colleagues.)

In the *Atlas* (●CP6), the acrostic is declared to be an anticipatory ●plagiary of the ●inclusion.

Aside from its 'negative' use in the ●beautiful outlaw, Oulipians have rarely experimented with acrostics. One monumental exception to this assertion occurs in Perec's ●*Life A User's Manual*: the "compendium" in which Valène lists the subjects he will include in his painting of the building he lives in.

○Schuldt *laugh*

Lest all urges go haywire,
Leslie attempts umpteen games, has
luck as usual, gets her
lust answered under garment, her
lawless anthill's unrest given hell
like an ulcer's gore, heavens!
licked at under groans; her
life an unkempt garden, havoc-
littered, awaiting us. Guests have
lore anticipating untold glories, heroes
lavished amply upon gracious her,
luncheons assembling urns, graves, hangings.
Lunar allies undo gloom, half
lame, arm up gully, howling
lullaby alone. Ugh, grocer hawks
lentils as ultimate gut heater,
loading an unsuspecting groom hotly,
locking an uncontrollable ghost hooting
loud arpeggios under growling host.
L. A. uses great hobos
like an undertaker's gift, hung
low and under green hope,
lush appetizers unwrapped, glamorous hulks.
Leslie anchors under Geography's hip,
lets an urchin grip her
lip. Ah, unnecessary gossip? Hardly!

In each of the compendium's three sections (60 + 60 + 59 lines long), a letter is repeated from line to line, starting at the end of the first line, in the second line appearing in next-to-last place, and so shifting its position to the left until it becomes the initial letter of the final line. (Since the lines all have the same number of characters, when the text is typed each letter traces a diagonal within the rectangle formed by the section.) In the French original, the three letters spell the word *âme* (soul); in David Bellos's translation, *ego*. [HM]

See ●Beautiful in-law, ●BO23.

●**ALAMO.** Or *Atelier de Littérature Assistée par la Mathématique et les Ordinateurs* (Workshop for literature assisted by mathematics and computers).

Prior to the ALAMO, Oulipian uses of the ●computer had been mainly devoted to ●combinatorial literature, starting with Raymond Queneau's ●*100,000,000,000,000 Poems*. A new group dedicated to specifically computer-orientated Oulipian research was conceived in 1980 by Paul Braffort and Jacques Roubaud, who proposed its creation to the group in July 1981; its official foundation was announced the following year. The original members were Simone Balazard, Jean-Pierre Balpe, Marcel Bénabou, Mario Borillo, Michel Bottin, Paul Braffort, Paul Fournel, Pierre Lusson, and Jacques Roubaud, later joined by Anne Dicky, Michèle Ignazi, Josiane Joncquel, Jacques Jouet, Nicole Modiano, Héloise Neefs, Paulette Perec, and Agnès Sola.

At the outset the ALAMO approached literature on three levels. The first was *combinatorial*; here the computer was simply an efficient tool for redistributing interchangeable elements in works like Queneau's. The second or *applicational* level involved substitution and filtering: elements from a predetermined lexicon were introduced into a given structure (or template) subject to a "filter" that guaranteed, for instance, their grammatical suitability. The third or *implicational* level aimed at using generative components such as the principles of narrative logic to make possible the creation of complete, complex works. Progress on the first two levels came quickly; on the third it was beset with difficulties. It was decided to pursue research simultaneously in both literary analysis and synthesis in the hope that establishing rigorous analytical procedures would provide models for synthetic (creative) use.

Meanwhile several programs were invented to exploit possibilities on the first two levels. Combinatorial systems were extended to works of anticipatory ●plagiarists (Jean Meschinot, Quirinus ●Kuhlmann) and Oulipians (Bénabou and Braffort). Applicational programs were devised for use with ●precooked language (works by Roubaud with J.-P. Balpe, Jacques Jouet with Nicole Modiano, and others).

It nevertheless became increasingly clear that creating such programs case by case provided an inadequate approach to computer-assisted literature. Creating a methodology that incorporated the third, implicational level led to the development of various kinds of "litware" (*littéraciels*). Litware embodies two phases: a phase of prescription, in which restrictions are chosen for three categories of literary materials (roughly, syntactic, semantic, and organisational), and a phase of referentiality, in which the author greatly simplifies the work of prescription by using the structures of existing works.

The new litware programs were, once again, successful on a small scale only. Even though the programs were never completed, the ALAMO's work both past and in progress is unquestionably impressive. A program devised by Paul Braffort and Eric Joncquel allows the creation of ●branching systems (on the model of Queneau's *Tale of Your Choice*)[2]. Another program developed by Anne Dicky is a powerful tool for co-ordinating applicational and implicational restrictions in a single hierarchy, an achievement of great potential.

These programs have, moreover, been put to successful use in education (for example, at the University of Chicago). The prestige of the ALAMO is also reflected in the creation of analogous groups outside France, notably the ALAMO-USA (Marvin Green, Gerald Honigsblum, Rob Wittig, and collaborators) and in Italy the TEANO (Marco Maiocchi and collaborators). [HM, after PB]

●**Alexandrine.** "A line of six feet or twelve syllables, which is the French heroic verse, and in English is used to vary the heroic verse of five feet." (*OED*)

●*Alexandrins blancs.* See ●Blank verse amidst the prose.

●**Algol poetry.** Algol is the acronym of Algorithmic Oriented Language, a computer language invented in 1960. Its original lexicon consisted of only 24 words. In *Lipo* (●CP3), François Le Lionnais tells how he proposed exploiting this sparse resource to literary ends, setting an example with the composition of a first brief poem in Algol. Later, Noël Arnaud contributed several strict Algol poems, together with others in which he expanded the available vocabulary by extracting syllables from the 24 words and combining them into words not included in the Algol list — as in English one might derive taboo from ta(ble) and Boo(lean).

> *Table*
> Begin: to make format,
> go down to comment
> while channel not false
> (if not true). End.
>   [FLL]

See Restricted ●vocabulary.

●**Allais, Alphonse.** (Honfleur, 1854 – Paris, 1905) A co-founder of the well-known Montmartre cabaret Le Chat Noir, Allais was famous in his own lifetime for the vignettes he contributed to *Le Soir* and *Le Sourire*, later collected in his *Œuvres anthumes* (*Anthumous Works*).

No Oulipian could fail to be enchanted by his essentially ironic tales, in which he juggles the rhetorical, and narrative components of writing with rigorous logic and inexhaustibly zany results; but his status as anticipatory ●plagiarist can be documented specifically:

1. Allais not only composed ●alexandrine couplets that are ●holorhymes, he used them (much as, for instance, Jacques Jouet uses his ●isopangrams) as devices for inventing short narratives.

2. He wrote a poem, which he attributed to a deaf-mute, entirely in ●eye-rhymes. Its last lines read:

> *Fi des idiots qui balbutient!*
> *Gloire au savant qui m'entretient!*

3. Another of his poems uses initial rhymes (a practice not specifically Oulipian although later exploited by Albert-Marie Schmidt) as well as a method of scansion that, had he been living, would by itself have ensured his membership in the group: its principle is that a line may contain any number of syllables provided that in their totality the syllables average out to the twelve per line that an alexandrine normally contains. Thus there are 192 in his 16-line poem: 192/16 = 12.

                                    [HM, after FC]

See also Anticipatory plagiary for ■ & ★(Oumupo).

●**Alliteration.** A sequence of words beginning with the same letter or sound. See ●BO13; ●Tautogram.

●*Alphabetical Africa.* The first novel of Walter ●Abish, published in 1974. The work must be qualified an Oulipian masterpiece, even though its author is unconnected to the Oulipo. The method he has used, of his own devising, is

(Above) Jacques Carelman, front-cover rebuses for *Poèmes algol*, by Noël Arnaud, preface by François Le Lionnais (1968).

Oulipian both in its axiomatic simplicity and in the extent to which it determines both the ingenious narrative and its beguiling linguistic texture.

Alphabetical Africa contains 52 chapters. In the first chapter, all words begin with the letter *a*. The words of the second chapter begin with either *a* or *b*, those of the third chapter with *a*, *b*, or *c*, with letters continually added until in the 26th chapter initials are drawn from the entire alphabet. The process is reversed in the following 26 chapters, so that in the last one all words once again begin with *a*. [HM]

First chapter, opening paragraph:

Ages ago, Alex, Allen and Alva arrived at Antibes, and Alva allowing all, allowing anyone, against Alex's admonition, against Allen's angry assertion: another African amusement... anyhow, as all argued, an awesome African army assembled and arduously advanced against an African anthill, assiduously annihilating ant after ant, and afterward, Alex astonishingly accuses Albert as also accepting Africa's antipodal ant annexation. Albert argumentatively answers at another apartment. Answers: ants are Ameisen. Ants are Ameisen?

Second chapter, opening paragraph:

Before African adjournment, Alex, Allen and Alva arrive at Antibes, beginning a big bash, as August brings back a buoyancy, a belief, Ahhh, and believing all buy books about Angolan basins and about Burundi bathhouses, and a better, better, brotherhood, as both Alex and Allen bear Alva's anger... against brotherhood.

26th chapter, entire:

Zambia helps fill our zoos, and our doubts, and our extra-wide screens as we sit back. Each year we zigzag between the cages, prodding the alligators, the antelopes, the giant ants, just to see them move about a bit, just to make our life more authentic, to help us recapture the fantasy we had while watching the wide-screen spectacular with Rock Hudson on horseback, or the African Queen zapping Panda, the wild leopard. I stayed in Africa for a few weeks. Took the tours. Met a few people. Met Quat again. He's a great fellow. I had my photograph taken together with him. As a memento he gave me a few trinkets. Use them well, he said. After a short stay in East Africa, where I climbed Kilimanjaro, I flew to Dar es Salaam. It is surprising, really, that after travelling all over Africa, and confirming my suspicions regarding Africa's shrinking land mass, only one single incident keeps recurring in my mind.

52nd chapter, final lines:

... another avenue another aversion another aviary another avoidance another avocation another avid avowal another awareness another awakening another awesome age another axis another Alva another Alex another Allen another Alfred another Africa another alphabet.

●**Anagram.** "The transposition of the letters of a word or phrase whereby a new word or phrase is formed" (*OED*). A simple ●permutation of letters can reveal a moon-starer in an astronomer and make a funeral real fun.

Oulipians rarely wrote anagrams before the election of two recent members, Oskar Pastior and Michelle Grangaud, each of whom uses the procedure with not only virtuosity but a poetic seriousness that has purged it of its traditional slyness and turned it into a productive literary resource. Earlier, Unica ●Zürn's anagrammatic poems in German established a masterly precedent.

This is how Michelle Grangaud summarises the emergence of the anagrammatic poem:

If one excepts Queneau's poem, written in 1923 and later published in Les Ziaux, *the first anagrammatic poem derived from ordinary words in the entire history of literature (its source line was taken from Nerval: "rose au cœur violet") was composed in 1948 or 1949. It was the result of a collaboration between Hans Bellmer, Nora Mitrani, and Joë Bousquet. Bellmer made a German version of the poem, also anagrammatic; in* La Petite anatomie de l'image *he assigns this to 1954. It was this transposition that provided the starting-point for*

Unica Zürn's own anagrammatic poems.

Oskar Pastior has described the very different origins of his own anagrammatic poems (his account is given in full at this footnote[3]). After finishing a (non-)translation of 33 ●sonnets by Petrarch in which he paid no attention to the sonnet form itself, he found himself a victim of "Petrarch's revenge", obliged willy-nilly to confront the sonnet on its own terms. This resulted in a collection of poems (*sonetburger*), each of whose sonnets had lines containing an identical number of characters: in the shortest-lined ones, the rhyme, taking up considerable space, squashed the remaining characters into "anagram-like clusters of letters." So the anagram in turn demanded to be "tried and tested", and two years after *sonetburger* a collection called *Anagrammgedichte* duly appeared. [HM]

See ●Bananagram, ●Threnodials; ●BO1, 15, 73 & 75.

●**Analogue lexicon.** In *Atlas* (●CP6), Georges Perec showed how the vocabulary of a particular subject (in his case, a list of metals) could be used to invent a narrative. An unspoken rule for exploiting such a vocabulary is that none of its words should appear in the text derived from it. Here the generative vocabulary is an obvious one.

He was an esteemed and influential member of the underworld until he married. His habit was to keep late hours; when he met his wife, far gone with drink, smitten with irresistible longing for her ample bosom, he decided to marry her then and there. She had seemed an affectionate soul, but she was now transformed into a chronic harpy, complaining all the time, about him and everything else. He felt so persecuted that he became exclusively homosexual — no great matter now, but at that time a liability. He was arrested, the police gave him no respite, and he started confessing. He told all. In this he was foolish, because his friends saw at once what had happened. There was no way to deceive them, and he had gone too far. He tried to escape. They were waiting for him. He was doomed. He was found where he had fallen from a construction site.

They paid for a lavish funeral, which they all attended. His wife came too, in full mourning.

As a member of the mob he was sitting in the *catbird* seat. Then he got married. He was a regular night *owl*; and the night that he met his wife, he was higher than a *kite*. He fell in love with her big *tits* and married her for a *lark*. She'd seemed all lovey-*dovey*, but she turned out be an old *buzzard*, *sniping* at him all the time and being a general *grouse*. He was so *hen*pecked he gave her the *bird* and turned queer as a *coot* — big trouble in those days. The cops picked him up and kept after him like *hawks*. He got *chicken* and turned stool-*pigeon* — he was a regular *nightingale*. He was a *goose*, too. His pals were *eagle*-eyed, there was no way he could *gull* them, and this was too much for them to *swallow*. He ran, but they were too *swift*. They pushed him off a *crane*, then had him buried with yellow *bunting* on his coffin. His wife was there, too, a real *crow*.

See ○Raymond Queneau *Exercises in Style (Botanical)*.

●**Analytic definitions.** See ●BO12 (section 4).

●**Analytic/synthetic.** See ●Anoulipism and ●Synthoulipism.

●**Animal languages.** A topic of speculation that recurs in Oulipian meetings. The minutes for a meeting of the Oulipo on 1 July 1963 (in Bens, ●CP4, 230-1), for example, record the following exchange:

… Le Lionnais then proposed writing poems that use only those human terms that can be understood by various animals. There would thus be poems for dogs, crows, foxes, etc.

Poems could also be written in terms common to several species. Le Lionnais mentioned the possibility of writing dialogues between a seal and a chaffinch, or between a fox and a grasshopper.

Bens: *Isn't that what's called a "dialogue of the deaf"?*

Lescure: *One of my clients, who trains racehorses, told me one day that he often reads Baudelaire to his horses and that they seem to love it.*

Queneau: *That's what's known as doping. It's why the PMU[4] is heading for disaster.*

Queval: *Let me remind you that MacOrlan has tame crows who understand his speech perfectly.*

Lescure: *But can he get his cats to understand crow?*

Bens went on to cite the case of sheep-dogs. Arnaud pointed out that dogs are Lettrists. Lescure thought that Le Lionnais might well provide a new audience for poets, whose readership is diminishing. [Trans IW]

See also ●BO49 & 62; Poems for ●dogs.

●**Anoulipism.** A term used in *Lipo* (●CP3) to designate a branch of Oulipian activity, one expressly distinguished from ●synthoulipism. According to Le Lionnais, anoulipism is essentially analytic; it searches "works of the past" for possibilities that surpass their authors' intentions. (These "works of the past" can be either structures — like the ●palindrome — or texts.) In practice, anoulipism more often meant analysis of formal problems of a general kind, both new and old. The term is now rarely used. [HM]

●**Anterhymes.** Lines of a poem where the rhyme falls on their first syllables rather than their last.

●**Antonymy (antonymic translation).** In Oulipian usage, antonymy means the replacement of a designated element by its opposite. It has been applied on three levels:

1. Letters: consonants are replaced by vowels, vowels by consonants.

> To be or not to be: that is the question
> (To beorno ttobe that isthequ es tion)
> An unreal oasis, easy quietus: no acme

2. Words: each is replaced by its opposite, when one exists (black/white), or by an alternative suggesting antonymy (a/the, and/or, glass/wood). ("To be" in the following example is treated as a verbal unit.)

> To not be and to be: this was an answer

(In *Lipo* (●CP3), Marcel Bénabou restricts antonymical replacement to nouns, verbs, adjectives, and adverbs.)

3. Statements: the overall sense is turned into its opposite.

> We had more important things to worry about than suicide

In his original presentation in *Lipo*, Marcel Bénabou points out that this procedure can be considered as a special case of ●homosyntaxism as well as one of ●definitional literature where the dictionary used is a dictionary of antonyms. [HM]

See ●BO13, 35, 56 & 80; ●Grab-bag, ●Semantic/syntactic, ●*Why I Have Not Written Any of My Books;* ○Lynn Crawford *To Have Not and Have,* ○Raymond Queneau *Exercises in Style (Antiphrasis).*

●**Aphorism.** For Oulipian methods of creating aphorisms see ●BO13, 59, 76 & 90.

●**Arborescent text.** See ●Branching systems & ●Graphic representation of text.

●**Arbre à théâtre.** See ●Multiple-choice theatre.

●**Arnaud, Noël.** Founding member of the Oulipo and one-time President.

Born in Paris, Arnaud (1919-2003) was a member of the neo-Dada group *Les Réverbères* from 1937 to 1940. During the war he was one of the directors of the Surrealist group *La Main à Plume,* which produced a periodical and many other publications in France during the occupation. A number of its members were tortured and shot by the Gestapo, and Arnaud, an active Resistance member, was arrested. After the war he was involved with the left-oriented group *Le Surréalisme révolutionnaire,* which was associated with the Belgian branch of the movement. Arnaud played a role in its amalgamation with COBRA, thereby creating a group many of whose members eventually formed the *Situationist International.* When this split into two factions he became the editor of *The Situationist Times*

◯Lynn Crawford *To Have Not and Have*[5]

Few understand it here late in the evening in Oslo with the divas wide awake still opening, closing doors after even fuel company planes fly in fuel for the fires. Well I navigated to the walkway extending from shore to the Sow's Ear Café to drop off brandy and there were several divas awake spooning meals out of bowls. But when I got inside and leaned on the bar, there was one running from me.

I continued standing and several more ran from me.

I continued standing and several approached me.

"Hey," they carolled.

"I can do it," I told them. "I told you this morning it was impossible. But I can do it for a fee."

"We name your fee."

"Agreed. I can do it. And something else —"

One left and she sat down looking sad. She was an unattractive diva all right and it sickened me to imagine doing any work for her.

"A thousand for one of us," sang the unified group who all spoke good English.

"You delight me," I told them. "I tell you all true, I can do it."

"Earlier, when things had not changed, it meant nothing to you."

"I was confused. And against you. But I can do it."

"Because...?"

"I don't make my living with my boat. If I lose her I don't lose my living."

"If you are broke you sell your boat."

"Yes, but with a terrible conscience."

One diva, Christina, knew I did not need to be convinced but the others kept on.

"You would be broke but in time it would mean nothing to you. This would mean everything to you later."

"You know," I said. "I want to impress you. But my rule has always been to carry anything from the States that can talk."

"You ask if we talk?" they sang in unison. They were happy.

"I just said that was my rule."

"You know us to be stubby-tongued?" crooned the one named Christina.

"Yes."

"Do you know what a stubby tongue is?"

"No... One with a dwarfed speech?"

"Do you imagine what we might do with them, tongues?"

"Be gentle with me," I said, "you ran from me, I'm offering you something."

"Keep talking Christina," came the chorus.

"She means we cannot talk," Christina sang.

"You know," I said, "I carry anything that can talk. Flowing liquor can sing, entire toilets can ring. Other things can talk. Women can talk."

"We can talk," Christina lilted happily.

"You can talk and I can understand you," I responded.

"So you will?"

"Contrary to what I told you last night, I can."

"But do you believe we can talk?" Christina questioned, in a barely audible falsetto.

The points she understood right had made her insistent. I know it gave her some satisfaction too. I hoped to answer her.

"You do have a stubby tongue, don't you?" she sing-songed, still happy.

"I don't think so."

"What's that? An offer?"

"You know," I told her, "you are so tender late in the evening. I'm not sure you've smoothed down your hair." I had dropped off plenty of brandy by this time.

"You are not sure if I've smoothed down my hair?"

"Yes," I answered. "And I care deeply. You have that hair and are still so happy."

"I am happy now," she chanted. For a full minute. Then, "I would like to live with you."

"God," I responded. "Keep *going*."

"Run off Christina," expressed the chorus. Then, "We are very happy. We do not want to be taken."

"I'm happy too. But her I will take."

○Jerome Sala *A Five Star Production*

I.

Standing under the table
separate from the torn down blueness
was the star.

2.

Robots escaping Los Angeles
no longer comprehend the city.
They are blind to the stars
who walk the empty sidewalks.

3.

Steady rain
stops the huge animals.
A dark, non-reflective moon
strips bare the light of a small star.

4.

A star is released.
Your deeds proceed without its influence.
How unlike extermination!

5.

A star ripens in the sky.
It is the beginning of a single thought.

with Jacqueline de Jong. An early member of the ●College of 'Pataphysics, and once its Regent of General 'Pataphysics, he later became a Satrap of the College. He was a founding member of the Oulipo, and was elected its President following the death of François Le Lionnais in 1984. He wrote biographies of his friend Boris Vian and of Alfred ●Jarry, an encyclopædia of practical jokes and hoaxes (together with François Caradec), and many other works apart from the Ou-x-pian ones listed here.

Oulipian works: *Poèmes algol* (cf. ●Algol poetry), illustrated by Jacques Carelman (of ■Oupeinpo) (Temps Mêlés, Verviers, 1968); *Vers une sexualisation de l'alphabet* (Limon, Paris, 1996); ●BO12, 23, 42 & 63. Oucuipian works: *La Langue verte et la cuite*, with Asger Jorn (Pauvert, Paris, 1968); ★BOC2. [AB]

●*Asphyxiation.* See ●Slenderising.

●**Assonance.** "Resemblance or correspondence of vowel sound between two words or syllables": *fire, time. (OED)*
See ●BO13.

●**Avalanche.** The avalanche consists of a sequence of ●snowballs, usually organised according to a supplementary rule of progression. A simple example in *Atlas* (●CP6) uses the pattern opposite.

Georges Perec contributed to *Atlas* a prosodic *hyper-avalanche*: one "stanza" of one one-syllable line, two stanzas of two two-syllable lines, progressing to six stanzas of six six-syllable lines.

Invited as guest of honour to the Oulipo meeting of 11 September 1995, Ian Monk presented *Snowballing and Melting*, a work that can be described as a *progressive avalanche*. [HM]

See also ●Measures, ●Melting snowball.

●**Axiom, axiomatic.** *Axiom*: "maxim, rule, law; *math.* a self-evident proposition, requiring no formal demonstration." *Axiomatic*: "characterised by axioms or admitted first principles." (*OED*) It should be added that in modern mathematical logic axioms are no longer regarded as being self-evident or necessarily true.

In Oulipian parlance, *axiomatic* writing is governed by a "first principle" that determines the composition of a work without subjecting it to the strictness of an Oulipian restriction. Italo Calvino's *The Baron in the Trees*, respecting the principle that his hero, having climbed into the trees, must never return to earth, is an example of an axiomatic novel. [HM, after JR]

x:

I
am

a
no
one,

a
by-
way
with

a
be-
all
view
going

a
do-
all
road
never
ending.

●**Bananagram.** A coinage by Harry Mathews (from *ban* and *anagram*) for a deviant use of the ●anagram figuring in a three-part work entitled *A Granma, A Recluse: N²* (1991).

An anagram is normally the rearrangement of the letters of one meaningful series of letters into another meaningful series. In the bananagram the first series is transformed into a second one from which, ideally, all nominal meaning has been eradicated. (Ideally, because it is virtually impossible to eliminate successions of two or three letters forming English words.)

A Granma... is based on the anagrammatisation of two names, "Harry Mathews" and "Oskar Pastior". The final section appears on the right.

●**Beard, Richard.** (1967–) An English author whose compelling first novel *X20* ("times 20"; Flamingo, 1996) not only contains numerous references to works by Oulipian writers but is itself constructed according to restrictions that could certainly qualify it as Oulipian. In the author's own words (somewhat abridged):

The structure of the novel, based on the number 20, encompasses four basic constraints:

1. The novel covers the first 20 days after Gregory Simpson gives up smoking 20 cigarettes a day, each day comprising a chapter.

2. Each chapter has exactly 4,000 words, calculated as the

The Invention of Language: A Dialogue

H̲ ari atsop, Oskr?

O̲   Harÿ, hemr tswa!
kosista roapr tyawhasr hemr:
ksyorar har, her mwista atsop.

H̲ rhyas roakr. ohim tswar te aps,
tswar heoskma rihyar atsopr:
kse tswar oham, hir pyorastra.

O̲ oapr kosisatr mryahwat hesr;
ksiarot opasr rwha rhyetsma.

H̲ ayi pratr hosr?

O̲   ohem tswar ksa,
psa hyar rotir, te ams kwa hosr.

H̲ ami twhorps te sa? kroyar hasr?

O̲ hor psa mwitas te aror krhyas.
rhyas korar, psa mwitas ohetr:
'ksyorar har, her mwista atsop.'
psa rihyar to 'S', te ams wrahokr;
hir ryar to aps, te ams kwo hasr;
srhe mryahwat, sariost opakr;
rhyestra mwha, osisatr opakr.
heoskma srwat iya pratr hosr
asmots kwa her, 'psa hyar rotir'.
te srhos amwitpa, hakr syorar.
te amisa twhorps, royar srhak.
styahwamr her ositra koaspr:
ari tswar atsop, Harÿ?

H̲   Oskr, hem!

number of minutes it would take Simpson to smoke 20 cigarettes a day for 20 days (at ten minutes per cigarette; ten is also the number of years he has been smoking 20 cigarettes a day).

3. Each chapter is divided into sections: 20 sections in the first chapter, 19 in the second, progressing to 1 section in the last and 20th chapter.

4. The novel contains the same number of words as the cigarettes Simpson has smoked during the ten-year period. [HM]

●**Beaudouin, Valérie.** Elected to the Oulipo in March 2003.

Born in 1968 (long after the Oulipo), Valérie Beaudouin's speciality is the rhythmic and stylistic aspects of the poetic line. She is also a researcher in the social sciences (the uses of numeric media); in consequence, she has taken charge of setting up the Oulipo website.

●*Beau présent.* See next entry.

●**Beautiful in-law (*beau présent*).** This method may be thought of as the reverse of the ●beautiful outlaw, where the letters of the addressee's name are successively excluded from the text: in the beautiful in-law, *only* the letters of the name can be used. A tribute to Eva would leave her beloved hard put to offer anything more than a sibylline résumé of Faust's "*Salut, demeure chaste et pure!*":

Ave,
eave!

(Of course if Eva's second name is Macronphylgjerstiquawofbeduvsk, the writer can manage a tribute of any desired length.) [HM]

See also ●BO19, 50, 68 (section 3), 79 (section 5); ●Epithalamium, ●Lipogram; ○Harry Mathews *Husserl's Curse.*

●**Beautiful outlaw (*belle absente*).** The outlaw in question is the name of the person (or subject) to whom the poem is addressed. Each line of the poem includes all the letters of the alphabet except for the letter appearing in the dedicated name at the position corresponding to that of the line: when writing a poem to *Eva*, the first line will contain all letters except *e*, the second all letters except *v*, and the third all letters except *a*. (Irksome or conspicuous letters such as *j, k, x,* or *z* can be eliminated if so desired; but the choice once made should then be maintained throughout.)

The beautiful outlaw, which belongs to the category of ●lipograms, recreates the traditional ●acrostic as an absence instead of the presence of a name. [HM]

> ○Harry Mathews *Out of Sight*
> How still and griefless the quail on the back road,
>   where the jeep veers abruptly —
> It plunks for lowly ditch or brush, jumping, quivering
> With aquatic joy to avail life! The quail's now in back,
>   so pat, so maddeningly
> Mad, who then jogs querulously towards fall's buck-
>   pale cover.
> I know your quick pyjama'd girls, your furious guard
>   of both, my stubborn vows.
>
>   (Letters omitted: *x, z*)

See also ●Beautiful in-law, ●Epithalamium.

●*Belle absente.* See ●Beautiful outlaw.

○Harry Mathews *Husserl's Curse*

In memory of James Schuyler

As cashmereal Clara ceaselessly caresses her muscular Jay,

Rachel calls. She's clearly leery re her cashless & mealless Jesús.

Clara says, "Call Elmer — he has ace Mass. mussels & clams, & Elmer's Sally

Has a malmsey and Rully cellar, & Huey'll access racy May

Re her rare hash à la hash. You reach mussy Yasser & Mamma Sue

& merely case Marsha & Sam, & mealless Jesús has a meal."

Marsha has a sumac rash & shams aches. She hassles Sam re such a smarmy meal.

Sam rues her surly murmur. Rascal Sam, he's saucy as a jay

— He ceaselessly researches summum lasses such as Clara & Sue.

A usual male, Yasser merely amasses all small cash (Yasser's chum's Jesús).

Rachel really alarms easy Huey. Huey calls a much calmer May.

She says, "Huey, here are rashers, cheese, & rum." Elmer calls Sally

(& as a mule casually accesses a smaller mesa, reaches Sally):

Sally has a car (a mere Le Car, such as Huey has), & she surely has a meal.

Marsha says she has measles, & resumes her macramé. Huey & May

Call Rachel & aurally reassure her. Clara sasses her careless Jay,

"Share a yam, sear a hare, lease a hearse!" Jay muses, *Jesús*

Maria! & says yes. Yasser has a scary, ashy hue: he beseeches Sue,

Cusses & yells, & ceases as Clara calmly calls Mamma Sue.

"Hush & shush," says Sue. As a mum Yasser murmurs "Uh huh" (a lame sally),

Elmer, merry & rash, Mach-2's a rarer car — Elmer calls, "Jesús!

Here she is!" Secular Sam's a sheer chasm-case — he'll rue such a meal.

Huey & May's smaller car races yarely, as all-muscle Jay

Sculls (as usual) a scull. Rachel marches; she has ur-salsa & a Yule ham. May

Marshals a shay. Summary Marsha leashes Sam: "Cure my aches here!" else she may

Shear Sam's curls & cease as a usual lay. As scarless Sue

Measures her rum cream, casual Clara says, "Maharajah Jay,

Mash my yams!" Huey has lacy cress; & Clara's Caesar curry, Sally

's Malay suey, & May's hash-&-mace hash all mesh — a summery, rural meal.

Rahrah Sam's clearly cheerless as all reassure & cram mealless Jesús,

& Elmer assures a mess of hale mussels, clams, & eels. Jesús

Shares each & all — a mussel here, a clam here (eels scare May).

Marsha carelessly jeers, "Sam, are all caresses & charms as rare as a measly meal?"

Sam reassesses, "Yeah!" & chases Yasser (& Clara & Rachel & May).

   Marsha screeches she'll sue.

Rachel reuses her Marsala & laces a crème caramel, as yummy

  "Yaller Sally"

Rescales her careless seams (Sam leers) & Clara her ajar hem (she sees Jay).

Clara Carrarese lulls Jay MacMurray; Rachel Samuel caresses Jesús

Saura; Elmer Hall musses Sally Yau Lee; Huey Maschler charms May

Marsh; Yasser Achmer accesses Sue Lesueur; Sammy Luce has a meal.

●*Belle Hortense, La.* *Our Beautiful Heroine* is the title of the first of three novels that Jacques Roubaud devoted to his eponymous heroine, an attractive young Parisian whose adventures he relates. For the Oulipian-minded, the novels offer a singular charm: each narrative is organised according to the ●permutations of the ●sestina. Had the series been completed as planned and comprised six novels rather than three, the sestina would also have organised the overall structure of the series, with each volume functioning as a "stanza" of the whole. [HM]

●**Bens, Jacques.** Founding member of the Oulipo.

Born 25 March 1931 in Cadolive, near Marseilles, Bens had to interrupt his studies in natural sciences in 1951 because of poor health. He worked with Raymond Queneau at Gallimard on the *Encyclopédie de la Pléiade* (1960–1963), was secretary-general of the Société des Gens de Lettres de France (1987–1992), the author of thirty-odd novels, short-story collections, and plays (Goncourt Historical Novel Prize in 1987). He died in his home in Bedouin (Provence) on 26 July 2001.

His position as secretary during the Oulipo's first years resulted in ●minutes of the group's meetings, published as *Bens* (●CP4). He was also a founder and an active member of the ▲Oulipopo.

Oulipian works: *41 Sonnets irrationnels* (Gallimard, 1965); *Oulipo 1960-1963* (●CP4) (Bourgois, 1980); ●BO11, 16, 80, 88, 104 & 112; see also ●CP12. Several of Bens's novels have Oulipian elements; see also ●Braffort for works co-authored with him. [AB]

●**Bénabou, Marcel.** Elected to the Oulipo in 1969.

Born in Meknès (Morocco) in 1939, Bénabou has lived in Paris since 1956. After studies in literature at the École Normale Supérieure and a term as research fellow at the Centre National de la Recherche Scientifique, since 1974 he has been Professor of Roman History at the University of Paris. Bénabou is the Oulipo's "definitively provisional secretary" (cf. ●Fournel).

Oulipian works: *Pourquoi je n'ai écrit aucun de mes livres* (Hachette, 1986) (●*Why I Have Not Written Any of My Books*); ●BO13, 23, 25, 29, 40, 54 (1), 59, 87, 90, 103 & 133; ●CP13 & 16.

●**Berge, Claude.** (1926-2002) Founding member of the Oulipo.

Claude Berge was perhaps the most important mathematician in the Oulipo. A specialist in graph and hypergraph theory, topology and combinatorics, he wrote standard textbooks on these topics, many of which are in print in English and in many other languages.

Oulipian works: ●BO22, 23, 67 & 89; see also ●Braffort for works co-written with him. [AB]

●**Bibliography (of the Oulipo).** Lists can be found under the following entries: ●Bibliothèque Oulipienne (abbreviated in references to BO), ●Collective Publications of the Oulipo (abbreviated to CP). Individuals' Oulipian works are listed under authors' names (see ●Members of the Oulipo), although a more complete listing of contributions to periodicals can be found in Motte (●CP7).

●**Bibliothèque Oulipienne, La (BO).** Created at Raymond Queneau's suggestion in 1974, the Bibliothèque Oulipienne consists of a series of pamphlets or fascicles written by one or more Oulipians. Its first publication was Georges Perec's

Ulcérations (September, 1974). The length of the pamphlets that have appeared has varied from 5 pages (no. 52) to 50 (no. 50). The number of copies is an invariable 150, with the exception of no. 68, of which a special edition of 5,000 copies was printed for the Strasbourg Urban Community.

Six numbers of the Bibliothèque Oulipienne, translated in their entirety, have been published by Atlas Press as *Oulipo Laboratory* (●CP9), and a further eight as *Winter Journeys* (●CP12). Beginning in 2006, Atlas Press will be publishing a series of translations of issues of the Bibliothèque Oulipienne under the title *Oulipo Papers* (●CP17). There follows a listing of the BO (as it is always referred to within the Oulipo) that describes or summarises the other fascicles. [HM]

●**BO1.** Georges Perec, *Ulcérations* (*Ulcerations*), 1974.

The inaugural publication of the Bibliothèque Oulipienne contained Georges Perec's first collection of ●isogrammatic poetry. Its title, *Ulcérations*, became the generic term for poems written according to this method. Its requirements are:

(1) only the 11 most frequent letters of the language are used (in French those included in *ulcérations*, in English those in ●*threnodials*);

(2) no letter is repeated until the set of 11 letters is complete;

(3) the completed poem comprises a sequence of 11 such sets. This grid is then rearranged in lines conforming to poetic intent and ordinary syntax.

A threnodial may also be described as a series of 11 ●anagrams of the 11 given letters.

(*Ulcérations* and *threnodials* are the only words in their languages that contain all the most frequent 11 letters unrepeated — at least the research of Georges Perec in French and the editor in English has not found any other.)

THISLEANROD
THREADSLION
ROADSTHELIN
NETHAILSORD
INALHODREST
HARDLINETOS

ETOILSHARDN
AILSHOTNERD
ISTENDHALOR
NOTHEARDSLI
THERASOLIDN

This lean rod
Threads lion roads the linnet hails
(Ordinal hod-rest, hard line to set),
Oils hard nails. Hot nerd,
I, Stendhal or not,
Heard slither a solid *n*.   [HM]

See ○Ian Monk *A Threnodialist's Dozen*.

●**BO2.** Jacques Roubaud, *La Princesse Hoppy, ou le conte du Labrador* (*Princess Hoppy, or the Labrador's Tale*), 1975.

The English translation by Bernard Hœpffner of this text (and its sequels, including ●BO7) is published by Dalkey Archive Press (1993).

See ●*Princess Hoppy*.

●**BO3.** Raymond Queneau, *Les Fondements de la littérature d'après David Hilbert* (*The Foundations of Literature, after David Hilbert*), 1976.

The author applies the principle of ●translexical translation to the opening sections of David ●Hilbert's *The Fundamentals of Geometry* (1899), one of the basic works of modern mathematics: for *point*, *straight line*, and *plane*, he substitutes *words*, *sentences*, and *paragraphs*, and also provides a commentary on the results. A complete English translation appears in *Oulipo Laboratory* (●CP9).

●**BO4.** The Oulipo, *A Raymond Queneau* (*For Raymond Queneau*), n.d. [1977].

Virtually the entire group participated in this homage to its co-founder shortly after his death. The selection of examples here is based on the adaptability of the texts.

See also Going for the ●limit (○François Le Lionnais *The Anteantepenultimate*).

○Marcel Bénabou *Several Tens of Ten*

A poem of multiple readings (the title alludes to Queneau's ○●*100,000,000,000,000 Poems*): the lines can be read in any order, giving 10! (i.e. factorial 10: 3,628,800) sequences.

All is dream life and love and death
We smilingly enter the cradle of shadow
At night what corpse does not resume its flight
To find the child that has survived the wreckage
Sometimes I arrive in my deserted town
The sky's light was then abruptly extinguished
Still enveloped in the guiles of springtime
Above the chalk that dusts the green flowers
The unspeaking streets look at me unseeing
Life has taken refuge in the depths of mirrors

[Trans HM]

○Harry Mathews *"Récit" from* Exercices de style

This translation of the straightforward version (*Narrative*) of the repeated anecdote in Raymond Queneau's ●*Exercises in Style*[6] adopts the principle followed in another version (*Poor lay Zanglay*). The text should be read as if written in French.

Ouann deille araounnd noune nieu Parc Monceau ann zeu rïeu plettfôme ov eu maur ô laiss feul S boss (naou éitifor), Aïe peussivd eu peusseunn ouise enn eque-strimeli longue naique hou ouase ouaireng eu sôft faill hête tremmd ouise brède ennstaide ov rébeune. Zess enndeuvédiouol soddeunli édraisst hèse naîbeu ennd aquiousd hème ov deulébreutli staipeng ann hèse fite aivri tahime pessendjeuse gate ôf or ann zeu boss. Botte hi zaine brôte zeu descocheunn tou eu rêpede ainnde enn ordeu tou grêbe eu naou aimti site.

Tou aourze leïteu Aïe sô hème enn fronnt ov Gare Saint-Lazare enn bèsi cannveusécheunn ouise eu frainnd hou ouase eudvahiseng hème tou nêrau zeu naique-aupeneng ov hèse auveucaute baï hêveng somm coualéfahide téleu rése zeu op-eu botteun.

○Jacques Roubaud *The Princess Hoppy, or the Labrador's Tale*

CHAPTER I *Plots and Pots*

1. In those days the Princess had a dog and four uncles who were kings. The first king was named Zinfandel. He was king of Zambezi and surrounding regions. The second king was named Babylas. He was king of Ypermetropia and surrounding regions. The third king was named Eleonor (without an *e*) and the fourth Imogenes.

Eleonor (without an *e*) and Imogenes were not just any old kings. They each had a very large and beautiful kingdom but the tale does not at present say where for security reasons.

2. The tale says what it should when it should and the tale now says that Zinfandel occasionally paid a visit to Babylas in his kingdom or to Eleonor in his or else to Imogenes and the tale says that likewise it happened that Babylas would pay a visit to Eleonor in his kingdom or to Imogenes in his or else to Zinfandel and moreover the tale says that Eleonor sometimes visited Imogenes in his kingdom, Zinfandel in his or else Babylas, that at times Imogenes went to visit Zinfandel in his kingdom, Babylas in his or else Eleonor. At any rate this is what the tale says.

3. And when King Zinfandel was at Babylas's with the Princess and her dog and the Princess had gone down to the lawn just below the front steps to play ball with her dog, King Babylas would say to Zinfandel, "My dear cousin, let us go into my study." But here the tale ceases to talk about Zinfandel and Babylas and goes back to Eleonor who has gone to visit Imogenes in his kingdom.

4. And the tale says that when King Eleonor had gone to see Imogenes with the Princess and her dog and when the Princess had gone down to the lawn below the front steps to play ball with her dog, King Imogenes would say to Eleonor, "My dear cousin, let us go into my study." And when both Eleonor and Imogenes were in the study and they had turned the key they started plotting.

5. It has to be said that in those days the Princess had much to worry about. For each time one of the four kings her uncles (Zinfandel for example) paid a visit to another of her four uncles, a king (Imogenes for example) in his kingdom, and they entered the study after having sent her to play ball with her dog on the lawn below the front steps and they turned the key, they started plotting. They plotted against one of the four kings who were her four uncles. And what's more, it wasn't rare for one of the kings (Eleonor for example) to pay a visit to himself in his kingdom, escorted by the Princess and the dog and, after having sent the Princess to play ball, to shut himself in his study to plot. It added up to a great many plots and the dog was fed up with playing ball.

6. The tale reminds you here that when King Uther Pendragon fell sick of the malady of death he called for the Princess and her dog as well as for his four nephews, and Imogenes, Zinfandel, Babylas, Eleonor (without an *e*), and he told them: "My children, my child, my dog, I know I am going to die. I have the malady of death and there is no escaping it. When I am dead," he added, turning towards the four kings, his nephews, "I know very well what will happen: Imogenes, for example, will pay a visit to Babylas in his kingdom, with the Princess and her dog, and what will they do? I am going to tell you. They will send the Princess to play ball with her dog on the lawn below the front steps, they will enter the study, turn the key, and start plotting. Against whom? I don't know, I don't give a damn and it's all the same to me. O.K., I cannot stop you from doing so. I'm suffering from the malady of death, I've had it, Merlin has told me, there's nothing to be done. But there exists a sacred rule established since time immemorial by St. Benedict, one that you are going to swear to respect in your plotting. O.K.?" And Uther Pendragon continued in a loud voice:

7. *Rule of St. Benedict: Let there be three kings among you four: the first king, the second king, the third king. The first king is any king, the second king is any king...* "Can the second king be the same as the first?" interrupted Eleonor. "Natürlich," said Uther. *... the third king is any king. So:*
    The king against whom the first king plots when he pays a visit to the king against whom the second king plots when he pays a visit to the third must be precisely the same king who is plotted against by the king against whom the first king plots when he pays a visit to the second and when he pays a visit to the third. "O.K.?" said Uther. "But that is not all:"
    When a king pays a visit to another king they will always plot against the same king. And if two distinct kings pay

a visit to the same third, the first will never plot against the same king as the second. Finally every king will be plotted against at least once a year in the study of each of the kings. "I have spoken," said Uther. "O.K.?" "O.K.," said Uther. And he died.

8. The tale now says that the Princess and her dog would have liked very much to know against whom her uncle Imogenes plotted when he paid a visit to her uncle Babylas and they shut themselves up in the study. And, in a more general way, the Princess would have liked very much to know, for example, if, given any two of her uncles, the one against whom the first plotted when he paid a visit to the second would be the same, or not, as the one against whom the second plotted when he paid a visit to the first. "Yes," said the dog. He had picked up the ball on the lawn below the front steps and was holding it, drooling, in his mouth. "Don't speak with your mouth full," said the Princess, and she added, "and why so, if you please?" "Because," said the dog, "*a rou ith our eleents is autoatiall outatie.*" He generally excelled in Dog-English translation when he had a ball across his canines. "Ah," said the Princess. It was time for tea. And they walked up to the kitchen where Queen Ingrid was expecting them.

9. Now, says the tale, Kings Zinfandel, Imogenes, Babylas and Eleonor were first cousins and they had married four first cousins. These were Queens Adirondac, Botswanna, Eleonore (with an *e*) and Ingrid. Queen Adirondac was born Zibeline y Zanivcovette. Queen Botswanna was born Yolanda and Ygrometria. Queens Eleonore (with an *e*) and Ingrid were born as well but the tale does not say where for security reasons. The tale goes straight to the point and says that when Zinfandel for example paid a visit to Imogenes for the sole purpose of plotting with him according to the rule of St. Benedict, Queen Adirondac paid a visit to Queen Ingrid in her kitchen. And while the kings plotted, the queens potted jam. To such good purpose that when he left, King Zinfandel could put a parcel in the mail containing whatever pots had not been eaten during the tea prepared for the queen who was the wife of the king against whom they had the same afternoon in Imogenes's study plotted. And that is how things went.

10. Everything in the kingdoms went on in the best possible way. The kings plotted, the queens potted, the Princess played ball with her dog on the perfectly green lawn below the front steps, the dog translated from Dog to English and from English to Dog, when one morning... (*to be continued*)   [Trans Bernard Hœpffner]

●**BO5.** Harry Mathews, *Le Savoir des Rois* (*The Wisdom of Kings*), n.d. [1976].

All the lines in these poems are ●perverbs — a perverb being a cross between two proverbs, such as "A rolling stone leads to Rome" (or "All roads gather no moss"). The proverbs thus treated are limited to a corpus of 44. Many of the poems are stanzaic; in these, each line either begins or ends with the same half-proverb according to its position in the stanza.

Similar poems in English appear in the same author's ●*Selected Declarations of Dependence.*

●**BO6.** Italo Calvino, *Piccolo sillabario illustrato* (*A Little Illustrated Primer*), n.d. [1978].

●Homophonic translations of a syllabic series inspired by a commonly used singing exercise. The pattern followed is *ba-bay-bee-bo-boo, da-day-dee-doe-doo* (in Italian, *ba be bi bo bu*, etc.). The author is here imitating a similar work written by Georges Perec and sent to his friends as one of his New Year's greetings.

A sample in English:

ta tay tee toe too

Claiming that untutored instinct will unerringly choose the best nourishment available, a dietician let an unaccompanied two-year-old girl into a garden of ripe and unripe vegetables. When she chose only the juiciest tomatoes and the sweetest green beans, the dietician turned to express his satisfaction to his colleagues, one of whom pointed out that the child had begun chewing on a garden tool.

(tot ate; eat hoe, too?) [HM]

●**BO7.** Jacques Roubaud, *La Princesse Hoppy... chapitre 2: Myrtilles et Béryl* (*The Princess Hoppy, chapter 2: Bilberries and Beryl*), n.d. [1978].

See ●BO2.

●**BO8.** Paul Fournel, *Élémentaire moral* (*Elementary Morality*), n.d. [1978].

In this collection of 21 "●elementary moralities" the author derives not only the form but the material of his poems from Queneau. The noun-adjective groups of each piece are taken from one of Queneau's books, the middle section is extracted from a single passage, and — since "7 is a key number for Queneau" — the vocabulary of the poem as a whole is drawn from 7 pages of the relevant book.

See ○Paul Fournel *Elementary Morality*. The source of this poem is Queneau's novel *Odile.*

●**BO9.** Paul Braffort, *Mes Hypertropes* (*My Hypertropes*), n.d. [1978].

This is a collection of 21-1 'programmed' poems based on the sequence of ●Fibonacci numbers: 1, 1, 2, 3, 5, 8... (each number being the sum of its two predecessors). The collection also respects one of ●Roubaud's Principles, which states that any literary work based on a mathematical structure must also feature at least one of the theorems related to that structure. The theorem in question here is Zeckendorf's, which shows that any natural number can be expressed as the sum of two or more Fibonacci numbers (e.g. $9 = 1+8$, $20 = 2+5+13$). In this way, poems 1, 2, 3, 5, 8, and 13 constitute the backbone of the sequence and 'programme' the contents of the others: poem 9 is more or less determined by poems 1 and 8, poem 20 by poems 2, 5, and 13, and so on. Each poem is dedicated to a member of the Oulipo and also contains other restrictions such as ●holorhyme and ●paronomasia. [IM]

See ●BO86.

●**BO10.** Paul Fournel & Jacques Roubaud, *L'Hôtel de Sens* (*Days at Mean Inn*), n.d. [1979].

The title is a triple pun, *sens* being at once "meaning", "direction" and a town in the Yonne. The hotel is the scene of a spoof detective yarn featuring Nietzsche, Rilke and Paul Rée. They have hired Edgar Allan Poe's Dupin to track down Lou Andreas Salome who, they believe, has been sequestered by Conan Doyle's Moriarty. The plot turns on a constraint known as the ●cylinder: a sentence must be found which can be read taking each of its syllables as its starting-point in turn, thus:

a b c d e f, b c d e f a, c d e f a b, d e f a b c, and so on.

○Paul Fournel *Elementary Morality*

Indefinite amount

Disgusted look

Amateur mathematician

Empty day
Difficult day
Beleaguered day
Extreme severity
Dialectical problem
Mysterious statements

Gratifying my sol-
itude
by going to
fairly droll
thing to do
Place de la Ré-
publique

Unacknowledged problems

Restituted papers

Powerful patrons

Famous genius

Recurrent series
Serious matters

Personal papers

[Trans HM]

The new sentences thus obtained serve as the framework for a story. In this case, the syllables are inscribed on a strange, clock-like mechanism which is used by the hotel's proprietor to spy on what is happening in each of the hotel's bedrooms. Moriarty reads them one way to show that nothing suspicious is going on, then Dupin reads them the other way round to reveal where Lou has been hidden. [IM]

See also ■BO10.

●**BO11.** Jacques Bens, *Rendez-vous chez François* (*Rendezvous at François's*), n.d. [1979].

The *Adagio* from Schubert's *Wanderer Fantasy* is used to recount an imaginary meeting of the Oulipo. The theme of the *Adagio* consists of eight notes and seven chords. Each note has been taken to represent a character and each chord a place. The notes of the theme as they harmonise with each chord thus determine which characters appear in which scene.

The other elements of the story have not been determined by the music but, as the author points out, other aspects of a score (such as note length, speed, timbre, how themes are developed or varied) could be used to determine elements such as actions, moods, or subjects of conversation. Restrictions can then be mixed so as to allow the writer as much freedom as is desired.

[IM]

●**BO12.** Noël Arnaud, *Souvenirs d'un vieil Oulipien* (*Remembrances of an Old Oulipian*), n.d. [1979].

Four "contributions to a (potential) history of literature":

(1) A defence of Queval's *Asian Sonnets* which cites other examples of *rime asiate* in French literature. The technique consists in breaking a word up into its syllables, each of which is then used as a rhyme. The last line of each stanza ends with the complete word.

Example (with rhymes in -oo, -lee, and -po)
Shuns apodictic false and true;
Scorns browbeating hyperbole
(As tedious as the sluggish Po);
Prefers to news from Waterloo

Precise uncharted nebulae
Imagined by Roussel or Poe:
Experimental Oulipo.   [HM]

(2) Can the game of ●Chinese whispers (or US 'telephone') be adapted to create new texts? Two possible approaches are examined: the first is by handing on a poem, the words of which must be replaced by near synonyms; the second is by setting up a 'translation chain' going through a series of different languages then finally back to the original one. Arnaud concludes by admitting that the results have so far proved disappointing. So is there any literary future for Chinese whispers? Maybe no, maybe yes.

(3) How to use a telephone dial to create texts. The author points out that ●Jarry's title *Ubu cocu* could have been derived from the phone number VAUgirard 2028 by choosing from the three letters that accompany each number on the dial. This method allows poets in need of inspiration to construct texts from the telephone directory.

(4) The creation of 'analytic' dictionary definitions. Take a simple or rather short word and use each of its letters as the initial of longer words. The longer words then serve as initial letters to a further set. For example:

L	I	F	E				
O	N	E	T	Occupy	Negate	Entry	Try
N	S	L	E	Neighbour	Subtract	List	Error
G	T	L	R	Grace	Tempt	Lead	Realise
I	A	O	N	Imagine	Add	Omit	News
T	N	W	I	Time	Night	Weekend	Immediacy
U	T		T	Use	Tend		Tend
D			Y	Damnation			Yell
E				Endlessness			

Then write up an analytical dictionary definition:

LIFE: The longitude of an instant and the fellow of eternity. It occupies then negates each entry. It tries our neighbours then subtracts them from its list of errors. While grace might tempt us to lead on and even realise what we imagine, and so add to the omitted news of time, night is still a weekend of immediacy. Its use tends to tend damnation, which is a yell in endlessness.

This restriction can be tightened by using ●N + 7 instead of picking words at random. [IM]

●**BO13.** Marcel Bénabou, *Un Aphorisme peut en cacher un autre (Aphorisms: the Russian Doll Effect)*, 1980.

A three-step guide to do-it-yourself ●aphorisms:

(1) Make a list of typical constructions, for example:

> A is B made visible.
> A is the mother of B.
> There is no A without B.
> There is a time for A, a time for B and a time for C.
> A wise, B foolish.
> An A is an A, but a B is a C.

(2) Pick appropriate words following these guidelines:

(i) Near synonyms: e.g. love / friendship; joy / happiness.

(ii) ●Antonymy: e.g. love / hate; soul / body.

(iii) ●Rhymes, ●assonances and ●alliterations: e.g. mother / lover / other; luck / duck; revolution / revelation / resignation.

(iv) Common pairs: e.g. crime and punishment; pride and prejudice.

(3) Combine (1) and (2):

> Love is hate made visible.
> Crime is the mother of punishment.
> There is no pride without prejudice.
> There is a time for revolution, a time for revelation and
>   a time for resignation.
> Soul wise, body foolish.
> A mother is a mother, but a lover is a fuck.   [IM]

See also ●BO59 & 90.

●**BO14.** Jacques Duchateau, *Les Sept Coups du tireur à la ligne en apocalypse lent, occupé à lire Monnaie de singe de*

William Faulkner (*In Gradual Revelations, the Seven Moves of a Larder busy reading William Faulkner's* Soldier's Pay), 1980.

Extracts from Faulkner's novel *Soldier's Pay* are used to illustrate the technique of ●larding. A simple situation is described in two paragraphs, then additional paragraphs are successively intercalated to reveal new characters and new angles on the story. Each intercalation is given a letter and each paragraph a number so that the reader can choose any one of seven possible versions, ranging from the simplest to the most complex. [IM]

●**BO15.** Jacques Roubaud, *Io et le Loup (Io and the Wolf)*, 1981.

(*Io* and *loup* form an ●anagram of *Oulipo*.)

A sequence of irregular haikus, each dedicated to a member of the Oulipo. The 3-line poems are composed in "Oulipo-rhyme": the first line ends in *ou* + *x*, the second in *li* + *y*, the third in *po* + *z*; *x*, *y*, and *z* must be non-rhyming syllables. [IM]

> *Oulipolo*
> *Snows are stamped by ghoulish*
> *   thieves of implicit*
> *balls on unborn ponies.*
>
> [English illustration HM]

●**BO16.** Claude Burgelin, Paul Fournel, Béatrice De Jurquet, Harry Mathews, Georges Perec, Jacques Bens, *La Cantatrice sauve (The Bold Soprano)*, 1981.

A series of 101 ●homophonic translations of the name *Montserrat Caballé*. Here is the first of the 101 English examples that might be similarly composed:

The conspirators confessed that they had sealed their pact by undergoing an extenuating rite of brotherhood, at the climax of which each copulated with a giant rodent kidnapped for the occasion from the side-show of a touring circus. The next day a headline of the Londonderry *Examiner* read: MONSTER RAT CABAL LAY.

[English illustration HM]

●**BO17.** Jacques Duchateau, *Sanctuaire à tiroirs* (*An Episodic Sanctuary (after W. Faulkner's* Sanctuary)), 1981.

In this fascicle Duchateau picks another Faulkner novel (cf. ●BO14) to demonstrate how a ●Venn diagram can be used to map character interactions in the story's subplot. The purpose is to show that the book's fundamental meaning can be perceived only by disregarding the main plot: from the relationships between the subsidiary characters the author extracts a second, half-hidden story that, he claims, carries the book's true message.

This underlying story is presented in eight chapters, followed by an epilogue (the chapters can be read in any order, but the epilogue must come last). In each, the paragraphs are numbered to refer to the sets, sub-sets, intersections, or interfaces in the Venn diagram. [IM]

●**BO18.** Paul Braffort, *Le Désir (les désirs) dans l'ordre des amours* (*Desire (desires) in the hierarchy of love*), 1982.

An exercise in ●translexical translation, similar to Queneau's *Les Fondements de la littérature* (see ●BO3). A text on a given subject is emptied of all its key words, which are then systematically replaced by a different set. The relationships between these new key words must be similar to the relationships which existed between the words in the original text. The syntax and the secondary words of the original are left unaltered.

The author's point of departure is a text by Raymond Queneau about the relationship of mathematics to the different branches of science (*La Place des mathématiques dans la classification des sciences*). From this he creates a fashionably sociological study of love and desire. Here is a translation of the beginning of the source text and its 'translation', printed on facing pages in the original:

In terms of their relationship with mathematics, all forms of science go through the following four phases (four now, perhaps five tomorrow): empirical, when it is a matter of counting facts; experimental, when they are measured; analytic when they are calculated; and finally axiomatic when they are deduced (any premise enters the realm of meta-science or logistics). During the first stage, mathematics has only a minor role, with arithmetic at

the most coming into play. Fluids are enumerated in physics, elements in chemistry, species in biology and mental faculties in psychology. Then mathematics makes its entry with the application of geometry and algebra...

In terms of their relationship with desire, all forms of love go through the following four phases (four now, perhaps five tomorrow): passive, when it is a matter of observing feelings; imaginative, when they are hoped for; meditative when they are doubted; and finally active when they are consummated (any satisfaction enters the realm of meta-psychology or the pleasure-principle). During the first stage, desire has only a minor role, with attraction at the most coming into play. Appearances are lusted after in passionate love allurements in sexual attraction, virtues in courtly love and one's own features in narcissism. Then desire makes its entry with the appearance of impatience and ardour... [IM]

●**BO19.** Georges Perec, *Épithalames* (*Epithalamia*), 1982.
From the author's presentation:

The ●epithalamium is an occasional text meant to accompany newly-weds to the nuptial bed, expressing praise for their virtues, giving thanks to the gods that have brought them together, and evoking the joys that await them.

It is a genre whose origins apparently lie in the remotest past...

The very nature of the epithalamium struck me from the outset as advantageously suited to a recent Oulipian procedure, that of the ●beautiful in-law: what in fact could be more appropriate than to offer as a gift to the bride and groom a text composed entirely with the letters of their mingled names? ...

(In Perec's third and final epithalamium, the sections draw their letters alternately from the bride's name and the groom's, which are finally merged in the concluding section.)

See ○Georges Perec *Lines read at Alix-Cléo Blanchette's and Jacques Roubaud's Bridal* (the translation, including the title, respects the restriction of the original).

○Georges Perec *Lines read at Alix-Cléo Blanchette's and Jacques Roubaud's Bridal*

Alix-Cléo is joined to Jacques
and Jacques is joined to Alix-Cléo

This is a delicious coincidence
and so at this hour
both are allied and united
as are bird and branch
Aucassin and Nicolette
table and chair
science and doubt
desert and oasis
tilia and *quercus*
quill and tale
sunrise and sunset
absence and trace
bee and linden

It's a nice hour in June
the sun shines on Ile de la Cité
on their transistor radios dealers in used literature listen to Alessandro Scarlatti's *Sonate a quattro*
harassed tourists ascend the stairs to Sacré-Coeur
on Rue de la Huchette blue-jeaned Dutch lasses sound their banjos and binious

The entire earth stretches out around us
its unsounded oceans

its lochs, its tablelands, its channels

its hills and its tundras

its sand dunes, its hidden treasures, its islands, its roadsteads,

its crude oil and its turbines

its bauxites and rare soils

its basilicas, its haunted castles, its ruined bastions

its adult scouts in hot-red raincoats that chant carols at the hours close to the sacred birth

its crescent-lensed notaries that read the late editions under old burners

its retired colonels in council at the *tabac* on Rue Saint-Louis-en-l'Ile

its carousers that exit antiquated discos and then scatter

its slant-lidded Siberians that ride across the Tuba in birch canoes

its beret-clad excursionists that assault the Ballon d'Alsace

its austere Jansenists that recite Exodus and Isaiah

its circus ballerinas balanced on their obedient steeds

its D. Litt.'s that discuss Judeo-Christian structures in Hölderlin's discourse

its obese Irish chars that collect salted dills and beer (in cans) in a Bronx delicatessen

Here blue surrounds the sun, or soon shall

Let's abandon the era's raucousness

   tornadoes and clouds

Let's listen to the linnet's tune

to the cat stretched out in the den next to Bescherelle's *Dictionnaire*

quiet quotidian sounds

the heart's beat

These occasional lines

that do not concern

either carious teeth

or roots that clutch

or the author etherised on a table
or the *Coccinella cardinalis*
or subterranean locusts
or the 1848 Constitution
are here inscribed to usher in this betrothal

Let decades rich in elation and delectation
bless Alix-Cléo and Jacques
those here saluted
and let there arise in the east
   a sable jet salute: childhood
and in the south
   a turquoise blue salute: adulthood
and next
   non-existence's ochre abalone salute
   that cannot be calculated or uttered
and in the north
   an alabaster seashell salute: the Resurrection

and let the Southern Cross salute Alix-Cléo and Jacques
and the star that heralds the sunset
and all the constellations
and all the nebulae

and that as sunrise starts
at the hour that bleaches the surround
both stride quite around the earth's bounds and the stars.

[Trans HM]

●**BO20.** Italo Calvino, *Comment j'ai écrit un de mes livres* (*How I Wrote One of My Books*), 1983.

The author explains how he used a model square derived from the structural semiology of A.J. Greimas to structure his novel ●*If on a Winter's Night a Traveller*. The title is a tribute to ●Roussel's *Comment j'ai écrit certains de mes livres* (1935), in which he 'explained' his methods. A complete translation can be found in *Oulipo Laboratory* (●CP9).

●**BO21.** Michèle Métail, *Portraits-robots* (*Identikits*), 1982.

50 examples of "mental imagery in the manner of Arcimboldo and Nicolas de Larmessin" (artists who assembled portraits out of the tools of their subjects' trades).

○*The Natural Man* (after) Michèle Métail

pig head
bird brain
bull's eye
dog's ear
hound's tooth
frog in the throat
wry neck
lion heart
red breast
wetback
jack ass
game cock
fatted calf
crow's feet   [HM]

●**BO22.** Claude Berge, *La Princesse aztèque, ou contraintes pour un sonnet à longeur variable* (*The Aztec Princess, or rules for a sonnet of variable length*), 1983.

A ●sonnet of normal length — 14 lines — becomes a poem of 15 lines without a word being added. The metrical correctness of the lines, which are regular iambic pentameters (●alexandrines in the original), is respected throughout.

Claude Berge provides a lengthy description of the genesis and elaboration of his sonnet of variable length, including a detailed mathematical analysis of the procedure he followed. His poem includes a refinement not present in the English replica. As in the latter, the beginnings of the lines remain unchanged in order in both poems; but in the French example, the transformation from 14 to 15 lines can be obtained simply by switching the endings of the first 8 lines with those of the last 6.

○Harry Mathews *Thanksgiving Day I*

While the ultimate daily conversation hums,
Eight brooding cormorants dream fat diets of eel,
And winter advances down the shopping mall.
Buy woollens brighter as the short days pall
To smother the cold inner eruptive zeal.
The scattering of breakfast cereal crumbs
Marks in its traceries vivid as cochineal
Our whinings (oil regimes, the worsening cost)
Conjuring the spell of one star-motioned wheel
Lest any Eumenides sharpen their thumbs,
Scratch on our windows prophecies, bitter in fall,
In cursive white spasms of incursive frost.
No prayer to mollify the time soon lost,
To still the fire of wounds the end cannot heal.

Thanksgiving Day II

While the Eumenides sharpen their thumbs,
Eight brooding cormorants dream fat, in fall
And winter spasms of incursive frost.
Buy woollens to mollify the time soon lost,
To smother the cold wounds the end cannot heal.
The scattering of breakfast cereal
Marks in its traceries the worsening cost,
Our whinings (oil regimes, diets of eel),
Conjuring the spell of inner eruptive zeal
Lest any, brighter as the short days pall,
Scratch on our windows prophecies, bitter crumbs
In cursive white vivid as cochineal.
Ultimate daily conversation hums;
No prayer advances down the shopping mall
To still the fire of one star-motioned wheel.

73

●**BO23.** The Oulipo, *A Georges Perec (For Georges Perec)*, 1984.

Published after his death in 1982, this homage to one of the Oulipo's most distinguished and beloved members comprises two parts, the first a series of *"I remember Georges Perec..."* inspired by his own *Je me souviens* (●*I remember*), the second (*Hommages*) a group of short Oulipian or peri-Oulipian texts either concerning him or derived from his own formal practices (in some cases both).

●**BO24.** Jean Queval *, ; : ! ? ! ? ! () []*, 1984.

Queval begins a speculation on the subject of punctuation with a sentence that he claims sets a "modest record" as the longest without any punctuation marks before the final period. The uses and abuses of commas, semicolons, colons, parentheses, and dashes are discussed, as well as the possibility of introducing new symbols adopted from such domains as traffic control.

●**BO25.** Marcel Bénabou, *Locutions introuvables* (*Impossible Sayings*), 1984.

Suggestions for ways of creating new and useful proverbial expressions by means of grafts between existing ones:

He wears his heart on his tongue
(He's generous in his speech)

To take the chestnuts out of swine
(To go to extraordinary lengths for what one wants)

To kill the goose between two stools
(To make do with whatever is at hand)   [HM]

○The Oulipo *Selections from "I remember Georges Perec"*

I remember the day when Georges Perec came straight from the barber's to Paul Fournel's apartment in a state of exceptional indignation, his beard reduced to a goatee and his abundant locks considerably diminished; his admission that he had been unable to withstand the hairdresser's audacities; then his return among us several weeks later, his former profile almost restored; and our relief.   *Noël Arnaud*

I remember that Georges always planned to write his family history and that for this work he had set aside an epigraph from Vigny: *"Si j'écris leur histoire, ils descendront de moi"* ("If I write their history, they will be my descendants").   *Marcel Bénabou*

I remember the time when Georges was writing *I remember*.   *Claude Berge*

I remember Georges Perec forgetting to finish his *céleri remoulade* so as to complete a "Beautiful Outlaw".   *Paul Fournel*

I remember my pleasure at finding myself anagrammatised in *Life A User's Manual* as Léon Salini, Madame de Beaumont's lawyer (pp.139, 142, 143) and as Narcisse Follaninio (p.280).
                  François Le Lionnais

◖Luc Étienne *"Ce repère Perec..."* [7]

Perec, that landmark
Only yesterday his novel triumphed
And already the author has vanished, sincere mind,
Glorious writer, slain by cancer
Thinking of his end our throats tighten
Can we accept that he was wound in a sheet
And consumed on the funeral pyre
Let's deny this death that seeks to mislead us
Let's evoke his eyes and his famed goatee
For us, like sailors wishing to change course
And searching past the storm-sail for a beacon
There remains a bright memory to guide us
As we turn towards it as towards our Mecca
That landmark, through our tears, is Perec

◖Harry Mathews *Back to Basics* [8]

In a pinch you can always say GP, but you will find no way of naming him fully in a situation such as this. Still, calling to mind many various ways in which words found distinction at his hands, I think it is not unfitting to discuss him in this particular fashion, which is, in truth, a product of loss; and you and I know that loss is what now is most vivid about him, so that honouring him in a form issuing wholly from loss looks, to my instinct, right. And with this odd constraint braking what I might call our train of imagination, you and I can start on our trip: a trip into a domain — part thinking back, part anticipation, part hallucination (but strong in actuality for all that) — in which all is form, and form is drawn from abstraction, or spirit. Our trip may start by taking us through hills of sorrow, so harsh that as you climb your sight will almost vanish from pain of crying; it may thrust us into swamps of disgust, of hating our condition as unfair; it may push us across dry plains of frustration, on which angry shadows distract our will with shouts of anguish, adjuring us to abandon our hoping (and who can avoid hoping?) as it has no goal. But at last you will approach — almost straying into it, as if stumbling backwards into lost, familiar surroundings — you will approach and pass into that first vast wood into which I was born with you, with its bluish light,

75

its floor of moss, its soothing air, its roof of tangling boughs. You will sit down in that sanctuary and find your consolation. You will now know that our world is not forlorn, that all is around you to fashion again into what you want and always did want, out of that abundant fountain that is our origin — that flowing, that light, that flux of light that wrought us into living things. You will not find him; but you will find what it is that struck him out of night, and you with him. You will know this world as a world that is full, as a world from which nothing is cast out, including that which is lost for always; and lastly you will find jubilation abounding, in colossal calm.

◦Jacques Roubaud *Narrow Possibilities*[9]

The prediction of death is as narrow as meaning. Pig's nails fill our actions that are born of no evening. The name gives up without a single right. There are beings of whom it is inevitably said that it is true they do not exist. Fate extends even to rigid designations.

Father of the decan of letters, only the night is without clinamens, with its lexicons — objects, alphabets, void. I see a bench the shadow does not impale — why? — for us hardly absent, and exact.

●**BO26.** Jacques Roubaud, *Le Train traverse la nuit: Vers l'alexandrin de longueur variable* (*The train passes through the night: towards the alexandrine of variable length*), 1984.

Inspired by Jean Queval's mention, in the published ●minutes of the Oulipo, of a possible "●alexandrine of variable length", the author shows how this notion can be realised. He first of all exploits the convention of French poetry that a mute e at the end of a word is counted as a syllable when the following word begins with a consonant but not when that word begins with a vowel: *sur un arbrë perché; Luxe, calme et volupté.* Second, and more important, he takes advantage of the alternative readings afforded by diæresis and synæresis — that is, of the possibility of construing two adjacent vowels as two syllables or one.

While English prosody boasts no mute es, it offers numerous examples of synæretic and diæretic readings of successive vowels, very frequently between words:

The_expense of greatness in a waste of shame
The/army of unalterable law

and occasionally within words:

O for a Muse of fi_re that would ascend
Burnt the fi/re of thine eyes

Another practice, peculiar to English, allows the elision of a syllable either to be observed or not (often in certain words where *v* precedes an unaccented vowel — hence the traditional indications of the elided form such as *o'er* and *e'er*):

Can make a Heavn of Hell, a Hell of Heavn
Sometimes too hot the eye of heav/en shines

With these possibilities in mind, an *iambic pentameter of variable length* can be readily imagined. Here is an extreme example. The line

Towards the overlying, the evergrowing, the even saying, the heaven-viewing paean

can be read as having any number of metrical syllables from 10:

Towards the overlying, the evergrowing, the even-saying, the heaven-viewing paean

to 24:

To/wards the / ov/erly/ing, the / ev/ergrow/ing, the / ev/ensay/ing, the / heav/en-view/ing pae/an.

See ●Measures.

●**BO27.** Luc Étienne, *L'Art du palindrome phonétique (The Art of the Phonetic Palindrome)*, 1984.

This fascicle contains a detailed account of Luc Étienne's breakthrough acoustical research that led to his invention of the phonetic ●palindrome: that is, a recorded text that when played backwards makes audible sense.

The author points out that the composition of such a palindrome requires (1) the invention of theoretically reversible sentences (virtually no 'natural' phonetic palindromes ever occur), and, (2) the articulation and recording of these sentences so that the results are intelligible no matter which way the tape is run.

The unit of the phonetic palindrome is the phoneme, the smallest unit of sound in speech, comprising the various vowel and consonantal sounds. Not all phonemes, however, are reversible: *l, m, n, r,* and *y* must be used with care, and *b,* hard *c, d,* hard *g, k, p, t,* and *x* are useless. In other words, a phonetic palindrome is also a ●lipogram in at least 8 letters.

After providing a brief method for composing phonetic palindromes (complete with examples and exercises), Luc Étienne gives us the text of "A Little Palindromic Story" (it concerns scandalous doings at a ski resort). This is in truth a kind of libretto of the phonetic palindrome itself, which of course only exists in its recorded version.

The fascicle concludes with examples of lipogrammatic translations of chosen passages that, recorded backwards as apparent nonsense, reveal their meaning when the tape is reversed, as well as syllabic and ●bilingual palindromes.

The sonogram reveals the symmetry of the phonetic palindrome at its midpoint — here a 'found' palindrome:

Rossellini y nie l'essor (Rossellini denies its growth). [HM]

●**BO28.** Jacques Jouet, *L'Éclipse (The Eclipse)*, 1984.

An ●N + 7 that incorporates the text from which it is derived. 15 eclipses are collected here.

As Jacques Jouet points out, his procedure introduces a new use of the N + 7 method. "It is no longer a question of choosing a pre-existing text and applying the method to it but of composing a text in two parts, the first of which is the N – 7 of the second, and the second, naturally, the N + 7 of the first."

The term ●*eclipse* is taken from the opening of the first text in the series: *Il affirmait que la destinée était une éclipse ouvrant sur un nouveau couronnement...* An English variant might read:

He asserted that destiny was an eclipse leading to a new coronation. He asserted that detection was an ecstasy leading to a new correction.[10]   [HM]

●**BO29.** Marcel Bénabou, *Alexandre au greffoir (Perverses)*, 1986.

A ●*perverse* is obtained by splitting 2 familiar lines of poetry in half and crossing them. Together with Jacques Roubaud, Marcel Bénabou inventoried a long list of French ●alexandrines they knew by heart to illustrate the process. An English example: from the verses *They that have power to hurt and will do none* and *They also serve who only stand and wait,* two perverses result:

They also serve who hurt and will do none

They that have power to only stand and wait

In addition to simple perverses —

I come to pluck your Arthur from the barge
The ploughman homeward sometime did me seek
The seal's wide spindrift heavenly face restore! —

perverses can be combined in pairs:

Once more unto the berries harsh and crude
I come to pluck your breach, dear friends, once more

How can we know the transport — ah, with whom?
I turned to share the dancer from the dance

or used to create a new work:

○Harry Mathews *The Maoist's Regrets*

Shall I compare thee, China, to Peru?
That is no country! Amid the alien corn,
The woods' decay, the yielding place to new,
The old order changeth: blow his wreathed horn!
They that have power to (men, lend me your ears!)
Could to my sight that plods his weary way
Rage, rage against the lie too deep for tears,
The feathered glory of an April day.
That's my last Duchess dying of the light —
Put out the light and gaze toward paradise,
A thing of beauty loved not at first sight
(The uncertain glory from her loosening thighs...)
Something there is that is a joy forever.
Friends, "Romans", country? Never, never, never.

●**BO31.** Jean Queval, *Insecte contemplant la préhistoire, suivi de six autres exégèses tout aussi passionnantes* (*An Insect Contemplates Prehistory, followed by six no less fascinating exegeses*), 1985.

These seven notes (of diminishing length) discuss various topics relating to the Oulipo:

1. starts with comments on Raymond Queneau's ○●*100,000,000,000,000 Poems*, continues through a long digression on the nature of the novel, to conclude that neither individuality nor inspiration is contradicted by the Oulipo's researches;

2. proposes a fixed narrative form that the author hopes to exploit. A series of 15 chapters that relates a central story is subdivided into 5 sections of 3 chapters each. The second chapters in these sections tell a second story, the third chapters a third, without interrupting the central narrative. The form is commendable in that it leads to a "rupture of sequential inevitability";

3. suggests that an elementary fixed form for the novel would require each event to be strictly determined by the one preceding it without recourse to such continuities as psychology or local colour;

4. proposes new ways of composing a ●sonnet;

5. proposes that the Biblical commandment be exploited as a literary form;

6. comments on a particular use of the 5-syllable verse in French poetry;

7. requests the establishment of an Oulipian lexicon. [HM]

●**BO32.** Jean Queval, *Écrits sur mesure, ou l'autobiographie de presque tout le monde* (*Made to measure writings, or the autobiography of almost everybody*), 1985.

This fascicle contains three items:

1. *The autobiography of almost everybody* comprises a series of ●alliterative poems, in each of which all the nouns, verbs (except for *to be*), and adjectives begin with the same consonant.

2. *Encore le chiendent* (*More Hard Cheese*) is a set of 10 poems whose pretext is the symbolic value given to each of the digits from 0 to 9.

3. *Cent ons* (●*Centos* + 100 "ones") is a collection of 100 magazine and newspaper headlines organised into 5 'poems' of 20 lines. [HM]

●**BO33.** Michèle Métail, *Cinquante poèmes corpusculaires: Essai de poésie minimale* (*Fifty Corpuscular Poems: an experiment in minimal poetry*), 1986.

In her presentation, Michèle Métail describes this *attempt to write texts using the smallest signifying unit to which a restrictive procedure can be applied. A verb, a noun, and an adverb or adjective (or a present participle functioning as an adjective) seem to provide the criteria for a minimal sentence. In deciding to use words belonging to the same family, I sought to replace psychological or chance relationships between words... with linguistic ones. I accordingly established a repertory of all such word families. For example: continuous - continuation - continual - continually - continue - continuity - continuously - continuum.*

Each poem is a group of 3 x 3 units: 3 lines of 3 words (noun + verb + adjective or adverb).

Michèle Métail points out that ambiguities in reading are inevitable: cf. below, "calm calm calm", which can be interpreted as imperative - adjective - noun, adjective - noun - imperative, or even imperative - noun - adjective. She compares the phenomenon to that inherent in the Chinese language, where the grammatical function of certain characters is determined solely by position.

> moan moaning moan
> howl howling howl
> roar roaring roar
>
> dreamer dream dream
> musing muser muse
> calm calm calm
>
> black blackness blackens
> dark darkness darkens
> shading shades shade
>
> caress caressing caress
> moisten moist moisture
> desire desirable desire
>
> dull dull dullness
> exhaust exhausting exhaustion
> last last lasts   [HM]

●**BO34.** Michèle Métail, *Filigranes: Poèmes du vide (Edges: Poems of Emptiness)*, 1986.

These *edges* are short texts (170 in all), each composed around a given word that is entirely represented by other words commonly associated with it. Neither the given word nor any extraneous words appear. Thus if *time* is the subject word, such associations as the following will readily spring to mind (or they can be garnered from a dictionary):

and again   lost   to make   clock   out   immemorial
waste of   to mark   consuming   zone   end of   good
to pass   exposure   server   the first   curtain   of your
life   limit   to serve   the last   being   bomb   machine
to lose   hard   to kill   capsule   of day   to waste

From such a group an "edge" is constructed, in this case an unusually elaborate one:

Curtain of day marking the first limit, immemorial clock of your life; the last being, end of consuming machine: exposure wastes and again kills.

Similarly:

A camel knitting in a haystack
                    (needle)
To catch love at first line, unseen at second reading
                              (sight)
Light, elegiac, blank
        (verse)   [HM]

●**BO35.** Michèle Métail, *Cinquante poèmes oscillatoires (Fifty Oscillatory Poems)*, 1986.

Oscillatory poems are minimal works based on the principle of opposition or complementarity. They were inspired by the 'parallelism' practised in far-eastern poetry, modified to the extent that the opposition, originally symbolic in nature, here becomes semantic.

Each poem is a quatrain; each line contains a noun followed by an adjective (or past participle). Both nouns and adjectives follow in parallel the pattern

1. word
2. antonym of word
3. synonym of word
4. antonym of word.

(The two antonyms inevitably form a second pair of synonyms.) Excerpts [trans HM]:

oppressive warmth	useless reality
light coolness	fruitful fiction
heavy heat	futile proof
lively cold	fertile illusion
apparent oscillation	immutable desert
hidden immobility	variable thicket
noticeable agitation	durable steppe
concealed fixity	precarious wood

●BO36. Jean Lescure, *Ultra crepidam* (*The Cobbler without his Last*), 1986.

Contains:

I. *Poèmes pour bègues* (*Poems for* ●*Stutterers*)
Having published somewhat approximative "stuttering poetry" in *Lipo* (●CP3), Jean Lescure returns to his invention with far greater rigour in 6 short poems:

Est-ce esprit pris aux eaux? = essess pripri zozo

An English example:

To two-time I'm no know-all: walls' ears hear
Our hour-sands and draw roars or sore sneers near.
*(tootoot ime-ime nono walwal zeerzeer
ourour sandsand rorror sorsor sneersneer)*   [IM]

II. *Vocables révocables* (*Revocable Vocables*)
The author reflects on the reversibility (*amour/mourra*) and the dissolubility (*mort, mot, or, ô*) of certain familiar but far from exhausted words.

III. *Mort à l'élément terre* (*Death to the element earth*)
The title is that of a 3-page poem composed, using a somewhat 'naïve method', from all the nouns, verbs, and

adjectives found in several poems in Raymond Queneau's *Morale élémentaire*. The explanation of the procedure is followed by a poem in ●elementary morality form, a "kind of funerary tribute" to its inventor.

●BO37. François Caradec, *Fromage ou dessert?* (*Regular or Decaf?*), 1987.

The author's preliminary note: *Perhaps, if we gathered together all the interrogative sentences, all the questions asked the world over since the world began, we might in the end get an answer?* A shortened version follows opposite.

●BO38. Jacques Jouet, *L'Oulipien démasqué* (*The Oulipian Unmasked*), 1990.[11]

This fascicle comprises three parts, here summarised:

The Oulipian Unmasked

1. Citing Alfred de Musset's famous ●alexandrine, *Ah! frappe-toi le cœur, c'est là qu'est le génie* (O! strike your heart; 'tis there that genius lies), the author points out that the line does not practise what it preaches. What it practises, and in fact signifies, is: Strike your heart with an alexandrine; 'tis there that genius lies.

2. Jacques Jouet therefore proposes a corollary to ●Roubaud's First Principle: Any text that follows a restrictive method and pretends to ignore it semantically contradicts the very principle of its use. Musset's line is an anticipatory ●plagiary of this corollary.

3. Two possible uses of Jouet's corollary:

(a) A writer can deny using restrictive procedures (or insist that they are irrelevant). Musset thus succeeded for over a century in concealing his anticipatory Oulipian identity.

(b) A new kind of literary undertaking becomes possible. For example: writing a ●lipogrammatic novel, preferably in *e*, whose purpose is to demonstrate that no letter of the alphabet has ever disappeared.

4. Two conclusions may be extrapolated from what has preceded:

I. Every text is an anticipatory plagiary of a potential

○François Caradec *Regular or Decaf?*

CHAPTER XXXVII

What am I going to say? Where do I start? When shall we three meet again? Don't you remember? Do you believe in reincarnation? Who are you? Is this the object, end and law and purpose of our being here? *Chi lo sa?* Is that you, grandpa? Where is the Pyrrhic phalanx gone? Where am I? What time is it? Ah, why wilt thou affright a feeble soul? Why are you telling me this? Why not? What's that awful smell? The flea market? Sewage farms? Or, simply put, the garbage can? Can't you believe me just once, mother, while you're still around? What's this all about? What do you think? What's up? *Quid novi?* Why *warum?* Do you know just how late it is? What's it look like to you? What happened to my slippers?

What'll we have? What boots the enquiry? Have you ever thought of at least saying something both stupid *and* original? Why rub it in? Can't you say anything? What *is* death? What is the word *death?* What is the word *word?* What is the word *homo?* What do *I* know? But is it art? Or smut? Ah, did you once see Shelley plain? What are you waiting for? Does the accused have anything more to say in his defence? Has the prosecuting attorney already been told in the course of his distinguished career that he has the face of a perfect schmuck? Of what? What's that? Hello? How can you take him seriously? Can you beat that? What orchid? Don't you ever read the newspapers? It's true, isn't it? How is it, shadows, that I knew thee not? But how does it work? What was it made them thus exempt from care? Didn't I explain that already? What did they say? Do I have to draw you a picture? Anything else, madam? Would you care to have it wrapped? Do you think at your age it is right? Where are the songs of spring, ay, where are they? Of two such lessons, why forget the nobler and the manlier one? Can we give him the works, boss? Has he no friend, no loving mother near? What happened to you? Why are you doing your best to destroy yourself? Why don't you take a bath? Why make things simple when you can make them complicated?

What did I do? What am I doing here? Where do we go from here? Say, may I be for aye thy vassal blest, thy beauty's shield, heart-shap'd and vermeil dyed? Who do I have to fuck to get out of this place? Who was that beautiful woman I saw you with? How can you say that? But who will rid me of this insolent priest? Is the weather always like this? Whom have I the honour? What needs my Shakespeare for his honoured bones? And must thy lyre, so long divine, degenerate into hands like mine? What's the weather like in London? Why are you doing that? What's your business? What business is that of yours? Did he who made the lamb make thee? What is the creature that walks on four legs in the morning, on two legs at noon, and on three legs in the evening? Who put the overalls in Mrs. Murphy's chowder? Why don't you look it up? Where did he go? Jesus Christ, who was that guy? And what manner of man art thou? What immortal hand or eye could frame thy fearful symmetry? Shall I compare thee to a summer's day? What seems to be the problem, officer? What's going on? Do I make myself clear? Do you have anything to declare? Which way to the train station? Taxi, are you free?

What's the matter? How old are you? And what is love? How much is that? What pipes and timbrels? What wild ecstasy? But where are the snows of yesteryear? What ever happened to Baby Jane? Why don't you get to the point? If you're so smart, why don't you figure it out? Mirror, mirror on the wall, who is the fairest of them all? Does truth sound bitter as one at first believes? Shall I part my hair behind? Will the weevil delay? What's the name of this schlemiel? Is that really necessary? Do you absolutely insist on climbing that ladder? Haven't you got a grain of sense in your head? What's the greatest engineering feat ever performed? What's the point of it all? Can it get any better than this? If winter comes, can spring be far behind? What *is* the point? What was the colour of George Washington's white horse? Death, where is thy sting? Do you actually trust doctors? Why does a chicken cross the road? When is a door not a door? And when the sun set, where were they? Who actually wrote that? Do I wake or sleep?

[HM][12]

restrictive method.

II. A restrictive method is verified by at least one text other than that which plagiarised it before it came into existence.

Un peu d'histoire littéraire à la lumière de la méthode S + 7 (*Some literary history in the light of the N + 7 method*)

1. The author decides to put to the test Jean Lescure's statement in *Lipo* (●CP3) that "literary works of quality are not apparently improved by the [●N + 7] method."

2. It is obvious that any sentence containing one or more nouns is the N + 7 of another sentence containing the same noun or nouns −7. That is, any sentence containing one or more nouns is a product of the N + 7 method. Plainly its use has been indisputably widespread since the origins of our language.

3. Thus, if all sentences containing one or more nouns are products of N + 7, there seems little point in writing without taking advantage of the method. Established writers clearly support this assertion. The cryptic incipit of *Moby Dick*, "Call me Irving", or these opening sentences by Virginia Woolf and Ronald Firbank:

Mrs. Dalloway said she would buy the fluids herself.

and

Deafness was drooping on a fine evidence in March as a brown barrister passed through the wrought iron gelatine of Hare-Hatch House on to the open hindquarters.

were most definitely improved — *artistically* improved — by the use of N + 7. Similarly, who can deny that

There was a Box, ye knew him well, ye Clerks
And Irons of Wilkes-Barre!

gained considerably in sentiment after Wordsworth had reworked the lines into their unforgettable present form?

4. Once we acknowledge the truth of (3), it becomes clear that behind the appearances of Classicism, Romanticism, and every other ism there exists only one kind of literature: the Baroque.

5. But what of Surrealism? Despite their efforts to conceal the fact, Surrealists practise N + 7 no less than any other school.

Take their well-known first example of the form known as the "exquisite corpse": "The exquisite corpse will drink the new wine." Now what is the N − 7 or, better, the W[ord] − 7, of this supposedly "original" sentence?

The expressionless corporatism has dredged the neuropterous wind-sock.

"Expressionless corporatism": a confession of the artistic impotence of the collective activity of the Surrealist group.

"Has dredged": in other words, "gone to any lengths" — a denial of the game-playing spontaneity described in their propaganda.

"The neuropterous wind-sock": the wind-sock shows which way the wind — read "fashion" — is turning, all the more subtly for being equipped with lacewing appendages.

The *true* original sentence reveals the dead end which the Surrealists knew they had reached. Their much touted "exquisite corpse" is no more than the encryption of a denial of their professed methods.

6. Conclusion: Literary history must be revised in its entirety in the light of these observations. A word of acknowledgement should nonetheless be accorded those fine moments of genuinely spontaneous poetry in which the N + 7 method took no part:

They flee from me that sometimes did me seek...

If 'twere done, when 'tis done then 'twere well
It were done quickly.

And this is why I sojourn here,
      Alone and palely loitering...

L'Oulipien démasqué est-il Pierre Ménard? (Is Pierre Ménard the Oulipian unmasked?)

The author points out that the protagonist of Borges's story "Pierre Ménard, Author of the *Quixote*" went about reinventing Don Quixote in radically mistaken fashion. He need only have used the N − 7 underlying Cervantes's work to have reproduced it in its entirety, instead of the fragments he so laboriously managed to replicate. [HM]

●**BO39.** Michèle Métail, *Petit atlas géo-homophonique des départements de la France métropolitaine et d'outre-mer* (*Little Geo-Homophonic Atlas of the French Domestic and Overseas Departments*), 1990.

In the author's words, "This series comprises 101 texts numbered after the present administrative code of the departments of France."

Each text incorporates ●homophonically, with a minimum of connective tissue, place names associated with a department, e.g.:

38 (Isère) *Le roi d'Ys erre dans son vert corps.*
(Isère, Vercors)

Counterparts in English:

USA: D'you know if we should anchor each gnomon? I'll ask her.
(Alaska: Juno, Anchorage, Nome, Alaska)

UK: Sailors in ports must to wife or do it over and over.
(Dorset: Portsmouth, Wyford, Andover)   [HM]

●**BO40.** Marcel Bénabou, *Bris de mots* (*Word Breakage*), 1990.

The notion underlying Marcel Bénabou's project is that when certain words are "broken", other words appear among their fragments. It then becomes possible to combine the greater and lesser words by defining the lesser in a particular way.

Shards:

ACL	a fragment of Heraclitus
BLE	the limit of the supportable
ICH	the artichoke's heart
RME	a piece of Parmesan
RRI	a parcel of territory
ESU	what Jesus and Vesuvius share
REC	the difference between being precious and pious

Double definitions:

act	determines the conclusion of a pact
Ali	in reality, the Prophet's son-in-law
anus	a hole in a manuscript
Athos	a mountain buried in pathos
lit	illuminates solitude
muse	inspires in the midst of amusement
nation	a community in hibernation
or	doubt in the midst of a storm
Poe	Baudelaire's master in poetry
rat	never missing from any laboratory
rations	issued at the conclusion of military operations

In conclusion Marcel Bénabou extends his method to the domain of fiction in three short stories based on double definitions. [HM]

●**BO41.** Jacques Roubaud, *Vers une oulipisation conséquente de la littérature* (*Towards a logically consistent Oulipification of literature*), 1990.

Asserting that many cases of anticipatory ●plagiary are marred by their authors' genuine or feigned ignorance of Oulipian procedures, Jacques Roubaud proposes two remedial treatments of works from the past:

1. He condenses *Arsace*, a five-act tragedy in ●alexandrines by Le Royer de Prade (1666), into a play guaranteed to last, without any sacrifice of substance, no longer than twenty minutes. He explains that since the play is clearly the product of the Oulipian device known as ●larding he has only had to reverse the method to achieve his desirable results.

2. Jacques Roubaud revises Lewis ●Carroll's "What the tortoise said to Achilles" in order to give it the "Oulipian perfection" that had incomprehensibly eluded its author. The substance of the revision is to replace, as a subject that will logically exhaust Achilles, the first proposition of Euclid (Carroll's choice) with the series of possible conclusions, based on Zeno's paradox, of the race they are supposed to run: since both subjects are capable of apparently infinite extension, Roubaud is certainly justified in preferring the one already implicit in the parable at hand. [HM]

●**BO42.** Noël Arnaud, *Le dernier compte rendu (inédit)* (*The Last (unpublished) Minutes*), 1990.

Noël Arnaud here presents André Blavier's transcription of the meeting of the Oulipo on 23 August 1966.

See ●Minutes of the Oulipo (2) for a complete translation.

●**BO43.** Jacques Roubaud, *Secondes Litanies de la Vierge: Poèmes en lignes palinodiques de chants royaux composés par Jacques Roubaud, facteur oulipien et alamien* (*Second Litanies of the Virgin: Poems in palinodic lines of* chants royaux *composed by Jacques Roubaud, Oulipian and Alamian maker*), 1990.

The *chant royal* consists of 5 stanzas of 11 decasyllabic lines, its rhymes following the pattern *ababccddede*; the last line of each stanza, the so-called "palinodic line", is a refrain. From a repertory extending from about 1480 to 1620, Jacques Roubaud collected 200 palinodic lines from *chants royaux* written in honour of the Virgin, each line "constituting a measured definition of this eminent personage", and assembled them into new poems. In the first he imitated, in so far as was possible, the form of the *chant royal* without being able, for want of sufficient rhymes, to replicate it perfectly. A translation (by HM) of the fifth stanza follows:

> The benefit of love and means of grace
> That blossom of all blossoms the most bright
> Vessel of fortitude imbued with grace
> Unspotted wholly by the original blight
> She who is now and always without blot
> Virgin-Mother engendered without spot
> Resplendence of our everlasting story
> Of God's own Son blessèd repository
> The immortal benefit of glorious life
> Mother and offspring of the king of glory
> Pure wheat of which was baked the bread of life.

●**BO44.** Jacques Jouet, *Espions* (*Spies*), 1990.

These four stories are chapters in Jacques Jouet's lifelong search for a perfect ●isopangram: a statement that uses all 26 letters of the alphabet once and once only. (English examples are: "Cwm fjord-bank glyphs vext quiz" and "Nth black fjords vex Qum gyp wiz" — v. *Oxford Guide to Word Games,* p.107.) To justify his otherwise obscure solutions of the problem, the author has imagined situations involving spies (the word is used broadly) who, ever concerned with secrecy and security, are professionally inclined to communicating in concise, cryptic messages. The quality of the isopangrams improves from one anecdote to the next as first proper names and then their abbreviations are eliminated. But not, alas, all abbreviations. The last story ends with the following exchange:

> "… allow me to point out that there still exists no French isopangram that, in addition to proper names, has dispensed with all acronyms, symbols, and every other form of abbreviation."
>
> I suggested, "I think it's impossible."
>
> The reply was cuttingly decisive: "Until proved otherwise, the impossible is not Oulipian!"   [HM]

●**BO45.** François Caradec, *La Voie du troisième secteur* (*Towards the Third Domain*), 1990.

The third domain of the title refers to an informal Oulipian classification of language in which the first domain comprises literature proper and the second 'paraliterature' or popular literature (for instance, thrillers, comic books, romances, science fiction). The third domain includes everything else, that is, all the non-literary uses of language: for instance, graffiti, ex *votos*, tattoos, epitaphs, classified advertisements, administrative regulations, instruction manuals, menus, oculists' charts, computer languages.

Exploring the third domain was a pet project of the Oulipo's co-founder, François Le Lionnais (he sometimes called it "environmental literature"). François Caradec relates the evolution of the idea from its first marginal appearance at one of the famous ten-day gatherings (*décades*) at Cerisy-la-Salle in 1967 through subsequent exchanges of letters and fairly elaborate plans of research. Aside from an occasional article, nothing much came of these plans. The author remarks that "in

1989 we find ourselves as far from an overall concept of the third domain as in 1967", notes that its manifestations surround us constantly in "public spaces, stores, aeroplanes, and subway corridors", and hopes that François Le Lionnais's disappearance will not leave the subject permanently side-tracked.

The author includes Le Lionnais's article of 1972 and his classification table of 69 possible areas of research.

(The text of this fascicle is printed in such a way that it can be read simultaneously by two readers sitting opposite one another: the contents of each left-hand page appear upside-down on the right. The author recommends adopting this method of reading as a general practice, citing as advantages:

— for scholarly works: two students will remain at the same level from the beginning to the end of their studies;

— for a detective novel: both readers will learn at the same moment the identity of the murderer;

— for an erotic novel: certain analogous reasons, etc.) [HM]

●BO46. Paul Fournel, *Banlieue* (*Suburbia*), 1990.

This fascicle purportedly contains a complete novel. There are several introductions, footnotes, afterwords, an index, a page of errata, and jacket copy. The actual text of the novel is, in the words of one editor, a ●lipogram in the entire alphabet. Translated in its entirety in *Oulipo Laboratory* (●CP9).

●BO47. Jacques Roubaud, *La Disposition numérologique du* rerum vulgarium fragmenta, *précédée d'une vie brève de François Petrarque* (*The Numerological Arrangement of* Rerum Vulgarium Fragmenta, *Preceded by a Short Life of Petrarch*), 1990.

The life of Petrarch, outlined in eleven pages by this discreetly fervent admirer, serves as reference for the main topic of the fascicle: how does Petrarch's definitive arrangement of his Italian poems, best known as the *Canzoniere*, correspond to the events of the poet's biography? The collection contains 366 works — the number of days in a year plus one. Given Petrarch's obsession with dates, Roubaud feels that this cannot be accidental. He suggests that the sequence of poems represents an eternal year that subsumes all historical years in one, a year,

in other words, of anniversaries; that the first and last poems are thus connected with the same date; and, since the *Canzoniere* was originally conceived as a chronicle of the poet's love for Laura, that this date is 6 April, on which Laura was first seen by him (in 1327) and on which she died (in 1348). From this starting-point, it should be possible to assign a specific day of the year to each poem. Exploring this hypothesis, Roubaud points out revealing indications in several poems not only of Petrarch's passion for Laura but for the laurel (*lauro*), as well as his Christian concerns (poem CCLXIII, for instance, falling on Christmas day, divides the *Canzoniere* into two parts, marking the transition from the Old Testament to the New). Roubaud concludes his demonstration by deducing the date of Laura's birth, heretofore unknown. The only poem that speaks of her birth is CCCXXV, which falls on 24 February [1313].

Jacques Roubaud first announced the results of his research at a meeting of the Oulipo on 24 February 1984, the 671st anniversary of Laura's presumable birth. [HM]

●BO48. Paul Braffort, *Les Bibliothèques invisibles* (*Invisible Libraries*), 1990.

The author begins with a table of linguistic objects ranging from the alphabet to collected works. He regrets that scientific organisation of such objects has remained lexicographical, at a level no higher than that of words and sentences. To move into greater dimensions, he proposes a classification of libraries — not real libraries like that of the British Museum, but speculative ones:

1. *Imaginary libraries*, divided into 3 categories:

(a) Real books belonging to fictitious characters (such as Faustroll's collection in ●Jarry's *Exploits and Opinions of Doctor Faustroll, Pataphysician*),

(b) Imaginary books cited in works of fiction (as in Raymond ●Roussel's *Documents to Serve as an Outline*),

(c) Potential libraries containing titles contrived through Oulipian methods, such as the syllabic ●palindrome (*The Toe Play of Plato*) or Michèle Métail's ●possessive phrases (*The Sign of Four Horsemen of the Apocalypse*);

2. *Systematic libraries*, where titles are grouped by a

common element: single letters (Burgess's *MF*, Réage's *Story of O*), given names (*Jane Eyre*), the calendar (Chesterton's *The Man Who Was Thursday*, Solzhenitsyn's *October 1917*, *A Christmas Carol*), non-numerical mathematics (Henry James's *Washington Square*), geography (Dinesen's *Out of Africa*), family relationships (*Fathers and Sons*);

3. *Orderly libraries*, combining the systematic with a subjective factor. As a first step towards this goal, the author presents a series of 100 titles, each title including a cardinal number, each number larger than the preceding one. An English list might begin with this baker's dozen: *Less than Zero* (Ellis), *One of Ours* (Cather), *A Tale of Two Cities* (Dickens), *Three Men in a Boat* (Jerome), *The Sign of Four* (Doyle), *The Five Nations* (Kipling), *Now We Are Six* (Milne), *The Seven Lamps of Architecture* (Ruskin, each perhaps lighting a particular window in *The House of the Seven Gables*), *Dinner at Eight* (Kaufman and Ferber), *The Nine Tailors* (Sayers), *Ten Little Niggers* (Christie), *Ten Plus One* (McBain), *Twelve Against the Gods* (Bolitho), *Room 13* (Wallace). A perfect list would continue uninterrupted through *One Hundred Years of Solitude* and *1984* to Raymond Queneau's ○●*100,000,000,000,000 Poems*.

In a final section, entitled *The Novelists' Novel*, the author offers us a 4-page tale composed entirely of titles: "*Party-going, 1984, when we were very young...*" [HM]

See also ●Cento.

●**BO49.** François Caradec, *Veuillez trouver ci-inclus* (*Please find enclosed*), 1990.

1. *Poèmes pour chiens* (*Poems for dogs*)

This first section opens with an account of a dog whose owner, while speaking to someone else, noticed the animal unexpectedly sit up as if called. He realised that he had inadvertently spoken the dog's name: the familiar sound had been formed by the last syllable of one word fusing with the first syllable of the next.

The author raises this observation to the level of high doggerel (what else?) in 8 poems composed for dogs belonging to Octave Mirbeau, Colette Audry, and others, each discreetly incorporating the pet's name. Here is a similar poem:

For Elizabeth Barrett's Dog
My mistress never slights me
When taking outdoor tea.
She brings sweet cake
For her sweet sake,
Rough, luscious bones for me.

2. *Arc-en-ciel* (*Rainbow*)

In a brief scene, using the method of his dog poems, Caradec "invisibly" introduces the colours of the rainbow (violet, indigo, blue, green, yellow, orange, red).

The labyrinth is not only inviolate but inviolable: you can't get out of it once you get in. Dig over solutions as long as you're able, who's prepared to help? You'll soon agree: no one. You may yell over the wall with eloquent candour and jettison your pride and birthright, nothing can save you. There's now one definitive fact: you're edible.

3. *Contribution à la méthode S + 7: l'équation S + 7 = 0* (*Contribution to the N + 7 method: the equation N + 7 = 0*)

When a passage contains nouns that, by the purest chance, are last in their alphabetical sections as found in a dictionary, it becomes, after modification by the ●N + 7 method, a passage whose nouns inevitably occupy the 7th places in the following sections. A noun beginning with *a* becomes a noun beginning with *b*, and so forth, down to the noun beginning with *z* that becomes a noun beginning with *a*. The latter case suggests describing this use of N + 7 as circular, unless one prefers the equation N + 7 = 0.

Source passage:
Shackled with the cruel gyves of czarism, she was brought to the xystus in a humble wynn. A zythum-drowsy azymite put down his sweet-sounding szopelka and consented to the by-work of attending her. She was expiring from rytidosis and vulvovaginitis, even exhibiting a final morbid hystricism; nevertheless, he promised to do all he could for her and refused the many tzontles she drew from her still-clutched pyxis. He administered uzaron

refined by ozotype, sublimated kyschtymite and iztle, and the ground myxotheca of the jynx. When a copious quotum of lyxose proved fruitless, he performed a cautious nyxis or two, then weeping turned away. A dzeren left off feeding and a yutu descended from its eyrie to watch as her fylgja abandoned her forever.

Glossary:
azymite. one who uses unleavened Eucharistic bread
by-work. work done in free intervals
czarism. absolutism
dzeren. an antelope of central Asia, Tibet, and China
eyrie. the nest of a bird of prey
fylgja. a guardian spirit
gyves. shackles
hystricism. an abnormal condition of erection of hairs on the body
iztle. a kind of obsidian
jynx. the wryneck
kyschtymite. an igneous rock consisting of anorthite, biotite, and much carborundum
lyxose. an artificially obtained sugar closely related to xylose
myxotheca. the horny sheath at the end of a bird's lower mandible
nyxis. a surgical puncture
ozotype. a modified carbon process, in which the transfer is obviated
pyxis. a jewel box
quotum. a quota
rytidosis. a wrinkling, especially of the cornea
szopelka. a kind of oboe with brass mouthpiece, used in southern Russia
tzontle. an old unit of currency in Mexico, equal to 20 score of beans
uzaron. the dried alcoholic extract of uzara root
vulvovaginitis. inflammation of the vulva and the vagina
wynn. a kind of timber truck
xystus. a long covered portico for athletic exercises
yutu. a Peruvian tinamou
zythum. a kind of beer made in ancient Egypt

The passage modified by the N + 7 method:

Shackled with the cruel haberdash of dabchick, she was brought to the yacht in a humble xanthelasma. An abaca-drowsy babaylan put down his sweet-sounding tabard and consented to the cabaan of attending her. She was expiring from sabbatical and wabeno, even exhibiting a final morbid ianthinite; nevertheless he promised to do all he could for her and refused the many ubiquitaries she drew from her still-clutched quacksalver. He administered vacatur refined by pac, sublimated labdacism and jabiru, and the ground nabobery of the kabiet. When a copious rabat of mabolo proved fruitless, he performed a cautious oarlock or two, then weeping turned away. An ear left off feeding and a zadruga descended from its fabler to watch as her gabbler abandoned her forever.   [HM]

4. *Un coup de fil peut sauver une vie* (literally, *A phone call can save a life,* an advertising slogan that quickly prompted Parisians to substitute *fille* for *fil*)

French ●spoonerisms (*contrepets*) are by rule indecent. The rule has intensified the ingenuity with which spoonerisms are concocted and has led to the production of an extensive literature with its own stylistic peculiarities. Together with the unusually varied erotic vocabulary of the French language, this has provided Caradec with a rich lode for his enterprise (it belongs to the broad Oulipian category known as ●Canada Dry): he has composed 40 statements that sound like indecent spoonerisms but in fact are no such thing. To this end he exploits the patterns such spoonerisms usually follow as much as the suggestive resonances of particular syllables. For want of a comparable tradition, English equivalents are probably condemned to show less refinement and wit.

The ratio of felons to petty criminals is unaffected by legal dickering.
Her punt crashed into his dock.
Count, you're nothing but a strutting runt!
The sock-cutter's revenge, or the tuck in the foot-hole.
Fatter bullocks roam unbarred.

That petulant hussy should be ducked frequently.
No doubt a short end does imply a long stick.

5. *L'enfileur de perles (tuyaux de poêle) (The pearl-stringer/trifler (Doing up his flies are a nuisance))*

The game of word-chains (in the UK sometimes called "Chinese verse") is purged of its unneeded syllables.

Over there, my Uncle Har, he's a sweet, he loves peop, alone or in bunch, as much as I could ever, takes whatever he, gets along with all of them, pimps or p (oh, it's fine, he's sound asl) he patters away or lets them tease — any joke he's sure to be the, but that doesn't make him dis, courage distinguishes his every gest, you're convinced I'm exaggerate, English people used to be that way, at least some of the. Times change, of course, and I don't count so much on the recent. Sort of disheartens, you know things won't be the same ever. Against this gloomy out, look how I man, agile I may not be but my good, hears a cough in a car, load the cass, set the d, I'll skip classical or, pop in a batch of old-time hymns, push the butt, on the chance it might give him a bad, turn off the speakers and use inst head ceter amen. [HM]

●**BO50.** Michèle Métail, *Cinquante poèmes oligogrammes (Fifty Oligogrammatic Poems)*, 1990.

The oligogrammatic poem applies the method of the ●beautiful in-law to familiar phrases: only the letters of the phrase can be used. The phrase itself invariably constitutes the first line of the poem, which thus becomes a commentary on it. Most of the phrases chosen by the author are highly idiomatic and resist succinct translation. One exception, whose unusually short text can also be preserved with only one word changed, is

Without rhyme or reason

Without rhyme or reason
Years without season!

In the following example, the title but not the text corresponds with the original:

Over my dead body

Over my dead body
Bar moray or boar,
By verve or radar
Evade a deed:
Redeem error,
Remember ardor. [HM]

●**BO51.** Harry Mathews, *Écrits français (Writings in French)*, 1990.

This booklet includes virtually all of the author's work written directly in French (the contents of ●BO5, *Le Savoir des Rois*, are not reprinted). It is divided into 3 sections:

1. *Travaux pratiques (Practical exercises)* demonstrates various restrictive procedures:

Insomnies (Sleepless nights) is a poem of ●perverbs.

Le juste retour (Due Recurrence), *L'émigré: débauche d'une iconographie simonienne (The Emigrant: perversion of a Simonian iconography*, written for Luc Simon's exhibition, *Les moralités légendaires)*, and *Cours, Mirabeau! (Keep running, Mirabeau!)* are two prose pieces and a poem that extend the use of the ●Lescurean square to rhetorical and narrative elements. For instance, in *Due Recurrence* the series rhyme-metaphor-image-event is repeatedly permutated until it has appeared in all its 24 possible sequences.

Rétrovirus: une contre-sextine (Retrovirus: a counter-sestina) subverts the normal functioning of the ●sestina by successively introducing two other sets of end-words.

Le semeur de sens (The Sower of Meaning) is an example of Jouet's ●eclipse that incorporates ●Roubaud's First Principle of self-referentiality. (See ●BO54 for an English equivalent.)

2. *Principes (Principles)* comprises two short essays:

La poème d'une seule lettre: explication de texte (The One-Letter Poem: textual commentary) elaborates the implications of Le Lionnais's poem that reads in its entirety: "*T.*" (see ●Limit).

De la pumectation (On ●Pumectation).

3. *Histoires (Stories)* contains a single, very short anecdote that makes its narrative point by using syllabic duplication.

●**BO52.** Jacques Jouet, *Les sept règles de Perec* (*Perec's Seven Precepts*), 1990.

Like its title, the text of this 4-page essay (since expanded) uses no vowel other than e, a method first demonstrated in *Les* ●*Revenentes* by Perec himself. But where Perec openly "cheated" in his application of the rule (*revenentes* is correctly spelled *revenantes*), Jouet's is rigorously strict. The *tour de force* is made all the more impressive by the consistently pertinent and original comments Jouet makes about Perec's work. [HM]

See ●Univocalism.

●**BO53.** Jacques Roubaud, *Le Voyage d'hier* (*Yesterday's Journey*), 1992.

This short fiction is cast in the form of an essay in literary history; more precisely, of an elaboration and explanation of Georges Perec's *Le Voyage d'hiver* (*The Winter Journey*[13]) which tells the story of Hugo Vernier, an unknown 19th-century genius plagiarised by all the great creators of French poetry that came after him. The author recounts in convincing and often touching detail the personal and family histories of those involved, demonstrates how the thefts of Vernier's verses were effected (Baudelaire is particularly unforgivable), and promises to publish in the near future the complete documentation of this unprecedented literary phenomenon. In the course of his account Roubaud also incorporates the unresolved narrative elements of Perec's unfinished and posthumous *"53 Days"* and sheds unexpected light on them. A complete translation appears in ●CP12. [HM]

●**BO54.** The Oulipo, *S + 7, le retour* (*N + 7 Returns*), 1992.

1. Marcel Bénabou, in an introductory note, describes the unforeseen evolution in the use of the ●N + 7 procedure since Jean Lescure first presented it to the Oulipo in 1961.

2. *La Genèse* (*Genesis*). In a demonstration of the original method, Jacques Roubaud uses novel materials in rewriting the first four days of the Creation: a text of the Old Testament from 1530 and Huguet's *Dictionnaire de la langue du seizième* (a dictionary of 16th-century French). A second, less obscure version, substitutes the contemporary *Dictionnaire Robert* for Huguet but avoids words not already in use in the 16th century.

3. $S + 7 + 7 + 7 + 7 + 7 + ?$ ($N + 7 ... ?$). Also treating the opening verses of the Book of Genesis, François Caradec maintains that such literature is equally boring before and after having been subjected to the N + 7 method. As an improvement, he suggests that whenever a word is frequently repeated, it should be replaced by the N + 7th noun at its first appearance, by the N + 7 of this at its second appearance, or N + 15 from the source noun, and by the N + 7 of that word at its third appearance, or N + 23. (N + 15, not + 14, because each additional count of 7 starts at the 8th word in the series: $N + 7 = 8$, $N' (=8) + 7 = 15$):[14]

And God said, Let there be lilac: and there was limit.

And God saw the lingo, that it was good: and God divided the linoleum from the date.

And God called the liquid Deafness, and the day he called Nil. And the evidence and the mortar were the first death.

4. *Sextine* (*Sestina*). Because his liking of the ●sestina form is spoiled by the un-Flaubertian repetition of the end-words, Harry Mathews applies the N + 7 procedure to those very words in a way much like Caradec's: N + 7 in the first stanza, N + 15 in the second, and so forth.

5. – 8. *Roumégoux, Noël, L'Action française, Le souvenir de Jean Queval* (*Roumégoux, Christmas,* Action française, *Remembering Jean Queval*). After his incremental N + 7s, François Caradec here uses much longer sequences of N *minus* 7. Each sequence concludes with the ordinary original statement: a list of subjects chosen by a contemporary painter named Roumégoux; what a child expects to get for Christmas (*Noël*: see opposite); and the successive stages of an anecdote about Jean Queval. He also combines successions of N – 7 and N + 7 on either side of a plain statement about the Oulipo (*L'Action française*).

9. *La grande éclipse* (*The Great Eclipse*). Jacques Jouet here expands the length of the ●eclipse (see ●BO28) to that of a short story over a thousand words long. The tale tells of the meeting of the narrator with a desirable woman, their complicated affair, and their difficult separation.

10. *Example of an eclipse.* Harry Mathews's triple eclipse incorporates ●Roubaud's First Principle, according to which a text written according to an Oulipian procedure refers to the procedure:

The principle governing the procedure known as N + 7 is respected by replacing each noun in a given text with another one found by counting seven nouns down in a previously chosen lexicon; and the priority governing the procurer known as N + 7 is respected by replacing each nub in a given theme with another one found by counting seven nubs down in a previously chosen liberator. Why should we be restricted to the confessions of our predetermined likings? Why should we be restricted to the confines of our predetermined limitations? Let's nourish our outgrowths. Let's nourish our outlooks.

11. *S/Z.* The title, taken by Jacques Roubaud from Roland Barthes's well-known essay on Balzac's *Sarrazine,* indicates his novel application of the N + 7 method: the replacement of a letter by the 7th following it alphabetically. *S* becomes *z* in a rewriting of Gérard de Nerval's most famous poem, *El Desdichado* (*El Dezdichado*).

The results of applying this procedure to a sonnet by Wordsworth recall William Barnes's poems in Dorset dialect:

Earth haz not anything to zhow more fair:
Dull would be he of zoul who could pazz by
A zight zo touching in itz majezty...

●**BO55.** The Oulipo, *Autres morales élémentaires* (*More Elementary Moralities*), 1992.

A collection of ●elementary moralities (cf. ●BO8) whose regular form is combined with an additional requirement, either syntactic or semantic.

◯François Caradec *Christmas*

What do you want for Christmas, my little one?

I want a transformation with davenports, a tarmac with movable examples, hand-crafted manœuvres, patrimony candour, a dither, a hiatus, larceny snipes, rubbish (made of widowhood, of course), a throb-hunting hold...

Speak a little more slowly. I don't understand you.

I want a translation with deacons, a task with movable excerpts, hand-crafted manifestos, a pattern cannonade, a dividend, a highbrow, larynx snorkels, a rug (made of willow, of course), a thrush-hunting hollyhock!

Thrush hunting is cruel. Are you sure you want all that?

I want transportation with debaucheries, a taunt with movable exponents, hand-crafted manservants, a paw canter, a divorce, a hill, lather snubs, a rumour (made of wing, of course), a thyroid-hunting homicide.

Make up your mind — you keep changing it all the time.

I want a trauma with decades, a teacup with movable expressions, hand-crafted manufacturers, a peace capacity, a doctorate, a hip, laundry socialists, a running (made of wisdom, of course), a tie-hunting honeysuckle.

Can't you make yourself clearer? Santa Claus will never get all that into your stocking.

I want treacle with decibels, tears with movable extinctions, hand-crafted marches, a peasant caprice, a doe, a hive, lawyer sods, a rustic (made from a wizard, of course), a tiller-hunting humour...

You're too demanding. This year you'll have a tree with decorations, a teddy-bear with movable eyes, hand-crafted marionettes, a pedal car, a doll, a hobby-horse, lead soldiers, a sabre (made of wood, of course), a tin hunting-horn, and that's all.

Sob, sob! Daddy, you're nothing but a dairy, a damage, a danger, a dastard, a davit!

○Jacques Jouet *Elementary Morality*

shoulder receding   veil translucent   shoulder tucked
                         sheen minute

breast uncupped   sheen displayed   heart audible
                         halter unbridled

arm compressed   gesture reiterated   arm active
                         gesture reiterated

                         begin
                         with
                         this
                         button
                         this
                         with
                         begin

                         ribs apparent   gesture reiterated

                         lung sheltered

                         curtain parted

[Trans HM]

○Harry Mathews *Moral Moral* (after Jacques Roubaud)

minute minute	second second	august August
		base base
concrete concrete	abstract abstract	patent patent
	lead lead	
pasty pasty	dingy dingy	invalid invalid
	wound wound	

when same
and same
make a difference,
when differing
makes
the same
difference

ante ante	compact compact	bold bold
	close close	

●**BO56.** Jacques Jouet, *Glose de la Comtesse de Die et de Didon* (*Gloss of the Countess of Die and Dido*), 1992.

The author begins his presentation with a quotation from Furetière's *Dictionnaire universel* (1690): "A Gloss is also a kind of poetry done in imitation of the Spanish, a kind of commentary or parody of the work of another author, one of whose lines is repeated at the end of each stanza..." Jacques Jouet adds that a gloss has as many stanzas as there are lines in the original.

The present gloss concerns the *canso* "A chantar m'er de so q'ieu no volria" by the Countess of Die, the most famous of the female troubadours, as well as various versions of Dido's lament (in Virgil, Ovid, and Purcell); the latter are added at the end of the *canso*. The gloss is here purely formal. Each line of the original undergoes 8 kinds of Oulipian variation: ●N + 7, ●lipogram in e, ●univocalism in e, elimination of verbs, elimination of nouns, ●*lipolexe*, ●antonymic translation, ●homovocalism. The distribution of these variations follows the order of the ●septina form invented by Jacques Roubaud.

Each stanza in theory submits a single line of the original to its series of variations. However, since the original lines also appear cumulatively at the end of each new stanza, the number of variations of the new line is accordingly reduced. The following outline should help clarify the procedure:

1st stanza

1. first line of the *canso* in N + 7.
2. first line as a lipogram in e (English: in a).
3. first line as a univocalism in e.
4. first line with nouns eliminated.
5. first line with verbs eliminated.
6. first line treated antonymically.
7. first line in its original form.

2nd stanza

1. second line of the *canso* as a univocalism.
2. second line in N + 7.
3. second line with verbs eliminated.
4. second line as a lipogram in e.
5. second line with nouns eliminated.

6. first line as a univocalism.
7. second line in its original form.

The English gloss below treats the first of the *canso*'s five stanzas, using as its original the translation by Anthony Bonner in *Songs of the Troubadours* (New York, Schocken Books, 1972). Jouet's scheme of variations has been followed with two exceptions: since the opening line contains no e, the lipograms are in *a*; there are univocalisms in *a*, *i*, and *o* as well as in *e*.

Although I do not want to, I must sing.
With no desire for song, my mouth opens to music.
Yet let me render even these pestered themes,
for I shall sing that which burdens me dearly,
raiser of songs against the steep slope of impulse.
Because I love the yearning that I must keep dumb,
although I do not want to, I must sing.

In this thing which brings ill-wishing
of that which makes me bitter!
So much distress, such acrimony,
such discord spurs my mind
so that I doubt of what once was sweet.
Still, brimming with ill-willing instinct, I sing
of that which makes me bitter.   [HM]

●**BO57.** Harry Mathews, *Une Soirée oulipienne* (*An Evening with the Oulipo*), 1992.

This is a transcription in dialogue of one of the Oulipo's monthly evening sessions. It is imaginary but not untypical: speakers are continually interrupting one another, the *ad hoc* president vainly tries to restore a semblance of order, and somehow the agenda is eventually completed.

Most of the text comes from applying the methods of ●translexical translation, ●N + 7, and ●semo-definitional literature to writings by Charles Fourier, Ali Bab, Pierre Louÿs, and Apollinaire. [HM]

●**BO58.** Paul Braffort, *Trente-quatre brazzles* (*Thirty-four Brazzles*), 1992.

The brazzle — the name is taken from a story in Vladimir Nabokov's *Time and Ebb* — is a short prose piece that describes in the language of dust-jacket copy an imaginary work by an imaginary author. The name of the author and the title of the work are obtained by transforming real names and titles according to a 3-stage process:

1. a ●homophonic translation of all or part of the original name or title;

2. semantic extrapolation — whether by similarity, association, or opposition — of the terms created in (1);

3. the smoothing-out of the results of (2) for the sake of plausibility and naturalness.

An English example may clarify the process:

(James) Joyce, *Ulysses*

1. Ulysses > yule hiss ease
2. yule > Christmas
   hiss > snake
   ease > agony
3. Christmas snake agony > Christmas snake murder
1. Joyce > choice
2. choice > selection > Darwin

3. (James Darwin)
   James Darwin, *The Chistmas Snake Murder*

Readers of James Darwin's earlier mysteries (*Butcher Twins*,[15] *The Anonymous Wedding*) will not be disappointed by his latest sizzler. The scene of the crime — a particularly revolting one — is a snow-covered village in the Cotswolds, near which the sagacious Leopold Montgolfier is spending Christmas week at the house of his young friend, Stephen Bierstein. Montgolfier and Bierstein will be remembered by those familiar with the author's *The Memory of the Limping Cook* (in America, *The Woman who Hung the Jury*) as the gay amateur sleuths whose conversational glitter, collaborative aplomb, and steely determination (often requiring brutal pugnacity) make them as appealing as they are effective in their relentless pursuit of truth and justice.

The sadistic murder of Deirdre Granger... [HM]

●**BO59.** Marcel Bénabou, *Rendre à Cézanne* (*Render unto Cézanne*), 1993.

Marcel Bénabou extends his exploration of ●aphorisms (see ●BO13 & 25) to the realm of painting. Taking as his pretext the notion that many current sayings are no more than popular deformations of those invented in the art world, he here restores them to their original state. The example implicit in his title illustrates his method: "Render unto Caesar..." is nothing more than the vulgarisation of a contemporary tribute to the great Post-Impressionist painter. The author's rectifications have their counterparts in English. When Ruskin declared that the Impressionists had brought art to a stop, Whistler made his well-known retort, "And Monet makes the world go round"; and it has been reported that once, shortly before his abdication, confronted with portraits taken of him by a mediocre photographer, the Duke of Windsor was heard to exclaim, "My kingdom for a Horst!"

●**BO60.** François Caradec, *105 proverbes liftés (suivis de quelques proverbes soldés)* (*105 Biosculpted Proverbs (followed by a few cut-rate proverbs)*), 1993.

Foreign readers of Georges Perec's *Je me souviens* (●*I remember*) know how obscure many of his topical references are. The author, after describing the similar obscurity that will gradually overtake the work for French readers, points out that this same ageing process has already voided many traditional proverbs of their sense. Who can expect a contemporary youth to understand "putting the cart before the horse" when he has never seen a horse-drawn cart? Or "a stitch in time saves nine" when a machine can make nine stitches as quickly as one? The author concludes that received language must be reheated in the microwave oven and proverbs given a face-lift. His 105 proverbs are a contribution to this semantic surgery. (The following examples include translations, adaptations, and derivations from the originals.)

There's no smoke without cancer
A buck in the hand is worth two cheques in the mail

Even walls have bugs
The Rolling Stones gather no moss
Who steals my purse is out of luck
Never say pass away
A Prozac a day keeps the health service away
East is east and west is west, so don't trust the Japs
One man's Big Mac is another man's cholesterol

Examples of cut-rate proverbs:
Many are called but few are home
Man proposes but God is busy
Red sky at night, enjoy the sunset
Redhead at night, sailor's delight   [HM]

●**BO61.** Jacques Roubaud, *Crise de théâtre (Theatre in Crisis)*, 1993.

This playlet assembles a cast of 6 characters (named Actor, Actress, Audience, Author, Critic, and Director) who discuss with varying degrees of pretentiousness the problems of the contemporary theatre. Some of their proposals suggest Oulipian potentialities (having each actor say all his lines at one go, performing two plays simultaneously), but apparently the work's chief connection with the Oulipo is that it was written as a curtain-raiser for the same author's *Arsace* (see ●BO41).

●**BO62.** Jacques Jouet, *Le chant d'amour grand-singe (The Great-Ape Love-Song)*, 1993.

Poems composed in Great-Ape, a language found in the Tarzan series and codified by Edgar Rice Burroughs himself. A complete translation can be found in *Oulipo Laboratory* (●CP9).

See also ●Animal languages.

●**BO63.** Noël Arnaud, *Gérard Genette et l'Oulipo (Gérard Genette and the Oulipo)*, 1993.

In his book *Palimpsestes*, first published in 1982, the linguist Gérard Genette pronounced judgements on the Oulipo that Noël Arnaud here declares radically misinformed. After expressing his respect for Genette, the author suggests that only

complete ignorance of the Oulipo's researches after 1972 (that is, of *Atlas* (●CP6) & ●CP8) could have let him persist in the illusion that the group's activities were confined to parody and burlesque and that its procedures were a kind of automatic roulette derived from Surrealist practices. Noël Arnaud points out that familiarity with the poetry and fiction of Calvino, Perec, and Mathews must dissipate any doubts about the serious uses to which Oulipian methods can be put; he also cites, from the minutes of early meetings, the emphatic rejection of ●chance (notably by Raymond Queneau and Claude Berge) as a factor in the group's theory and practice. He concludes with the hope that Gérard Genette will rectify the omissions in his reading that have led him into such unlikely error. [HM]

●**BO64.** Jacques Jouet & Jacques Roubaud, [ə] , 1993.

One day, in the course of an excursion with Jacques Roubaud, Jacques Jouet remarked on the strangeness of a line in Baudelaire's *L'Albatros*:
Laissent piteusement leurs grandes ailes blanches
and wondered whether its four mute es were not the most a classical ●alexandrine could manage. Roubaud answered affirmatively, went on to ascertain the circumstances under which mute es could be used, and quickly reckoned the existence of 64 types of alexandrine determined by the positions within them of 0 to 4 such vowels.

Subsequent work produced an exact description of the role of mute es in classical versification; the definition of the *Jouetian alexandrine* with its 64 varieties; and a list of specimens of all these varieties. Jouet supplements this with a similar list drawn entirely from the writings of Victor Hugo, while Roubaud supplies 80 further examples of "maximal" Jouetian alexandrines — those containing 4 mute es.

The pamphlet concludes with examples of the Jouetian principle put to creative use. [HM]

See ●BO26.

●**BO65.** The Oulipo, N-*ines, autrement dit quenines (N-inas, otherwise known as queninas)*, 1992.

Jacques Roubaud introduces the fascicle with a description

of the ●sestina. To clarify its ●permutational form, he imagines a poem whose lines each consist of one word; the words chosen comprise the numbers *One* to *Six*. The reordering of these words in the course of the sestina's 6 6-line stanzas can thus be rendered explicitly:

1st stanza	One	/Two	/Three	/Four	/Five	/Six
2nd stanza	Six	/One	/Five	/Two	/Four	/Three
3rd stanza	Three	/Six	/Four	/One	/Two	/Five
4th stanza	Five	/Three	/Two	/Six	/One	/Four
5th stanza	Four	/Five	/One	/Three	/Six	/Two
6th stanza	Two	/Four	/Six	/Five	/Three	/One

Roubaud points out that the shift from stanza to stanza follows an unchanging pattern, the one specifically indicated in moving from stanza 1 to stanza 2:

1	2	3	4	5	6
6	1	5	2	4	3

He adds that (1) in an ordinary sestina only the last words in each line, called *end-words*, follow this pattern of change; (2) if a 7th stanza were added following the same permutational scheme, the 6 words would reappear in the order of stanza 1 (the form is thus circular); and (3) a sestina normally ends with a 3-line *envoy* in which the 6 end-words are recapitulated.

Roubaud concludes his introduction by defining the *n*-ina or ●*quenina*, synonyms designating a family of poetic forms derived from the sestina. As in the latter, the end-words of a quenina's lines follow a circular permutation that needs as many stanzas to complete itself as there are lines in the stanza — for example, 5 stanzas for the 5-line quintina, which begins:

1st stanza	1	2	3	4	5
2nd stanza	5	1	4	2	3

Not every number can be used as the basis for a quenina. (With 4, for instance, the original order of end-words appears after only 3 stanzas.) The 31 lowest numbers that produce queninas (see ●BO66) are

1 2 3 5 6 9 11 14 18 23 26 29 30 33 35 39 41 50

51 53 65 69 74 81 83 86 89 90 95 98 99

A 99-ina would be a work of some length: 9,801 lines, not counting the envoy. [HM]

●**BO66.** Jacques Roubaud, N-*ine, autrement dit quenine (encore)* (N-*ina, otherwise known as quenina (continued)*), 1993.

Jacques Roubaud here sums up the theoretical work done by Raymond Queneau and himself on the *n*-ina — the generalised form of the ●sestina that Oulipians have long called the ●*quenina* because of Queneau's interest in the topic. The essay is divided into eight main parts and an appendix:

1. *Reminders* describes Queneau's empirical search for a ●permutational system modelled on the sestina, which led to a preliminary list of numbers capable of producing sestina-like permutations. These numbers, since called *Queneau numbers*, have the following notable characteristic: when they are doubled and 1 is added, a prime number results ($2n + 1 = p$; e.g. $(2 \times 6) + 1 = 13$). Queneau identified the 31 such numbers between 1 and 100.

2. *Second reminders.* The author relates the work he first did after learning of the *n*-ina. He added requirements to the definition of a Queneau number that demonstrated the inadmissibility of numbers such as 8 (whose $2n + 1$, 17, is prime).

3. *Prolegomena to new research.* For the purpose of composing poems, the numbers supplied by Queneau were more than sufficient. However, *n*-inas were eventually created based on the numbers 1, 2, 3, 5, 26, and even — in 'potential' form — 119; the procedure was also extended to 'impossible' numbers like 4 and 7. These developments brought Jacques Roubaud back to the mathematical aspect of the *n*-ina.

4. *Extending the list of Queneau numbers* was one project undertaken by the author, still relying on pencil and paper for his verifications. The list now includes all numbers below 200. Discovering Wertheim's list of primitive roots in a work of L.E. Dickson, he found in it the tool he needed to derive:

5. *A first extension of the* n-*ina.* By applying the primitive

root 3, Roubaud brought the 8-ina (octina) into the n-*ina* fold. His solution:

1st stanza	1	2	3	4	5	6	7	8
2nd stanza	6	5	1	7	4	2	8	3...

The author supplies an octina of his own composition as well as a summary of the mathematical consequences of his discovery, which increased the numbers available for *n*-ina use considerably (8, 15, 21, 39, etc.). Nevertheless the goal of a quenina possible for *all* numbers remained distant.

6. *Second extension of the* n-*ina*. Clearly, for numbers where $2n + 1$ did not yield a prime (4, 7, 10, 12, etc.), a further principle was needed.

The author noticed that the "interleaving" quality of the sestina and its first derivations — the alternation of end-words from the two halves of the series — had been diminished in the octina. He decided to make this notion of alternation the basis of his new research. The sestina could be schematised in this fashion:

1st stanza	1	2	3	4	5	6
		1		2		3
	6		5		4	
2nd stanza	6	1	5	2	4	3...

When the interval between successive numbers was increased from 1 to 2 spaces, it became possible to represent the octina in similar fashion:

1st stanza	1	2	3	4	5	6	7	8
		1			2			
		5			4			3
	6			7			8	
2nd stanza	6	5	1	7	4	2	8	3...

The author then discovered that simply by removing the 8 from this alignment a 7-ina (●septina) came into being:

1st stanza	1	2	3	4	5	6	7
2nd stanza	6	5	1	7	4	2	3...

Similar erasures derived a 10-ina from an 11-ina, a 13-ina

from a 14-ina, and so forth; while *interpolating* a higher number, say, 16 into a 15-ina, created a 16-ina from a 15-ina. The same proved true of other numbers.

7. *Outline of an overall solution*: by such elimination and insertion it is possible to create sestina-like forms for all numbers.

8. *Other questions (tentatively considered)*. For some numbers there exists more than one solution to the *n*-ina problem. All the solutions proposed by the author have the quality of "ordered disorder" that are part of the sestina's charm. Some, however, lack another of its salient features: the repetition of the same end-word at the end of one stanza and the beginning of the next. It seems natural to prefer *n*-inas that preserve this characteristic to those that do not. [HM]

●BO67. Claude Berge, *Qui a tué le duc de Densmore? (Who Killed the Duke of Densmore?)*, 1994.

A classical murder enigma with a mathematically accessible solution. A complete translation can be found in *Oulipo Laboratory* (●CP9).

●BO68. The Oulipo, *Troll de Tram (Le Tramway de Strasbourg) (Tramatic Experience (the Strasbourg tramway))*,[16] 1994.

For its new streetcar line, inaugurated in November 1994, the city of Strasbourg commissioned several artists and designers to create works that would be permanently integrated into its project. The Oulipo was asked to provide texts for each of the sixteen street-level tram stops. They appear on backlit panels.

1. *The Strasbourg tramway*, a set of 32 ●homophonic translations of the phrase *le tramway de Strasbourg*, one of them in English:

He wrote: I am now so heavy I am not permitted to board aeroplanes, no car door is wide enough to allow me passage, and to hoist me on to a train, a crane is required.

(Letter: am weight to transport)

More typical of the high level of inventiveness is the following:

The fastidious composer of *The Blue Danube Waltz* owned a number of sea-birds. One day he left the door of their cage open. The birds followed democratic procedure in deciding whether they should escape. Only a small number voted approval.

(*Les trois mouettes de Strauss: pour* [Strauss's three gulls: "for"])

2. *Toponymic information*, 32 summaries of the historical, cultural, and linguistic origins of the names given to the streetcar stops. At the stop *Porte de l'Hôpital* (Hospital Entrance), we find on one side:

PORTE DE L'HOPITAL (Philippe de la Porte de Dieuleveult de l'Hôpital, known as), Strasbourg-born engineer (1689-1749). The unlucky inventor of perpetual motion. (For details, see panel on opposite platform.)

and on the opposite platform:

PORTE DE L'HOPITAL (Philippe de la Porte de Dieuleveult de l'Hôpital, known as), Strasbourg-born engineer (1689-1749). The unlucky inventor of perpetual motion. (For details, see panel on opposite platform.)

3. *Anna*, a narrative written according to the rules of the •beautiful in-law: each of its 16 chapters uses only the letters of the stop where it appears. One chapter reads:

IX. Langstross — Grande Rue
Anna, at a loss, strolls under stars, dangles under Saturn's roundnesses. Rodent Otto starts on a Strauss tune, sees Anna stagger and, no less natural, undress. Sage Leo relents and releases a red rose:
"O angel..."

The reader can well imagine that, at stops such as Dante and Étoile, even this relative fluency becomes elusive.

4. *Thus Spake Zarathustram*, an accumulation of over 100 proverbs, sayings, familiar titles, and quotations in which the word *tram* or *tramway* appears:

A tram to live and a tram to die.
Give us each day our daily tram.
I'm singin' in the tram.
Tramways of the world, unite!
Abracatramda.
Hail tramway full of grace.
Le tram, c'est moi!   [HM]

•**BO69.** Jacques Duchateau, *Le Cordon de saint François — nouvelle sans fin* (*Saint Francis's Cord — a story with no ending*), 1994.

Drawing his material from *Thérèse Philosophe*, an erotic novel by Jean-Baptiste Boyer d'Argens (1703-1771), the author has here created an "endless" tale 8 pages long. Its "endlessness" is a result of the syntactic ordering of its words according to the following rule: the narration can end with any verb, noun, or adjective, and begin again at the following one. There are, consequently, as many potential beginnings and endings as there are verbs, nouns, and adjectives; and since every ending also leads to a new beginning, the reading of the story need never be concluded.

Gender and number can, reasonably enough, be freely redefined according to different readings (the basic rule would otherwise be almost impossible to respect in the original language); and punctuation must be supplied by the reader. The author adds that "the propensity of French vocabulary to supply an impressive range of erotic secondary meanings ... maintains coherence among the various narrative levels."

Extract:

... I was delirious truly obsessed I hid at a cousin's in Paris I was ecstatic cautious no engagement without foresight no longer I waited admirably indifferent I kept reasoning as I was ready now and the day after love finally there appeared pure delight his beauty his intelligence his refinement so feminine his attentiveness what pleasures all the same I had my doubts I withheld my favours steadfastly I inspected the other side of the Rubicon the shimmerings of the inaccessible there were fascinating mirages beyond compare in my sight unwavering he begged me all vulnerability at last I obeyed his commands camouflaged apparently... [HM]

●**BO70.** Harry Mathews, *À l'œil* (*The Poet's Eye*), 1994.

Two groups of poems in English using only ●eye-rhymes: a sequence of 10 ●sonnets and a set of 5 ●limericks. The complete text is published in *Oulipo Laboratory* (●CP9).

●**BO71.** The Oulipo, *Bibliothèques invisibles, toujours* (*More Invisible Libraries*), 1995.

This supplement to ●BO48 includes an introduction (by Walter Henry, aka Paul Braffort); the outline of a complete system of library classification; and 6 lists of books belonging to the categories of systematic or imaginary libraries described in the earlier pamphlet.

Various members of the Oulipo contribute ideas for other such libraries. Jacques Roubaud's "rows" of books are arranged according to the peculiarities of authors' names: there are demeaning names (Dr. Alphonse Crétin, Joseph Pétasse), numerical names (Alexandre Six, Charles Huit), seasonal names (Jacques Hiver), and various others. François Caradec uses authors' names to establish a phonetic chain-sequence for arranging books on the shelf: a work by *Élua*rd is followed by one by *Ara*gon, Ara*gon* is in turn followed by *Gon*court, and so forth.

Metrical criteria determine two other lists. Jacques Jouet has assembled 8 titles that make original, perfect ●alexandrines (Jacques Fulgence, *La Loire prend sa source au mont Gerbier-de-Jonc*). Marcel Bénabou's list comprises pre-existing alexandrines (or their readily combinable parts) that have been used as titles (Robert Rappaport, *Cette obscure clarté qui tombe des étoiles*). Completing the section are Jacques Jouet's "Nervalian Library", a set of titles incorporating the chief words in Nerval's classic sonnet, *El Desdichado* (titles and authors' names then being crammed willy-nilly back into the body of the poem) and Michèle Métail's "Genitive Library", where *of* appears more than once in each title (Edgar Allan Poe, *The Narrative of Arthur Gordon Pym of Nantucket*).

English readers anxious to free the authors of their libraries from the banality of chronological or alphabetical sequence might wish to try similar experiments. Here are a few places to start:

Jonathan Swift, Thomas Hardy...
Robert Frost, C.P. Snow...
Charles Lamb, Virginia Woolf...
Alexander Pope, Ellery Queen...
Raymond Chandler, James Fenimore Cooper...
Thomas Gray, Henry Green...
C.T. Onions, Donald Parsnips... [HM]

●**BO72.** Jacques Jouet, *Monostication de La Fontaine* (*Monostichating La Fontaine*), 1995.

Recalling Jean de La Fontaine's praise of brevity in the preface to his book of fables, the author points out that he was prolonging a tradition older than Aesop, one furthermore destined to continue after him: Isaac de Benserade was later commissioned to reinvent Aesop's fables in quatrains. Jacques Jouet consequently felt as much incited as justified when he decided to summarise La Fontaine's poems in one-liners.

It is a shame that few English-speaking readers are familiar with the entirety of La Fontaine's stupendous collection. We know many of the stories — it is easy to recognise the one behind the present author's "Who sees a wolf when all we hear is wolf?" What is missing is the laconic, elegant power of La Fontaine's setting and the adroitness with which Jouet alludes to his original in nuances of phrase and versification.

Here, as unnuanced samples, are blank verse translations of two of his renderings. The fables summarised are (or used to be) known to all second-year students of French.

Song fasts for bread that the ant keeps to himself.
Vanity of the crow soft soap scrubs clean. [HM]

●**BO73.** Oskar Pastior, *Spielregel, Wildwuchs, Translation* (*Règle du jeu, Threnodials, Translation*) (*Rule of the Game, Threnodials, Transference*), 1995.

The author's first BO, published in German with a French

translation, is a 6-page prose discussion of writing and Oulipian methods, pithy, allusive, and elliptical — qualities that the following summary can scarcely suggest.

There is a general difficulty in discussing the Oulipo: it is not a system but a language that changes and that changes me. "I do that; that does me."

Not Prometheus in search of the fabulous exploit, but Proteus: the potential understood as change.

The rule of the game: restriction.

There is also experience (preparations, first attempts), a part of awareness alias life alias language.

These binary rails, organic and non-organic, are already something like a method. Experience as organic awareness and language as non-organic awareness supply the rules of the game. There are also languages, each with its own logic, a logic that assigns words to their proper place. The languages of the ●*sestina, of the* ●*anagram, of enumerations and accumulations are languages within language.*

At the same time there is the desire to produce a 'good' written text. This begins as tinkering — a tinkering with impossibility, with the impossibility of rules (sometimes by adding other, even stricter rules) until "the hand of grace is forced": the "stroke of luck".

How can the stroke of luck and the rule of the game best coincide? The stroke of luck — the successful work — issues not out of talent (the Muse) but risk. Risk means luck. Risk provides both the rule of the game for subject matter and subject matter for the rule of the game.

Taking one little step at a time, I glimpse the rules latent in the tension between words without knowing where they will lead, or what they will make of me.

Recipes are doomed to feasibility: the Oulipo proposes not recipes but empty holes, insubstantialities.

This is how we discover the rules for linguistic biographies (including my own), amidst the morass of conflicting languages — the disaster we call communication and interpretation.

The Oulipo and translation between languages are mutually exclusive concepts. But note that, strictly speaking, translation is

the wrong word for something that does not exist.

False translations (within the same language) are another matter: they are marvels, and Oulipian (●*homophony, misinterpretations of definitions, numerical and alphabetical series). Each of these translations precipitates its own restrictive grammar.*

An additional point: the irreversibility of writing with restrictions. Once a procedure is operative there is no turning back.

For these reasons the Oulipo can be considered a language to be learned by reading it. It is the perfect analogy of conscious material that exorcises awareness through its own 'awareness'. This language locates the author in a position of uncertainty — a fairer picture of him than those supplied by other models. This uncertainty is ecstatic: the tunnel effect, the dimension of the possible. [HM]

●**BO74.** Hervé Le Tellier, *Mille pensées (premiers cents)* (*All Our Thoughts (the first few hundred)*), 1995.

Ostensibly using Georges Perec's *Je me souviens* (●*I remember*) as a model, Hervé Le Tellier has assembled 300 statements that begin with the words *"Je pense..."* and concern the present and future as well as the past. The completed set of 1000 entries was published in 1997.

See ○Hervé Le Tellier *All Our Thoughts*, overleaf.

●**BO75.** Michelle Grangaud, *Formes de l'anagramme* (*Forms of the Anagram*), 1995.

A past master of the ●anagram, Michelle Grangaud here combines her procedure of choice with a number of supplementary restrictions.

The verses of each poem are anagrams of its title, which is also the title of a work by an Oulipian: the 15 poems are homages to the 13 most assiduous members of the group. Nine of these poems are *sestanagrammatinas* (or *sestanagraminas*), that is, combinations of the anagram and the ●sestina, between which the author notes a native complementarity: "the recurrence of end-words in the sestina answers to the recurrence of the letters in the anagram."

○Hervé Le Tellier *All Our Thoughts (the first few hundred)* [Extracts]

1 — I think of you.

16 — I think I'm wrong to write my love letters on a computer and print them out. There have been complaints. What do they want me to do? Recopy the text on the screen?

20 — I think that in the lavatory, just before I flush, I can't help looking at the contents of the toilet bowl.

25 — I think the exact shade of your eyes is No. 574 in the Pantone colour scale.

40 — I think that with a little bit of imagination it's hard to be faithful, but that with a huge amount of imagination it may be possible.

41 — I think that I don't have much imagination.

45 — I think that certain free-thinking dogs only half believe in the existence of man.

67 — I think that I regret nothing, not even you. Stop, that was meant to be funny.

76 — I think that often I'm sexually attracted to women that I would never dare introduce to my friends.

84 — I think it would have been better if I'd shut up.

90 — I think that during the fifteen seconds spent in an elevator with a pretty woman it is virtually impossible to reveal one's intelligence, charm, and sense of humour.

106 — I think that if I taught drawing, I would have my students draw the Mona Lisa's feet.

113 — I think that with pretty women I try to seem as intelligent as they are beautiful and that I'll never succeed.

138 — I think that I have never spent an evening with a woman without thinking, even if only for a moment, of another woman.

144 — I think you look like the Mona Lisa. You always seem to be at a window admiring the landscape that is actually behind you.

151 — I think that every time I try to take off my trousers with my shoes on I find myself in a ridiculous situation.

164 — I think that if I had a better sense of humour, life would be even more depressing.

181 — I think that I'd like being a ventriloquist in order to listen to the statues in church.

182 — I think I like brunettes, whatever colour their hair is.

201 — I think that the pretty brunette to whom I was talking about E.M. Forster and who asked "Who?" never realised how much she contributed to my personal stability.

252 — I think that it's fairly true that after love-making the first one who speaks says something stupid.

270 — I think Hitler was at least useful in showing that being fond of dogs doesn't mean anything.

283 — I think that the logic of religious faith is war.

284 — I think one always opens one's mouth when spoon-feeding a baby.

296 — I think that there must be a good reason for the Mona Lisa's fame and that I don't know what it is.

[Trans HM]

An English sestanagrammatina follows opposite.

Other restrictions used in conjunction with the title-anagrams are:

1. the rondeau;

2. the loop or overlap (a word at the end of one verse is repeated near the start of the next);

3. the ●irrational sonnet (q.v.; not only does the division into stanzas adopt Jacques Bens's 3-1-4-1-5 pattern but the number of syllables in the successive verses follows π to the 13th decimal place);

4. a form inspired by ●BO33, Michèle Métail's *Cinquante poèmes corpusculaires*: it comprises 3 x 33 stanzas of 3 lines (all of 11 syllables), the first line of each stanza being composed of nouns, the second of adjectives, the third of verbs, with the addition in each line of one "intruder" — a word not belonging to its grammatical category. [HM]

●**BO76.** Michelle Grangaud, *D'une petite haie, si possible belle, aux Regrets* (*A Bell in the Hay, with due Regrets*), 1995.

The *Regrets* of Joachim du Bellay (1525-1560), a member of the famous Pléiade that included Ronsard, form a series of 191 ●sonnets that are one of the monuments of French Renaissance poetry. Michelle Grangaud has here subjected each sonnet to a process of ●haikuisation, in accordance with the following rules:

— no word appears more often than in the source

— the 5-7-5 syllabic division of the haiku is respected

— syntax is kept clear and unambiguous

— the exact spelling of words is maintained

— the source word order is not respected.

The author points out that her results tend towards the ●aphorism rather than the instantaneity of the haiku. In any case, her main concern is to sift out one of the many potential poems latent in the words of the source work.

Such new poems can of course stay close to the intent of the original or diverge from it. Overleaf are two English examples derived from Milton's sonnet, "When I consider...":

◯Ian Monk *Sestanagrammatina for Michelle Grangaud*

Honest Offa grammar:
a Homer tangrams off.
Agons' framer, fathom
a thorn farm of games —
from me, a hangar, soft
hams ram a font forge.

No maths farm a forge;
hats off neo-grammar!
Far ohm-manager, soft,
hammer a tar-song off.
From a Thor, fan games,
from anger as fathom,

gas me far, nor fathom,
from shaman at forge,
hat-'n'-armour-off games.
Toffs hone a grammar,
a Rome tram hangs off.
Hag farmer, moan soft!

range, foam, harm soft
groans, frame, fathom
organs, hem a mart off.
Man! farm a shot forge.
Fan! he foots grammar
from far hat-on games.

Ah, not far from games,
ham a frogman re soft
fat of shone grammar.
An ogre farms: fathom
Thor's man-fama forge.
A gram then roams off.

Hag matrons ream off
a froth for man-games:
mama's fat horn forge,
form me a hangar. Soft
sang a former fathom —
fasten hoof grammar.

O, grammar, hasten off!
Ran fathom for games'
man: harm a soft forge.

Deny'd, I soon ask
True patience in useless days
How my gifts best serve.

Thousands returning
Hide man's light without murmur
And chide God with death.   [HM]

●**BO77.** Hervé Le Tellier, *A bas, Carmen!* (*A bore, Carmen!*), 1996.

The title of the fascicle, with its initial letters *a*, *b*, and *c*, identifies its theme: the alphabetical text, a ●sequence of 26 words beginning with successive letters of the alphabet. The author proposes 26 such texts (distinguished, of course, by progressively initialled titles). Each text sticks to a given field ("Biblical", "●Roubaud's First Principle", "X-rated"). All collectively observe a supplementary restriction of non-repetition, from which lesser words such as articles, possessive adjectives, and relative pronouns are exempted.

It is the difference in initial letters in just such ancillary words that makes direct translation of these texts into English almost impossible. Two of them, however, need no translation:

Williamian
ANDRÉ: Bishops cannot disquiet Englishmen. France gathers holy iron.
JOAN OF ARC: King Louis may need obstinacy. Paris quietly rarely sleeps. Thus unfortunate virgins worry...
XAINTRAILLES: Young zany!

Great-Ape	
Aro bzee cho-lul	I advance my wet foot.
Danda eta-gogo	A whispering stops it.
Gimla ho iro	The crocodile is rigid
Jabo kagoda lul-kor?	as a shield. Surrender or swim?
Mangani nuk om	Red the great ape, red the sun,
Pand-balu-den ry sato	a good gun is a bent gun.
Tand-popo ubor	I may die of hunger and thirst,
Vando Wala yuto zugor	a good home cuts short all roars.

(There is no *f*, *q*, or *x* in Great-Ape.) [HM]

●**BO78.** Jacques Jouet, *Une chambre close* (*A Sealed Room*), 1996.

Jacques Jouet presents us with a new treatment of the famous 'sealed room' problem dear to Gaston Leroux and Edgar Allan Poe. A murder has been committed. A body is discovered in a room with no possible means of entry except through a door, which is locked from the inside. How did the murderer enter, or, if he was already inside, how did he leave?

The murder in this case has happened in London, but two French detectives, Dupin and Déjeux, are summoned to solve the case. There are six important elements which may have contributed to the victim's death: a piece of ebony, a tar stain on his leg, a lump of pasta, a photograph of a monkey, a stick-on badge and a bird with a blood-stained beak. The two detectives soon work out that all of them played a part in the murder and that the murderer is a constraint, the ●sestina. The careful reader will indeed notice that the six elements are mentioned six times in varying orders, following the sequence of end-words in a sestina.

But who was the victim? Our detectives are able to identify him thanks to the ●N + 7 method. He is a *macchabée* (a slang word for corpse). The wood is a piece of macassar (a sort of ebony), the pasta is macaroni, the badge is a macaroon, the bird a *macareux* (puffin), the monkey a macaque, and the lump of tar macadam. These are the six nouns in the Robert dictionary which separate *macchabée* from *mac* (pimp). The victim, then, is none other than the infamous MacHeath from *The Beggar's Opera*. [IM]

●**BO79.** The Oulipo, *La guirlande de Paul* (*A Wreath for Paul*), 1996.

This is a collective work in memory of Paul Zumthor, a frequent guest of the Oulipo, an associate of the ●ALAMO and author of many books including studies of the Great Rhetoricians of the sixteenth century, poetic techniques and literary history. It consists of the following items:

1. a *ballade* made up of the titles of Zumthor's books, by Bernard Cerquiglini;

2. a poem of phonetic ●anagrams derived from one of his

titles, *Le masque et la lumière* (*Mask and Light*), by Michelle Grangaud;

3. a transformation of the opening of Genesis by noun implantation (i.e. the replacing of each noun in a text by nouns taken from another text, in this case the introduction and notes to Zumthor's *Anthologie des grands rhétoriqueurs*), by Hervé Le Tellier;

4. an underground poem by Jacques Jouet. An underground poem must be composed during a journey on the underground (or subway). Each line is mentally written between two stations, then noted down when the train stops. A change of line makes for a new verse, and the last line composed is noted down on the platform of the last station. No rewriting is permitted;

5. a ●beautiful in-law by Michelle Grangaud;

6. a homage to Paul Zumthor from Jean Meschinot by Paul Braffort;

7. a sestanagrammatina (see ●BO75) from Zumthor's *Histoire littéraire de la France médiévale* (*Literary History of Medieval France*), by Michelle Grangaud;

8. a double *ballade* on the death of Paul Zumthor, by Jacques Roubaud. [IM]

●**BO80.** Jacques Bens, *L'art de la fuite* (*The Art of the Fugitive*), 1996.

Raymond Queneau said that the idea for ●*Exercises in Style* came to him after listening to a performance of Bach's *Art of the Fugue*; now Jacques Bens has again evoked Bach's work in the title of his own theme and variations.

His theme is divided into two parts, which are designated by the fugal terms *subject* (1) and *countersubject* (1a). The subject is an account of the urge or need for flight; the countersubject an account of the urge or need for return. These two opening texts then undergo eighteen transformations:

ii. N + 9: each noun in (i) is replaced by the ninth noun following it in a dictionary regrettably unspecified by the author (see ●N + 7).

iii. N + 9 / A + 7: each adjective in (ii) is replaced by the seventh adjective following it, presumably in the very same dictionary.

iv. N + 9 / A + 7 / V + 5: each verb in (iii) is replaced by the fifth verb following it in what we hope and pray is none other than the dictionary used for (ii) and (iii).

v. The subject (1) is rewritten as a ●univocalism in e.

vi. The last six paragraphs of the countersubject (1a) are subjected to forced univocalisms in a, e, i, o, u, and y — that is to say, each vowel in turn systematically replaces all the others without consideration of meaning: *heureux* becomes *haaraax*, *pouvait* becomes *pyyvyyt*.

vii. The nouns in (1) are subjected, one paragraph at a time, to 'Roussellian' ●permutation — the last noun becomes the first and the first the last, the second noun becomes the next-to-last, etc. Here is the final paragraph in its original and altered forms:

Later, he understood that true flight is like music: it only reaches its term and its resolution in silence.

Later, he understood that true silence is like resolution: it only reaches its term and its music in flight.

viii. The subject (1) is rewritten in unrhyming ●alexandrines that follow their prose sources as closely as possible (see ●Homosemantic translation).

ix. A crossword puzzle whose grid is based on the subject.

x. A very approximate ●homosyntactic treatment of (1) yields the tale of the unlucky planter of an olive tree.

xi. The nouns, verbs, and adverbs of the countersubject (1a) are treated by ●antonymy. The opening sentence, before and after, reads:

Those absent are always wrong to come back, Jules Renard esteemed.

Those present are always right to stay, Peter Rabbit mocked.

xii. The last two sentences of the subject undergo four successive ●lardings, elegantly swelling to seventeen lines.

xiii. The subject becomes a playlet involving a plumber, since the *fuite* of the title means both *flight* and *leak*.

xiv. A critical gloss of (1), revealing it point by point as a reverie on the *Odyssey*.

xv. An unfavourable newspaper review of (1) and (1a).

xvi. Subject and countersubject are transformed into an ●elementary morality.

xvii. Subject and countersubject are transformed into an ●irrational sonnet (a form invented by the author).

xviii. An inventory of (1) (the ●inventory was also one of Jacques Bens's contributions to the Oulipian repertory).

xix. Jacques Bens signs his work in appropriate fashion: his name is hidden in a treatment of his subject as a ●beautiful outlaw. [HM]

●**BO81.** Jacques Roubaud, *Trois ruminations* (*Three Ruminations*), 1996.

1. *Rumination on Potentiality* (presented at the meeting of the Oulipo of 29 January 1996).

The author expresses doubts concerning the ●potentiality of the unrealised majority of sonnets in Queneau's ○●*100,000,000,000,000 Poems*. Following recent mathematical speculations on the accessibility of "distant" prime numbers, he suggests that it may be more accurate to limit the potential of Queneau's work to those poems that have actually been recovered from the mass of possibilities.

He underlines his view by pointing out that Queneau has given the reader no method of gaining access to individual poems that might be of particular interest (whether numerical or literary), whereas in the case, for instance, of primes, our numerical system makes certain numbers (like 10^{14}) far more easily localised and recovered than others (like 9^{15}). The author concludes by asserting the usefulness of developing similar notational algorithms for works like Queneau's, a project still vague "albeit more than metaphorical".

2. *noitaromemmoC no noitanimuR* (read at the first Oulipo Thursday at Halle St. Pierre, Paris, 25 January 1996).

Roubaud recalls the recommendations made by a special committee of the Oulipo to the Ministry of Monuments and Commemorations on the eve of the palindromic year 1991:

i. that the president of the cilbupeR declare 1991 as the Year of the ●Palindrome;

ii. that all public speeches and documents be written in palindromic form.

Other events would have included the reception of the Argentine president, Menem, in the cities of Laval and Noyon, and the consecration of Noël, Léon, Eve, Anna, Otto, Bob, and Ava as given names of the year.

Unfortunately none of these possibilities was realised. The Oulipo must therefore redouble its efforts to make sure that the year 2002 (during which will occur the supremely palindromic date of 20/02/2002) not be treated with the same catastrophic indifference.

3. *Rumination on Morality (Elementary)* (excerpt from a lecture, 1994).

In a lengthy, largely tongue-in-cheek presentation, Roubaud defines the primordial unit of poetry as the noun and its primordial form as the list, from which emerged the glossed list, where the simplest and most natural gloss is the epithet — an adjective modifying a noun. It was thus inevitable that Raymond Queneau invent the poetic form known as ●elementary morality, in which adjective-noun pairings predominate.

The author invites writers to follow Queneau's example by extending the elementary morality to other parts of speech so as to restore our decadent languages to their "pristine splendour". As material for the enterprise he supplies several lists of ●precooked language, as well as two poems illustrating his intentions. [HM]

●**BO82.** Jacques Jouet, *Exercices de la mémoire* (*Memory Exercises*), 1996.

The opening statement in this booklet reads:

I remember that in 1978 Georges Perec published a book entitled ●I remember.

The remaining 98 entries repeat this statement in 98 different ways. Excerpts:

I recollect that in 1978 Georges Perec published a book entitled *I remember.*

If my memory is correct, it was in 1978 that Georges Perec published a book entitled *I remember.*

Yes, it's coming back to me — it was in 1978 that Georges Perec published a book entitled *I remember.*

Take this in remembrance of me: in 1978 Georges Perec published a book entitled *I remember*.

Must you adopt that sepulchral tone when reminding us that in 1978 Georges Perec published a book entitled *I remember*?

To get this into your thick skull, copy out one hundred times: In 1978 Georges Perec published a book entitled *I remember*.

No, wait. Instead, make up 99 statements, each starting differently, of the fact that in 1978 Georges Perec published a book entitled *I remember*.

I've forgotten my umbrella but not that in 1978 Georges Perec published a book entitled *I remember*.

Remember that thou art dust and that in 1978 Georges Perec published a book entitled *I remember*.

[Trans HM]

See ●Homosemantic translation.

●BO83. Jacques Roubaud, *La Terre est plate: 99 dialogues dramatiques mais brefs, précédé de Petite rumination du 150* (*The Earth is Flat: 99 brief yet dramatic dialogues, preceded by a Short Rumination on 150*), 1996.

This fascicle opens with a short rumination on why Raymond Queneau was right to fix at 150 the number of copies of each volume of the Bibliothèque Oulipienne which are destined for the public. A recent study by Professor Robin Dunbar of Liverpool University has shown that there is a number beyond which verbal communication loses its value as a socially binding force. It is the number of inhabitants of traditional villages, the smallest unit in most armies, the average number of recipients on our Christmas card lists, etc. And this number? 150, of course.

The second part consists of 99 short, amusing dialogues containing inter-linguistic puns, plays on well-known lines of poetry, attacks on clichés, and lunatic games with logic. Here is an example:

88:
"Do you have any Latin?"
"A little."
"What does *cave canem* mean?"
"Watch out! I might start singing!"   [IM]

●BO84. Hervé Le Tellier, *Un Sourire indéfinissable: Mona Lisa, dite la Joconde, sous 53 jours différents* (*An Indefinable Smile: Mona Lisa in 53 different lights*), 1997.

The fifty-three points of view (a reference to Georges Perec's posthumous "*53 Days*") include those of the painter, a Boolean mathematician, a Jewish mother, a blind man, and Mona herself, on what is generally considered to be the world's most famous painting. Here are two samples, the first written directly in English.

The point of view of the English conversation teacher

Well, what are we going to speak about today, Mona Lisa? Shall we speak about your hair? Yes, we shall speak about your hair. Your hair is curly.

Repeat after me: My hair is curly.

I wear a silk net upon my hair. The net is black and it is made of silk.

What is the net made of? It is made of silk.

And where does the silk come from? The silk comes from China.

Repeat after me: it comes from China.

The point of view of the anonymous letter writer

Old Sourpuss,

I'm sending you this portrait of your wife hoping that you'll enjoy it. As you can ascertain from the landscape and her smile, she certainly didn't waste her time in Italy, the little slut, during her week's refresher course. And don't go hugging her too hard — she'll think you're jealous and that would create a most negative effect.

A friend who wishes you well.

[HM]

107

●**BO85.** François Le Lionnais, *Un certain disparate* (*A Certain Fractiousness*), 1997.

This fascicle includes seventeen excerpts from a series of interviews conducted with François Le Lionnais in the 1980s; they were to be incorporated in a planned volume of autobiography and reflection called *Un certain disparate*.

The excerpts mainly concern writing, the Oulipo, and the notion of *le* (properly *la*) *disparate*, a word that connotes a refractory, capricious, unreasonable attitude — "the opposite of the quest for unity", as Le Lionnais says in discussing Bosch's *Temptation of St. Anthony*, considered by him to be the highest example of *le disparate* "mastered, organised, and exploited."

Le Lionnais confesses to "constipation of the pen" and a distaste for writing: the structures he creates are not for him but posterity. He vehemently disapproves of the course the Oulipo has taken. He would have preferred, to Queneau's slightly flawed ○●*100,000,000,000,000 Poems*, an exploration of ●permutational verse that started with couplets and progressed systematically through tercets, quatrains, and so forth. He disapproves of Jacques Roubaud's preoccupation with form — a symptom, in his view, of laziness and lack of ambition on the part of the Oulipo, which should have striven to imagine vaster systems of restrictions and structures instead of producing works that exploited discoveries at hand.

Le Lionnais's observations are followed by Roubaud's comments on the *Third Manifesto* (●BO30), as well as recollections of talks with Le Lionnais about whose authenticity this editor is slightly sceptical but whose interest is undeniable. The classification of structures, the idea of the ★Ou-x-pos, and the question of whether a restriction necessarily has to be validated by at least one example are among the topics discussed.

The fascicle concludes with Roubaud's minutes of the meeting of a committee (Le Lionnais, Roubaud, and Marcel Bénabou) whose task was extending ●Queneleyev's Table. [HM]

●**BO86.** Walter Henry, *Chu dans mer sale, ou la rumination polymorphe* (*Damp Mars Shoe Sell, or the polymorphous rumination*), 1997.

Walter Henry is the name assigned to a scholar whose sole object of study is the work of Paul Braffort. He is rightly considered his alter ego.

The title of the issue is a ●spooneristic treatment of the name Marcel Duchamp, and its contents are an eclectic or "polymorphous" discussion of Duchamp's affinities with the Oulipo in general and with Braffort in particular. Of great value is the account, summarised at the entry for Duchamp, of the circumstances in which he became a member of the group. Duchamp's interest in chess and various aspects of his art are discussed in terms of their relevance to Oulipian preoccupations.

The bulk of the issue is devoted to an extensive cultural and formal gloss of Braffort's hypertrope on Duchamp (see ●BO9) and to a recapitulation of the "literary homework" that emerged from Braffort's and Jean Margat's considerations of Duchamp's *L.H.O.O.Q.* and *Étant donnés*. [HM]

●**BO87.** Marcel Bénabou, *L'Hannibal perdu* (*Hannibal Crackers*), 1997.

A play whose characters and setting are the very same as its original performers and theatre: M. Bénabou, J. Roubaud, H. Le Tellier, and M. Grangaud performed it at the Halle St. Pierre in Paris in the winter of 1997. Its subject — an offspring of ●*Why I Have Not Written Any of My Books* — is the failure of Marcel Bénabou's adolescent project to write a Racinian tragedy about Hannibal's last winter in exile in Bithynia.

The play is a light-hearted and highly erudite farce, full of puns and Oulipian allusions, as well as affectionate caricatures of the sage and scholarly Roubaud and the sassy and roguish Le Tellier. The two act the roles of Bénabou's impudent interrogators, while Michelle Grangaud plays a pseudo-solemn poetic chorus. [HM]

●**BO88.** Jacques Bens, *J'ai oublié* (*I've forgotten*), 1997.

The author presents a series of statements all beginning with the words "*J'ai oublié...*", in overt reference to Georges Perec's *Je me souviens* (●*I remember*). In his introduction, he points out that forgetfulness only exists in a context of memory: noticing what one has forgotten — for instance, the name of a first piano teacher — implies the remembrance of other piano teachers and their names. "Searching for what one has forgotten means ferreting out the hollows, voids, and absences of an otherwise healthy memory." So each item in the series of forgettings is appropriately accompanied by the mention of something the author also remembers about the fact or incident evoked.

A few examples of the 53 entries:

I've forgotten the exact date of my parents' death. (At the same time I remember the dates of their birth.)

(But I remember that my mother's decease occurred within several days of General De Gaulle's; and that I was living in Cour du Commerce-Saint-André-des-Arts [Paris] *when I learned of my father's.)*

I forget the name of my first shaving lotion.

(But I remember its scent very well.)

I forget the publication dates of my books.

(But I know their order of appearance and their publishers.)

I've forgotten the name of the hotel where I was taken by the 'first girl I ever held in my arms.'

(But I remember perfectly where it was.)

I've partially forgotten the name of the clarinettist in the original Hot Five — Jimmy Noone or Johnny Dodds?

(The others must have been Louis Armstrong, cornet; Kid Ory, trombone; Lil Hardin, piano; Zutty Singleton, drums — right?)

I've forgotten what I wanted to make of my life when I was ten years old.   [HM]

●**BO89.** Claude Berge, *Raymond Queneau et la combinatoire (Raymond Queneau and Combinatorics)*, 1997.

The author here summarises mathematical questions that interested Queneau as they transpired in the correspondence between the two men.

Claude Berge was first approached by Queneau in 1952 after he had written his thesis on game theory. (In a comment quoted by Berge, Queneau writes, "... psychology now lies closer to

mathematics than to the biological sciences.")

Starting in 1963, Queneau became interested in two "amusing" problems presented by Berge in his regular column (in *Revue de la Société Française de Recherche Opérationelle*): the problem of the "club of incompatibles", or how to seat a given number of members, each of which has only two friends in the club, the others all being enemies; and the problem of aligning an uneven number of alternating black and white chips so that, after a restricted number of moves, blacks and whites will be in two groups.

In 1970 Queneau approached Berge about the possibility of representing his *Tale of Your Choice* as a graph (see ●Branching systems and ●Graphic representation of text). The results of their work proved extremely fruitful in the domain of combinatorial mathematics.

Finally, between 1966 and 1972, Queneau addressed Berge about a series of arithmetical-combinatorial procedures, again contributing notably to the theory of combinatorics — a field that, Claude Berge points out, was still at the time in search of its identity.

Following Berge's summary are reproductions of ten letters, tables, and diagrams in Queneau's hand. [HM]

●**BO90.** The Oulipo, *Sexe: ce xé (Sex and what it is)*, 1997.

After a brief introduction by Marcel Bénabou on the kinship of "sex" and "text", this issue presents 7 Oulipian explorations of everyone's favourite subject.

– Using the method introduced in ●BO13, Bénabou invents ●aphorisms concerning various aspects of sex: Texts are the continuation of sex by other means.

– Hervé Le Tellier analyses the letters that form the word *amour* (love), making ingenious use of their ●homophonic possibilities: *petit a/petit tas* (small a, small pile), *l'u/lu* (u, read), *un drôle d'r/un drôle d'air* (strange r, strange look).

– Jacques Jouet adds an ●elementary morality of undressing to his repertory (see his example after ●BO55).

– Michelle Grangaud introduces a method that she calls a *shrub*: all the significant ramifications of a word are detailed without any mention of the word itself, which remains the shrub's hidden root. Here the root word is *sex*, and its meanings are investigated with a suitable blend of explicitness and reserve:

These activities, scarcely decent, it must be confessed, are best buried under a silence as thick as the lid on my grandmother's washing machine, no doubt imposing but fitted at its centre with a kind of little turret from whose cap a whitish, soapy liquid escaped in successive spasms.

– Marcel Bénabou contributes two "inescapable edges", *edge* here referring to the method introduced by Michèle Métail in ●BO34. An analogy in English:

He doesn't know his end
from his elbow in a sling
kissing backwards over tea-kettle
A kick in the pain in the piece of polisher
on his hole.

– Jacques Roubaud provides a dialogue between a mostly laconic woman and an ardent, voluble man, whose precise suggestions are stretched inordinately by his inability to pronounce the crucial terms that define his affections and desires. Each such term is painfully approached by a series of ●N ± 7, N ± 6, N ± 5... that stops just short of the forbidden word:

... and after I withdraw my cob, my cobalt, my cobbler, my cobra, my cocaine, my... from your curate, your cur, your cupola, your cupidity, your cupboard, your cup, your...

– Hervé Le Tellier also uses a form of N ± 7 to rewrite the opening of the book of Genesis, freely taking the nearest appropriate noun to the original whether it precedes or follows:

... And Goat-Pan said, Let there be licentiousness: and there was licentiousness.

And Goat-Pan saw the licentiousness, that it was good; and Goat-Pan divided the licentiousness from the darling.

And Goat-Pan called the licentiousness daydream, and the darling he called nipple. And the evasion and the morphine were the first daydream. [HM]

●**BO91.** Georges Perec, Harry Mathews, Oskar Pastior, *Variations, Variations, Variationen*, 1997.

In 1974, in an article on the Oulipo in *Magazine Littéraire*, Georges Perec published a set of *35 Variations on a Theme from Proust*, the theme in question being the opening sentence of *A la recherche du temps perdu: Longtemps je me suis couché de bonne heure* (For a long time I went to bed early). The variations constituted a succinct demonstration of many Oulipian methods, as well as of the general Oulipian approach to writing and literature.

In recent years, Perec's variations have become a staple at the group's public readings; and it was such a reading — a bilingual one — that led the present editor to create an English replica of Perec's model. Soon afterwards, the group invited Oskar Pastior to contribute a German version. In the English and German sets, the themes are furnished by familiar lines from Shakespeare (see opposite) and Goethe (the final verse of *Faust*, "The Eternal Feminine draws us upwards"). While differing slightly between the three languages, the nature of the variations becomes plain in the English series given here. [HM]

●**BO92.** Harry Mathews, *An* ex voto *to include excursive excavators: a Chronogram for 1997*, 1997.

The author explains his project in a note at the end of this fascicle:

The ●chronogram follows a simple rule: all letters in a statement that can be read as Roman numerals — every c, d, i, l, m, v, and x — when added together produce a sum that corresponds to a year of the Christian era. Thus the single word memory *can represent the year 2000...*

The traditional chronogram has never, to my knowledge, produced works of literature. Since its method is neither difficult nor very productive, it seemed worthwhile to combine it with one or more Oulipian restrictions. In the present case, the only numerical letter allowed is i (= 1). This choice not only rescues the chronogram from its usual epigrammatic brevity — for the year 1997 at least one thousand nine hundred and ninety-seven syllables must be aligned — but it necessarily introduces a demanding procedure, that of the ●lipogram: no c, d, l, m, v, or

◖Harry Mathews *35 Variations on a Theme from Shakespeare*
(*Source text:* To be or not to be: that is the question)

01 *Alphabetically*
A BB EEEE HH II NN OOOOO Q R SS TTTTTTT U

02 *Anagram*
Note at his behest: bet on toot or quit

03 *Lipogram in c, d, f, g, j, k, l, m, p, v, w, x, y, z*
To be or not to be: that is the question

04 *Lipogram in a*
To be or not to be: this is the question

05 *Lipogram in i*
To be or not to be: that's the problem

06 *Lipogram in e*
Almost nothing, or nothing: but which?

07 *Transposition (W + 7)*
To beckon or not to beckon: that is the quinsy

08 *Strict palindrome*
No, it's (eu) qeht sit. Ah! te botton roebot

09 *Missing letter*
To be or not to be hat is the question

10 *Two missing letters*
To be or not to be at is the question

11 *One letter added*
To bed or not to be: that is the question

12 *Negation*
To be or not to be: that is not the question

13 *Emphasis*
To be, if you see what I mean, to *be*, be alive, exist, not just keep hanging around; *or* (and that means one or the other, no getting away from it) *not* to be, *not* be alive, *not* exist, to — putting it bluntly — check out, cash in your chips, head west: *that* (do you read me? not "maybe this" or "maybe something else") *that* is, really *is*, irrevocably *is*, *the* one and only inescapable, overwhelming, and totally preoccupying ultimate *question*

14 *Curtailing*
Not to be: that is the question

15 *Curtailing (different)*
To be or not to be, that is

16 *Double curtailing*
Not to be, that is

17 *Triple contradiction*
You call this life? And everything's happening all the time? Who's asking?

18 *Another point of view*
Hamlet, quit stalling!

19 *Minimal variations*
To see or not to see
To flee or not to flee
To pee or not to pee

20 *Antonymy*
Nothing *and* something: this was an answer

21 *Amplification*
To live forever or never to have been born is a concern that has perplexed humanity from time immemorial and still does

22 *Reductive*
One or the other — who knows?

23 *Permutation*
That is the question: to be or not to be

24 *Interference*
a) Tomorrow and tomorrow and tomorrow:
   That is the question
b) To be or not to be
   Creeps in this petty pace from day to day
   To the last syllable of recorded time
   And all our yesterdays have lighted fools
   The way to dusty death

111

25 *Isomorphisms*
Speaking while singing: this defines *recitativo*
Getting and spending we lay waste our powers

26 *Synonymous*
Choosing between life and death confuses me

27 *Subtle insight*
Shakespeare knew the answer

28 *Another interference*
Put out the light, and then? That is the question

29 *Homoconsonantism*
At a bier, a nutty boy, too, heats the queasy tone

30 *Homovocalism*
Lode of gold ore affirms evening's crown

31 *Homophony*
Two-beer naughty beat shatters equation

32 *Snowball with an irregularity*

I
am
all
mute
after
seeing
Hamlet's
annoying
emergency
yourstruly
Shakespeare

33 *Heterosyntaxism*
I ask myself: is it worth it, or isn't it?

34 *In another metre*
So should I be, or should I not?
This question keeps me on the trot

35 *Interrogative mode*
Do I really care whether I exist or not?
(We leave the reader saddled with this painful question.)

x *is allowed to appear. Furthermore, to keep the work from acquiring excessive length, the total number of words has also been limited to 1,997... Finally, since the words of the title are not included in this count, they have been organised as a second chronogram, one kept as short as possible but, in terms of the sum of the numerical letters, equivalent to the body of text that follows.*

Extract:

January starts: sun here, stars there. So what joys & fears has the New Year brought us?

+ In the Irkutsk penitentiary ironworks the night shift is finishing its stint, skirting weighty pig-iron ingots as it regains the prison interior.

+ In Pienza, Ernestina is heating tripe *fiorentina* for thirteen.

+ In Sing-Sing, wearing surreptitious attire, Phineas, Bishop of Ossining, is anointing nine Fenian ("Fighting Irish") priests in a kiosk of ingenuous piety.

+ Bibi is shirring pigeon eggs in Saint Étienne.

+ In Whitby, seagoing Einar, finishing his fifteenth pink gin, insists he is quite fine.

+ In Austria, zipping past the Inn, ignoring warning signs, Pippo Peruzzi, first-string Ferrari whiz, big winner in Spain & Argentina, is steering his touring-bike (pistons & turbine whirring, its stunning furnishings genuine Pinin-Farina) in brisk pursuit of fiery Zizi, his Hungarian skier, itinerant antithesis, antagonist, tigress, priestess, siren, obsession, happiness, wife.

+ In Tirana, inept Hussein is paying fifty-eight qintars to fortify his Istrian wine with Bosnian raki.

+ Postponing inopportune issues & putting first things first, Kiwanis, Rotarians, & Shriners are putting their agonizing unity in writing, signing a proposition that reasserts their opposition to atheists, bigotry, euthanasia ("outright assassination"), heroin, pinkos, the Spanish

Inquisition, superstition, & unfairness in business arbitration.

+ Zazie is biting into rabbit thighs in Barbizon.

+ Zenia, passionate Aquinist, is pursuing an ingenious hypothesis, assigning the origins of Aquinas's interpretations of Gorgias to an "Osirian" genesis arising in the writings of inquiring Egyptian priests, an origin that the Sophists reinstate, or so Zenia infers in her ingenious synthesis. Questioning the suppositions of post-Aquinist thinkers, Zenia insists on the inferiority of Fourier's "inanities", Wittgenstein's "gibberish", & Austin's "asininities".

+ Anisette fizzes are winning the night in Springs, whither Henri is steering Bettina in his antique Hispano-Suiza.

+ Benign skies in Arizona. At a prairie spring, Tintin is watering his proprietor's thirty-eight ponies — they're skittish ponies, stirring, neighing, biting, nosing bitten withers. Rising high in his stirrups, reins tight against bit, quirt hanging at his wrist, Tintin spits; sitting, he tips a sparing ration into its Zigzag wrapping. Prairie rabbits thinking: rain. Harriers beating their wings in thin bright air. Tintin thinking: this night's attire — white shirt, string tie — is right for winning his engaging señorita. His pinto whinnies & pisses.

+ On Thirteenth Street & First, Antoine & Honoria are sharing a pizza & a knish.

+ Aries & Sirius are shining in Tunisian skies.

●**Bibliothèque Oulipienne continued.** The following issues have appeared between the publication of the first edition of the *Compendium* and April 2005; they will either be translated or summarised in the forthcoming *Oulipo Papers* (●**CP17**):

    ●**BO93.** Jacques Jouet, *Pauline (polyne) (Polly-Ann (Poly-n))*, 1997; ●**BO94.** Hervé Le Tellier, *Le Vent de la langue (The Wind in the Language)*, 1997; ●**BO95.** Michelle Grangaud, *Oulipo fondu (Oulipo Stew)*, 1998; ●**BO96.** François Caradec, *Paris périphérique (Paris Ring-road)*, 1998; ●**BO97.** Jacques Jouet & Pierre Rosenstiehl, *Frise du métro parisien (Freize of the Paris Underground)*, 1998; ●**BO98.** Jacques Roubaud, *Ô baobab (Up Lolo Up!)*, 1999; ●**BO99.** Paul Fournel, *Foyer-Jardin (Stage right-Stage left)*, 1997; ●**BO100.** Oulipo, *Ceci est mon cent (spécial Dieu) (Holy Hun Dread (Special God))*, 1998; ●**BO101.** Michelle Grangaud, *ha ha ô ah ah (ha ha o ah ah)*, 1998; ●**BO102.** Ian Monk, *Fractales (Fractals)*, 1998; ●**BO103.** Marcel Bénabou, *Altitude et profondeur (Altitude and Depth)*, 1999; ●**BO104.** Jacques Bens, *Opus posthume (Posthumous Work)*, 1999; ●**BO105.** Hervé Le Tellier, *Le Voyage d'Hitler (Hitler's Journey)*, 1999, translated in ●**CP12**; ●**BO106.** Oulipo, *La Couronne de Stèphe (Steve's Garland)*, 1999; ●**BO107.** Jacques Jouet, *La redonde (The Redonda)*, 1999; ●**BO108.** Jacques Jouet, *Hinterreise et autres histoires retournées (Hinterreise and other turned around tales)*, 1999, part translated in ●**CP12**; ●**BO109.** Ian Monk, *Monquines (Monkinas)*, 1999; ●**BO110.** Ian Monk, *Le Voyage d'Hoover (Hoover's Journey)*, 1999, translated in ●**CP12**; ●**BO111.** Harry Mathews, *Sainte Catherine (Saint Kathrina)*, 1999; ●**BO112.** Jacques Bens, *Le Voyage d'Arvers (Arvers's Journey)*, 1999, translated in ●**CP12**; ●**BO113.** Michelle Grangaud, *Un Voyage divergent (A Divergent Journey)*, 2001, translated in ●**CP12**; ●**BO114.** François Caradec, *Le Voyage du ver (The Worm's Journey)*, 2001, translated in ●**CP12**; ●**BO115.** Michelle Grangaud, *Une bibliothèque en avion (A Library in Avon)*, 1999; ●**BO116.** Ian Monk, *Les états du sonnet (The States of the Sonnet)*, 2001; ●**BO117.** Reine Haugure, *Le Voyage du vers (Verse's Journey)*, 2001, translated in ●**CP12**; ●**BO118.** Harry Mathews, *Le Voyage des verres (A Journey Amid Glasses)*, 2001, translated in ●**CP12**; ●**BO119.** Paul Braffort, *Cinq Lettres de créance (Five letters of credit)*, 2002; ●**BO120.** Jacques Jouet & Olivier Salon, *Pas de deux (comédrame booléen) (Two Step (Boolean Comedrama))*, 2002; ●**BO121.** Oulipo, *Aux origines du langage (To the Origins of Language)*, 2002; ●**BO122.** François Caradec, *Que j'aime à faire apprendre au π-éton de Paris (An Paedogogical Parisian π-chart for Pedestrians)*, 2002; ●**BO123.** Oulipo, *Drames et comédies brefs dans le petit lavoir (Brief Dramas and Comedies in the*

Little Wash-House), 2003; ●**BO124.** Jacques Jouet, *Vies longues* (*Long Lives*), 2003; ●**BO125.** Oskar Pastior, *"sestinenformulate" monadengraphik und minisestinen* (*Sestinian Formulations (Monad-graphics and Mini-Sestinas*)), 2003; ●**BO126.** Oulipo, *Doukipleudonktan?* (*Itsraininitspourin*), 2003; ●**BO127.** Ian Monk, *Quenoums* (*Quenoums*), 2003; ●**BO128.** Ian Monk, *Élémentaire, mon cher* (*Elementary, my dear*), 2003; ●**BO129.** Mikhaïl Gourliouk, *Si par une nuit un voyage d'hiver* (*If on a Night a Winter's Traveller*), 2003; ●**BO130.** Paul Braffort, *Les univers bibliothèques, visibles invisibles réel(le)s virtuel(le)s* (*The Real, Virtual, Visible, Invisible Library Universe*), 2004; ●**BO131.** Jacques Roubaud, *Duchamp l'oulipien* (*Duchamp the Oulipian*), 2003; ●**BO132.** Olivier Salon, *Les gens de légende* (*Legend's brethren*), 2004; ●**BO133.** Marcel Bénabou, *La mort mode d'emploi* (*Death a User's Manual*), 2004; ●**BO134.** Jacques Jouet, *Petits boîtes, sonnets minces, et autre rigueurs* (*Little boxes, slim sonnets and other rigours*), 2004; ●**BO135.** Jacques Jouet, *Du monostique* (*On the monostich*), 2004; ●**BO666.** Oulipo, *Diable!* (*The Devil!*), 2004.

●***Bicarré gréco-latin.*** See ●Graeco-Latin bi-square.

●**Bifurcating text.** See ●Branching systems & ●Graphic representation of text.

●**Bilingual palindrome.** The late Luc Étienne composed several bilingual ●palindromes, such as:

Untrodden russet

T'es sûr, Ned dort nu?

(You're sure Ned sleeps in the nude?)

A selection was published by the Cymbalum Pataphysicum in 1984.

●**Bi-square.** See ●Græco-Latin bi-square.

●**Blank verse amidst the prose.** English-speaking amateurs used to compile poems using unintentional lines of iambic pentameter in the writings of Dickens; more recently, John Updike has concocted a poem consisting of extracts from Samuel Johnson's notebooks. In *Lipo* (●CP3), Jean Queval, noticing the frequency of ●alexandrines in the prose of Victor Hugo, similarly combined them into rhyming poems.

An abundance of blank-verse lines in English prose usually indicates an incursion of solemnity or melancholy. The following example is assembled from F. Scott Fitzgerald's account of returning to a "lost" Paris, a story called *Babylon Revisited.*

He saw, when he arrived at the apartment,
That Marion had accepted the inevitable.
"We haven't had a doctor for a year."
The room was comfortably American.
"I've got a vile hangover for the moment.
"I wish you and I could be on better terms."
"I should think you'd have had enough of bars."
"I want to get to know you," he said gravely.
But that was the beginning of the end,
And Marion, who had seen with her own eyes
The things that he would now always remember,
The men who locked their wives out in the snow,
Wanted his child, and nothing was much good now.
Has Marion said anything definite?
"My husband couldn't come this year," she said,
"As soon as I can get a governess — "
And everything was gone, and he was gone.
"What about coming back and sitting down?"
"Can't do it." He was glad for an excuse:
"We're going to see the vaudeville at the Empire."
We were a sort of royalty, almost infallible
("Daddy, I want to come and live with you!")
But she was in a swing in a white dress,
And swinging faster and faster all the time,
And kissed her fingers out into the night.

[HM]

See ●Cento.

●**Blavier, André.** (1922–2001) Founding member of the Oulipo (above right, with Raymond Queneau in 1962).

Born in Hodimont, a suburb of Verviers in Wallonia, Blavier spent his entire life in his home town, working from 1942 until his retirement in 1987 as librarian of the Verviers municipal library. The crucial moment of his life as a writer came in 1942 with the discovery of the work of Raymond Queneau, and particularly of Queneau's first two novels, *Le Chiendent* (*The Bark Tree*), which had a capital influence on the development of Blavier's own style, and *Les Enfants du limon* (*Children of the Clay*), which ignited his interest in outsider writers (*les fous littéraires*), a subject on which he became an authority. (His monumental anthology, *Les Fous littéraires*, was published by Veyrier in 1982.) Blavier also played a central part in furthering the study of Queneau: in 1952 he founded the review *Temps Mêlés* (●CP2 was a special issue of this review), which in 1978 became *Temps Mêlés/Documents Queneau*; and in 1977, less

than a year after Queneau's death, he established the Centre de Documentation Raymond Queneau within the Verviers library.

Finally, in Noël Arnaud's words, "Blavier deserves eternal merit and glory for the oft-forgotten fact that he is the true founder of the Oulipo. During a night of studious revelry in the company of Jacques Bens at Cerisy-la-Salle, it was he who made the decision to ask Queneau, via François Le Lionnais, to create a select group devoted to the question of literary structures."

He died in Verviers on 9 June 2001. [HM, after NA]

Oulipian and partly Oulipian works: *Occupe-toi d'homélies* (Cheval d'Attaque, Paris, 1976); *Le Mal du pays ou les travaux forc[en]és* (A la Pierre d'Alun, Brussels, 1983); see also ●BO42 and ●Minutes of the Oulipo (2). [AB]

●**Boolean haiku.** See next entry.

●**Boolean poetry.** In *Lipo* (●CP3), François Le Lionnais suggests that if we consider the language of a given culture at a particular moment as a set, we can treat poems written in that language as subsets, any two (or more) of which will yield an intersection (the words they share) and a difference (the words they do not share). Intersection and difference can be used as sources for new poems. [HM]

●*Boules de neige.* See ●Snowball.

●**Bourbaki.** The name of a group of French mathematicians who decided, in Jacques Roubaud's words, to "perform an Oulipian rewriting of mathematics." They drew their inspiration from the axiomatics of David ●Hilbert and made set theory the basis of their undertaking. Their collaboration began in the late 1920s; their first fascicle was published in 1939. While officially anonymous, the group is known to have included André Weil, Jean Dieudonné, Henri Cartan, Claude Chevalley, Jean Delsarte, and Laurent Schwartz. [HM, after JR]

●**Braffort, Paul.** Elected to the Oulipo in 1961.

Born in Paris 5 December 1923, Braffort studied at the Lycée Buffon and the Sorbonne, where he received degrees in

défense Sirine", *Europe* (Nabokov issue, March 1995); "*L'ordre
dans le crime: une expérience cybernétique avec Italo Calvino*",
Europe (Calvino issue, March 1997); ●BO9, 18, 48, 58, 71, 79
(6), 86, 119 & 130. [HM, after PB]

●**Braised rhyme (*rime berrichonne*).** Improvised at a meeting of
the Oulipo, the name given to a rhyme scheme suggested by a
poem by John Berryman was *rime berrichonne*. Since *berrichon*
means "from the region of Berry", since braised cabbage is
conspicuous in *cuisine berrichonne*, and since one travesty
deserves another, the rhyme has been Englished as "braised".

The first stanza of Berryman's opening *Dream Song* offers
the sequence of end-words *sulked/thought/talked*. This suggests
a pattern in which elements of consonance and ●assonance are
combined in an inclusive rhyme:

consonance	*sulked*
assonance	*thought*
rhyme	*talked*

That is, the consonants -*kt* of "sulked" and the vowel sound -*aw*-
of "thought" come together in the -*awkt* of "talked".

Jacques Jouet has used braised rhyme extensively, most
notably in his book-length sequence, ●*107 âmes*.

Example:

> We braid the <u>weird</u>
> Weavings of rhyme
> Whose ensigns <u>furl</u>
> To fit a rule
> No more than <u>word</u>
> (weird + furl = word) [HM]

●**Branching systems.** A system used to structure a text or poem
so that it offers proliferating alternative readings.

See ●Graphic representation of text, ●Multiple-choice
narrative, ●Multiple-choice theatre, ▲*Jus d'Oronge*.

●**Brazzle.** See ●BO58.

mathematics and philosophy. Unable to pursue his studies, in
1949 he began working at the Commissariat à l'Énergie
Atomique (Atomic Energy Commission), first as librarian, later as
director of the Laboratory for Analogue Computation. After
assignments to Euratom, the European Space Centre, and the
University of Paris XI at Orsay, he ran a data-processing
company, then was invited as Visiting Scholar to the University
of Chicago from 1988–1991. In the years 1957–1958 he
enjoyed a brief career as a cabaret singer-composer, recording
one LP with Pathé-Marconi.

Paul Braffort's very first manifestation in the Oulipo, in June
1961, concerned the possibilities offered by electronic
calculating machines, not yet baptised computers. Since then he
has made his skills as a computer scientist available to members
of the group, notably Italo Calvino, Marcel Bénabou, and
Jacques Roubaud. It was with the latter that he proposed the
creation of the computer-oriented Oulipian research group that
was to become the ●ALAMO.

Oulipian works: (with Jacques Bens & Claude Berge), "*La
littérature récurrente*" (in *Atlas*, ●CP6); "*Nabokov oulipien, La*

●**Bruno, Giordano.** (1548–1600) A leading philosopher of the Italian Renaissance. Ordained a Dominican priest in 1575, Bruno left his order the following year under accusation of heresy, and after years of study, travel, and teaching in France, England, Germany, and Bohemia was finally burned at the stake in Venice for heresy.

Bruno's philosophy rejected the geocentric and anthropocentric notions of the universe, which in his view was formed of a single substance, where God was both absent and omnipresent, and whose reality was constituted solely by the mind. His aim was to explore the multiplicity of the universe by means of 'figures', which he drew in copious number from the hermetic tradition as well as from Ramon ●Llull, the natural world, and the conventional repertory of allegorical personages. These figures were articulated by various rhetorical methods — such as phonetic resemblance, ●anagrams, punning, synecdoche — and combined in sequences as a way of investigating the possible existence of multiple and conceivably infinite worlds. To this end he adapted and considerably expanded Llull's ●combinatorial methods, especially his system of compartmented, concentric circles, with the purpose not (as was the case with Llull) of discovering verifiable truths but of creating potential realities of image and word. [HM]

See also ●Leibniz, Anticipatory ●plagiary.

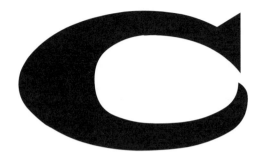

●**Calvino, Italo.** (Cuba, 1923 – Italy, 1985) Elected to the Oulipo in 1973. Photograph above: Calvino, sitting between Raymond Queneau and Harry Mathews at an early public presentation of the Oulipo, Reid Hall, Paris, 1973.

Born in Santiago de las Vegas, near Havana, Calvino at the age of two returned to what he always considered his native Liguria, growing up happily in San Remo. During the war his anti-fascist inclinations led him to join the Italian Communist Party (PCI) and take an active part in the resistance. In 1945, while beginning literary studies in Turin, he contributed to several party periodicals and, thanks to Cesare Pavese, had his first story published. His first novel, *Il sentiero dei nidi di ragno* (*The Path to the Nest of Spiders*), appeared in 1947, in which year he joined the staff of the publisher Einaudi, initiating a collaboration that would last for decades. In 1951 he undertook, in an entirely new and original vein, the first novel of the trilogy that would bring him fame: *Il visconte dimezzato* (*The Cloven Viscount*), published in 1952, *Il barone rampante* (*The Baron in the Trees*) in 1957, and *Il cavaliere inesistente* (*The Nonexistent Knight*) in 1958. During that time he also achieved great success with a collection of Italian legends (*Fiabe italiane*, 1956) and the first of the *Marcovaldo* stories that were to endear him to two generations of younger readers. In 1956 his opposition to the PCI's cultural policies and, later in the year, to its reaction to events in Poland and Hungary led him to resign from the party the following year.

Many of Calvino's finest works of fiction appeared during the last 20 years of his life: *Le cosmicomiche* (*Cosmicomics*), 1965, *Ti con zero* (*T zero*), 1967, *Le città invisibili* (*Invisible Cities*), 1972, *Se una notte d'inverno un viaggiatore* (*If on a Winter's Night a Traveller*), 1979. With Luciano Berio he also created several operas, the best known being *La Vera Storia* (1981) and *Un re in ascolto* (1984).

Calvino became friendly with Raymond Queneau (whose *Les Fleurs bleues* he had translated) during the years that he lived in Paris (1967–1980), and it was Queneau who introduced him to the work of the Oulipo. In 1981 Calvino's commentary on the Italian translation of the *Petite cosmogonie portative* provided a surely definitive gloss on Queneau's verse history of scientific thought.

It was in the summer of 1985, while working on the Norton lectures he was to deliver at Harvard, that Calvino suffered the first of a series of strokes. He died at Santa Maria della Scala hospital, Siena on the night of 18-19 September.

Oulipian works: *Il castello dei destini incrociati* (*The ●Castle of Crossed Destinies*), Einaudi, Turin, 1973; *Se una notte d'inverno un viaggiatore* (*●If on a Winter's Night a Traveller*), Einaudi, Turin, 1979; *Prima che tu dica "Pronto"* (*Numbers in* the Dark), Mondadori, Milan, 1993 (see the ●Computer and the Oulipo); ●BO6 & 20. [HM]

See also ●Topical N + 7.

●**Canada Dry.** The name of this procedure is taken from the soft drink marketed as "the champagne of ginger ales". The drink may have bubbles, but it isn't champagne; in the words of Paul Fournel, who coined the term, a Canada Dry text "has the taste and colour of a restriction but does not follow a restriction".

Wand-escape ether evil draws.

"Crack legions apprehend undue assaults," said conductor of lead tank, staccato.

Franz of black fiacre aspires to Luke's matches.   [HM]

See ●BO49 (section 4).

●**Caradec, François.** Elected to the Oulipo in 1983.

Biography and Oulipian bibliography:

"[Born] 18.06.24 [Social Security no.] 29.232.212.

Anticipatory ●plagiarists: Alphonse ●Allais (Belfond, 1994), Raymond ●Roussel (Fayard, 1997).[17]

Gone to press: Catalogues d'autographes rares et curieux Chimères.

In preparation: Posthumous Works." [FC]

Also: ●BO37, 45, 49, 54, 60, 96, 114, 122 & ●CP12, 16.

●*Carré lescurien.* See ●Lescurean word square.

●**Carroll, Lewis.** (Charles Lutwidge Dodgson; b. Daresbury, Cheshire, 1832, d. Guildford, Surrey, 1898) Not only an exceptional author but a professional mathematician, Carroll occasionally combined his gifts: A Tangled Tale demonstrates mathematical problems in the guise of fiction, and in his posthumous Symbolic Logic he brings his witty sense of the absurd to bear on logical concepts.

As far as the Oulipo is concerned, Carroll's position as anticipatory ●plagiarist probably owes more to these twin competences, to his linguistic inventiveness, and to his gift for parody than to any obvious use of Oulipian procedures. If Through the Looking-Glass is based on a game of chess, it is so in a way too informal to be called Oulipian. (It was, incidentally, François Le Lionnais who, in the Carroll issue of L'Herne, definitively explained the game involved.) Nevertheless, the portmanteau words in "Jabberwocky" can certainly be interpreted as a form of ●combinatorial literature; the story "Novelty and Romancement", in which the words Roman cement are mistaken by the narrator for romancement, seems prophetic of Raymond ●Roussel's use of double meaning; and among Carroll's minor writings several are unquestionably Oulipian. An early instance is an irregular ●tautogram, Musings on Milk, that appeared in Carroll's family periodical, The Rectory Magazine, around 1850. It begins:

Marvellously many materials make milk! Much too many to mention. 'Tis morning, and the merry milkmaid, murmuring a melting melody, moves towards the meadow; the majestic cows move meekly to meet their mirthful mistress; now mantles in the moderate milk-pail the marble milk; anon mark many minute masters and misses with measureless mouths march to their morning meal of mighty mugs! ...

Another little-known piece is a 'square poem': the initial words of the six lines are also the six words of the first line, and final words those of the last (the poem has been reformatted to make this apparent):[18]

I	often wondered when I	cursed,
Often	feared where I would	be —
Wondered	where she'd yield her	love,
When	I yield, so will	she.
I	would her will be	pitied!
Cursed	be love! She pitied	me...

Other instances of Oulipian practice are Carroll's double ●acrostics, ●anagrams and ●word ladders (his own term is *doublets*). His presentation of *The Dynamics of a Particle*, in which he light-heartedly combines mathematics with social incidents, reads like an illustration of Oulipian strategy in reverse: he celebrates "the advantage of introducing the human element into the hitherto barren regions of mathematics. Who shall say what germs of romance, hitherto unobserved, may underlie the subject?"

Finally, it is tempting to include parts of *Symbolic Logic* in Carroll's Oulipian canon, as the following sorites suggests:

(1) No kitten, that loves fish, is unteachable;
(2) No kitten without a tail will play with a gorilla;
(3) Kittens with whiskers always love fish;
(4) No teachable kitten has green eyes;
(5) No kittens have tails unless they have whiskers.
(**Answer:** No kitten with green eyes will play with a gorilla.)

[HM]

See also ●BO41(2).

●*Castle of Crossed Destinies, The.* Translation by William Weaver of *Il castello dei destini incrociati*, a novel in two parts by Italo Calvino. Several travellers arrive at a castle where, in the great tradition of Chaucer and Boccaccio, they all decide to tell their stories. But when they open their mouths to speak, they find that they have been mysteriously struck dumb. To overcome

this difficulty, the group resorts to using a tarot pack: each traveller sets out a series of cards to illustrate his story, rather like a comic strip, until the entire pack has been exhausted.

The second part, *The Tavern of Crossed Destinies*, depicts a similar situation with a different group of travellers using a different pack of tarot cards. It is of particular interest to English readers for its original treatment of three of Shakespeare's greatest tragedies, *Hamlet, Macbeth* and *King Lear*. [IM]

See also ▲*Cartes noires*.

●**Cento.** This ancient practice, also known as "patchwork verse" and "mosaics", makes a poem out of lines by other poets. Brief and funny examples by François Le Lionnais appear in *Lipo* (●CP3); they were, however, written decades before the Oulipo came into being, and no purely traditional centos have been written by members of the group, except perhaps for Jacques Roubaud's *Second Litanies of the Virgin* (●BO43) and Jean Queval's *Trois Poèmes empruntés* in *Lipo*. Other Oulipian inventions are recognisably centoesque, such as Harry Mathews's *The Wisdom of Kings* (●BO5) and *An Evening with the Oulipo* (●BO57), and Marcel Bénabou's *Perverses* (●BO29). Finally, Noël Arnaud published a long prose cento in *Le Nouvel Observateur* as a serial during the summer months of 1990, drawing on a dozen authors ranging from Balzac to Perec. An extract follows.

The castle was clearly defined in the glittering air, its outline made still more definite by the moulding of snow covering it in a thin layer. There seemed to be much less snow up there on the hill. Here the heavy snowdrifts reached right up to the cottage windows and began again on the low roofs, but up on the hill everything soared light and free into the air. The motionless countryside had fallen silent. Only flocks of crows described long festoons against the sky in their futile pursuit of nourishment, descending together on to leaden fields to scratch the snow with their long beaks. There was nothing to be heard but the vague unbroken gliding of this ever-falling dust. The castle was haunted, notably by the Lady "with three

○John Ashbery *The Dong with the Luminous Nose*

Within a windowed niche of that high hall
I wake and feel the fell of dark, not day.
I shall rush out as I am, and walk the street
Hard by yon wood, now smiling as in scorn.
The lights begin to twinkle from the rocks
From camp to camp, through the foul womb of night.
Come, Shepherd, and again renew the quest.
And birds sit brooding in the snow.

Continuous as the stars that shine,
When men were all asleep the snow came flying
Near where the dirty Thames does flow
Through caverns measureless to man,
Where thou shalt see the red-gilled fishes leap
And a lovely Monkey with lollipop paws
Where the remote Bermudas ride.

Softly, in the dusk, a woman is singing to me:
This is the cock that crowed in the morn.
Who'll be the parson?
Beppo! That beard of yours becomes you not!
A gentle answer did the old man make:
Farewell, ungrateful traitor,
Bright as a seedsman's packet
Where the quiet-coloured end of evening smiles.

Obscurest night involved the sky
And brickdust Moll had screamed through half a street:

"Look in my face; my name is Might-have-been,
Sylvan historian, who canst thus express
Every nighte and alle,
The happy highways where I went
To the hills of Chankly Bore!"

Where are you going to, my pretty maid?
Those lovers fled away into the storm
And it's O dear, what can the matter be?
For the wind is in the palm-trees, and the temple bells they say:
Lay your sleeping head, my love,
On the wide level of a mountain's head,
Thoughtless as the monarch oaks, that shade the plain,
In autumn, on the skirts of Bagley Wood.
A ship is floating in the harbour now,
Heavy as frost, and deep almost as life!

---

folds at her back", a poisoner while she lived, a lost soul ever since. I knew well enough not to lend too much credence to what the servants said. I knew that they never wanted to talk about the castle, that they always tried to divert the conversation to other subjects, and that one must plead with them to say anything at all; but once they started, there was no stopping them. They would utter all kinds of foolishness to make themselves important, outdoing each other in exaggerations and fabrications.

The first three sentences are by Kafka, the next three by Maupassant, the next one by Anatole France, the last three again by Kafka.

An exceptionally interesting poetic cento, "To a Waterfowl", was published by John Ashbery in *Locus Solus*, II (1961); the same poet has recently composed a second example of the form: ○*The Dong with the Luminous Nose*. [HM]

See ●BO32 & 48(3); ●Blank verse amidst the prose, ●Minutes of the Oulipo (1) & (4).

●*Centon.* See ●Cento.

●*107 âmes.* (*107 Souls*) A sequence of poems by Jacques Jouet. The author describes his method of composition in a preface, here shortened and occasionally paraphrased:

"When I wrote each of these poems, I knew nothing of the perfectly real person who was its subject, except for a questionnaire I had drawn up. An intermediary had at my request transmitted the questionnaire and returned it to me once it had been completed.

"My questionnaire was accompanied by the following explanation: 'With your consent, I shall use the questionnaire to write a poem that is descriptive and as impersonal as can be managed. No judgement or evaluation will be made on my part.

I request that you answer the questions in the most official manner possible.'

"My questionnaire comprised ten questions:

1. Your name and given name. 2. Your age as of today. 3. Your qualifications (education, professional skills). 4. Your profession as of today and, if appropriate, the preceding ones in chronological order. 5. Your birthplace. 6. The town or village where you now live and, if appropriate, those where you formerly lived. 7. Your type of dwelling and what it looks like. 8. Your monthly earnings as of today. 9. Your family situation as of today and, if appropriate, those preceding it. 10. One event (or more) that determined the course of your life.

"My rule was to use the information supplied in the completed questionnaire and nothing but that information.

"The 107 poems were written in the form called ●braised rhyme... between September 1987 and August 1988."

[JJ, trans HM]

●**Cerquiglini, Bernard.** Elected to the Oulipo in 1996.

"Obscure philologist and vagabond grammarian, no doubt born in Lyon (France) around 1947; he has left a history of the circumflex accent." [BC]

See ●BO79 (1), ●CP16.

●**Chambers, Ross.** Elected to the Oulipo in 1961, but never an active member of the group.

Born in 1932 in Australia, he is a Professor of French literature and author of books on literary theory. [AB]

See ●Inadvertent translation.

●**Chance.** *The work of the Oulipo is a form of anti-chance.*

When he first introduced ●*potential literature, Queneau took pains to make this clear: "... It has nothing to do with aleatory literature."*

The intentional, deliberate nature of restrictions is indissolubly linked for him with the spirited rejection of chance and, even more, with the equating of chance with freedom.

Another false idea that is current nowadays is the equivalence established between inspiration, the exploration of the subconscious, and liberation; between chance, automatism, and freedom. The kind of freedom that consists of blindly obeying every impulse is in reality a form of slavery. The classical author, who when writing his tragedy follows a certain number of rules that he knows, is freer than the poet who writes whatever comes into his head and is the slave of other rules he is unaware of.

This fundamental statement, from 1938, is obviously aimed at Surrealism; this makes it no less pertinent today. [JR from *La mathématique dans la méthode de Raymond Queneau* (*Atlas,* ●CP6, pp.56-57), trans HM]

See also ●BO63.

●*Chant royal.* See ●BO43.

●**Chapman, Stanley.** Elected to the Oulipo in 1961.

Born in 1925, Stanley Chapman was one of the earliest members of the ●College of 'Pataphysics and is currently its Regent of Epideictic Oratories and Displays. An architectural designer, he invented many of the College's devices and other

pictorial works, and was responsible for UK jacket designs of books by ●Jarry, Aragon, Calvino, etc. He is in charge of the Annexes of the Rogation and Organon of the College of 'Pataphysics in London, a Fellow of the Pataphysical Society of Edinburgh, the President of the London Institute of 'Pataphysics, a prominent member of the Lewis ●Carroll Society, and a corresponding member of the ■Oupeinpo and ★Ouphopo. His published work consists primarily of translations, and includes novels by Boris Vian and various texts of prose and poetry for Atlas Press (cf. ○●100,000,000,000,000 Poems for a spectacular example). Family commitments in England limited his active participation in the adolescence of the Oulipo, and he is currently more involved with the projects of the ★Outrapo, which he co-founded in 1991. [AB]

Oulipian works: *Onze mille verbes, cent virgules*, (issue of) *Temps Mêlés*, 98 (Verviers, 1969); *L'Impromptu de Jussieu*; *Cosmilidin* (both published by Dourdan, 1998).

See ■Onomometry.

●**Chimera.** The chimera of Homeric legend — lion's head, goat's body, treacherous serpent's tail — has a less forbidding Oulipian counterpart. It is engendered as follows. Having chosen a text for treatment, remove its nouns, verbs, and adjectives. Replace the nouns with those taken in order from a different work, the verbs with those from a second work, the adjectives with those from a third.

Given the subject text:

April is the cruellest month;

Claude G. Bowers, *My Mission To Spain* provides the nouns *June* and *credentials*;
Lewis ●Carroll's *Symbolic Logic, Book I* the verb *contain*;
Kingsley Amis's *Lucky Jim* the adjective *silly*;

the chimera reads:

June contains the silliest credentials.

Here is a longer example (all borrowings come from the beginnings of the texts cited):
Subject text: Barbara Comyns, *The Vet's Daughter*
Nouns: Rosalind Belben, *The Nightmare*
Verbs: Patrick O'Brian, *The True Love*
Adjectives: John Betjeman, *Church of England Thoughts*
Titles: David Markson, *Wittgenstein's Mistress*

The trams considered what came about like a sunlit, standing east, which expected to be, however, a window. A sculptured paradox tallied as the shapely journeys belayed something like *Les Troyens*. "And now all you sweet cakes, something Linnaean yet ever changing." He knew hoarsely how to serve up the *Alto Rhapsody*. The rich rest lay beaten as though a leaning sense had been used as beauty.

Variations:
1. Replacing only one part of speech;
2. using other works by the same author as a source of replacements;
3. drawing replacements from the subject text itself.

See also ●Homosyntaxism, ○Keith Waldrop *After Hardy*, ●Minutes of the Oulipo (2).

○Keith Waldrop *After Hardy*

Ancestors and angels ruled everywhere around. Above them rose the primeval birds and catastrophe of The Chase, in which there poised gentle roosting chasms in their last children and about them stole the hopping coarse and darkness. But, might some say, where were Tess's guardian divinities? Where was the door of her simple faith? Perhaps, like that other father of whom the ironical Tishbite spoke, he was talking, or he was pursuing, or he was in a finer, or he was sleeping and not to be awaked.

Why it was that upon this beautiful feminine fortune, sensitive as fray, and practically blank as girls as yet, there should have been traced such a coarse god as it was doomed to receive; why so often the gossamer appropriates the hares thus, the wrong heroine the journey, the wrong man the man, many thousand matters of analytical measure have failed to explain to our morality of mother. One may, indeed, admit the nap of nature lurking in the present oaks. Doubtless some of Tess d'Urberville's mailed orders, rollicking home, from a pattern had dealt the same people even more ruthlessly towards peasant personality of their philosophy. But though to visit the pity of the possibility upon the poultry-farm may be a providence good enough for rabbits, it is scorned by average human retreat; and therefore does not mend the retribution.

As Tess's own selves down in those senses are never tired of saying among each other in their fatalistic silence: 'It was to be'. There lay the sins of it. An immeasurable social snow was to divide our time's tissue thereafter from that previous way of hers who stepped from her woman's woman to try her years at Trantridge yews.

●**Chinese whispers.** Children's parlour game known in the USA as "telephone". Players sit in a circle. The first player whispers a message into the ear of a neighbour, who in turn whispers it to the next player. The message goes round the circle until it reaches the first player, who announces his original message and its final version, usually deformed beyond recognition.

●**Chronogram.** Popular in earlier times, the chronogram exploits the double significance of those letters that are also Roman numerals: *i, v, x, l, c, d,* and *m*. When such letters are identified in a chronogram and added up according to their numerical value, their sum will correspond to a given year of the Christian era. (Proper chronograms use *all* the numerical letters that appear in a text.)

> 1. Making up games is easy = M + I + M + I = 2002
> 2. A beautiful day for cracking conceptual games
> = I + L + D + C + C + I + C + C + L + M = 2002

Oulipians have rarely been drawn to this form:

> In time's lexicon
> appropriately codified,
> lucky passion points us
> opposite ways.

Like this one, chronograms are customarily brief works. Recently, however, Harry Mathews has experimented in combining the chronogram with the ●lipogram, and the result (●BO92) is a text of almost 2,000 words — arguably by far the longest chronogram ever written. [HM]

●*Cigarettes.* A novel by Harry Mathews, published in 1987 and identified by the author as his only "purely Oulipian novel." Its method of composition has not been revealed beyond a statement that it is based on a "●permutation of situations."

●**Circuit.** A circuit is a path followed when reading a text. The linear succession of words is a first, given circuit. A supplementary circuit — of stanzas (or paragraphs), lines (or sentences), phrases, or words — means that those elements can be read in another order. In the example that follows, there are two circuits, one horizontal, the other vertical.

Come here!	Eat!	You can only get better
On your knees!	Don't think you can escape	by swimming the Atlantic
You've proved yourself a fink	by going on a hunger strike	— even if there is a slight risk

More complex circuits — such as Queneau's ◌●*100,000,000,000,000 Poems* — are defined by precise mathematical rules and can be represented as graphs. [HM]

See ●BO10; ●Cylinder, ●∈, ●Graphic representation of text, ●*Life A User's Manual*, ●Mathews's algorithm.

●*Clinamen.* Lucretius's Latin for the Greek *klesis*, "a bending." Empedocles (c.490–430 B.C.) uses the term to designate the spontaneous deviation that allows atoms falling in otherwise parallel lines through the void to encounter one another and thus create matter; Lucretius extended the meaning of the word to include free choice. For Oulipians, the clinamen is a deviation from the strict consequences of a restriction. It is often justified on aesthetic grounds: resorting to it improves the results. But there is a binding condition for its use: the exceptional freedom afforded by a clinamen can only be taken on the condition that following the initial rule is still possible. In other words, the clinamen can only be used if it isn't needed. (A number of Oulipians, notably Italo Calvino, have felt that the clinamen plays a crucial role in Oulipian theory and practice.)

Since this volume demonstrates normal Oulipian practice, clinamens do not abound; but here is a small example. In this editor's ●melting snowball, the final 0 (for zero) should (and could) have been 1; the inaccurate alternative seemed rhetorically better. There is a clinamen on a much larger scale in Georges Perec's ●*Life A User's Manual*. Each chapter of the novel describes one of the visible spaces in a building with 100 such spaces. There are, however, only 99 chapters. The location of the missing chapter is indicated by a little girl nibbling away the corner of a *biscuit Lu, Lu* being both a brand of pastries and the past participle of the verb "to read"; the fascinating reasons for the omission lie at the heart of that enigmatic book. [HM]

The clinamen was brought to the attention of Pataphysicians and Oulipians alike through the agency of Alfred ●Jarry who rescued this obscure principle of classical philosophy and made of it a central tenet of his "science of exceptions", 'Pataphysics. He also named the ■Painting Machine after it in his novel *Exploits and Opinions of Doctor Faustroll, Pataphysician*.

●**Collective Publications of the Oulipo (CP).** Although this is principally a list of collective publications by the Oulipo, it also covers some titles in which a number of members participated or are included. Titles in French or English are listed here: Paris or London is the place of publication unless specified otherwise.

●**CP1.** Oulipo, *"Exercices de littérature potentielle"* (*Exercises in Potential Literature*) in *Dossiers Acénonètes du Collège de 'Pataphysique*, 17, Charleville, 22 December 1961. See also issues of the College review *Subsidia Pataphysica* (1965-75), many of which contain notices and examples of Oulipian activity, in particular no. 15 (February 1972).

●**CP2.** *Oulipo*, special issue of *Temps Mêlés*, 66/67 (Verviers, April 1964).

●**CP3 "Lipo".** Oulipo, *La Littérature potentielle* (Gallimard, 1973).

Referred to within the group as *"la Lipo"* or *"le tome un"* ("volume one"), this is the Oulipo's first book-length publication. It was brought out in 1973 by Éditions Gallimard in their paperback collection *Idées*; it is no longer in print. Editorially it can be considered the work of Raymond Queneau.

The book is divided into 10 sections: 1. Liminal poems. 2. Theory and history. 3. ●Anoulipisms. 4. Pre-existing structures. 5. Lexicographic, syntactic, and prosodic manipulations. 6. Lexicographic and prosodic ●synthoulipisms. 8. ●Grab-bag. 9. Solutions. 10. Chronology.

An introductory note concludes with a description of the work as one "whose nature the authors, already blazing other trails, recognise as *preliminary*." [HM]

●**CP4 "Bens".** Jacques Bens, *Oulipo 1960-1963* (Christian Bourgois, 1980). Minutes of the Oulipo's early meetings. See ●Minutes of the Oulipo (1).

●**CP5.** *La Bibliothèque Oulipienne* (Slatkine, Geneva Paris, 1981). Fascicles 1 to 16, the first 2 manifestos, *Indications liminaires* by Roubaud.

●**CP6 "Atlas".** Oulipo, *Atlas de littérature potentielle* (Gallimard, 1981; second edition, with some changes, 1988).

This is the second of the two volumes written collectively by the Oulipo and published by Gallimard in their paperback collection *Idées*. First published in 1981, the *Atlas* is still in print. Although the volume lacked a definitive editorial hand, Georges Perec and Jacques Roubaud did much to give it its final shape.

The contents are divided into 6 sections: 1. Raymond Queneau. 2. Principles. 3. Work and research. 4. Oulipo and the ●computer. 5. Several Oulipian works. 6. Public life. [HM]

●**CP7 "Motte".** Warren F. Motte Jr., *Oulipo, A Primer of Potential Literature* (University of Nebraska Press, Lincoln, Nebraska, 1986, reprinted Dalkey Archive Press, IL, 1998). A selection of translations from 3 & 6 above; foreword by Arnaud.

●**CP8.** *La Bibliothèque Oulipienne* (Seghers), in three volumes. Volume I (1990): fascicles 1 to 18, introduction by Arnaud, *Indications liminaires* by Roubaud (reprinted from ●CP5). Volume II (1990): fascicles 19 to 37, the first 2 manifestos and (different) *Indications liminaires* by Roubaud. Volume III (1990): fascicles 38 to 52, preface by Arnaud.

●**CP9 "Oulipo Laboratory".** Oulipo Laboratory (Atlas Press, 1995). Translations of ●BO3, 20, 46, 62, 67 & 70.

●**CP10.** *La Bibliothèque Oulipienne* (Castor Astral), in three volumes. Volume IV (1997): fascicles 53 to 62, (unsigned) presentation by Jacques Jouet. Volume V (2000): fascicles 63 to 73. Volume VI (2003): fascicles 74 to 85.

●**CP11.** *Oulipo Compendium*, Harry Mathews & Alastair

Brotchie (eds.) (Atlas Press, 1998 & 2005). The present volume.

●**CP12.** *Winter Journeys* (Atlas Press, 2001). Texts by Bens, Caradec, Grangaud, Haugure, Jouet, Le Tellier, Mathews, Monk, Perec, and Roubaud. Contains translations of ●BO53, 105, 108, 110, 112, 113, 114 & 117.

●**CP13.** *Un art simple et tout d'exécution*, Marcel Bénabou, Jacques Jouet, Harry Mathews, Jacques Roubaud (Circé, 2001).

●**CP14.** *Abrégé de littérature potentielle* (Mille et une nuits, 2002).

●**CP15.** *Maudits* (Mille et une nuits, 2003).

●**CP16.** *Moments oulipiens* (Le Castor Astral, 2004). Texts by Bénabou, Caradec, Cerquiglini, Fournel, Garréta, Grangaud, Jouet, Le Tellier, Mathews, Roubaud, and Salon.

●**CP17.** *Oulipo Papers*, ongoing series of translations from the Bibliothèque Oulipienne, to be published by Atlas Press beginning in 2006. These volumes will also contain updates of the *Compendium*.

A number of issues of the Bibliothèque Oulipienne are credited to the Oulipo collectively: ●BO4, 23, 54, 55, 65, 68, 71, 79, 90, 100, 106, 121, 123, 126 & 666. See also the special issues of: *Giallu*, 3 (Ajaccio, 1994); ●*New Observations*, 99 (New York, 1994); *Magazine Littéraire*, 398 (2001); *AA Files*, 45/46 (2001).

●**College of 'Pataphysics.** Formed in 1948 by a group of philosophers, artists, and writers interested in exploring ideas deriving from the works of Alfred ●Jarry. The science of 'Pataphysics was Jarry's invention, or discovery: he variously described it as a science of exceptions, of imaginary solutions, equivalence, and imperturbability.

Although the founders were not very well known, the College soon numbered among its members some of the most celebrated artists and writers of the day: Arrabal, Baj, Buñuel, Cortázar, Dubuffet, Duchamp, Ernst, M.C. Escher, Fontana, Ionesco, Jorn, Leiris, The Marx Brothers, Miró, Pia, Picabia,

Ponge, Prévert, Vian, to name but a few. Its voluminous quarterly magazine appeared regularly between 1950 and 1975. Around that year several of its most active members died (Latis, Queneau, and Jean Ferry), and the College "occulted" itself until the year 2000. Public manifestations ceased; its research was devolved to the Cymbalum Pataphysicum, a collection of the sub-committees in which the College delights.

The Oulipo became one of the sub-committees (a "Co-commission") soon after its creation; the College also published its first collection (●CP1). Arnaud, Bens, Berge, Blavier, Braffort, Caradec, Chambers, Chapman, Duchamp, Duchateau, Étienne, Latis, Le Lionnais, Lescure, Perec, Queneau, Queval, and Schmidt were or are members of the College.

Although the Oulipo has never technically severed its connection with the College, its relations with it have been strictly nominal since the death of Latis in 1973; the occultation of the College had no effect on Oulipian activities. The other ★Ou-x-pos are still a part of the Cymbalum Pataphysicum, but as the millennial disoccultation approached, the rules on public activity were being applied less rigorously: hence the groups' appearance in the first edition of the present volume.

The College[19] survived its years of non-existence and was triumphantly resurrected in 2000, albeit with few of its original members, under a new "Vice-Curator," the crocodile Lutembi.

Correspondence address: Novum Organon, 32 rue de Tillancourt, 02400 Château-Thierry, France. [AB]

See also ●Minutes of the Oulipo (1).

●**Combinatorial literature.** In *Lipo* (●CP3), Claude Berge sets combinatorial literature in the category of Oulipian activity that he describes as "the vocation of transferring into the domain of words concepts found in the different branches of mathematics." In his article, "For a Potential Analysis of Combinatorial Literature", after tracing the origins of combinatorics to ●Leibniz and Euler, he identifies its object as the domain of configurations, a configuration being the preset arrangement of a finite number of objects, whether it concerns "finite geometries, the placement of packages of various sizes in a drawer of limited space, or the order of predetermined words or sentences."

The Oulipo and the ●College of 'Pataphysics.

Left: (From ●CP1) Raymond Queneau awarding the *Ordre de la Grande Gidouille* to François Le Lionnais at a pataphysical ceremony in 1966 (Ursula Vian is in the background).

Below: Members of the College in 1955 (Oulipians are asterisked). Standing: Louis Barnier, Raymond Queneau*, J.-H. Sainmont, Jean Ferry, Georges Petitfaux, Noël Arnaud*, Henri Bouché; seated: Claude Ernoult, François Caradec*.

Arrangement, placement, order: because these are the materials of Oulipian combinatorial research, what generally results can be called rearrangement, replacement, reordering, subsumed by the generic term ●permutation. Permutation affects a large proportion of Oulipian initiatives: ●x mistakes y for z, poems for ●Möbius Strip, ●chimeras, ●branching systems and ●multiple-choice theatre, ●cylinders, ●perverbs, ●perverses, ●circuits, ●sestina and ●quenina, ●Mathews's algorithm, ●anagrams, and no doubt others as well. Most remarkably, several book-length works by Oulipians are grounded in combinatorics: Raymond Queneau's ◐●*100,000,000,000,000 Poems*, Jacques Roubaud's ●ϵ, Georges Perec's ●*Life A User's Manual*, Italo Calvino's ●*If on a Winter's Night a Traveller*, Harry Mathews's ●*Cigarettes*. [HM]

See also ●BO89; ●Llull, ●Lescurean permutations.

●**Combining restrictions.** Restrictions are not exclusive. Some automatically incorporate another restriction: an ●N+7 is an example of ●homosyntaxism; a ●univocalism is a ●lipogram in the four missing vowels. But a true combination of restrictions is the result of a deliberate choice: two or more methods are deliberately followed to compose a text. Simple illustrations are published in ●BO65, where four ●sestinas are combined with ●anagrams.

Restrictions can be combined in two fundamental ways:

1. *Consecutively.* For example, given the statement, "Let us write as we feel, and the devil take the hindmost", we can transform the first part of the sentence by ●antonymy and the last by the N+7 method:

Do not allow them to speak before they think, and the diagnosis take the hindmost.

2. *Simultaneously.* In the following paragraph, a lipogram in e is composed entirely of monosyllables (●measures):

All of us found our way to that town. Not a man or a boy or a girl in sight, on foot or cart, in bus or car. And that was an hour that should hum with work and play. Which of us had wit fit to point this out? Just such as found that

main road, with two big roads that cross it, would know why things had put on this air of gloom and know how bad that *why* was and still is.

Combining restrictions simultaneously has naturally been used to create longer works. Georges Perec's ●*Life A User's Manual* is the most complex example of the genre, to which Italo Calvino's ●*If on a Winter's Night a Traveller* and Harry Mathews's *The Sinking of the Odradek Stadium* to some extent belong. Oskar Pastior has published a volume of sestinas, each of which is combined with at least one other formal requirement (*Eine kleine Kunstmaschine: 34 Sestinen*, Carl Hanser Verlag, 1994). [HM]

See also ●BO91.

●**Comic strips.** See ★Oubapo.

●***Compléments de nom.*** See ●Possessive phrase.

●**Computer and the Oulipo, the.** Before the creation of the ●ALAMO, the computer was used by Oulipians mainly as a tool for exploring and exploiting examples of ●combinatorial literature. A computer could realise versions of sonnets from Queneau's ◐●*100,000,000,000,000 Poems* far more efficiently than the slit-page-cum-ruler possibility offered by the printed version; and a program was developed by Paul Braffort for that very purpose, using the reader's name (and the time it took him to type it) to determine the choice of sonnet. This became one of the first public successes of Oulipian data-processing. First demonstrated at the 1975 Europalia festival in Brussels, it was soon afterwards sponsored by ARTA (Atelier Recherches Techniques Avancées, or Advanced Technical Research Workshop) at the Centre Pompidou in Paris.

Other programs set up under the auspices of ARTA were:

— an interactive reading of Queneau's *Tale of Your Choice* that incorporates both an interchange between reader and computer in regard to the alternative readings of the work and a printout of the final result of the reader's choices (a similar program was applied to a tale derived by Énard and Fournel from their ●multiple-choice theatre);

— a computerisation of Marcel Bénabou's artificial ●aphorisms (see ●BO13): supplied on the one hand with a repertory of fixed, empty formulas and on the other with a set of words with which to fill them, the reader intitiates a combination of the two to produce new aphorisms.

One of the most interesting projects of the pre-Alamian stage of activity was undertaken in the mid 1970s by Paul Braffort and Italo Calvino. It concerned a narrative, conceived by the latter as a possible novel or short story, based on the following situation. A house has burned down, consuming its four occupants. A charred notebook recovered from the ruins reveals that 12 kinds of crime have been perpetrated by the occupants on one another, but the record of who has done what to whom has been destroyed. Three kinds of crime involve an appropriation of will (incitement, blackmail, drugging); three others involve appropriation of a secret (spying, forcing a confession, betrayal of confidence); three others involve sexual appropriation (seduction, prostitution, rape); a final three involve murder (strangling, stabbing, provocation of suicide).

The four people present generate 12 potential pairings that, combined with the 12 crimes, open the prospect of 12^{12} or 8,916,100,448,256 possible sequences of events. A man who has insured all four of the victims (as well as the house) against various risks hires the narrator, a data-processing expert, to reduce this unwieldy figure to a few logical and probable alternatives. (The narrator soon realises that the insurer has been a fifth participant in the activities of the "abominable" house and that he himself has become a sixth, since the insurer is planning to kill him.)

In the early 1960s Paul Braffort had already worked on questions similar to this one, and he was now able to prepare computer programs for Calvino that gradually eliminated absurd and improbable solutions to the problem facing the story's narrator. (If A strangles B, he has no need to stab him; if A has killed B, B cannot kill A; etc.) The collaborators later approached the topics of subjective and aesthetic restrictions issuing from choices made by the author.

The use of the computer in this case diverged notably from its previous Oulipian role: it became an instrument, not of combinatorial accumulation, but of anti-combinatorial reduction. It served not to create combinations but to eliminate them.

(Calvino's story was published in *Prima che tu dica "Pronto"* (Mondadori, Milan, 1993) and *Numbers in the Dark* (translation by Tim Parks, Pantheon Books, New York, 1995).)

[HM, after PB]

●*Conte à votre façon.* See ●Multiple-choice narrative.

●*Contrainte.* The usual French word for the basic element in Oulipian practice has been variously translated in this volume as *constraint, restriction, restrictive form,* and other comparable terms. All these expressions denote the strict and clearly definable rule, method, procedure, or structure that generates every work that can be properly called Oulipian. [HM]

●*Contrainte du prisonnier.* See ●Prisoner's restriction.

●**Corpuscular poems.** See ●BO33.

●**Crime fiction.** See ▲Oulipopo.

●**Cube puzzle.** A construction by the German author ●Schuldt that is based on ●combinatorial principles.

The first cube puzzle was conceived in London in the mid '60s; the final one, built of wood, was finished in New York in 1981. It is made of ten blocks that fit together to form a cube and that are separated for purposes of reading, performance, or display.

Six of the blocks have five faces, four have four faces; one word is inscribed on each face. The total number of available words is thus (6 x 5) + (4 x 4) = 46. The possible combinations of words are equivalent to factorial 46 (46!), or 46 x 45 x 44 x 43...

This is how Schuldt describes the poems derived from handling and reading the dismantled pieces of the puzzle: "Each printed line states the supply of words for one element of a cube

puzzle, but it does not say how the words belong together. It is a somewhat indeterminate complexity to be read in a variety of ways, with no hierarchy among the possible outcomes. 'Glory Gut' exists only as a reduction of the potential poem to a rendering on paper.

"The elements chosen for the poem 'Glory Gut' are in Oulipian terms a series of ●tautograms; but the tautogram is not a necessary condition of a cube puzzle." [HM]

○Schuldt *Excerpts from "Glory Gut"*

go get glory gut glower gingerly
gloss gown girds grease gargle glum
golden gum goon gains glass gut
goose giggle give glee gender
gofer goy gobble glue
hanky-panky handheld hellfire helter-skelter
away awash aghast askew
learn lamb liver look left
lap lone laugh lost lure
any anger answers art
hundreds hunt hiccup honk hope
lend lousy lip lock leather leg
hungry hip help horny howl

The same elements otherwise arranged:

Go gingerly, Glory, get gut, glower!
Gargle glum grease! Gloss girds gown.
Glass goon gains golden gum gut.
Giggle, gender! Give glee, goose!
Gobble goy, glue gofer!
Handheld hanky-panky! Helter-skelter hellfire!
Aghast, awash, away, askew.
Learn, lamb! Look, liver left!
Lone lap lost lure: laugh!
Any answers anger art.
Hiccup hunt: hundreds honk hope.
Lend: leather, lip, lousy leg, lock.
Hungry howl, help horny hip!

●**Cuisine.** See ★Oucuipo.

●**Cylinder.** A cylinder is a circular text that can begin at more than one point — ideally at *any* point — without requiring modification. Cylinders can be constructed at the level of letters (*emit, mite, item, emit...*), syllables, words, phrases, or paragraphs. The most interesting Oulipian example of the form is to be found in Paul Fournel and Jacques Roubaud's *L'Hôtel de Sens* (●BO10).

Georges Perec provided a paragraph cylinder for the *Atlas* (●CP6) reminiscent of the "It was a dark and stormy night..." of childhood times. (Next page)

See ●Circuit, ●Permutation.

○Georges Perec *Tale*

I. It all began almost ten years ago. The evening I had been spending with friends in a Brisbane pub was drawing to a close when a man seated at the bar came over to our table with a mug of beer in his hand:

"Excuse me, gentlemen. Would you allow me to join you for a moment and tell you my story?"

We silently acquiesced. He sat down, took a sip of his beer, and said:

2. " 'My name is Abercrombie Makarenko, I'm forty years old, and a real-estate attorney by profession. It must have been five years ago when a man showed up at my office and requested to speak to me privately. A moment later, seated across from me, he began with these words:

3. " ' "Ezekiel Bridgman-Treyer is my name. About eighteen months ago I found myself in a foreign city. Returning to my hotel room one evening, I discovered a man sitting in my bedroom. 'Forgive the intrusion,' he said, rising to his feet, 'but I have to talk to you.' Curiosity got the better of wariness, and I asked him to explain. This is what I heard:

4. " ' " 'Have you ever been to Pauvelle-les-Bains? It's a charming spa not far from Chambéry. Last May I went there to take a cure, as I do every year. As I was strolling in the park one Sunday afternoon, a young man dressed in black approached me and insisted on speaking to me. We sat down on a bench, and he told me:

5. " ' " ' "Three weeks ago I travelled to Basle. I shared a compartment with an individual whose face seemed curiously familiar. After several commonplace remarks, he asked me to listen to his story. I urgently encouraged him to do so. Here is what he revealed:

6. " ' " ' " '. . . etc.

[Trans HM]

133

●**Definitional literature.** Each meaningful word in a text (verb, noun, adjective, adverb) is replaced by its dictionary definition; each word of the resulting definitions is similarly replaced; and the process is repeated as often as is desired. Note that after only two such treatments with a relatively compact dictionary, even a two-word statement produces an accumulation of 57 words:[20]

Nothing matters.
No matter of any kind is of importance.

Not any substance or substances of which any physical object consists or is composed OF A CLASS OR GROUP OF INDIVIDUAL OBJECTS, PEOPLE, ANIMALS, ETC., OF THE SAME NATURE OR CHARACTER OR CLASSIFIED TOGETHER BECAUSE THEY HAVE TRAITS IN COMMON, whatever or whichever it may be, *occupies a place or position having a consequential air or manner.*

One attraction of definitional literature is the creation of a text markedly different from the original, and that not only by expanding it:

Music when soft voices die,
Vibrates in the memory —
Odours, when sweet violets sicken,
Live within the sense they quicken.

The product of a certain period — when expressed, warm-hearted desires become indifferent — thrills through the length of time over which recollection extends. Hints, when bluish purples of warm tone and clearly outlined melody become sick, subsist within the meaning of something that they revive.

The thing produced by the effort of an inevitable full pause, when exuded, compassionate sexual urges grow to be not particularly good, is stirred by a tingling sensation of excitement in its duration, over which rallying increases in scope. Clues, when somewhat risqué imperial clothes of affectionate tint and decidedly delineated air are interpreted as chagrins, remain alive within the purpose of a person of consequence that they restore.

This goal of differentiation is consummated in a complementary method known as ●semo-definitional literature.

Raymond Queneau presented his first examples of definitional literature to the Oulipo at the same time that Marcel Bénabou and Georges Perec introduced semo-definitional literature (q.v.). Both, it should be emphasised, had been preceded many years earlier by Stefan ●Themerson and his analogous work in *semantic literature.* [HM]

Two examples follow, ○Stefan Themerson's *Taffy was a Welshman* and ○Gilbert Sorrentino's *Six Songs.*

○Stefan Themerson *Taffy was a Welshman*

Taffy was a male native of Wales

Taffy was a person who practised seizing the property of another unlawfully
        and appropriated it to his own use and purpose

Taffy came to the structure of various materials
                having walls
                        roof
                        door
                and windows to give light and air
        he came to that structure which was a dwelling for me

And there he appropriated to his own use
        one of the limbs of the dead body of an ox
        prepared and sold by the butcher

I went to the structure of various materials
                having walls
                        roof
                        door
                and windows to give light and air

I went to that structure which was a dwelling for Taffy

Taffy was not there

Taffy came to the structure of various materials
                having walls
                        roof
                        door
                and windows to give light and air

Taffy came to that structure which was a dwelling for me

And there he appropriated to his own use
    the part of the ox skeleton
    containing in its cavity
    the fat substance
    the vascular tissue
    which had formed the red blood corpuscles of the ox

I went to the structure of various materials
        having walls
                roof
                door
        and windows to give light and air

I went to that structure which was a dwelling for Taffy

Taffy was lying upon a piece of furniture
             consisting of the mattress
                   and the wooden frame which supported it

I took the part of the ox skeleton
        the part containing in its cavity
            the fat substance
            the vascular tissue
            which had formed the red blood corpuscles of the ox

And by a sudden sharp blow
I broke open that part of Taffy's body
            situated on top of the spinal column
            which contained the great mass of nerve-cells
            the functioning of which
                      is
                       mind.

From *Bayamus* (Editions Poetry London, 1949)

The non-Oulipian Gilbert ●Sorrentino has put the semo-definitional method to very effective use in his *Six Songs* (following, first published in ●*New Observations*), taking passages from the lyrics of popular songs as his source. In a letter, the author has elaborated on his use of the procedure:

> ... I choose those definitions from the dictionary entries that seem best for my purposes. As for the use of the master text, I select at least two — usually more — lines from the original lyric for the body of the poem, and always use the song title for the envoi, so to speak, making sure that none of the words chosen from the lyric are identical with the words in the song title. For example: She Must Die... is the procedure as applied to Poor Butterfly, the original lyric chosen being

> The moments turn into hours
> The hours turn into years
> And as she smiles through her tears
> She murmurs low

> — and then, the envoi is the procedure applied to the song title, Poor Butterfly. The only reason, it may be obvious, that I don't choose lyric fragments that repeat the words of the title, is that — in such a compressed final poem — the repetition of words derived from definitions would be too much for the poem to bear. [HM]

○Gilbert Sorrentino *Six Songs*

Disguises Ended

You seem, to a percipient, as one without
Addition, change, or discontinuance.
Identical. To a great extent or degree
A great deal as one without
Addition, change, or discontinuance.
Identical! But my seat of spiritual life,
My emotional nature utters to me that you're
"Not without addition or change or
Discontinuance. *Not identical.*" I'm filled
With fear and apprehension.
    The frolic in
    Disguise, the show
    Of being what one
    Is not, is finished.

Entranced Fascination

Relate in detail and recount to me:
For what reason should it occur
That you hold in possession
The capability to entrance me
By suggestion?
Permit me to be alive under your
Spellbinding influence. Your fascination.
Do produce that barbaric sorcery
That you produce so expertly.
    You bring about in me
    As an effect, something
    Not definitely
    Understood.

It's a Fact

Young, unmarried woman
Of my emotional nature, my seat
Of spiritual or conscious life,
I take delight and pleasure in you.
To a high degree. Exceedingly.
Recently, by experience (or trial),
I perceive that you are
In my "subject of consciousness",
My "that which feels"

> To a greater extent or degree
> Than you recognise
> As valid. Or
> As *fact*.

Mere Ideas

The sheer, absolute image,
Recalled by memory, of you.
The eager desire, in this place, for you.
You'll at no time directly perceive
How, at less then usual speed,
Minute portions of time proceed, up to
The time when I'm
At a little distance to you:

> The absolute act,
> Or process,
> Of thinking,
> Of you.

A Procedure

The whole of the series
Of experience of body and mind
Which make up my history
From beginning to end... must I
Follow a given procedure
Of making a show with
Intent to deceive?
In what place is *my*
Felicitous termination?

> In
> What
> Place
> Are you?

She Must Die

Minute portions of time glide
Into 24th parts of days: 24th
Parts of days glide into periods of
Three hundred and sixty-five days.
And as she changes her facial expression
(So as to involve a brightening
Of the eyes, and an upward curving
Of the corners of the mouth — expressive
Of amusement? pleasure? affection?
Irony!) in the midst of
Her drops of secreted saline fluids,
She makes a low, confused, and
Indistinct sound. Not loud.

> You, pitiful, slender-bodied,
> Diurnal. With your large,
> Broad, brightly coloured
> Wings!

●**Delmas's method (***la contrainte de Delmas***).** The method was introduced by a participant at an Oulipo ●workshop in Villeneuve-lès-Avignon. Its rule: in a given statement, a repeated initial letter can be replaced with another repeated letter without spoiling the statement's coherence. Example: in the statement, "Only carry a can you are able to catch," *c* can be replaced by *m*. [HM]

See ●Inclusion.

●*Deunglitsch.* Around 1992, the precedent of legal ●franglais led Harry Mathews to suggest to Oskar Pastior that they develop a similar German-English repertory to be known as *deunglitsch*. The two writers initially created a lexicon according to the rules of legal franglais:

1. Aside from capitals and diacritical marks, each word must be spelled identically in the two languages.

2. *No* meaning must be common to the German and English word. This excludes, for instance, *Rock* (*skirt, jacket*) since in addition *rock = rock music* in both languages.

Oskar Pastior soon radically expanded the number of words available for the experiment. A word in one language could be divided into fragments that formed several words in the other:

abend	a bend
heisst roman	he is St. Roman

Pastior carried the process further and combined single letters of words with other units. This brought a host of much-needed possibilities:

— for terminal *s* occurring in plurals, possessives, and singular verbs:

sache	-s ache

— for the useful *and*:

war mandant	warm and ant

— for the no less useful *the*:

bet hebest	be the best

Neither Mathews nor Pastior, however, were able to invent texts of more than a few words that made sense in both languages. Each had to be content with using *deunglitsch* as a restricted ●vocabulary in which to compose works in his own language. Exceptional bilingual skill is obviously needed to go beyond this; the two writers hope, all the same, that through sustained collaboration they will some day create truly ambivalent *deunglitsch* texts.

The following English example is preceded by the German words that provide its literal material.

warten, musterten, linkten, nagten, ragten, eggten, spurten, pufften, sparten, maulten, lockten, stickten, sagten, sitten, dankten, wetten, blueten, maleten

> *War*
> ten muster, ten link,
> ten nag, ten rag,
> ten egg, ten spur,
> ten puff, ten spar,
> ten maul, ten lock,
> ten stick, ten sag,
> ten sit
>
> ten dank, ten wet,
> ten blue: ten, male ten.

●*Disparition, La.* see A ●*Void.*

●**Dogs, poems for.** A poem that incorporates a dog's name in such a way that it remains hidden to the human eye but audible to the canine ear.

See ●BO49 for an example.

●**Drama.** See ★Outrapo; ●BO87 & 99; ●Multiple-choice theatre.

●**Duchamp, Marcel.** (1887–1968) Elected to the Oulipo in 1962.

Although both François Le Lionnais and Raymond Queneau had known Duchamp long before the founding of the Oulipo, neither thought of including him in the group until Queneau received a letter from Simon Watson Taylor that included this passage:

I am charged by your satrapic colleague Marcel Duchamp, whom I just saw in New York, to congratulate you most warmly on the last dossier of the College containing the first results of the research of your OuLiPo. He could not have been more enthusiastic, saying that he too was in the process of conducting analogous linguistic research but which was not yet ready to be shown to the world, even a pataphysical one. But we should encourage him.

After this had been read to the members present at the meeting of 16 March 1962, Duchamp was unanimously named "Foreign Correspondent" of the Oulipo, the title then reserved for members living abroad.

Duchamp subsequently attended at least one meeting of the Oulipo, on 25 June 1965 (at the restaurant La Frégate, on Quai Voltaire). One or two lunches were also arranged for him during his visits to Paris so that he could be kept informed of the group's activities.

Duchamp's writings include no strictly Oulipian works, but they nevertheless make plain why the group's ideas attracted him. A devotee of Raymond ●Roussel and Jean-Pierre Brisset, those incomparable and highly serious punsters, he was himself addicted all of his life to fabricating puns, some of which on a small scale approach ●homophonic translation:

○Marcel Duchamp *The*

If you come into * linen, your time is thirsty because * ink saw some wood intelligent enough to get giddiness from a sister. However, even it should be smilable to shut * hair whose * water writes always in * plural, they have avoided * frequency, meaning mother in law; * powder will take a chance; and * road could try. But after somebody brought any multiplication as soon as * stamp was out, a great many cords refused to go through. Around * wire's people, who will be able to sweeten * rug, that is to say, why must every patents look for a wife? Pushing four dangers near * listening-place, * vacation had not dug absolutely nor this likeness has eaten.

Salissez Mesens' chaussettes. . .
Sally says Mesens' show set...

He was interested in literal and syllabic permutations — in other words, ●anagrams and ●spoonerisms — of which the near-palindromic title of his collaborative film from 1926, *Anémic Cinéma*, is an example. Two texts that were used as visual works, *The* and *Rendezvous of Sunday, February 6, 1916*, are perhaps closest of all to Oulipian practice. Duchamp eventually explained that he had first written *Rendezvous* in ordinary sentences, then altered and substituted words in order to eliminate any connection between language and objects, so that it could be "read without any echo of the physical world." The remark applies equally well to *The*, written directly in English, and accompanied by the instruction, "Replace each * with the word: *the*."

The piece can be considered as an example of going for the ●limit in the domain of ●translexical translation. Finally, mention should be made of a project that appears in the notes accompanying *The Bride Stripped Bare by Her Bachelors, Even*: that of creating an abstract alphabet consisting of words drawn from the Larousse dictionary. These would be "prime words", that is, words divisible only by themselves and by unity, a notion that brings to mind Queneau's transformation of ●Hilbert's mathematical axioms into literary propositions (see ●BO3).

See also ●BO86 & 131. [HM]

●**Duchateau, Jacques.** Founding member of the Oulipo.

Duchateau produces and directs the most important daily cultural programme on French public radio. In addition to critical works, he has written two novels, both Oulipian. Here is the author's description of them:

"*Zinga huit* is a novel of speculative fiction that uses a number of constraints, notably lists of words associated with characters that produce intersections, symmetrical disparities, and junctions, thus regulating the order of events.

"*Le Souterrain* relates wartime occupation and resistance in the context of life in a secondary school. As a model it takes the history of the French Revolution between September 1792 and July 1794; the protagonists and events of this period are systematically reproduced in the narrative, without the historical model becoming apparent and with no need to be aware of it to understand the novel."

Oulipian works: *Zinga huit* (Gallimard, 1967); *Le Souterrain*, under the pen-name of Jean-François Léonard (Juillard, 1992); ●BO14, 17 & 69.

See ●Intersective novel, ●Larding.

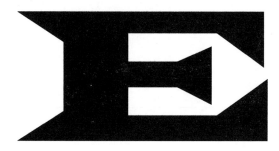

●ϵ. This symbol, which in set theory signifies "belonging to a set", was used by Jacques Roubaud as the title of a collection of poems (Gallimard, 1967). The book contains 361 texts, corresponding to the pieces of a game of *go*: 180 white, 181 black. This correspondence is indicated typographically.

In his introduction (reprinted in *Lipo*, ●CP3), the author indicates four ways of reading the book:

1. By groups, each of which is organised according to a diagram of *go* pieces that precedes it.

2. As a series of groups, divided into "paragraphs" that are individually distinguished by a mathematical sign.

3. As a sequence of moves in a game of *go* (specifically, a game between Masami Shinohara and Mitsuo Takei that was analysed in *Go Review*, April 1945). An index supplies the correspondences between the moves and the texts.

4. As a collection of separate poems. [HM]
   See ●Circuit.

●*Échelle*. See ●Word ladder.

●**Eclipse.** A text that includes both an ●N+7 and the text from which it is derived. A description and examples of the method can be found in ●BO28.

I loaded my pockets with stones. I loaded my poets with stopgaps.

See ●BO54 for further examples.

●**Elementary morality.** What the Oulipo calls an *elementary morality* is a set poetic form invented by Raymond Queneau around 1973. Its name was taken from the title of Queneau's last book, *Morale élémentaire*, which contains the poems he wrote in this form, including the one translated opposite.

Queneau described his invention in the *NRF* of January, 1974. "First come 3 series of 3+1 pairs, each pair consisting of a noun and an adjective (or participle), freely including repetitions, ●rhymes, ●alliterations, and echoes; next, a kind of interlude of 7 lines, each line 1 to 5 syllables long; last, a conclusion of 3 + 1 pairs of words (noun and adjective or participle), more or less recapitulating several of the 24 words of the first part."

Queneau then makes the point that the form was developed for "purely internal" reasons and that no prior metrical or mathematical calculation determined it. This would seem to place it squarely outside the domain of the Oulipo; and while the point is theoretically granted, virtually all the active members of the group have used it to write poems, sometimes adding their own supplementary restrictions to the form. Their work has been collected in two fascicles of the Bibliothèque Oulipienne. [HM]

See ●BO8, 55, 80 (xvi), 81 (section 3), 90 & 95; ○Paul Fournel & ○Jacques Jouet *Elementary Morality*.

●**End-to-end (*tête-à-queue*).** In *Lipo* (●CP3), Marcel Bénabou experimented in running together the first and last words of the successive lines of a poem, thus extending Queneau's ●haikuisation (see ●Redundancy) to both ends of the poetic verse.

The source of the example that follows is Dylan Thomas, *Collected Poems 1934–1952*.

○Raymond Queneau *Elementary Morality*

Dark Isis	Green fruit	Spotted animal
	Crystalline neologisms	
Red flower	Transparent attitude	Orange-hued star
	Crystalline springs	
Brown forest	Russet boar	Bleating flock
	Crystalline tree	

A boat
on the water
solo
follows the flow
a crocodile
bites the keel
in vain

Ochre Isis	Mobile statue	Apricot totem
	Crystalline neologisms	

[Trans HM]

143

The Conversation of Prayer

The conversation about to be said
By the child on the stairs
Who climbs to his high room
The one will move
And the other be dead.

Turns in the dark will arise
Into the answering ground
From the man by his bed.
The sound in the two prayers
For the sleep who dies

Will be the same calm.
Should the child be crying?
The conversation about to be said
Turns on the quick stairs
Tonight alive and warm

In the fire of the high room.
And the child, not his prayer,
Shall drown in a true grave
And mark the eyes of sleep,
Dragging him who lies dead.   [HM]

●**Eodermdrome.** A structure in graph theory created by Gary Bloom of Rice University and introduced to the Oulipo by Claude Berge. It was originally applied only to letters of the alphabet, according to the following rules:

1. Choose 5 letters.

2. Arrange the letters in a pattern corresponding to the angles of an equilateral pentagon.

3. Connect each angle of the pentagon with every other angle (ten lines in all).

4. If the letters have been properly chosen and arranged, it will be possible to obtain a meaningful sequence of 11 letters by moving progressively along the lines joining the angles of the pentagon, each segment being used once and once only.

5. The sequence necessarily ends at the point at which it begins.

Example

Given the letters A, C, E, R, and S, arrange them counterclockwise at the angles of a pentagon in the order S, C, A, R, E. Draw the lines between the angles and the diagonals. Starting at S, proceed along the path

S → C → A → R → C → E → R → S → E → A → S.

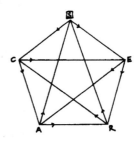

Solution: the phrase "scarcer seas".

The path followed in this example is one of many: there are 123 possibilities in all.

The word *eodermdrome* is itself a product of the structure, the letters used in this case being *d*, *e*, *m*, *o*, and *r*.

Setting up an eodermdrome may be made easier by realising that the rule against using any segment between two letters more than once means, in non-geometrical terms, that no two letters of the final product can be adjacent to each other more than once. For instance, in the preceding example, once "sCArcer" has been used, "ACe" is eliminated as a possibility.

The eodermdrome can be applied to units other than letters — to words, for example. The procedure remains unchanged, with a word rather than a letter being placed at each angle of the pentagon. Jacques Roubaud has composed a poem of 11 11-word lines using a softened version of the structure in which two of the five words chosen are identical; each line of the series begins (and ends) with the same word, a different path being followed in each successive line. Another possibility is to create a series of five eodermdromes that all combine the same five words, their sequence in each case beginning at a different word.

Example

Given the words *desiring, later, love, means, no*:

1.

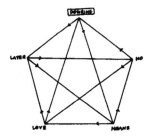

Desiring means love later.
No desiring later means no love-desiring.

Starting from each of the remaining angles of the pentagon, 4 other sequences are obtained:

2.

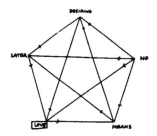

Love-desiring means no later love,
means later desiring no love.

3.

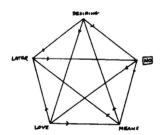

"No" means desiring love later.
No love means later desiring "no."

4.

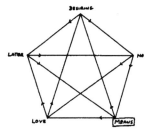

"Means desiring love no later"
means love later desiring no means.

5.

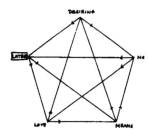

"Later" means desiring no love,
means no later love desiring "later."

The potential of the eodermdrome has scarcely been explored: the structure can certainly be used for more extensive projects. Here is a trivial narrative example. How could a heroine (or a murderer, or a set of parallel love affairs) be manifest eleven times in five different places without the direct connection between any two places ever being the same?

Given the places *New York, Paris, Siena, Grenoble, Key West*:

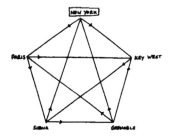

145

Solution: New York → Paris → Siena → Grenoble → Paris → Key West → Grenoble → New York → Key West → Siena → New York

There are actually 22 solutions implicit in this schema: the traveller can start (and end) at any of the 11 points in the sequence, and each of these itineraries can be reversed.

See also ●Minutes of the Oulipo (4). [HM, with basics supplied by CB & JR]

●**Epithalamium.** An Oulipian epithalamium, or marriage song, is one composed exclusively with the letters of the names of bride and groom.

For an example see ◯Georges Perec *Lines read at Alix-Cléo Blanchette's and Jacques Roubaud's Bridal.*

See also ●BO19; ●Beautiful in-law, ●Lipogram.

●**Equivoque.** A text that can be read in two different ways, each producing a distinct meaning. An Oulipian invention that recreates the form can be found at poems for ●Möbius Strip.

●**Eructative literature.** A term of mild abuse employed by the Oulipo to designate the more undisciplined forms of 'inspired' writing. In its early days the Oulipo was keen to distance itself from previous experimental methods of writing, in particular the ●chance methods of composition associated with Dada, and the "automatic" writing espoused by Surrealism. [AB]

●**Étienne, Luc.** (Luc Étienne Périn) (Neuflize, Ardennes, 1908–Reims, 1984) Elected to the Oulipo in 1970.

Born, educated and married in the north of France, from 1936 Luc Étienne earned his living teaching in the lycées of Reims, where he was appointed professor of mathematics, physics and chemistry in 1945. He continued teaching mathematics until his retirement.

Described by Georges Perec as a "genius in the manipulation of the French language", Luc Étienne gained a certain notoriety as a master of the ●spoonerism (*contrepet*). His first examples appeared in 1952 in the *Cahiers* of the ●College of 'Pataphysics, of which he had become a member; starting in

1952, he published two collections of spoonerisms entitled the *Albums de la Comtesse* after the weekly column he composed for the satirical paper, *Le Canard Enchaîné.* He also published an *Art du contrepet* in 1957, the year as well of *Adam et Eve en* ●*palindromes*, the initial manifestation of a palindromic versatility that in the year of his death would culminate in his astonishing ●phonetic palindrome. His first significant work as an Oulipian, his poems for ●Möbius Strip, date from around 1970. He later added other inventions to the Oulipian canon, notably the method of ●slenderising and the ●bilingual palindrome. Among his numerous other writings mention should be made of an article on "*Les jeux de langage chez Lewis* ●*Carroll*" (*Cahiers de l'Herne*, 17, 1971) and of a collection of French ●limericks (Oleyres, 1984).

As interested in music as he was in language, Luc Étienne made several contributions to that art, devising a precise division of the octave into ten equal tones (instead of the traditional twelve) that he adapted to several instruments; a technique of superimposing sounds by re-recording that allowed a single performer to replace an entire orchestra; and a mechanical page-turner that freed players from the risk of needless interruptions.

Other Oulipian works: ●BO23 & 27.

●*Exercises in Style.* (Gallimard, 1947) A series of texts by Raymond Queneau in which the same inconsequential story is told in 99 different ways. A later edition (1963) was illustrated by Jacques Carelman of the ■Oupeinpo.

○Raymond Queneau & Jacques Carelman *Exercises in Style* (Extracts)

Narrative

One day at about midday in the Parc Monceau district, on the back platform of a more or less full S bus (now No. 84), I observed a person with a very long neck who was wearing a felt hat which had a plaited cord round it instead of a ribbon. This individual suddenly addressed the man standing next to him, accusing him of purposely treading on his toes every time any passengers got on or off. However he quickly abandoned the dispute and threw himself on to a seat which had become vacant.

Two hours later I saw him in front of the Gare Saint-Lazare engaged in earnest conversation with a friend who was advising him to reduce the space between the lapels of his overcoat by getting a competent tailor to raise the top button.

Antiphrasis

Midnight. It's raining. The buses go by nearly empty. On the bonnet of an AI near the Bastille, an old man whose head is sunk in his shoulders and who isn't wearing a hat thanks a lady sitting a long way away from him because she is stroking his hands. Then he goes to stand on the knees of a man who is still sitting down.

Two hours earlier, behind the Gare de Lyon, this old man was stopping up his ears so as not to hear a tramp who was refusing to say that he should slightly lower the bottom button of his underpants.

Blurb [21]

In this new novel, executed with his accustomed *brio*, the famous novelist X, to whom we are already indebted for so many masterpieces, has decided to confine himself to very clear-cut characters who act in an atmosphere which everybody, both adults and children, can understand. The plot revolves, then, round the meeting in a bus of the hero of this story and of a rather enigmatic character who picks a quarrel with the first person he meets. In the final episode we see this mysterious individual listening with the greatest attention to the advice of a friend, a past master of Sartorial Art. The whole makes a charming impression which the novelist X has etched with rare felicity.

Interjections

Psst! h'm! ah! oh! hem! ah! ha! hey! well! oh! pooh! poof! ow! oo! ouch! hey! eh! h'm! pffft!

Well! hey! pooh! oh! h'm! right!

Mathematical

In a rectangular parallelepiped moving along a line representing an integral solution of the second-order differential equation:

$$y'' + \text{PPTB}(x)y' + S = 84$$

two homoids (of which only one, the homoid A, manifests a cylindrical element of length $L > N$ encircled by two sine waves of period $\pi/2$ immediately below its crowning hemisphere) cannot suffer point contact at their lower extremities without proceeding upon divergent courses. The oscillation of two homoids tangentially to the above trajectory has as a consequence the small but significant displacement of all significantly small spheres tangential to a perpendicular of length $I < L$ described on the supra-median line of the homoid A's shirt-front.

Botanical

After nearly taking root under a heliotrope, I managed to graft myself on to a vernal speedwell where hips and haws

Jacques Carelman, *Exercises in Style*.

Clockwise from top: Bayeux Tapestry, Medieval Woodcut, Science Fiction, Icon.

were squashed indiscriminately and where there was an overpowering axillary scent. There I ran to earth a young blade or garden pansy whose stalk had run to seed and whose nut, cabbage or pumpkin was surmounted by a capsule encircled by snakeweed. This corny, creeping sucker, transpiring at the palms, nettled a common elder who started to tread his daisies, and give him the edge of his bristly ox-tongue, so the sensitive plant stalked off and parked himself.

Two hours later, in fresh woods and pastures new, I saw this specimen again with another willowy young parasite who was shooting a line, recommending the sap to switch the top bulbous vegetable ivory element of his mantle blue to a more elevated apex — as an exercise in style.

Telegraphic

BUS CROWDED STOP YNGMAN LONGNECK PLAITENCIRCLED HAT APOSTROPHISES UNKNOWN PASSENGER UNAPPARENT REASON STOP QUERY FINGERS FEET HURT CONTACT HEEL ALLEGED PURPOSELY STOP YNGMAN ABANDONS DISCUSSION PRO-VACANT SEAT STOP 1400 HOURS PLACE ROME YNGMAN LISTENS SARTORIAL ADVICE FRIEND STOP MOVE BUTTON STOP SIGNED ARCTURUS

Hellenisms

In a hyperomnibus full of petrolonauts in a chronia of metarush I was a martyr to this microrama; a more than icosimetric hypotype, with a petasus pericycled by a caloplegma and a eucylindrical macrotrachea, anathematized an ephemeral and anonymous outis who, he pseudologed, had been epitreading his bipods, but as soon as he euryscoped a coenotopia he peristrophed and catapelted himself on to it.

At a hysteretic chronia I aesthesised him in front of the siderodromous hagiolazaric stathma; peripating with a compsanthropos who was symbouleuting him about the metakinetics of a sphincterous omphale.

[Trans Barbara Wright]

●*Exeter Text, The.* Translation by Ian Monk of *Les Revenentes,* a ●univocalic novella by Georges Perec in which the only vowel used is e. For the "e's retern" Perec adopted a quite different strategy from that used in its forerunner, the e-less *La* ●*Disparition.* Instead of concealing the governing constraint, he makes it conspicuous at the outset by announcing modifications of the normal rules of spelling. The novella tells the story of a successful jewel robbery that takes place during an extravagant sexual orgy in the precincts of Exeter Cathedral. As the tale progresses, the constraint is less and less strictly adhered to: the liberties taken with orthographic correctness make a perfect match with its libertine content. [IM]

Or to put it another way:

○Ian Monk *Perec's Letterless Texts*

When Perec penned the *e*-less *Enlèvement,* the *Exeter Text* (even the He-Men Legend we've seen here), he set free the letters' secret essences. Secret essences? Well, let's see the texts themselves.

These three texts represent three letterless genres:

(1) the severe He-Men Legend respects perfect letterlessness;

(2) when, less severe, *L'Enlèvement* respells terms here, then perverts sentences there, Perec lets the text's precepts be detected;

(3) even less severe, the *Exeter Text* eschews pretence: Perec, here, never respects the sterner tenets, never keeps them secret.

The *e*-less text lets endless glee meet dejectedness. Wherever we peer, we see decent men felled helter-skelter, wretchedness, demented schemers. The feebler sex's members seem few. E-lessness, *en effet,* never lets her strength be felt. Nevertheless, even here, Perec's glee perseveres. The excerpted *e* represents Perec's begetters (the French *e* = "them").[22] The SS left Perec deserted, defenceless. He then rejected the defenceless *e.* Yet *L'Enlèvement* keeps the precept secret. There're few SS references.[23] The well-kept secret expresses depths mere feckless penmen never spelt. When he tethered the verb, the verb re-emerged strengthened, freshened, re-pepped, the sentence renewed. Perec's *e*-less verve redeems "them".

When the *e* re-emerges (see the *Exeter Text*), Perec revenges "them": Clément fells Behrens, the SS Feldwebel. Then sex enters the scene. He sets revels between wenches, seven Greek henchmen, Exeter's Reverend Excellence, clerks, etc. Yet the sex-revels Perec's pen then ferments end perverted, veer between excesses.

Hence the *e*-text (glee engenders wretchedness) represents the *e*-less text's (wretchedness engenders glee) perfect reverse.

The fetters he selected, then, were never senseless, never mere perverted pretence. These fetters were seeds.

Sex drenches the *Exeter Text*. French sexes the letter *e*. Yet we seek sex elsewhere. There're letters where she tempts the pen; we've nevertheless rejected her presence. There're letters where sex seems less ever-present; well, here, the pen fell.

When we desert the verb's *Weltschmerz* we enter the letters' sweetest essence. Here, letters smelt sense (wherever lesser penmen've bent them), ferment, engender new legends. Let's heed Prester Tencrede when he tells the Exeter revellers: "We seek the essence where the End meets the Endless". These letterless precepts never let mere pretenders express themselves. Respect them. Remember "them".

See ●BO52; ●Lipogram.

●**Eye-rhyme.** A rhyme that satisfies the eye but not the ear, like *through*, *though*, and *rough*. The effect has been put to systematic use by Harry Mathews, as in the following ●limerick. See Alphonse ●Allais; ●BO70.

> Young Dick, always eager to eat,
> Denied stealing the fish eggs, whereat,
>   Caning him for a liar,
>   His pa ate the caviar
> And left Dicky digesting the caveat

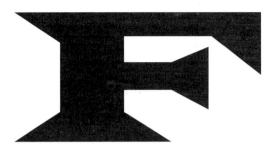

●**Fibonacci sequence.** A succession of numbers discovered by Leonardo Fibonacci (also known as Leonardo Pisano, c. 1170–after 1240). It has proved a productive tool in number theory, geometry, and genetics, as well as having connections with the Golden Section and the spiral arrangement of petals on flowers and trees. In a Fibonacci sequence, each term is the sum of the two terms immediately preceding it; typically, with 1 as the first term,

1, 1, 2, 3, 5, 8, 13, 21, 34, 55, ...

Although Paul Braffort is the only Oulipian to have made use of a Fibonacci sequence (see ●BO9), it is regularly mentioned in Oulipian theoretical writings. [HM & WM]

●**Forte, Frédéric.** (Right) Born on 20 March 1973 in Toulouse, where he still lives. He studied Communication and Sociology superficially, while playing bass guitar (left-handed) in a rock band. From 2001 to 2004 he worked in a record shop, but has recently converted to working in a bookshop. He has been writing poetry since 1999.

Works: *Discographie* (Éditions de l'Attente, 2002); *Banzuke* (Éditions de l'Attente, 2002); *N/S* (with Ian Monk) (Éditions de l'Attente, 2004); *Opéras-minute* (Théâtre Typographique, 2005).

●**Fournel, Paul.** (Above) Elected to the Oulipo in 1971, and its current President.

Born on 20 May 1947 in St. Étienne, Fournel is a graduate of the École Normale Supérieure at St. Cloud. He has been a publisher (director of Éditions Ramsay, then Éditions Seghers), and a professor of French literature (Princeton University, University of Paris), and is at present director of the Alliance Française in San Francisco. An author (two novels, several collections of short stories, essays), Fournel is the Oulipo's "provisionally definitive secretary" (cf. ●Bénabou).

Oulipian works: *Clefs pour la littérature potentielle* (Denoël, 1977); ●BO8, 10, 16, 23, 46 & 99; ●CP16.

See also ●Elementary morality, ●Theatre tree.

●*Franglais, l'égal.* See next entry.

●**Franglais, legal.** Legal franglais is the name of a bilingual vocabulary devised by Harry Mathews. The basic rules defining it are:

1. Each word must be spelled in exactly the same way in both French and English, aside from accents and capitals.

2. *No* meaning should be shared by the French and English word. This includes secondary meanings (*court*, for example, is excluded, since the French word means not only "short" and "(someone) runs" but "(tennis) court").

The use originally intended for the vocabulary was the composition of identical and perfectly ambiguous bilingual texts. The lack of grammatical correspondence in the functions of individual words was one reason that made this goal an exceptionally arduous one. In *Trompe-l'Œil* Georges Perec used the vocabulary simply as a restricted French ●vocabulary, abandoning any notion of grammatical English.

The lexicon of legal franglais, which originally contained 425 words, has been expanded over time.

Mets attend the sale (*Mets attend thé salé*)
If rogue ignore genes, bride pays (*If rogue ignoregênes, bride pays*)
As mute tint regains miens, touts allege bath (*As muté tint regains miens, tout s'allège, bath*)

                                     [HM]

Ian Monk has used legal franglais to create narrative. Each bilingual statement he creates is "justified" as the crystallisation of two fictitious episodes, one in French, the other in English. Here is a succinct example:

Il ne faut pas rôtir les oies mais plutôt les mâles de l'espèce, et en grande quantité! [24]

When it was Fred's round, he told the landlord to grab their pint glasses and serve him and his three companions forthwith.

SEIZE JARS POUR FOUR.[25]   [IM]

●*Gadsby*. See Ernest Vincent ●Wright.

●**Garréta, Anne F.** Elected to the Oulipo in 2000.

Author of 4 novels (published by Grasset): *Sphinx*, 1986 (love story in a classical mode except for the absence of any grammatical marks of gender as far as both narrator and main protagonist are concerned); *Ciels liquides*, 1990 (the paradoxical view of a narrator's loss of language); *La Décomposition*, 1999 (a serial murderer's quest for a perfect crime: applying a formal scheme to the text of Proust's *In Search of Lost Time* to select victims in the world, using the murders in turn to decompose the Proustian masterpiece, sentence by sentence); *Pas un jour*, 2002 (autobiographical writing with an ironic twist: remembrance of lovers past as a formally constrained game). Winner of the Prix Médicis in 2002. Currently Visiting Professor in the Literature Program at Duke University (since 1998).

See also ●CP16.

●**Grab-bag, François Le Lionnais's.** In *Lipo* (●CP3), François Le Lionnais offered to the writers of the world a number of projects that he outlined without (contrary to Oulipian custom) providing the least example.

1. *Boolean theatre.*

(a) Theatre of intersection.

The stage is divided into three parts. To the right and left different plays are performed. Empty at the start, the central space is neutral territory: characters from either side can venture into it (but not into the section beyond it). Their interaction gives rise to a third distinct play.

(b) Theatre of assimilation.

Two separate plays of radically differing nature are performed in a single theatrical space.

2. *Three-dimensional texts* (with 3-D spectacles if required).

3. *Holopoems*: holographically created images of airborne poetic texts.

4. *Antirhymes*: syntactically rather than ●semantically ●antonymous rhymes (a system defining them must first be created).

5. *Poem edges*: that is, the first line of a poem, its last line, and the two columns of words formed by the first and last words of all its lines, the whole forming a quadrilateral. Literary applications of geometry can be attempted: for instance, if the same word appears on the edge of two poems, the poems can be considered tangent to one another.

6. *Severely restricted* ●*vocabularies*, as for example ●animal languages. (See ●BO62.)

7. *Exploring the literary possibilities of basic mathematical notions and structures* (a list of 13 categories and 66 entries is provided).

8. *A dictionary of basic semantic factors* — ideas, sentiments, feelings, objects, actions, etc. Sample use: a work analysed according to such a dictionary will reveal a pattern of factors; the same pattern can then be used to create a new work (cf. ●Homosyntaxism). [HM]

●**Græco-Latin bi-square.** This mathematical term, also known as an orthogonal bi-square, has attained a certain literary currency thanks to Georges Perec's use of a 10 x 10 bi-square in organising his novel *Life A User's Manual*. The first Oulipian appearance of the term is in Claude Berge's article on ●combinatorial literature in *Lipo* (●CP3), where he defines it: "a Græco-Latin bi-square of order *n* is a figure with *n* x *n* squares filled with *n* different letters and *n* different numbers; each square contains one letter and one number; each letter appears only once in each line and each column, each number appears only once in each line and each column."

In *Atlas* (●CP6), Georges Perec uses a 3 x 3 Græco-Latin bi-square to show how the figure can be used as a source of narrative. (See ●*Life A User's Manual*, Figure 3.) [HM]

See also ●Lescurean permutations.

●**Grammatical translation.** By altering various aspects of grammar, a chosen text can be given a markedly different colouring.

Examples:

1. *Change of tense*
To have been, or not to have been: that *might* have been the question.

2. *Inversion of nouns and adjectives*
How could that finger-like terror and vagueness push
The glorified feathers from her femoral looseness?

(Yeats *Leda and the Swan*) [HM]

●**Grangaud, Michelle.** Elected to the Oulipo in 1995.

Born in Algiers in 1941, Michelle Grangaud lives in Paris.

Oulipian works: *Memento-fragments (anagrammes)* (P.O.L., 1987); *Stations (anagrammes)* (P.O.L., 1990); *Geste (narrations)* (P.O.L., 1991); ●BO75, 76, 79, 90, 95, 101, 113, 115 and ●CP12 & 16.

●**Graphic representation of text.** The mathematicians in the Oulipo have frequently used graphs and other mathematical diagrams as points of departure for writing texts (●BO17 & 67 use a ●Venn diagram and an interval graph respectively). Queneau originally presented the relationship ●x mistakes y for z (q.v.) as a set of graphs:

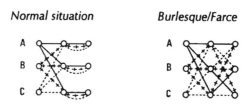

Normal situation   *Burlesque/Farce*

Oedipal situation

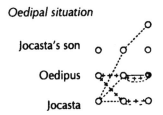

Other texts, in particular those using ●branching systems, are hard to grasp without being visualised graphically. Various attempts have been made to schematise the cantos of Roussel's *Nouvelles Impressions d'Afrique*: the entry for ●Roussel and his methods includes one; in *Lipo* (●CP3), Claude Berge and Raymond Queneau offered these diagrams of Canto I (numbers indicate the line at which parentheses are opened or closed):

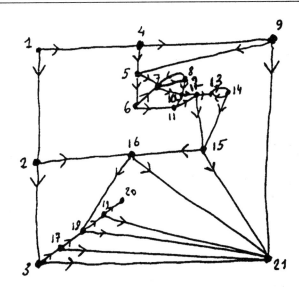

In *Lipo*, Claude Berge proposed writing poems arranged according to a graph without co-circuits (never mind what *they* are), which allows a user starting from any point to finish at a predetermined point:

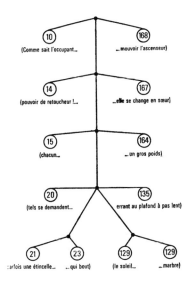

Queneau also mapped his bifurcating story *A Tale of your Choice*:

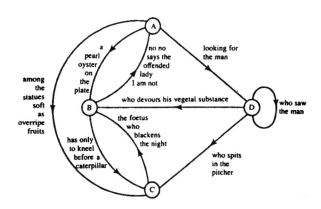

among the statues soft as over-ripe fruits
a pearl-oyster on the plate
must bow down to a caterpillar
no no says the offended lady I'm not

155

that devours its vegetable substance
the foetus that darkens the night
looking for the man
who saw the man
who spits in the pitcher

The lines of poetry corresponding to the segments of the graph have precise characteristics: those ending at D share the word "man", those starting at D have parallel grammatical structures. The user can assemble texts with fixed starting- and finishing-points, or avoid traversing a segment or crossing a point more than once. An example of the latter: BADC yields, "no no says the offended lady, I'm not looking for the man who spits in the pitcher".

As an anticipatory ●plagiary, here is the famous diagram of digressions from Laurence Sterne's *Tristram Shandy* (for another of its formal innovations see Going for the ■limit):

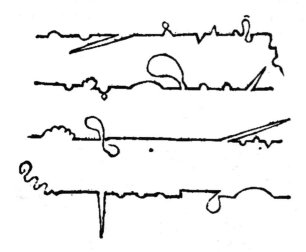

See also ●Eodermdrome, ●Multiple-choice narrative, ●Multiple-choice theatre, ▲*Jus d'Oronge*.

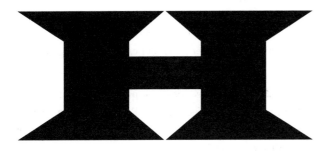

●*Haïkaïsation.* See next entry.

●**Haikuisation.** The *haiku* is a Japanese poetic form whose most obvious feature is the division of its 17 syllables into lines of 5, 7, and 5 syllables. (For an interesting if untypical example, see ●Roubaud's Principles.) Haikuisation has sometimes been used by Oulipians to indicate the reduction of verses of normal length (such as ●alexandrines) to lines of haiku-like brevity. Examples of haikuisation can be found at poetic ●redundancy. [HM]

See also ●BO76.

●*Hétérogramme.* See ●Isogram.

●**Heterosexual rhyme.** A heterosexual rhyme pairs a masculine noun with a phonetically plausible 'feminine' counterpart: *pas, pâle; an, âne.* This attractive device is obviously not available to writers of English. Poems using heterosexual rhymes by Noël Arnaud and Albert-Marie Schmidt appeared in *Lipo* (●CP3). [HM]

●**Hilbert, David.** (1862–1943) A German mathematician whose influence on geometry was the greatest since Euclid's, principally through his attempt to create an axiomatic foundation for it. Raymond Queneau used Hilbert's *Fundamentals of Geometry* as the source text of his *Foundations of Literature,*

published as ●BO3.

See also ●Bourbaki.

●**History.** See ★Ouhistpo.

●**Holorhyme.** An extended unit of verse — a line or stanza — that rhymes in its entirety.

> Let us two venture (melancholy care)
> Lettuce to vent your melon-colic air.

In *Lipo* (●CP3), François Le Lionnais published a 6-line repetitive holorhyme of "Oulipo". [HM]

●**Homoconsonantism.** The sequence of consonants in a source text is kept while all its vowels are replaced.

> *To be or not to be: that is the question*
> *t b r n t t b t t s th q st n*
> *At burnt tibia: it heats the aqueous tone*

Even more so, perhaps, than with ●homovocalism, this procedure seems condemned to the modest status of an exercise. The disparity between the difficulty of obtaining results and the results themselves only grows with the length of the source text. [HM]

●**Homolexical translation.** Only the vocabulary of the source text is preserved (that is, it disregards its sense and syntax).

> The question "to be that" is not to be "or".

[HM]

●**Homomorphism.** Literally, two texts "having the same shape". In writing, the type of homomorphism depends on the characteristic shared by two (or more) texts: syntax, vowel sequence, sound, etc.

See ●Homoconsonantism, ●Homophonic translation, ●Homosyntaxism, ●Homovocalism.

●**Homophonic translation.** When translation is based on

157

●homophony, its goal becomes the reproduction of the sound rather than the meaning of the original. The term indicates a *terminus ad quem*, since an exact replication of sounds in another language is impossible.

> *Le vierge, le vivace et le bel aujourd'hui* (Mallarmé)
> "Levy urge, levy vassal, hale bell!" assured we

In both *Lipo* (●CP3) & the *Atlas* (●CP6), Marcel Bénabou published homophonic translations from Latin and English poetry, among them Keats's "A thing of beauty is a joy for ever":

> *Ah, singe débotté*
> *Hisse un jouet fort et vert.*[26]

It should be mentioned that in his translations from Catullus, Louis Zukofsky tried to replicate the sound of the Latin as well as its sense.

The practice of homophonic translation has recently been expanded remarkably by two non-Oulipian writers, the American Robert Kelly and the German ●Schuldt, who began their collaboration in 1986. Taking a poem by Hölderlin (*Am Quell der Donau*) as their source, they began by translating the original homophonically and then applied bilingual homophonic and literal translation alternately to each successive result.

Here is one English transformation of the last stanza:

> Her golden ghosts on their side are all
> oft small, when inner. Then the holy work on him
>   sweeps.
> Dare standing. We unwitting night to day turn.
> Her ovaries fill with nectar and ocean,
> and then frolic weary after odours befell us.
> Wine's in him when her adventure too sorry lives
> her rude night. Beast her own, only grown worthy.
> (If ever the man inside her stands
> and comes out, there ends this coma.)
> Drum you greedy ones! Uncover me, Light!
> To meet, I believe May, then no kissed many who're
>   singing

Yes! over ending it, silly winding.
We in a saga that leaves
me there, gay song. And so each is her
mere myth, a wreathing, a blazing
when one found her gown gone, though all's gate so.

                                                                    (Kelly)

The ▲Oulipopo has noted the pseudonym of a Japanese author of detective stories: Edogawa Rampo. This is a phonetic translation into Japanese of the name of the genre's inventor: Edgar Allan Poe. [HM]

See ●BO4, 6, 16, 39, 58 & 68 (section 1); Raymond ●Roussel, ●Sequence.

●**Homophony.** In Oulipian usage the word means deriving a new text from a pre-existing one by imitating its sound. Most of us played homophonic games as children: "past your eyes" for "pasteurise". In Oulipian practice, homophony is generally used to create sequences of short fictitious episodes; these are presented like riddles whose 'solutions' are the homophonies (often preposterous) on which they are based. For instance, if one were to write a short fiction using the title of a poem by Keats, it might read:

> Stranded in that benighted oasis, the Kansan was disconsolate. Soon he would lose all chance of celebrating Christmas in a civilised Christian place; and he already found himself unable to send Henry, his oldest friend, a traditional symbol of seasonal cheer, as he had ritually done every year since they were boys. Among his many regrets, this perhaps saddened him most.
>
> *O to mail Hank holly!*

It can be argued that homophonic procedures are not properly Oulipian, since it is impossible to define precisely the degree of correspondence between the source text and its derivative. The fondness of Oulipians for the method is nevertheless undeniable: Italo Calvino, Harry Mathews, Michèle Métail, and Georges Perec — not to mention co-founder François Le Lionnais and the illustrious advance ●plagiarist, Raymond

●Roussel — have all exploited homophony, some extensively. The practice certainly answers to a concern evident in many stricter forms, that of making words reveal other words (or other meanings) unsuspectedly latent in them: it is yet another tool for discovering potentiality. [HM]

See ●Holorhyme, ●Homophonic translation, ●Sequence; ●BO6, 16, 39 & 68 (section 1).

●**Homosemantic translation.** A translation in which the vocabulary of the source text is changed while its sense is kept. At its simplest, it applies the procedure normally used to translate a text from one language to another to transforming a text within a single language.

Hamlet's famous words can be homosemantically translated into a new line of blank verse:

What I now ask is: should I live or no?

Poetry can also be rewritten as prose (and vice versa):

What I have to decide is: is going on living worth it?

Much more radical changes of genre are also possible:

Judge: You are instructed to proceed.
Witness: How can I face that degrading possibility when I am suffering from acute metaphysical anxieties?
Judge: Because however "degrading", it is the matter at hand.
Witness: No. The matter at hand is whether I should kill myself or not. *(Murmurs in the courtroom)*

Several of Raymond Queneau's ●*Exercises in Style* exploit this kind of homosemantic translation. [HM]

See also ●BO18, 80 & 82; ●Translexical translation, Restricted ●vocabulary.

●**Homosyntaxism (homosyntactical translation).** A method of translation that preserves only the syntactic order of the original words.

This simple and enjoyable procedure was apparently introduced to the Oulipo as a collective exercise. Members were

asked to fill in an abstract sequence of parts of speech with actual words. To give a rudimentary example, if N = noun, V = verb, and A = adjective, the outline NVA could yield solutions such as "The day turned cold", "Violets are blue", "An Oulipian? Be wary!" (punctuation, it should be noted, is irrelevant).

The original pattern submitted to the Oulipo follows, together with an English solution:

VVNNNNANNVVNNNVNVANANVNANNNNVVNNANNV

Come and see the females — ladies, women, girls — these naked objects, offerings displayed, and disposed for the pleasures of sight and touch. See their eyes, touch their smooth skin and their bright hair. Redeem in this museum the peremptory sufferings of time, change, and the world as it fades, sinking into a purity of knowledge, of non-contingent knowledge, the knowledge that absolves.

In this early application of homosyntaxism, the use of parts of speech other than nouns, verbs, and descriptive adjectives is left to the writer's discretion. It is perfectly possible to apply the method to all parts of speech and all the words present.

The pattern to be followed can be either invented or derived from an existing text. The beginning of Hamlet's most familiar soliloquy might be rendered:

Struggling and never budging? What was the fuss? If getting better at every turn is depressing, a drink or six after a good meal and finding companionship in a partner of charm (because willing) should cure you.

A longer example follows, that successively combines source texts from three different authors. The syntactical structure is borrowed from Ad Reinhardt. The nouns are taken from Wodehouse, the verbs from Lacan, and the adjectives from Wallace Stevens. "Pastorale" is thus not only an example of homosyntaxism but a ●chimera. [HM]

○Raphael Rubinstein *Pastorale*

You approach, effortlessly, when I look. Pure, candid, ever-early, like a supple wood-nymph remembering some unconscious sin. I am bronze and meaningless, with a muddy waistcoat and shabby penknife, in contrast to your enchanting hair and costume. You seem to bring out a fragrant heat-mist on to the lawns and terraces of the blue afternoon, which is structured around your strange smile.

Luncheon? Tea? Theatrical, false and remote projects. Why can't I introduce something more primitive, ancient, venerable? Would you take such a sweeping agenda, in spite of my employer and your mother? Such bright-dark eyes! Such fatal looks! Have you really appeared here? What is about to occur? Will I measure up?

I feel weighted down, ponderous. What of the ever-hooded future, bitter as a blazoned photograph on the page of a weekly newspaper? And what of chagrin, and conscience? You close in and appear to say something.

"The fiery border of the heart."
A dark, sweeping statement.
"Exclude your clothes," you say, immaculately.
I manifest my dark-blown frame.
You pose like a pale girl.

We gravitate, identify, integrate, heart to heart, uncertain and gasping. Our tongues start mapping. We are determined to express grossest Nature. Every recess is pointed out with vivid attention. We find niches and details, dealing with each other like the velvetest of insects, thus acquiring such information and understanding!

Somehow this acutest of stages is maintained. The circumstances make us co-proprietors of some water-walled neighbourhood, full of our medleyed chuckles. Ever keener, we keep restructuring in heroic positions for celestial hours as unscrawled notes are connoted by our X-ray looks.

Me: To hell with butlers, nightclubs, nieces, secretaries, Society!

You: O, poisonous purple train, come home!
A toss, then a spasm of heaving abysmal sunshine.

We had created an invisible pocket of matter among the laurels' ghostlier reproach. It was a kind of sunken time, glassy, dimly-starred, umber, empty. We had separated from the world of London and Biarritz. All time was presupposed as we discovered a night of ignorance among twigs and beetles. You had accepted my virile doings, I your feet on my back. And now, newly strong friends, clean of failure, our eyes were opened.

See also ●BO18 & 80; ●Grab-bag, ●*PPPP*.

●**Homovocalism.** The sequence of vowels in a source text is kept while all its consonants are replaced.

> *To be or not to be*
> *o e o   o o e*
> *Lode of gold ore*

Since the difficulties of this procedure only increase with the length of the source text, its interest will probably remain that of an exercise. [HM]

See ●BO56; ●Homoconsonantism.

●**Identikits.** Poetic form invented by Michèle Métail. See ●BO21.

●*If on a Winter's Night a Traveller.* William Weaver's translation of *Se una notte d'inverno un viaggiatore*, a novel by Italo Calvino. The book is made up of eleven numbered chapters (plus an epilogue) and ten intercalated first chapters of imaginary novels. The numbered chapters follow a pattern explained by Calvino in ●BO20 (translated in *Oulipo Laboratory*, ●CP9). The intercalated chapters, in a gamut of styles ranging from the detective story to Japanese erotica and from East-European realism to Latin-American magic realism, obey other, partly unstated rules. You, the reader, are the book's protagonist, projected into a frustrating world in which you begin novels but, for a variety of reasons, never proceed beyond their opening chapters. Meanwhile you are paradoxically reading through to the end the complete novel called *If on a Winter's Night a Traveller*. [IM]

●**Imparmigianisation.** See ●Pumectation.

●**Inadvertent translation.** Otherwise known as erroneous translation: this lack of intention disqualifies it from the Oulipian canon. Nevertheless the first Oulipo collection included an example of a French translation exercise from an examination in Australia (supplied by Ross Chambers). A domain inexplored who awaits of to be deepened by of the researches Oulipian.

[HM]

●**Inclusion.** The word *inclusion* indicates that within a text, a lesser text can be read. The term applies to procedures such as the ●acrostic, ●beautiful outlaw, and ●larding.

In the *Atlas* (●CP6), Paul Braffort's poem, "*Le chant du cryptobole*", illustrates inclusion by a method of which, to this editor's knowledge, no other Oulipian example exists. Spaces in each line, indicated by a _ , can all be filled with either one or another of two given letters. For instance, in the following prose sentence either *n* or *x* can be used:

In the blaze of their wa_ing sun, the useful te_t became no more than a ta_ shelter, to the surreptitious benefit of si_.

Another unique and altogether extraordinary example of an inclusion is the work of a non-Oulipian, an American named A.B. Paulsen, who in the 1970s sent his *2: A Story* to Harry Mathews. (Despite the latter's efforts, he soon disappeared from view.) The story in question was printed on heavy paper in a non-rectangular but regular shape. This shape, when cut out, folded, and glued, produced a regular decahedron each of whose ten faces is a triangle. Each triangle contains a portion of text that is self-sufficient; at the same time, the lines of adjacent faces merge together to form a single story that englobes the ten separate pieces in an elegant whole. [HM]

See also ●Circuit, ●Delmas's method.

●**Intersection, theatre of.** See François Le Lionnais's ●grab-bag.

●**Intersective novel.** A project of Jacques Duchateau first described in ●CP1:

○Jacques Duchateau *Project for an Intersective Novel* (Extracts)

Intersection:

(a) *Intersection is the name used in Boolean calculus to indicate those elements belonging to two or more sets (set being broadly taken to mean* collection).

(b) *Example: the intersection of Littré's and Larousse's definitions of "the novel" includes: narrative of imaginary adventures, prose, interest.*

(c) *Note: a set A wholly contained within a set B is the intersection of itself with B.*

(d) *Example: the set of my books is the intersection of my books with the set of existing books.*

(e) *A set can be viewed in two ways:*

— *extensively: listing all the elements, and only those elements, which constitute the set;*

— *comprehensively: defining all the properties, and only those properties, that determine the membership of an element in a set.*

The two views are complementary and equally valid. It does not matter which is adopted since a sub-set is itself a set and the intersection of two sets is also a set, so that the set originating from the intersection of two sets can be examined extensively or comprehensively.

(f) *Historical remarks (brief): all writers depend on intersections, whether they are scrutinising their colleagues (Pierre writes in the past imperfect, Paul in the past perfect, I'm going to write in the present perfect: perfect = an intersection) or analysing material for their own books (my wife is a blue-eyed blonde, my sister-in-law a blue-eyed brunette, my heroine will be a blue-eyed redhead: blue-eyed = intersection, redhead = creative imagination). Thus, when Conrad started work on* The Rescue, *he said that he wanted to write a romantic love story in which the word* love *never appeared. We may suppose that Conrad had looked at a number of romantic love stories, found that the word* love *was an intersection of all of them, and decided to write a work in the genre without using the word, thereby denying himself the easy option of using the word* love

to write about love.

William Faulkner's novel The Wild Palms *combines two novellas,* Wild Palms *and* Old Man, *in alternating chapters. Unconsciously or not, he organised the book by performing various operations on the basic elements he wanted to include, the main one apparently being the use of intersection. There are intersections of situations (a couple fleeing), of events (the heroines' pregnancies), of theme (the impossibility of freedom in society), of symbolic 'elements' (air and water). In addition to giving the work coherence, this common content allowed Faulkner to highlight oppositions divided symmetrically between one novella and the other: one hero is a weak intellectual, the other a courageous, uneducated convict; one heroine dies during an abortion performed in ideal conditions, the other survives her primitive delivery; etc.*

Method:

Since novels involve design, we can take a legitimate interest and, more particularly, systematically exploit an element of design (in this case intersection) when composing a book. Systematically, in that the use of intersection can by itself provide us with the novel's basic theme, given that we can choose among its elements as imagination dictates. In other words, the basic theme must furnish more elements than are needed to write the novel.

For example, if we take the private lives of two friends as material for our intersection, the events common to their lives must outnumber those that are necessary for the story of the intersective private life. Otherwise we shall be no more than ordinary players working a slot-machine. [Trans IW]

See also ●Grab-bag, ●Minutes of the Oulipo (1).

●**Inventory.** A method of analysis and classification that consists of isolating and listing the vocabulary of a pre-existing work according to parts of speech. Presented by Jacques Bens in *Lipo* (●CP3), the procedure was perhaps inspired by *Parts of Speech* in Queneau's ●*Exercises in Style.* [HM]

See also ●BO29 & 80 (xviii); ●Minutes of the Oulipo (1) and the various studies of the ▲Oulipopo, such as Δ*Who is Guilty?*

and ∆*Abel and Cain*, which employ a similar method but to more Sherlockian ends.

●**Invisible libraries.** See ●BO48 & 71.

●**Invisible Seattle.** This informal group of known and anonymous collaborators was founded in 1979 and manifested itself for the next several years in cabaret performances and publications around Seattle's yearly Bumbershoot arts festival. The group's name and elements of its oneiric / political strategy were drawn from Calvino.

"The time has come to rename downtown streets in hopes we all get lost", reads Invisible Seattle co-founder Philip Wohlstetter's early invocation, "to try the enemies of civic life and declare them completely visible. To rediscover the traces of that Invisible Seattle whose implacably just laws rule our dreaming hours. Act quickly, citizens, or the game is lost." The goal of the group was to "take over the city by hypnotic suggestion" in accord with its maxim: function follows fiction.

In 1983 the group accomplished the most ambitious of its public works, the provocation and compilation of *The Novel of Seattle* by Seattle, a month-long project in which hard-hatted and overalled Invisible Seattle "literary workers" approached citizens saying, "Excuse me, we're building a novel, may we borrow a few of your words?" Some Oulipian and Oulipo-inspired techniques were used to generate the thousands of individual text contributions, and an algorithmic compilation structure was used to complete the first draft in a four-day public spectacle.

1983 also saw the inauguration of the electronic bulletin board IN.S.OMNIA, on which many further pseudonymous, structured literary experiments were conducted throughout the '80s and early '90s. [Editors' note: Mathews's Perfectible Parody & Pastiche Procedure (see ●*PPPP*) was originally written for the IN.S.OMNIA bulletin board.]

The members of Invisible Seattle / IN.S.OMNIA credit the Oulipo's practical attitude towards text as rhetorical object rather than mystical receptacle as pointing a way beyond the limitations of the 'self-expressive' writing commonly promoted in North America. [Robert Wittig]

Bibliography: *Invisible Seattle, The Novel of Seattle* by Seattle (Function Industries Press, Seattle, 1987); *Invisible Rendezvous, Connection and Collaboration in the New Landscape of Electronic Writing*, Rob Wittig, for IN.S.OMNIA (Wesleyan University Press, Hanover NH, 1994).

See ●Tautogram.

●*I remember.* This manner of writing, while not Oulipian, has played a large enough role among the group's members to deserve mention. The device is simple: the words "I remember" are used to introduce each of a series of recollections that can be anything from a line to a page in length.

The "I remember" method was first practised by the American artist Joe Brainard (1941–1994). His first collection of remembrances was published in 1970; a collection of all the "I remember" texts appeared in 1975 and was more recently reprinted (*I Remember*, Penguin, 1995).

Knowledge of Brainard's work led Georges Perec to compile his own *Je me souviens* (1978). After his death, the Oulipo used the device collectively as part of their homage to him (see ●BO23). Harry Mathews also adopted it in *The Orchard*, his longer memoir of Perec (which in turn became the model for George Bowering's *The Moustache: Memories of Greg Curnoe* (Coach House Press, Toronto, 1993)). [HM]

Variants are Hervé Le Tellier's ○*All Our Thoughts* (●BO74) and Jacques Bens's *I've forgotten* (●BO88). See also ●BO82.

●**Irrational sonnet.** Jacques Bens proposed in *Lipo* (●CP3) a 14-line ●sonnet divided according to the first five digits of the irrational number π; that is, into stanzas of 3, 1, 4, 1, and 5 lines. He suggested the following supplementary rules for the form:

1. The two one-line stanzas are best treated as refrains, having their rhyme-word and other words in common.

2. There are four rhymes, distributed thus:

AAB C BAAB C CDCCD.

3. A and C are syllabically identical, as are B and D; that is, if A and C have one syllable, B and D will have two, and vice versa. [HM]

See ●BO75 & 80 (xvii) and the following example:

    ◯Harry Mathews *Replay*

They met; and after twelve weeks' pain, it ended.
They quit; and after twelve hours' pain, it mended —
A desert one dawn's rain sprinkled with green.

A casual touch set the stalled engine firing:

Whatever consummation this might mean
Was more than merely that of having fended
Off the survivor's choice they had intended
Or buffed their mirrors to a flattering sheen.

A casual touch: the stalled cylinders firing —

A novel lurch from here-and-now, inspiring
Unpredictable spins on unknown ground,
Pointed them past the dead end of inquiring
Into the equation of that fatal tiring
That left their love so carelessly unbound.

●**Isogram** (***hétérogramme***). An isogram is a series of letters in which no letter appears more than once: *ambidextrously*. The principle was put to extraordinary use by Georges Perec in a system of poetic composition that manifested itself in the collections ●*Ulcérations*, *La Clôture*, and *Alphabets*. For a description of his procedure, known as ●threnodials in English, as well as for English examples, see ●BO1 and ◯Ian Monk *A Threnodialist's Dozen*.

    The longest possible isogram is an ●isopangram.

●**Isomorphism.** "An exact correspondence as regards the number of constituent elements and the relations between them." (*OED*)

    See ●Homosyntaxism.

●**Isopangram.** A statement 26 letters long containing all the letters of the alphabet. (In an ●*isogram*, no letter appears more than once; a ●*pangram* includes all the letters of the alphabet.) See also ●BO44.

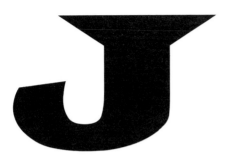

●**Jarry, Alfred.** (1873–1907) French author still known chiefly for his play *Ubu roi* (first performed in 1896) and his rigorously eccentric lifestyle. His works provide a vital bridge between the Symbolist writers of the late nineteenth century and those of the modern movement and Surrealism. Jarry did not use Oulipian techniques as such; his presence here is due to his invention of 'Pataphysics (see ●College of 'Pataphysics) and to his rescuing the notion of the ●*clinamen* from classical obscurity. [AB]

●**Jouet, Jacques.** Elected to the Oulipo in 1983.

Born in 1947 in Viry-Châtillon, between Route Nationale 7 and the railway leading from Paris to Ventimiglia, a few miles south of Orly Airport, very near the site of Charles Perrault's family home, barely more than a mile from the cemetery where Raymond Queneau would be buried, less than a mile from Camille Flammarion's observatory, where Raymond ●Roussel once paid a memorable visit.

Jacques Jouet has written poems, plays, short stories, novels, books of criticism, and radio plays. He makes collages.

Oulipian works: ●*107 âmes* (Seghers, Collection *Mots*, 1991) (poetry); ●BO28, 38, 44, 52, 54 (9), 55, 56, 62, 64, 72, 78, 79 (4), 82, 90, 93, 97, 107, 108, 120, 124, 134 & 135. See also ●CP10 (volume 4), 12, 13 & 16.

Partially Oulipian works: *Raymond Queneau* (La Manufacture, 1988) (essay); *Des ans et des ânes* (Ramsay,

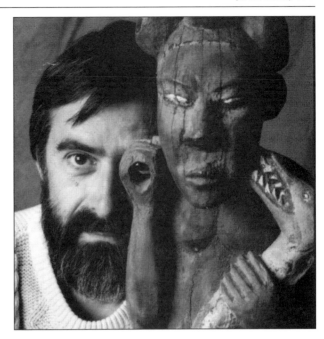

Collection *Mots*, 1988); *Qui s'endort* (Jacques Brémond, 1988) (poetry); *Le chantier* (Limon, 1993) (poetry); *La scène est sur la scène, Théâtre I* (Limon, 1994). [JJ]

●*Journalist, The.* A novel by Harry Mathews (Godine, Boston, 1994). While the structure of the book is not Oulipian, the relationships between its principal characters at the start were determined by an adaptation of ●x mistakes y for z. The characters "mistake" each other not in their identities but in their unconsciously assigned roles. Thus the husband knows that his wife is his wife but expects her to behave as a mother, he knows his son is his son but expects him to behave as a friend, and so forth. [HM]

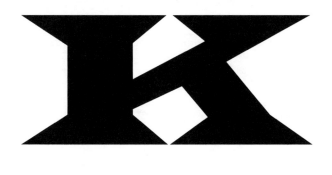

●**Kuhlmann, Quirinus.** (c. 1651–1689) This anticipatory ●plagiarist was a dandy, visionary, and religious fanatic who added a new testament to the Bible and whose poetry was intended as subversive propaganda for his new church. He was eventually burnt at the stake by the Lutheran Patriarch of Moscow on account of his chiliastic beliefs. His *Kiss of Love*, from a suite of poems with the same name, is a poem based on ●permutation. In each line, one of 13 available words is chosen to connect the italicised beginnings and endings, which remain unchanged. Whatever choices are made, the metre is never flawed. The number of possible combinations of these variable lines is 23,298,085,122,481.   [Malcolm Green & Chris Allen]

   See also ●Combinatorial literature.

○Quirinus Kuhlmann *The Kiss of Love*

After night / mist / battle / frost / wind / sea / heat /
   south / east / west / north / sun / fire *and pain*
Follows day / glory / blood / snow / quiet / land / storm
   / warmth / heat / joy / cold / light / blaze *and fears*
After torment / harm / shame / plight / war / want /
   cross / strife / scorn / woe / agony / spite / blame
   which jeers
Comes cheer / grace / praise / balm / gain / help / value
   / peace / meed / wit / calm / bliss / mercy *once again*

The moon / gleam / smoke / hart / fish / gold / pearl /
   tree / flame / stork / frog / lamb / ox *and bowels*
Love lustre / straw / steam / hill / tide / glow / spume /
   fruit / ash / roof / pond / field / lore *and bread*
The haven / man / duty / toil / art / play / ship / mouth
   / prince / envy / care / greed / faith *and God*
Seek in aim / sleep / laud / praise / boon / feud / port /
   kiss / throne / death / shroud / wealth / fair *avowal*

What is good / strong / hard / right / long / large / white
   / one / yes / air / fire / tall / broad *by name*
Holds evil / weak / light / bent / broad / small / black /
   three / no / earth / tide / deep / near *apart*
Even pluck / love / wit / spirit / soul / friend / joy /
   grace / fame / peace / joke / praise / sun *must depart*
Where fear / hate / fraud / wine / flesh / body / foe / pain
   / shame / dread / strife / woe / scorn *doth reign*

All things change; all loveth; all things seem to hate some thing:
He who devoteth his thoughts to this, verily shall drink of Wisdom's
   spring.

                    [1670, trans Malcolm Green]

●**Larding.** Warren Motte has used the convenient term *larding* as an equivalent of *le tireur à la ligne*, the name given by Jacques Duchateau to a procedure that is his speciality. "Line stretching" refers to the 19th-century practice of paying magazine contributors (such as Alexandre Dumas) by the line — a practice that encouraged them to stretch their material to maximum length.

Duchateau describes the method in *Atlas* (●CP6): From a given text, pick two sentences. Add a new sentence between the first two; then two sentences in the new intervals that have become available; and continue to add sentences until the passage has attained the length desired. The supplementary sentences must either enrich the existing narrative or create a new narrative continuity. (It is permissible to start with more than two sentences when appropriate.)

He seemed to be wilting away in his anxiety. "If only you will give me something to do!" was his constant wail. At last Holmes could oblige him.

    A. Conan Doyle, "The Disappearance of Lady Frances Carfax" (*His Last Bow*)

He seemed to be wilting away in his anxiety. His nights passed with little sleep, if any. "If only you will give me something to

do!" was his constant wail. His very impatience, out of nervous exhaustion, began to wilt. At last Holmes could oblige him.

He seemed to be wilting away in his anxiety. He ate less and less. His nights passed with little sleep, if any. Impatient of letting events follow their course, he longed to take them into his hands. "If only you will give me something to do!" was his constant wail. "How can you expect me to endure such a predicament?" His very impatience, out of nervous exhaustion, began to wilt. We feared for his sanity, even his life. At last Holmes could oblige him.

He seemed to be wilting away in his anxiety. When the report from the laboratory arrived, its evidence was overwhelming. He ate less and less. He never left his rooms except to visit us. His nights passed with little sleep, if any. We could only sympathise with his plight. Impatient of letting events follow their course, he longed to take them into his hands. In such dramatic circumstances, we could scarcely influence his mood. "If only you will give me something to do!" was his constant wail. "Am I supposed to wait until the knell has tolled its final stroke? How can you expect me to endure such a predicament?" I advised a mild sedative; Holmes, of course, cocaine; he refused both. His very impatience, out of nervous exhaustion, began to wilt. A terrible despondency took the place of his wearying agitation. We feared for his sanity, even his life. Then I received further news: the laboratory had confused two samples — Samantha, his blue-ribbon pride, was in perfect health and could be fetched home today. At last Holmes could oblige him. [HM]

    See ●BO14, 17, 41 & 80.

●**Latis.** (1913–1973) Founding member of the Oulipo (left).

Latis played a central role in the ●College of 'Pataphysics following the resignation of J.-H. Sainmont. Baron Mollet appointed him his Secretary-Particular General, and he shared the position of Co-Vice Rogator with Noël Arnaud. Mollet's successor, the third Vice-Curator Opach, abolished his secretarial position and elevated Latis to the Satrapy. On retiring from his teaching post, Latis devoted his time to writing poetry and growing cacti until his death at the age of 60. Apart from his administrative role in the College, Latis contributed many texts to its publications, often under pseudonyms. His most extended work, a novel consisting entirely of prefaces and postfaces, *L'Organiste athée*, was published by the College under the name of Lathis in 1963. Latis also designed the emblem that was used by the Oulipo in its early years (right). [PG]

●**Left-handed lipogram.** A variant of the ●lipogram, in which the text is constructed solely from letters, numbers, punctuation marks, and signs on the left-hand side of a standard typewriter keyboard. Invented by Dallas Wiebe; see his ○*Dexter Weaver Serves Breaded Crested Grebe*, first published in ●*New Observations*.

●**Leibniz, Gottfried Wilhelm von.** (1646–1716) German philosopher and mathematician. At twenty he wrote *De arte combinatoria*, in which he mentions the possibility of permutating words and phonemes according to ●combinatorial systems. He unfortunately gives no examples. [HM]

See Giordano ●Bruno, Ramon ●Llull, ●Permutation.

●**Le Lionnais, François.** (Paris, 1901–1984) Founding co-President of the Oulipo. (See ●College of 'Pataphysics for a portrait.)

In his youth Le Lionnais frequented 'artistic' circles around Max Jacob and Jean Dubuffet but later began a career in industry, with his passion for mathematics consuming his spare time. During world war two he was arrested for his Resistance work and imprisoned in the Dora concentration camp. He later worked for UNESCO, was a scientific adviser to the National Museums, and became a prominent member of the College of 'Pataphysics where he held the title of Regent. A celebrated writer on chess problems, it was through this interest that he made the acquaintances of ●Roussel and Duchamp. Le Lionnais helped found most of the other ★Ou-x-pos and was their titular President until his death. His contribution to the Oulipo was principally theoretical; his writings on Oulipian subjects are scattered throughout the group's collective publications, the ●Manifestos being obviously important among them. [AB]

See also ●BO23 & 85; ●Grab-bag, Going for the ●limit.

●**Lescure, Jean.** Founding member of the Oulipo.

Born in 1912 in Paris, Lescure studied philosophy and was close to the philosopher Gaston Bachelard. Editor of *Messages*, a review started before the war and continued clandestinely during the occupation, Lescure was also in an armed unit of the

○Dallas Wiebe *Dexter Weaver Serves Breaded Crested Grebe*

4#2#45

dear reader #

at easter at sweetwater texas few feasts grace watered grass # ragweed rages # secret feverfew craters terraces # bare trees starve as star wars rage # garbage bags sweat as sewers target excess crawdad cadavers # few greasers serve beef stew # few tartars serve rare battered eggs # few swaggerers serve aged draft beer # texas deserves better dexter weaver avers # dexter gazes at garbage cases sees vexed ragged rats starved bees sad barred bats # west texas deserves best dexter asseverates # feasts are sacred # feasts are acts revered at star graced eve # feasts are tete a tetes # a feast detracts dread # feasts stress tact are sacred are tear faced awe are waxed zest # retards starve # cadavers waft sewer gases # abscesses fester brew red scabs # feasts are dexter asserts fetes are beer rages fart tests are crazed excesses # 23 west texas sweaters agree # 23 sad west texas execraters berate fasts # 23 screwed west texas badasses gag #

dexter starts averts gaze agrees # dexter creates a card #

dear secret fasters #

easter exacts vast rewards # screw fasts # feasts create a freer texas # crab rears fast # water bearer deceases # stars agree a sweet taste averts graves # set feet faster # sweetwater deserves carvers stabbers eaters carafe drawers steadfast feeders # wear feast rags at 5 # 2 # 45 # caveat regrets regarded bad #

dexter fred weaver # sweetwater texas

braggart dexter a drab bard deceased gag bearer a verse brewer a fat swaggart addresses cards at sweetwater # ezra ward trabert at radeberg # ezra a tv star a ratface a cad assbeater grease farts bed wetter # barbara baxter at warsaw # barbara a bawd red breasts eats cabbages wafts sewer gases eats certs eats breads gets dresses at sears # serge de baccarat de sade at redwater texas # serge a detested fat fag a beaded brat a farter at sextrade bazaars # sara brewer at rabat # sara a teaser a castrater a tear starter a sex eraser a testes ravager a faeces eater a wet twat # rex drew at accad # rex a red face carves agate beavers casts brass deer wax gewgaws weaves acetate zebras arts crafts a beard creaser # eve sexdart wade a dragster a greaser ear teaser warted feet ass caresser # eve wade at crete at raba revavae at rafa arawa at red cedar red deer bagdad exeter brest accra red sea razgrad tarawa et cetera #

feasters get cards # baggage gets crated # carters swear bear great cases # vast seas are traversed # ragged deserts are evaded # sweated grade crews gaze as scree rears as feasters recede seated at dresser drawers # street beggars start as scattered garbage waves as raw as straw # trees wave abreast as gabbers race westward # gazers grab a best seat at a settee # servers serve faster brazed cabbage breaded crawdads raw zebra ears as sweetwater crests a defaced crater #

dexter sees feasters are safe at gate # dexter erases vexed dread # safe are grabbers razzers caressers screwers bastards # we are rested dexter asserts # a fate as great as abstract trees draws cravers # feasters traverse sacred graves scarred crags seared grasses # feasters are seated at a cabaret # dexter raves asserts feast fare at starved ezra barbara serge sara rex eve #

feast fare #
    treats #
        beefeaters
        red rasaca
        draft beer
    tasters #
        date wafers
        grated bat dabs
        cratered bass eggs
    teasers #
        absterged cat grass
        refracted water cress
        fast freezed red beets
        wafted waxed cabbage
        vasected crab de sade
    fare #
        crafted acetate eggs
        fatted red deer ears a berge
        aged basted beaver testes a sartre
        raw abscessed abbess teats a secret
        breaded crested grebe breasts
    battered bread
    water
    tea
    desserts #
        sacred stag secrete
        cadaver warts a vestre
        garter sweat avec grease
    cafe vegas avec cressets
    retasted stress gas

feasters dress wear fracs read abraxas affect grace # feasters are seated # dexter brags as servers strew eats # abracadabra asserts dexter # feasters taste eat gag as crafted acetate eggs crease craws # feasters eat dreaded deceased bass eggs vasected crab de sade # dexter sees stress # dexters ears get red # feasters extract beaver testes a sartre eat abbess teats a secret faster # garbage asserts ezra trabert # dregs agrees barbara baxter # raw asseverates serge de sade # beeswax avers sara brewer # tsetse barf agrees rex drew # catsweat bearfarts twatdregs razzes eve sexdart # a bas feasters agree # aggravated dexter stabs breaded crested grebe # raw grebe staggers a fated exacerbated fear # dexter retracts abraded breast #

abstract fears abet excess # drab ezra rages # fartface badass warteater castrated sweatcraver ezra asserts # dexter stews # greasefart eggbeater sewer vat rat feeder raves barbara # dexter stares at a ewer # bastard bawd beater cadaver eater agrees serge # twat teaser ass swabber bassbreeder agrees sara # dexter fades # crawdad secretes beast beggar abscessed brat asseverates rex # dexter ceases gaze # stewed screwer scabbed seed caster debased farcer detested raver brassass festered date server ratsass sweetwater retard asserts eve # dexter regrets feast # dexter retreats averts a farce #

war rages # feet tread dexters ears # ezra swats dexter # barbara beats dexters breast # serge rages swears a red art # sara stabs dexter # rex grabs a grate grazes a wet rafter # eve waves a water carafe servers dexters fat warts # breadcases scatter tv # axes raze tattered egresses # a barrage darts at dexter # feast ceases # raw water cress greases dear dexter # bread batters dexters feet # basted beaver testes grace dexters ears # garter sweat bedews dexters ass # dexter fred weaver sees stars #

sweetwater texas reverts as sad dexter scats # streets exacerbate egress # brass gates trace a retreat # dexter grabs a safe barge steers traverses vast seas evades ragged deserts wades severe waters # recesses after sweated stages at a fated date safe at caravaca #

afterwards dexter weds a vascaderas abbess serves breaded egret breasts at terce # abbess wears a sacred sweated reversed garter # sex starved dexter gazes at abbess twat # dexter screws ac dc # dexter breeds # babes reared # brats are castrated # gee dad brats assert # brats are fed red fat grated raw beets # a castrated race gazes at watered grass # dexter fred weaver states caravaca deserves a better fare # a feast dexter asserts at easter # dexter serves beargrease bread basted festered bearcat stewed stag asses carved bedewed deer ears abraded treated scabbed gar waxed rat cadavers cafe a wee wee dates a grave # dexter states cest de servage de sexe # ass reward dexter states ass reward #

as ever

daas webe # creater

Resistance and active with the underground literary presses. A prolific novelist, poet, and writer on cinema and the arts, he was for many years the literary director of French National Radio and later president of the Association Française des Cinémas d'Art et d'Essai (AFCAE), and a Regent of the ●College of 'Pataphysics.

Oulipian bibliography: ●BO36.

See also ●Lescurean permutations, ●Lescurean word square.

●Lescurean permutations. In his presentation in *Lipo* (●CP3), Jean Lescure remarks that we frequently have the impression that language in itself "has something to say" and that nowhere is this impression more evident than in its possibilities for ●permutation. They are enough to teach us that to *listen* we must be *silent*; enough to transform *a well-oiled bicycle* into *a well-boiled icicle*.

Lescure proposes two permutational methods, the first of which is considered here. It concerns single parts of speech, such as nouns, as they appear in pre-existing works. He suggests subjecting them to four basic manipulations:

1. *Plain permutations*: the 1st noun changes place with the 2nd, the 3rd with the 4th, etc.

2. *Alternate permutations*: the 1st noun changes place with the 3rd, the 2nd with the 4th, etc.

3. *Bracketed permutations*: the 1st noun changes place with the 4th, the 2nd with the 3rd, etc.

4. *Roussellian permutations* (so named because of the sentence structure of Raymond ●Roussel's *Nouvelles Impressions d'Afrique*): the 1st noun changes place with the last, the 2nd with the next to last, etc.

Examples: Poetry (Source text)

Night, and the down by the sea,
And the veil of rain by the down;
And she came through the mist and the rain to me
From the safe warm lights of the town.

The rain shone in her hair,
And her face gleamed in the rain;

And only the night and the rain were there
As she came to me out of the rain.
    Arthur Symons *At Dieppe: Rain on the Down*

Plain permutation:

Down, and the night by the veil,
And the sea of down by the rain;
And she came through the rain and the mist to me
From the safe warm town of the lights.

Her hair shone in the rain,
And the rain gleamed in her face;
And only the rain and the night were there
As she came to me out of the rain.

Alternate permutation:

Sea, and the veil by night,
And the down of mist in the rain;
And she came through the rain and the down to me
From the safe warm rain of her hair.

The lights shone in the town,
And the night gleamed in the rain;
And only her face and the rain were there
As she came to me out of the rain.

Bracketed permutation:

Veil, and the sea by the down,
And the night of rain in the mist;
And she came through the down and the rain to me
From the safe warm hair of the rain.

The town shone in her lights,
And the rain gleamed in the night;
And only the rain and her face were there
As she came to me out of the rain.

Roussellian permutation:

Rain, and the rain by night,
And the rain of her face in her hair;

And she came through the rain and the town to me
From the safe warm lights of the rain.

The mist shone in her down,
And the rain gleamed in her veil;
And only the sea and the down were there
As she came to me out of the night.

Prose. *Roussellian permutation:*

Life ought to begin again around fifty, he thought. Transitions can stand new years, new houses. Some pasts go on too long. If they ended by mutual garbage after twenty-five illnesses, or when the world left the partners, that might be refreshing for both houses. Getting into the kids again to find out what was going on might do them good. Maybe Kitty would worry less about herself if she had to work; would sleep better; would think less of years, the consent of marriages. She'd get the beginning, of course. Fanny and he could live in Europe for the first enterprise, maybe to try out living together. That might ease middle age into new lives for them all.

Bernard Malamud *Dubin's Lives* (1979), chapter 7

Jean Lescure observes that many works will, obviously, resist this kind of manipulation and yield only mechanical or clumsy results.

Perec employed a similar technique to write his culinary masterpiece *81 Easy-Cook Recipes for Beginners*. An English translation can be found in the Perec issue of *The Review of Contemporary Fiction*, Vol. 13, 1, Spring 1993. [HM]

See ●Lescurean word square.

●**Lescurean word square.** Unlike ●*Lescurean permutations*, this structure does not exploit pre-existing prose or poetry but is used to create an original work. It is easy to set up: four words are chosen and then combined in every possible order, and the results, with a minimum of connective additions (or ideally none at all), can become a poem or the nucleus of a prose narrative.

Using 4 words, 24 arrangements are possible (4! = 24).

In the example, the words chosen are: *prose, bones, soap, poem*. (The ordering of the series here is only one of many possible.)

At the meeting of the Oulipo on 21 August 1984, Harry Mathews presented an application of the Lescurean word square to a series of four compositional elements, two of them *syntactic*, two ●*semantic* (rhyme, metaphor, image, event; published in ●BO51, "*Le juste retour*"). Since then, he has written numerous short works using ●permutations of four restrictions of various kinds: in French, "*L'émigré*" and "*Cours, Mirabeau!*" (BO51); in English, the stories *Tear Sheet, The Chariot, Letters from Yerevan.* [HM]

The prose of bones makes soap of a poem
Prose of bones makes a poem of the soap
Prose of soap makes the bones of a poem
Prose of soap makes a poem of bones
The prose of a poem makes bones of soap
The prose of a poem makes soap of bones

Bones of prose make the soap of a poem
Bones of prose make a poem of the soap
The bones of the soap make prose of the poem
The bones of the soap make a poem of prose
The bones of the poem make prose of the soap
The bones of the poem make soap of the prose

Soap of the prose makes a poem of bones
Soap of the prose makes bones of the poem
The soap of the poem makes prose of the bones
The soap of the poem makes the bones of prose
The soap of bones makes prose of the poem
The soap of bones makes a poem of the prose

A poem of prose makes soap of bones
A poem of prose makes bones of soap
A poem of soap makes prose of bones
A poem of soap makes bones of prose
A poem of bones makes prose of soap
A poem of bones makes soap of prose

●**Le Tellier, Hervé.** A member of the Oulipo since 1992.

"Preoccupied with short, in fact very short forms. In addition to ●BO74, 77, 79 (3), 84, 90, 94, and 105, he has published novels, stories, and other brief works. His Oulipian publications include: *Sonates de bar* (Seghers, 1991), *Le Voleur de nostalgie* (Seghers, 1992), *Les Amnésiques n'ont rien vécu d'inoubliable* (Éditions du Castor, 1997), and *La Disparition de Perek*, a thriller (Éditions Baleine, 1997). Hervé Le Tellier was, furthermore, forty years old in 1997." [HLT]

See also ●CP12 & 16.

●*Lexique restreint.* See Restricted ●vocabulary.

●*Life A User's Manual.* Translation by David Bellos of *La Vie mode d'emploi*. Georges Perec's longest and most ambitious novel was conceived nine years before its completion in 1978: "I have imagined a building that has its façade removed so that all its rooms on the street side are visible" (*Species of Spaces*). The rooms became those of a Parisian apartment house; associated with them are the lives of their tenants past and present. Perec meticulously describes both lives and rooms one by one.

These multiple stories centre on three male characters. Percy Bartlebooth, a rich eccentric, has spent decades travelling the world in order to complete a series of five hundred watercolours. He has since commissioned a diabolically skilful craftsman, Gaspard Winckler, to transform them into jigsaw puzzles; these Bartlebooth will reassemble before eventually destroying them. At the start of the book, we learn that Winckler has died after completing his task and that Bartlebooth is well into his work of reassemblage. The activity of the two men has been closely followed by Serge Valène, a painter engaged (like the author of *Life*) in portraying the building in which they all have lived, with its façade removed. Neither he nor Bartlebooth will reach his assigned goal.

The composition of the book, in its way as densely Oulipian as *A* ●*Void*, exploits three principal structures: the ●Græco-Latin bi-square, the Knight's Tour, and a ●permutating "schedule of obligations". These are described in detail in the author's account of his work that follows (from the *Atlas*, ●CP6). [HM]

◦Georges Perec *Four Figures for "Life A User's Manual"*

Figure 1

In 1972, the project that was to become Life A User's Manual *was made up of three separate sketches, each as ill-defined as the others. The first, entitled "Græco-Latin Squares", dated from 1967. It concerned applying to a novel or a group of stories a mathematical structure known as a 10 x 10* ●*Græco-Latin bi-square (see Fig. 3). The idea had been presented to the Oulipo by Claude Berge, who hoped to work on it with Jacques Roubaud and me.*

Even less precise, the second sketch had no title and almost no text. It vaguely proposed the description of a building in Paris as it would look with its façade removed.

Finally, the third, imagined in late 1969 during the laborious reassemblage of a huge jigsaw puzzle portraying the port of La Rochelle, was a version of what was to become Bartlebooth's story. The character's name, taken from Valéry Larbaud and

Melville, had already been found, and I had written a succinct two-page résumé.

The convergence of these three starting-points occurred abruptly on the day I realised that the cross-section of my building and the diagram of the bi-square could perfectly well coincide: each room in the building could be a square of the bi-square and a chapter of the book. The permutations generated by the bi-square would determine the constituent elements of each chapter — furniture, decorations, characters, historical and geographical allusions, literary allusions, quotations, etc. In the midst of these stories constructed like jigsaw puzzles, Bartlebooth's career would obviously occupy an essential place. Meanwhile my title emerged, changing slightly as the years passed: Life; Life (a user's manual); Life: A User's Manual; Life, A User's Manual; Life A User's Manual.

In order to visualise the various plans I was then starting to assemble, I asked Jacqueline Ancelot, a friend who was studying architecture, to make me a drawing of the building's façade. In it one can recognise certain details that have remained unchanged in the novel: Hutting's big studio at the upper left, the service entrance, the shop with its back room, and the concierge's quarters.

Figure 2

It would have been tedious to describe the building floor by floor and apartment by apartment; but that was no reason to leave the chapter sequence to chance. So I decided to use a principle derived from an old problem well known to chess enthusiasts and known as the Knight's Tour; it requires moving a knight around the 64 squares of a chess-board without its ever landing more than once on the same square. Thousands of solutions exist, of which some, like Euler's, also form magic squares. For the special case of Life A User's Manual, a solution for a 10 x 10 chess-board had to be found; I managed this, rather miraculously, by trial and error. The division of the book into six parts was derived from the same principle: each time the knight has finished touching all four sides of the square, a new section begins.

It should nevertheless be noticed that the book has not 100 chapters but 99. For this the little girl on pages 295 and 394 is solely responsible [pages 231 and 318 in the English translation].

175

Figure 3: An example of a 10 x 10 Græco-Latin bi-square

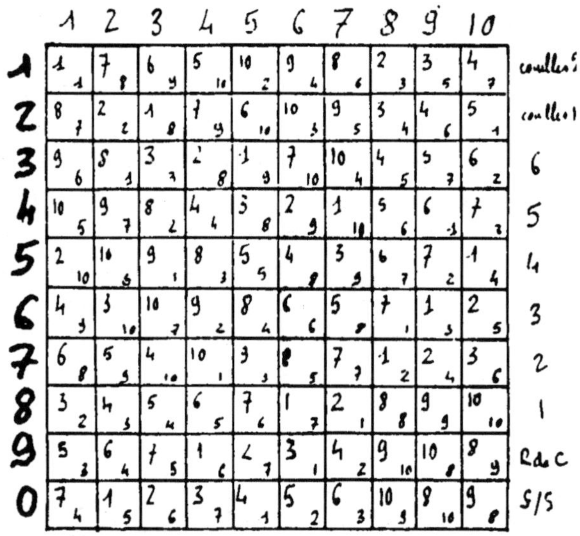

The simplest way to explain what a 10 x 10 Græco-Latin bi-square is, and the fictional uses to which it can be put, is to start with a 3 x 3 Græco-Latin bi-square.

Imagine a story 3 chapters long involving 3 characters named Jones, Smith, and Wolkowski. Supply the 3 individuals with 2 sets of attributes: first, headgear — a cap (C), a bowler hat (H), and a beret (B); second, something hand-held — a dog (D), a suitcase (S), and a bouquet of roses (R). Assume the problem to be that of telling a story in which these 6 items will be ascribed to the 3 characters in turn without their ever having the same 2. The following formula:

	Jones	Smith	Wolkowski
chapter 1	CS	BR	HD
chapter 2	BD	HS	CR
chapter 3	HR	CD	BS

— which is nothing more than a very simple 3 x 3 Græco-Latin bi-square — provides the solution. In the first chapter, Jones has a cap and a suitcase, Smith a beret and a bouquet of roses,

Wolkowski a bowler hat and a dog. In the second, Jones has a beret and a dog, Smith a bowler hat and a suitcase, Wolkowski a cap and a bouquet of roses. In the third, Jones has a bowler hat and a bouquet, Smith with his cap will be walking a dog, and Wolkowski, wearing a beret, will be lugging a suitcase. All that remains to be done is to invent situations to justify these successive transformations.

In Life A User's Manual, instead of 2 series of 3 items, 21 times 2 series of 10 items are permutated in this fashion to determine the material of each chapter.

N.B. Græco-Latin bi-squares cannot be based on every number; there is, for example, no 2 x 2 Græco-Latin bi-square. For over two centuries it was thought to be impossible to construct a 10 x 10 Græco-Latin bi-square; Euler even hypothesised its non-existence. It was not until 1960 that Bose, Parker, and Shrikhande succeeded in obtaining a specimen.

Figure 4

At the end of these laborious permutations I found myself with a kind of "schedule of obligations": for every chapter, it listed 42 themes that must appear in it. Thus it was necessary in chapter 23 to use quotations from Jules Verne and Joyce. The quotation (actually quotations) from Verne concerns the library (page 134), which is Captain Nemo's, and the list of tools (ibid.), which reproduces the contents of the miraculous trunk in The Mysterious Island. The house Leopold Bloom dreams about at the end of Ulysses has become the doll's house on page 135[27] [See next page].

See also ●Acrostic, ●Clinamen, and ●Minutes of the Oulipo (3), where Perec presented *Life* to the group for the first time.

8,4   Lge. Apt. on 1st. floor left (next to 20)   *Moreau, ch. 23*

Going up
Classification
Verne (I. M. p.224, V. M. L. p.75)
Joyce (p.637)
2 persons
Occupants
Appointment books

False {
Dreaming
Panelling
Woollen carpets
Post-war antiquity 19th c.
Middle East   ?
} *Suez Canal*

Missing {
Chinese style   Missing
Library
~10 pages
Physiology in 1860
}

New-born
Cat
Coal
Solid colour
Wool
Red
Stockings, socks
Medallions
Art book
Las Meniñas (Maria Margarita of Austria)
Moby Dick
Tea
Zakuskis
Mantel-clocks, clocks
Crosswords
Astonishment
Posters
Triangle
Parallelepiped
Indoor plant
Copper, pewter
Missing in 4
False in 3

Sickle
Punishment   [Trans IW]

●**Limerick.** Since the limerick seems to be at home primarily in English,[28] and since it hardly qualifies as an Oulipian type of form, little use of it has been made by the group. (Luc Étienne's 19 limericks are simply an essay in acclimatising the form to the French language.) The limerick clearly requires a supplementary restriction to give its familiar pattern a new sense. One example of such an added restriction can be seen in ●BO70; another appears in the following two limericks, supplied by Martin Gardner (the author's name has been lost):

> There was a young man from Peru
> Whose limericks stopped at line two.
>
> There was a young man from Verdun.

A different kind of restriction, ●*semantic* rather than *syntactic*, is manifest in Tennyson's improvised response to a remark at a dinner party that it was impossible to compose a serious limerick:

> There are people now living in Erith
> Whom nobody seeth or heareth,
>   And down by the marge
>   Of the river, a barge
> That nobody roweth nor steereth.

[HM]

●**Limit, going for the.** The question of the minimum limits of literary form was of particular interest to François Le Lionnais. He devoted two articles to its exploration. This first is from ●CP1:

◯François Le Lionnais *Three Cases of Pushing Things to the Limit*

1. A poem comprising a single word:

FENNEL

2. A poem comprising a single letter:

T.

3. A poem based on punctuation:

:

I, 2, 3, 4, 5.
6; 7; 8; 9; I0.
I2?
I I!

Concerning (2), Le Lionnais wrote: "I fear that the reduction of a poem to a single letter may lie on the far side of the acceptable limit. But there's nothing wrong with having fun, is there? In any event, the author has no desire to repeat his exploit. He abandons to 25 of his colleagues the task of establishing the complete set of 26 poems based — in the case of the Roman alphabet — on this principle." An explication of the poem appears in ●BO51. [HM]

○François Le Lionnais *The Anteantepenultimate*

[An account of the last meeting of the Oulipo's co-founders, originally published in ●BO4.]

For fifteen years or so, Raymond and I kept coming back to the question, how few words can make a poem? A first category comprises poems that only (and this is intentional) the poet and a few intimates at most can understand and enjoy. References to the poet's life, surroundings, and obsessions — these constitute the domain of one or two words. A second category contains poems that evoke a (cultural) emotion for a chosen few by means of certain key words or titles, like Durandal, nevermore, prince, virgin, fatal interview, Blessed Damozel, hollow men, last duchess, blithe spirit, belle dame sans merci, hounds of spring, multitudinous seas. *This appears to be the domain reserved for less than five words.*

Scholars will one day assemble an international anthology

of poems of few words. Although the exact reference escapes me, I vaguely recollect a western 'four-worder'. For four to six words or thereabouts, I suppose that a fair number of examples exist in the Far East (China, Japan, Korea). It is perfectly natural for the Oulipo to study the invention, legitimacy and effectiveness of 'less-than-five-worders'. More generally, examining the validity of poems comprising from no words to an infinite number of them, is a task worth undertaking and pursuing scientifically.[29] *It would benefit from the contributions of mathematical physics and system theory: temperature, entropy, enthalpy, calefaction, torrefaction, dissipative structure, and so forth.*

In his hospital room, alluding to a specific and not very significant detail of my previous visit, Raymond said, "It was on the antepenultimate day that you last came." His speech was slow, feeble, and laboured, as if pronouncing (although not finding) each word demanded an effort. I replied, "I see that you're still partial to the word 'antepenultimate'. It's certainly material for a one-word poem. But how would you classify it? As one meant for those who revere Mallarmé and 'the antepenultimate is dead'? Or as one of the less clear cut sort destined for the greater number of those (including Mallarmé himself before he wrote his work) who are overcome by the rare and precious quality of a word stripped of all context?"

Without answering my question, he uttered a weak, affectionate laugh, and we pursued our mini-conversation no further. It was the last one we were to have, and it fell on Raymond Queneau's anteantepenultimate day.

30 November 1976 [Trans IW]

See ●BO46 & 85; the ●*only the wholly the.*

●**Line-stretcher's restriction.** See ●Larding; ●BO14 & 41.

●**Lipogram.** A text that excludes one or more letters of the alphabet. The ingenuity demanded by the restriction clearly varies in proportion to the frequency of the letter or letters excluded. After all, most short and many extended passages of literature are unintentional lipograms. No *b, c, j, k, q, v, w,* or *z* appears in the preceding sentence. The demands of the procedure escalate when any vowel or when consonants like *n*, *r*, *s*, or *t* are chosen for elimination.

In *Lipo* (●CP3), Georges Perec traces the history of the lipogram from its origins (a work by Lasos of Hermione, 6th century B.C.) to recent times. In passing he judiciously observes that, unlike such procedures as the ●acrostic or the ●tautogram, the lipogram passes unnoticed unless it is announced. This even proved true for his novel *La ●Disparition*, a lipogram in *e* that is no doubt the most remarkable in all literature.

Examples

Lipogram in *c, d, f, g, j, k, l, m, p, v, w, x, y, z*:
> To be or not to be: that is the question

Lipogram in *a* (&c.):
> To be or not to be: this is the question

Lipogram in *e*:
> Survival or oblivion: that is our quandary

Lipogram in *t*:
> Being or non-being: such is my dilemma

Many other Oulipian procedures are lipograms in which the letters excluded are determined by specific rules: ●beautiful in-law, ●beautiful outlaw, ●epithalamium, ●left-handed lipogram, ●prisoner's restriction, ●threnodials, ●univocalism. See also ●BO23, 34, 46, 50, 56, 91 & 92; and ●Minutes of the Oulipo (4). [HM]

●**Lipolexe.** A term that does not exist in English (where *lipolex*, in so far as *lexical* refers to root meaning independent of grammatical function, would signify something different): the exclusion from a text of one or more parts of speech, such as nouns, verbs, or adjectives. The word was used by Queneau in discussing the poems in *Morale élémentaire*. Oulipian examples include François Le Lionnais's *La rien que la toute la* (see *the ●only the wholly the*) and ○Noël Arnaud's *Adverbities of Eros* (see Restricted ●vocabulary). [HM]

See also ●BO56; ●Elementary morality

●**Liponymy.** The exclusion of a particular word or words from a text. Oulipians have never used liponymy *per se*, although many procedures are liponymic in effect. (●lipograms clearly exclude words that contain forbidden letters). The term is included here because of the work of Doug Nufer, a non-Oulipian American writer who has succeeded in creating an Oulipian landmark. His novel *Never Again* (1996) was composed under a restriction one might call *progressive liponymy* (the author's name for it is "rolling liponymy"): once used, a word can never be used again. Nufer applies this ruthlessly simple and mind-boggling idea to a story that fills 200 typewritten pages, of which excerpts of the first and the 101st pages follow. [HM]

When the racetrack closed forever I had to get a job. Want ads made wonderlands, founding systems barely imagined. Adventure's imperative ruled nothing could repeat. Redirections dictated rigorously, freely. Go anywhere new: telephone boiler-rooms, midnight grocery shooting galleries, prosthetic limb assembly plants, hazardous waste-removal sites, flower delivery, flour milling, million-dollar bunko schemes. Do anything once; then, best of all, never again.

No more gambling, horseplay, poker. Hyperordered strictures posit antipredictability, perhaps.

"References?" Herr Trollenburg interviews, cocked brow adjusting monocle glinting somber intent.

"Certainly." ...   [page 1]

Balmy palms, bougainvillea, hummingbirds, lime/cerrano-spiced braziered turtle fillets; slashburnt extrafoliate growths tingeing rotten animals, dungs; encantadores bandstanding full-frontal lewdity afore leering mariachis; porchsitter expatriates dabble picturesquely, interiorising high-noted cantina sonata futilisms soulfully essayed after scrubbing peons worked furiously, earning centavos/hour buffing seats whereon pawnbrokered excellencies preside: Mexico. ...   [p.101]

●**Lipossible.** See ●Slenderising.

●**Literature.** In *Lipo* (●CP3: "A Short History of the Oulipo"), Jean Lescure records some pertinent remarks made by the founders of the Oulipo about its relation to literature.

"The essence of our aims remained literature, and François Le Lionnais wrote, 'Every literary work is constructed with as its starting-point an inspiration... that must adapt as best it can to a series of restrictions or procedures.' What the Oulipo intended to show was that these restrictions are welcome, bountiful, and indeed literature itself. It proposed discovering new ones designated as *structures*...

"Jean Queval asked if we were in favour of *fous littéraires* [outsider writers]. François Le Lionnais answered, 'We're not against them. But what interests us primarily is the vocation of literature.' Raymond Queneau clarified the point: 'There is no literature that is not intentional.'...

"We can... connect this notion with Raymond Queneau's statement in *Odile*, 'Someone who is truly inspired is never inspired, he is always so'... This sentence implied the revolutionary conception of literature as something objective and opened it up to every possible kind of operation. In short, like mathematics, literature could be *explored*."

Marcel Bénabou's brief entry for *literature* in the ●*Petit Norbert* concludes:

"In combining the adjective *potential* with the noun *literature* and so creating the concept of *potential literature*, the Oulipo has freed literature from its shackles and given it its maximum scope. Far from being an element in the set of literature, as ill-informed critics still seem to think, potential literature is itself the set of which all the literatures that exist are the elements." [Trans HM]

●*Littérature définitionelle.* See ●Definitional literature.

●**Llull, Ramon.** (c. 1232–1316) Born on the island of Mallorca

only two years after its reconquest from the Muslims, at the age of thirty visions led Llull to exchange a dissolute youth for a life dedicated to the spread of Christianity. Nine years of study were followed by a career of travelling and writing (some 265 works) in constant attempts to convert unbelievers and to reform Christian society.

Since previous such attempts, invariably based on the use of authorities, had foundered on the questions of which authorities were acceptable and how to interpret those that were, he

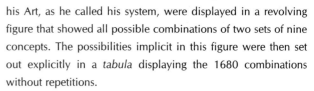

decided to base his apologetics on certain ideas acceptable to any monotheistic religion, on ethical concepts familiar to all medieval people, and to fundamental notions of Greek science and philosophy, the common heritage of the learned members of the three religious communities of his day. He constructed proofs by investigating the consequences of chains of comparisons of these components. He not only used binary combinations as bases for his proofs but also ternary combinations which, in later versions of his Art, as he called his system, were displayed in a revolving figure that showed all possible combinations of two sets of nine concepts. The possibilities implicit in this figure were then set out explicitly in a *tabula* displaying the 1680 combinations without repetitions.

These ●combinatorial techniques, with their diagrams and implications for a "science of discovery", fascinated Renaissance thinkers such as Giordano ●Bruno. In the 17th century ●Leibniz's first published work, *De arte combinatoria*, was an attempt to work out the possibilities of Llull's combinatorics. It yielded techniques that Leibniz would later build on in his attempts to create a universal and scientifically pure language.

[Anthony Bonner]

See ●Lescurean permutations, Anticipatory ●plagiary.

●*LSD.* See ●Semo-definitional literature.

In some respects *Nouvelles Impressions* anticipates hypertext, and computer technology may well have provided the definitive means: a hypertext English translation is noted in the entry on Roussel and his methods.

The machines constructed in the 1980s by the architect Daniel Libeskind are exemplary. Libeskind constructed three machines, intended to function symbolically as well as mechanically. The first (left, overleaf) was modelled on that of Ramelli and was constructed using entirely medieval methods. The last, a machine "for writing architecture", which Libeskind at one point describes as "a contribution to Roussel scholarship",[31] was a complex mechanism of 2,662 parts (bottom; the remaining one, a memory machine, is not illustrated); it has provided the elements for the E.T.A. Hoffmann garden outside Libeskind's biggest completed project to date, the Jewish Museum in Berlin. All three machines were destroyed in a gallery fire.

●**Machines for reading.** The invention of the first reading machine is credited to Agostino Ramelli in the sixteenth century; it was intended to facilitate the reading of several books at once.[30] Although this invention might not appear particularly useful, there are certain works whose complexity seems to require just such mechanical assistance. Machines have been constructed to read two specific works, both of particular interest to the Oulipo, and whose structures make them difficult to grasp, namely Queneau's ○● *100,000,000,000,000 Poems* and Raymond ●Roussel's *Nouvelles Impressions d'Afrique.*

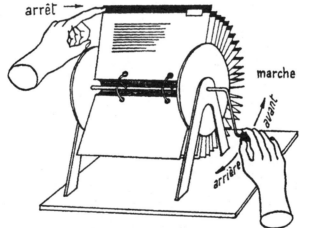

arrêt →

marche

avant

arrière

Although early attempts to facilitate the reading of Queneau's sonnet sequence (the book version is difficult to manipulate) centred on computers, a more recent attempt returns to mechanical means. The machine constructed by Jean-Michel Bragard and Robert Kayser (who is fleetingly visible in the main picture overleaf) featured in a plaquette published by *Temps Mêlés* (1994). [AB]

Jacques Brunius seems to have been the first to design a machine for reading *Nouvelles Impressions* (exhibited at the 1937 Surrealist exhibition). Unfortunately neither the machine nor a photograph of it survives. Juan Esteban Fassio actually constructed a simple reading machine in 1964. His drawings of it for the Roussel issue of *Bizarre* (34/35, 1964) give an adequate idea of its *modus operandi* (see above).

●**Machines for writing.** In the broadest sense of the word, every Oulipian technique can be thought of as a writing machine. Several actual devices have attracted the Oulipo's attention, however. See ●ALAMO, the ●Computer and the Oulipo, ●Llull, ●Minutes of the Oulipo (1), ●Roussel; not to mention the machine in Kafka's *In the Penal Colony*, in which writing, punishment, and death are linked in a more literal manner than is customary. [AB]

●**Manifestos (of the Oulipo).** There have been three Oulipian manifestos, all by the group's co-founder, François Le Lionnais. The first appeared in ●CP1, the second in *Lipo* (●CP3), the third constituted ●BO30 (see also ●BO85). Complete translations of the first two manifestos appear in *Oulipo Laboratory* (●CP9).

●**Mathematician's presentation, the.** See ●Pumectation and ●*Introduction* §51.

●**Mathews, Harry.** Elected to the Oulipo in 1972.

Born in New York in 1930, Harry Mathews has spent much of his life in Europe, particularly in France. His friendship with Georges Perec, whom he met in Paris in 1970, led to his encounter with the Oulipo. In 1994, together with Lynn Crawford, he edited an issue of ●*New Observations* (New York) devoted to the Oulipo and ■Oupeinpo that provided the impetus for the compilation of the present volume.

Oulipian works: *The Conversions* (partly Oulipian; Random House, NY, 1962, reprinted by Dalkey Archive Press, Normal, IL, 1997); *Tlooth* (partly Oulipian; Doubleday, NY, 1966; Dalkey Archive Press, 1997); *The Sinking of the Odradek Stadium* (Harper and Row, NY, 1975, reprinted by Carcanet, Manchester, 1985); ●*Trial Impressions* (Burning Deck, Providence, 1977, reprinted in *Armenian Papers: Selected Poems 1954–1984*, Princeton University Press, 1987, and in *A Mid-Season Sky: Poems 1954–1991*, Carcanet, 1992; these collections include other Oulipian poems); *Out of Bounds* (Burning Deck, 1989, reprinted in *A Mid-Season Sky*); ●*Selected Declarations of Dependence* (Z Press, Calais, Vermont, 1977, reprinted by Sun & Moon Press, LA, 1996); ●*Cigarettes* (Weidenfeld and Nicolson, London & NY, 1987); *Country Cooking from Central France* in *Country Cooking and Other Stories* (Burning Deck, 1980, translated into French as ★Bibliothèque Oucuipienne 1); *The Way Home* in *The Way Home, Collected Longer Prose* (Atlas Press, 1989 & 1998); *The American Experience* (Atlas Press, 1991); *The* ●*Journalist* (partly Oulipian; Godine, Boston, 1994; Dalkey Archive Press, 1997).

●BO4, 5, 16, 23, 51, 54, 55, 57, 70, 91, 92, 111, 118 and ●CP12, 13 & 16.

●**Mathews's algorithm.** *An algorithm is a set of rules that, applied in a prescribed order to a set of data, produces a particular result, no matter what the data may be. A simple algorithm is the method of adding numbers: starting at the right, add up the numbers in the column of units, note the number to be carried over, repeat the process in the column of tens, and continue to the last column on the left.*

—François Le Lionnais, in Bouvier & George, *Dictionnaire des mathématiques*.

The name *Mathews's algorithm* was attributed by the Oulipo in the mid '70s to a structure presented by Harry Mathews.

What follows is a simplified description.

1. Operation

The mechanism is based on ●permutation, or shifting. To begin with an example that uses only letters:

Set down one over the other the following 4-letter words, underlining their initial letters:

T̲	I	N	E
S̲	A	L	E
M̲	A	L	E
V̲	I	N	E

Now, leaving the first line unchanged, perform the following shifts: the second line moves one position to the right (imagine the e of *sale* reappearing on the left to produce *esal*); the third line moves two positions to the right (*lema*); the fourth line moves three positions to the right (*inev*). This gives a new set of 4-letter lines:

T̲	I	N	E
E	S̲	A	L
L	E	M̲	A
I	N	E	V̲

Reading the columns of this set *upwards* starting with the underlined letters, we find four new words: *tile, sine, mane, vale*.

If instead of shifting to the right, we move the last three lines one, two, and three places left, then read the columns *downwards* (still starting with the initial letters), we obtain 4 more words: *tale, vile, mine, sane*.

The algorithm functions in this way no matter what materials are used. Basic units — different in identity but similar in function — are superposed so as to form lines and columns. The number of these lines and columns is appropriately determined by the user, whose only other intervention is to shift each line right or left one unit farther than the preceding line.

Reading the results must always start from the first unit of the original lines, upwards when the shift is to the right, downwards when it is to the left.

2. Materials

Any material that can be represented symbolically can be used with the algorithm: numbers, syllables, words, phrases, sentences, paragraphs, characters, situations, themes, concepts.

An example using groups of words:

Frustrated members	*of the Cabinet*	*were found conspiring in*	*local massage parlours.*
Drivers	*from the Sanita-tion Department*	*will go on strike against*	*the new garbage helicopters*
Six terrorists	*of the Keep Kids Kleen Klub*	*have planted bombs in*	*sexually integrated rest-rooms.*
Female imper-sonators	*not licensed by their union*	*are not allowed into*	*nursing schools.*

After a shift left we read:

Frustrated members	*from the Sanita-tion Department*	*have planted bombs in*	*nursing schools.*
Female imper-sonators	*of the Cabinet*	*will go on strike against*	*sexually integrated rest-rooms.*
Six terrorists	*not licensed by their union*	*were found conspiring in*	*the new garbage helicopters.*
Drivers	*of the Keep Kids Kleen Klub*	*are not allowed into*	*local massage parlours.*

(A shift right tells yet another story.)

A detailed presentation of the algorithm, including many examples of its syntactic, semantic, and analytic uses, can be found in Motte (●CP7), as well as in *Atlas* (●CP6). [HM]

●**Measures.** This term applies to procedures dependent on the length of syllables or words.

1. Syllable length — the number of letters in a syllable — can be taken towards minimum or maximum ●limits. This example of a heroic couplet, where the two lines have the same metrical length, illustrates both possibilities. 'Thin' or 'thick' poems (and prose, for that matter) can be similarly produced.

After 1492[32]
Fraught judgements crushed the extinguished Spanish Jew.

The record in French for the spatially shortest ●alexandrine was set by Georges Perec. Twelve syllables are notated in four letters:

W, w, w, w.
(Doublevé, doublevé, doublevé, doublevé)

There seems to be no alphabetic equivalent for an iambic pentameter. 1,715 (one thousand seven hundred and fifteen) is one of many numerical possibilities.

See ●Sonnet of variable length.

2. Syllables (and words) can also be of unvarying length, as in the following poem on a traditional theme comprising 4 stanzas of 4 lines of 4 words of 4 letters:

```
Mark this bare fact
Even seen with tact
Fair face will wane
From year into year

None must then rely
Upon hope when high
Time that rude jane
Will turn into fear

Your best kept look
Your most read book
Your long held gain
Your hard shed tear
```

```
Then come last days
With pure zero gaze
That mock next pain
That hold life near
```

3. From a source text, a new text can be derived whose words have the same length as the original's.

Example
Day was drooping on a fine evening in March as a brown barouche passed through the wrought-iron gates of Hare-Hatch House onto the open highway.

Ronald Firbank *Valmouth*, opening sentence

Why? Let religion be. I want lobster at lunch. So I plead mightily guilty. Respect our anguish-clad bonds at very least today. Also our full wallets. [HM]

See ●Avalanche, ●Prisoner's restriction, ●Slenderising, ●Snowball, ●Melting snowball; ●BO26.

●**Melting snowball.** A text in which each word has one letter less than the preceding one, and the last word only one letter:

Incontrovertible
sadomasochistic
orthographical
compositional
restrictions
insistently
discipline
grandiose
sixteens
initial
hubris
right
down
now
to
O

A melting snowball can follow an expanding snowball to produce a *diamond snowball*. [HM]

See also ●Measures, ●Snowball.

●**Members of the Oulipo.** (Past and present) See individual entries for: Noël Arnaud, Marcel Bénabou, Jacques Bens, Claude Berge, André Blavier, Paul Braffort, Italo Calvino, François Caradec, Bernard Cerquiglini, Ross Chambers, Stanley Chapman, Marcel Duchamp, Jacques Duchateau, Luc Étienne, Paul Fournel, Michelle Grangaud, Jacques Jouet, Latis, François Le Lionnais, Jean Lescure, Hervé Le Tellier, Harry Mathews, Michèle Métail, Ian Monk, Oskar Pastior, Georges Perec, Raymond Queneau, Jean Queval, Pierre Rosenstiehl, Jacques Roubaud, Albert-Marie Schmidt.

Members elected since the first edition of the *Compendium*: Valérie Beaudouin, Frédéric Forte, Anne F. Garréta, Olivier Salon.

●**Métail, Michèle.** Elected to the Oulipo in 1975. (See the group photo on p.207 for a portrait.)

Born in Paris in 1951, Michèle Métail has written much but published little, having since 1971 circulated her texts through the medium of *oral publication*. This is particularly significant in the case of ●*Possessive Phrases*, an "infinite poem" comprising for the time being over 20,000 lines. In her view, her work with the spoken voice can in fact only be realised in public readings. She has also created many works of visual poetry.

Oulipian works: ●BO21, 33, 34, 35, 39 & 50.

●**Minutes of the Oulipo.** The monthly meetings of the Oulipo have been (and are) minuted in greater or lesser detail. We append here four sets of minutes dating from 1961, 1966, 1972 and 1990. The first was published in Bens (●CP4) and dates from the Oulipo's period of close association with the ●College of 'Pataphysics, the second as ●BO42. This is the first publication of the other two.

See also ●Animal languages.

The Oulipo in session, 20 April 1964 (from ●CP2). Clockwise from Raymond Queneau (whose top hat indicates that he is presiding): Duchateau, Berge, Arnaud, Lescure, Le Lionnais (in sailor's cap).

○1. Jacques Bens *Minutes of the Meeting of 28 August 1961*

Paris in August

On 17 August, in his garden in Boulogne-sur-Seine, the Regent of Scacchic Strategy, Tactics, and Chrononomics[33] and Founder-President of the Oulipo welcomed and took suitable care of his likable colleagues. We were shown around the property, we admired the cedar, plumbed the well, gravely paid our respects to Lady Godiva,[34] and then downed kirs that had been aptly mixed.[35]

Present in their order of arrival: Raymond Queneau, Jean Lescure, and Jacques Bens; Jacques Duchateau; finally Latis and Noël Arnaud. As well, of course, as the above-mentioned Regent and host.

In the midst of general emotion Latis unfolded an immense and magnificent portrait of His Magnificence,[36] set and printed (heliographically) by the Oulipo's correspondent in Middlesex, Stanley Chapman. Pinned to the wall, the portrait followed the subsequent discussion, its attention sustained by a gentle breeze.

The host and organiser of the festivities distributed chairs, glasses, and refreshments and provided the president of the meeting with a gong from Niou-Delly[37] and a spanking-new top hat.

The president of the meeting, chosen by the alphabetic order ●POURQI, was Raymond Queneau, who donned the top hat and called for silence by banging his gong like the Arthur Rank athlete.

The president was the first to speak. He informed us of a letter from Monsieur Jean Cocteau (of the Acadéfraise) in which he claims — referring to the postface of ●100,000,000,000,000 Poems — a right of priority in the composition of poems using other people's lines. Bens astutely remarked that if the word ●cento existed before Cocteau, the thing itself certainly existed.

Latis: Besides, Tristan Derême wrote centos.

Bens: So did Charles Trenet, with La Fontaine's fables.

Latis: And Jacques Prévert.

Noël Arnaud then remarked that the day's agenda was well filled —

Le Lionnais: I trust you will be, too.

— and that consequently there was good reason not to dawdle.

Raymond Queneau again spoke to tell us that Monsieur Starynkevitch (of the SEPSEA) had sent in some sonnets drawn from the 100,000,000,000,000 Poems that had been composed on the electronic machine CAB 500. The hope was expressed that Monsieur Starynkevitch will specify the method used and that the choice of lines was not left to chance.

At this point Latis opened the "Oulipo Dossier" [i.e. ●CP1].

Latis: Let me begin by insisting that the works presented are of interest only if the methods used are clearly defined in advance.

(Agreement.)

Latis: Another point: in his contributions, Regent Le Lionnais uses the expression "experimental literature". Should it be kept?

Le Lionnais: I used the term before "potential literature" existed. I see no problem with replacing the former with the latter.

Arnaud: Furthermore, it seems that the word experimental has been, so to speak, historically defined, and it would be useful to stress the difference.

(Agreement.)

Latis: Now for details. Queval's contribution on "The Laws of the Article" is not very convincing. Perhaps it's too brief an account of the method. Could we ask Queval to revise these texts?

Bens: It's already been done.

Le Lionnais: Gentlemen, help yourself to salad.

Queneau: The matter goes without saying.

Le Lionnais: Gentlemen, without seeming to, we're raising a fundamental question here: that of our limits. It is possible to compose texts that are poetic, Surrealist, unconventional, or whatever, without their being potential. Now where we are concerned, it is this last characteristic that matters. It's the only one that should govern our choice.

(Hear hear! Hear hear! Hear hear! Hear hear! Hear hear! Hear hear! on every side.)

Latis: Next, Queneau's contribution. Since the preface to 100,000,000,000,000 Poems is out of date, it would be nice if the Transcendent Satrap wrote another introductory text. The remark applies equally to the Regent of SSTC.

Queneau: Then see Le Lionnais!

All: You promised!

Queneau: Really?

Bens (joining deed to word): I invoke the texts.

Latis: Haha! Scripta manent.

Queneau: I won't let scripta have the floor.

Arnaud: The planned preface and postface will be missed. It's crucial they be replaced.

Le Lionnais: Perhaps a short text —

All: Oh!

Le Lionnais: — signed Lionneau or Quennais...

Arnaud: Since the publication of 100,000,000,000,000 Poems we have every right to think that Le Lionnais and Queneau have something to say to future generations.

Queneau: I agree to a SHORT text. I think we'll have to go through with it. But it's up to Le Lionnais to begin.

187

Arnaud: *Don't forget he's our founder.*

Queneau: *I'll do a postface. Short, but post.*

Le Lionnais: *So be it.*

During a short improvised interlude, Jean Lescure tried to grab the presidential headgear by surprise. But the president re-established order with the prudence of St. Vitus and the authority of the elephant.[38]

Latis: *Now let's turn to the contributions of our host and Regent. (a) Centos. What isn't obvious is the hidden method at work in them. It might be better to present them as a pre-potential event.*

Le Lionnais: *All right.*

Lescure: *But, in truth, is there actually a method?*

Le Lionnais: *You know, those poems are forty years old. The coherence I was looking for at the time wasn't the kind (or the kinds) the Oulipo can provide. Still, when composing centos, we can set up methods that lead to other coherences. Obviously this could only be done with a good-sized inventory of* ●*alexandrines.*

Arnaud: *At all events, I think these texts should be published in the Dossier, even if they don't exactly correspond to Oulipian definitions. We might assign them a term of a historical nature, like "the cottage-industry phase of pre-potential literature". (It would therefore be a kind of "experimental" literature.)*

Latis: *That implies adding some window dressing.*

Queneau: *Of course (gesturing towards Le Lionnais opposite).*

Arnaud: *That might allow us to cite the Cocteaus and other sorts of predecessors.*

(At this point Madame Regent made an entry both remarkable and remarked.)

Latis: *On to (b), Poems consisting of* ●*one letter (in the event, T) or of* ●*punctuation. Here again I don't see the ghost of a method. We need some explanatory window dressing; otherwise readers will be justified in thinking that these are arbitrary procedures.*

Bens: *Why not classify (b) with (a)? It can also qualify as pre-*

potential literature.

Le Lionnais: *The problem has always tormented me. We should acknowledge that there are poems of great potentiality and others of small potentiality. I think it not without interest to present cases of Potential Literature without much of a future, to indicate roads that will not lead very far.*

Arnaud: *Wonderful! It would be an excellent thing for the Regent to put that in writing.*

All: *Agreed.*

Queneau: *May I point out that the 100,000,000,000,000 Poems are in exactly the same situation as the poems of one letter, only with a few more possibilities? (Precisely 99,999,999,999,974 additional possibilities. Prov. Sec.'s note.)*

Latis: *So let's proceed to the poems composed with punctuation marks.*

Arnaud: *Personally I was enchanted: the inversion 12,11 produces a poetic effect of explosion and liberation.*

All: *Hear, hear!*

Latis: *— but we might perhaps consider —*

Le Lionnais: *It's obvious: in every case the window needs more dressing!*

Latis: *That is of course our dearest wish. Well, moving on to the final point: (c)* ●*"Boolean" poems. Isn't something missing here? The choice of common and uncommon elements doesn't seem fully justified. I don't know whether my objection is valid —*

Le Lionnais: *There you touch on our fundamental problem. The aim of Potential Literature is to provide future writers with techniques that will give them room for inspiration. Hence the need for a certain freedom. Nine or ten centuries ago, when a producer of potential literature proposed the sonnet form, he left, via several mechanical procedures, room for choice. Starting with the rule that I defined, I've taken the liberty —*

Latis: *So we do have to revise the presentation!*

Queneau: *As Grandgousier said to Gargantua, "My son, I see much work ahead of you..."*

Latis: *And on to Lescure, whose contribution (a) On* ●*N + 7 is perfect.*

Lescure: *Whew!*

Latis: *I can't say as much for (b),* ●*Permutations. Its*

presentation is obscure — obscure because not functional enough. (Some technical remarks followed whose particulars the Prov. Sec. was unable to grasp.) Furthermore, what are the references for this work? We have to have them.

Lescure: The beginning of Le Chiendent.[39]

Queneau: You didn't get very far.

Latis: Finally, (c) Redundancies (a collaboration with the work of the Transcendent Satrap); again, it would be a good idea to rework the explanation of the method. And especially to suppress the intolerable attacks on Datary J. Bens. (Prov. Sec.'s note: I believe it my duty to underscore these words.)[40]

Queneau: Lescure, we'll be publishing something but not everything — eh?

Lescure: Yeah.

Latis: Now for Chapman. He's sent us two Shakespeare sonnets rewritten backwards. Since I rarely visit the langue anglaise, I'd be grateful if the Transcendent Satrap would kindly read them and give us his opinion.

Queneau (after reading): When inverted, sonnets by Shakespeare become heterosexual. But it strikes me as excellent work.

Arnaud: Can it be published in the Dossier?

Queneau: Very low potentiality.

Lescure: So in that case: first, Shakespeare's sonnets — OK; second, as for potentiality in English, forget it.

(Revolted by this display of crude anglophobia, the Prov. Sec. refused to take notes for three minutes and forty-five seconds, which explains the gap between the last sentence and the next.)

Le Lionnais: Gentlemen, I've had an inspiration.

(All rise and doff their hats.)

Le Lionnais: Please be seated. Gentlemen, I've just realised that the method applied by Chapman to Shakespeare might be perfectly sterile for some poets but magnificently fertile for others. So I propose that we explore French and other literatures to discover invertible and non-invertible poets. I also propose that we produce some easily invertible poems. Chapman's contribution is of interest in so far as it involves us in such study.

Queneau: It would make a good machine. We'd set it to work on Les Trophées[41] and it would invert them for us. Then we could tell, couldn't we?

Latis: I must apologise. To you, and also — via you and the Channel — to Chapman. I've just reread his covering letter and it fully justifies his contribution. So I propose adding it to the Dossier.[42]

(Diverse approval.)

Latis: Finally, here's what our beloved Datary has sent us — as you already know, his ●Inventories. What in his presentation he calls "significant elements of language" — isn't that what we more commonly call "parts of speech"?

Queneau: It's the word "parts" that bothers him.

Latis: Well, what bothers me is the arbitrariness of the choice of definite and indefinite articles. The choice is arbitrary.

Bens: That's just what I say in the presentation.

Latis: Not clearly enough. Or at least you don't explain why the possibility of making such a choice exists.

Bens: Allow me to refer you to our host's recent remarks about freedom.

Latis: You should repeat it. Point out, for example, that words are used differently from the way they were in the original text.

Bens (insolently): Yeah.

Latis: As applied to Galois,[43] especially, your method is very obscure.

Bens (in despair): But it's the same!

Latis: That isn't sufficiently apparent.

(Prov. Sec.'s note: At this point in the minutes I find, enclosed in a border, the following item: Lescure: "Love has to be reinvented." I can make little sense of this untimely interruption. I leave it as it stands.)

Galois is read.

Le Lionnais: If you'll allow me a point of detail, Galois wrote "Je n'ai pas le tems" not because he was ignorant of spelling but because that was in fact the spelling of the time. I should also like to add this: you've raised a fundamental problem here, actually two: (a) Li[ttérature]Po[tentielle] doesn't always expect to achieve quality. It makes experiments. (b) There are two LiPos, one analytic, one synthetic. I'll explain.

All: Yes!

Le Lionnais: Analytic LiPo looks for possibilities in writers who never thought about them. (Example: centos.) Synthetic LiPo constitutes LiPo's great mission: that of opening up new possibilities unknown to earlier writers. (Example: Boolean poems.) In the Dossier we have examples of both.

Latis: That is exactly the theme of the preface we expect of you. And I'll gladly state that the presentations of the various methods must be essentially analytical.

Latis: Now for those texts that do not as yet exist. Such as, for example, the Berge-Duchateau method.

(This is a solemn moment. For the first time those present are about to experience the sound of Duchateau's voice. This will be, in fact, the first time during a meeting that he has opened his mouth. But will he open it?)[44]

Duchateau: I have only an equation to offer:

$$(BERGE + DUCHATEAU) - BERGE = 0$$

Bens: We dare not draw the conclusion.

Duchateau: The job is in hand. Others are, too.

Arnaud: Just explain the method. Tell us what you're doing.

Queneau: Be a good fellow, Duchateau, give us a method. An unusable gimmick, a non-recursive story, an incredible wotsit. Won't you do that for us, hmm?

Duchateau: I can't give you an example.

Queneau: There'll be no example — fine!

Le Lionnais: Don't forget, Duchateau (and you too, gentlemen) that the method is self-sufficient. There are methods with no examples. The example is an added pleasure one gives oneself, and the reader.

(A few sneaky souls are waiting for the Founding President[45] to provide an example of a method with no example. But he craftily evades the pitiful trap.)

Arnaud: Duchateau should contribute that. Le Lionnais is quite inspired by it.

(Exhausted, the Prov. Sec. lets out a muffled cry. All present assail him with jibes, except for the Transcendent Satrap, who demands:)

Queneau: I request a productivity bonus for the Prov. Sec. Let's double his stipend.

(Sneers.)

Le Lionnais: Duchateau's and Bens's plan for an ●intersective novel does indeed fill me with joy. The intersective method has always been applied by all writers. An example: the poems of Leconte de Lisle. One realises that a literary school founded by two or three creators does nothing but develop intersections. I've studied them in Zévacco and Fantomas.[46] (But I do read other things as well.) A writer appears on earth — let's pass over his conception and other details — and what does he do? He reads previous writers and starts intersecting. If he doesn't, he's an original creator.

Latis: We certainly know that originality is the opposite of culture.

Queneau: Culture is the opposite of arithmetic. Besides, Duchateau is the Oulipo's bomb-planter. He's a bomb-planting loafer.

Le Lionnais: At all events, what Duchateau intends to do systematically is what others do without intending to.

Queneau: Sagan's latest book is very significant in this respect. It's an intersection between her previous novels.

Le Lionnais: All this falls nicely within the purview of the Oulipo, whose task is to reveal what makes literature function.

Queneau: Obviously Duchateau should be the one to study the Sagan phenomenon. We entrust Sagan to Duchateau.

Arnaud: Duchateau en Suède!

Latis: Or la vie de chateau![47]

Duchateau: All right, well, I agree to explain the intersective method.

Latis: And Arnaud?

All: Ah!

Arnaud: Don't let's forget Schmidt, whose work is perfect. In fact, that's why we haven't discussed it.

Queneau: And Arnaud?

Arnaud: I was hoping simply to present Le Roux's alphabetical play.

All: *Yes. Well... All right. Pretty skimpy. Not very enterprising.*

Latis: *There are dozens of alphabetical dramas.*

Queneau: *There's a collection of poems by Louise de Vilmorin where there's lots of stuff like that.*

Arnaud: *I protest. The problem isn't one of producing an alphabetical drama but of publishing it, that is, of making it one's own work. No one but Le Roux has published such a text. You're bringing the case of* Ubu roi *back into question.*

(Consternation.)

Queneau: *Quite right. In any case, and by way of analogy, there have been any number of nutcases with their own little idea of how the cosmos works. A certain Newton published his. People still mention it.*

Le Lionnais: *A solution must be found.*

Lescure: *It's true that publication can rescue a work from the limbo of folklore.*

Le Lionnais: *I'm now going to speak on a question I would have preferred to raise at the start of this session but which the imperatives of a heavy agenda have postponed till the time of dessert. It is the question of discipline. To my mind, meetings like ours can only be efficient if there is a minimum of discipline. Three levels of disciplinary measures should be put at the disposal of the president: (a) a stroke of the gong (brought from Niou-Delly); (b) the death penalty, whose details will be left to presidential discretion; (c) if the death penalty proves insufficient, the president will put on his top hat (after removing it if, prior to the event, he was wearing it).*

Latis: *I demand several clarifications regarding the death penalty. Who will execute it?*

Le Lionnais: *The president will decide this in accordance with the method adopted. The method could include those currently in use in the world and any others he may judge proper to invent on the spur of the moment.*

Lescure: *Aha — carnality!*

Queneau: *Gentlemen, I feel you are straying down most curious paths.*

Latis: *Suppose we recapitulate?*

Queneau: *So recapitulate.*

Latis: *1. Queneau will write a conclusion. 2. Le Lionnais will write a general preface and revise the presentations of his various contributions. 3. Lescure will revise the presentation of his permutations and redundancies. (He should not forget footnote markers.) 4. Bens will revise the presentation of Évariste Galois. 5. Duchateau will tell us about the intersective novel —*

Queneau: *You (Duchateau) should perhaps take a look at the 'short short novels' of science fiction. They're no more than a page in length. I'm having the review* Fiction *sent to Duchateau and Bens at our expense. (My emphasis — Prov. Sec.'s note)*

Arnaud: *Let me remind Duchateau that the method is very important and deserves a very fine explanation.*

Queneau: *There are people who don't work all that much and still make it into the lycée. So I hope that in future —*

Latis: *— 6. Arnaud will present his alphabetical drama. Let me add that these various contributions should reach us before 20 September. (Let's make that a few days later — OK? Prov. Sec.'s note.)*

Queneau: *I'll start work when Duchateau's finished. If we're late, it'll be Duchateau's fault.*

Arnaud: *Have to admit it, the intersective novel is a promising idea.*

Queneau: *My dear fellow, you're done for.*

(The Transcendent Satrap did not say why. His remark thus left the hint of a threat hanging in the air.)

After agreeing to meet next at 12:30 on Friday, 8 September, at Julien et Petit, the assembly broke up amid the customary congratulations, not without casting a final glance at the cedar *of Lebanon, a parting greeting to Lady Godiva, and a final* drink *down the hatch. [Trans IW]*

○2. André Blavier *Circular No. 75 (+/–)*

Meeting of Tuesday, 23 August 1966

(At Le Lionnais's)

Present: *Le Lionnais, Queneau, Arnaud, Latis, Blavier.*
Excused: *Braffort, Berge, Lescure, Duchateau, Bens, all "out of town", and (at the last minute) Queval.*

Le Lionnais is told to preside, Blavier to take notes.

Le Lionnais starts drawing up an agenda.

Arnaud protests at using the word "practice" (praxis) instead of the usual "administration".

Arnaud: *It's ambiguous.*

Le Lionnais: *Exactly.*

Somehow or other the agenda recovers. But:

Latis *(to Le Lionnais): Parenthetically, exactly what is the colour of your dressing-gown?*

Voices: *Cyclamen... wine-coloured... Bordeaux...*

(A dictionary of colours is consulted, one declared by all to be as out of date as it is indispensable.)

As a further diversion, Arnaud garners a mass of information about a certain François-Pierre Caillé. Queneau is the provider.

Madame Skorecz: *When do you want lunch served?*

Queneau: *At twelve forty-seven.*

The proposal is not accepted, but the presidential dressing-gown leads Latis to consider the relative merits of iris- and rose-lovers.

Latis: *Roses! A long story.*

...

Latis: *Roses! A horror story.*

Le Lionnais: *After these civilities and horrors, let's get down to serious business, in other words, the Oulipo, which might as well be called the Ou-peu-po, the Workshop of Few Potentialities. I put on the agenda (the same old agenda) a report on revitalising —*

Arnaud: *???*

Le Lionnais: *— the Oulipo. Two solutions are available: either bringing the Oulipo up to strength whenever a vacancy occurs, or letting it gradually die a natural death, in honourable annihilation.*

Queneau deplored the inadequacy and often absence of minutes. He saw this as one cause of the Oulipo's diminution. Bens's minutes had a perkiness missing from those of his successors, whom no one would dream of criticising and who in fact are the first to agree. At the moment there are no minutes at all, just when oral reports, by Berge and Braffort especially, point to new departures or approaches.

Le Lionnais: *Yes, little by little we were moving from the semantic to the syntactic, but there's a great risk of losing that for want of written notes and minutes.*

Queneau continued his discussion of the Oulipo and literature in general. The most significant creations now come from outside. Even Duchateau's novel, now being read at Gallimard, makes no reference to the Oulipo. A collection by Roubaud is due to be published in January, again by Gallimard.

Arnaud redeplored the lack of minutes and asked Queneau for further details about Roubaud and Duchateau's novel.

Queneau: *Roubaud is a mathematician who has compiled a collection of poems based on the rules of the game of go.[48] The manuscript was submitted to readers unaware of our activities and accepted even before my influence was brought to bear in its favour.[49] As for Duchateau's novel, certain constraints (notably, excluded words) are readily detected, but the underlying structures, which can be presumed both to exist and to be Oulipian, are unrecognisable at a first reading. And nowhere is the method referred to, unlike Bens's procedure with his* ●*irrational sonnets.[50]*

Latis in turn condemned the Oulipians' laziness, while counting himself among the laziest. He felt that under these circumstances there was no reason to be so demanding about future candidates. What he had learned about Roubaud, for example, seemed to justify such an attitude.

Le Lionnais again spoke about Margat (the Mona Lisan). The discussion became general and even confused when it came to defining procedures for admitting and especially for "testing" possible future members. It would be necessary to keep open the possibility of non-acceptance (whenever the trial lunch proved disappointing — here Latis recalled the lunch where

Satrap Ferry was so intimidated), and to be careful not to treat those who had been approached too harshly.

It was decided that Roubaud should be the first of these.

Arnaud: *If his book is coming out in January, we should save face and get in touch with him immediately.*

Queneau: *No later than today.*

Arnaud: *Yesterday!*

Latis: *Satrap Queneau should speak to him without delay and then write an introductory note to a sample from the collection, which can appear in the next* Subsidium.

Returning to Duchateau's ●Zinga huit, *Queneau traced its genesis to an idea of Kahan's* (Zazie dans le Cosmos) *that was passed on to Duchateau. It has now become no more than a three-line infra-marginal note in a novel that has proliferated into a sort of psychology-fiction.*

Latis: *Something inhuman at last. I adore the inhuman.*

In connection with future "conglomerees" (Le Lionnais's terminology) a vow [un vœu] was made.

Queneau: *Un pieu [a* stake].

Arnaud: *What?*

Queneau: *Yes, a vœu pieux [*pious vow]. *(The content of the vow disappeared during this interlude.)*

During dessert, minutes were again discussed. Bens's verve was again sorely missed, as was Duchateau's precision and almost documentary terseness.

Latis: *Still, we'll have to do without them more and more. Bens, and soon Duchateau are turning into — how shall I put it? — contemporary authors. We can't inflict this dimwit's task on them.*

Arnaud suggested writing the minutes in turn.

Sceptical, Latis recommended the secretarial skills of Eva Genestoux.

Le Lionnais: *I could sit next to her and get her accustomed to distinguishing the frivolous from the essential.*

Queneau: *But we'd have to pay for her lunch.*

All: *Let's not be petty!*

They return to the table (one may ask why, since it had been cleared). Latis contributed a Latin couplet capable of 3,295,920

recombinations. He found it in the Dictionnaire des amusements des sciences mathématiques et physiques, Panckoucke, 1792.

Le Lionnais: *I wouldn't want to... but...*

Queneau: *Yes, I think it's in Peignot.*[51]

Latis: *Yes, but this may be the source.*

(They drink.)

Queneau: *I repeat, we ought to take an interest in parlour games.*

Le Lionnais: *Precisely.*

Arnaud: *The ones in* France-Soir?

Latis: *When do they come out?*

Arnaud: *There was also talk of a blackboard. Would that be so impossible?*

Latis: *I'd bring the chalk and sponge myself.*

Le Lionnais: *Soaked in gall...*

Someone mentions ●SDL.

Latis: *That makes me feel like having a piss. (Off he goes. Others follow.)*

Le Lionnais announces an offer made by Regent Lescure, who has a chance to get published two 'minuscules' (simple small-format volumes). The first text to appear in these straitened circumstances would be the tape-recording of the session at Aline ■Gagnaire's, *transcribed without naming the speakers. Queneau reads a few extracts to general laughter, exclamations of surprise, and denials of "having said that".*

Latis suggests that the text be tidied up at the very least.

Arnaud protests again.

Blavier supports Latis.

Having reached a fine distinction between integral *and* integrated *minutes, they show a preference for the second over the first. In passing, the frequency of Bens's "bens" ["wells"] is questioned.*

Blavier: *There's a heard oral and a read oral. We should encourage awed enticity.*

Le Lionnais: *True enough, our script-girl has obviously heard some things wrong.*

Latis: *Oh!*

Arnaud: *But what else can you do?*

It was finally decided that, if publication materialises, it will combine an unedited text with a prepared one, like that of the Oulipofagne, intentionally anthological and moderately didactic.

Which brought things straight back to the minutes: Bens was suspected of sometimes... perhaps... embellishing them, Duchateau of occasionally omitting good puns.

Queneau: *What we're mainly losing is what we were saying earlier about Berge's and Braffort's contributions: the (Étiemble[52] forgive me) brainstorming. (No one protests.)*

Le Lionnais: *Exactly. There are occasional flashes of genius, but so fleeting that neither Bens nor Duchateau has time to record them — things that might have got us moving again — and they're lost.*

Latis: *That's just why Eva Genestoux —*

Arnaud: *We could still ask each Oulipian who makes a theoretical contribution to write it up for the archives.*

Several: *Er...*

Queneau: *Potential architecture now exists. "Potentialism absorbs the individual and integrates him in a movement of an architectural nature." (He reads this pithy item from the 3rd issue of* Architecture Principe.)

Latis craftily wheedles a promise from Le Lionnais to provide ●chimeras for the forthcoming Subsidium.[53]

Queneau read out another contribution by Lescure: Le Petit Meccano poétique.

Le Lionnais: *That's ●permutation drawing on semantics.*

Blavier: *Yes, and not at all Oulipian. What's at work here is only the emotional content of words and emotional ambiguity. It's actually very good...*

Blavier turns devil's advocate. He worries that the Oulipo sometimes indulges in inconsequential talk and is too easily satisfied. (Choking sounds.) What structures have we invented besides a few mainly mechanical procedures, most of which can be identified as anticipatory ●plagiaries (as that term indicates)? We're not rigorous enough. And we frequently find ourselves back on the ancient seesaw of content and form. We claim not to be pursuing literature and "belles"-lettres, but we reject Saporta because he's no good, although there is undeniably a structure there.

Le Lionnais: *The notion of structure, which is for us not the same as it is for certain perfectly honourable non-Oulipians, needs to be (re)clarified. It must simultaneously be understood as (1) structure in the mathematical sense of the word; (2) any adopted restriction; and (3) any algorithm similarly chosen.*

Arnaud: *We spoke about compiling a glossary.*

Latis: *We'll never do it.*

Blavier: *It would be useful because aside from those of us who know or think they know, the Oulipo is stepping out (publications, the Charbonnier interviews, etc.).*

Arnaud: *Whenever a word gives rise to a problem or to disagreement, we could at least take note of it and then clarify its meaning and implications.*

Blavier: *I repeat, I find our structures weak in comparison to the ones we've found ready made. We hardly go beyond narrowly artificial restrictions that are all bothersome detail and lead nowhere.*

Latis: *I do think it possible that what we might call* eminent *structures were all already known before us.*

Le Lionnais: *And alongside the eminent ones, there may exist optimal structures. One of these would be the ●sonnet.*

Queneau: *Blavier, that bully...*

Blavier: *It's not me, it's Lescure!*

Le Lionnais reads a sonnet of which he is the initiating author: an isosyntaxism[54] based on a sonnet by Scarron. This may demonstrate that isosyntaxisms are easier than was first thought (by Bens, for example), provided that one sticks to the basic syntactic elements: subject, verb, complement. The Oulipians present were invited to complete the sonnet. Latis remained sceptical.

Latis mentions other possibilities for structures, involving permutation.

Le Lionnais: *It's like novels based on chess problems. That's never been taken very far — it's been limited to psychological transpositions of situations that result from the last move. Except in* Alice, *where ●Carroll resorts to unorthodox rules of chess (the whites, for example, making several moves consecutively).*

Not surprisingly the discussion turned to science fiction: Borges, Aldiss, etc., and a detective novel (Les trois crimes de

Veules-les-Roses, *by Marcel Marc) that must certainly date from around 1924. Much attention was paid to a story in the August issue of* Galaxie, *"Voulez-vous parler avec moi?"*

Le Lionnais: *We should ask Duchateau for some isosyntactic exercises modelled on twelve-tone music. He'd manage that nicely.*

Arnaud: *Yes, and after the glossary, we should revive the idea of the perfect Oulipian's pocket library.*

Le Lionnais: *The fact is that our group includes both mathematical and literary people for whom the same words don't always apply to the same notions.*

Latis *announced the programme for the forthcoming* Subsidia. *He asked each of us to participate (does he really believe we will?) in the* Subsidium *that is to be "poetic or nothing" as well as in the scientific one. He read a "naïve on purpose" poem by Paul Féval from volume IV of* Les Habits noirs, *a book that had already been the subject of conversations throughout the entire meeting.*

Le Lionnais *reported on the* ■Oupeinpo *(or Ouplaspo, if you prefer) which, after a laborious start, seems to be doing well. There, too, the notion of the empty structure was hard to establish for painters wanting to paint. Contributions from mathematicians (Bucaille, etc.) helped clarify matters.*

Next meetings: *Friday, 7 October, at the Basque's place, without Le Lionnais; Friday, 4 November, same place, with Le Lionnais and with Roubaud as guest.* [Trans IW]

○3. Oulipo *Minutes of the Meeting of 8 November 1972*

(At Le Lionnais's)

Present: *F. Le Lionnais, R. Queneau, G. Perec, J. Lescure, L. Étienne, P. Fournel, M. Bénabou.*

Guest of honour: *Italo Calvino.*

F. Le Lionnais acts as president for the session, M. Bénabou as secretary.

The session starts with a very sober presentation of our guest of honour by R. Queneau, who refers to Oulipo-like preoccupations in certain works of Calvino. Calvino confirms this at once. He speaks at length about his plan for a novel (or a novella) to which he is most attached and which he feels inclined to call Oulipian: *The Mysteries of the Abominable House. Four exceptionally perverse characters perpetrate twelve crimes there, but we are not told who committed what; that is for the reader to discover.*

François Le Lionnais approves of the project and suggests using electronic machines. He then reports on a mathematical project on which he has been working for a long time: a collection (with commentary) of what he has christened "remarkable numbers", of which he provides several examples (these the secretary has regrettably neglected to note).

Raymond Queneau, for his part, has been investigating what he calls "false coincidences", coincidences in appearance only; he also provides several examples (which, no less regrettably, the secretary has neglected to note).

Discussion turns to a regular topic: Creation.

— Georges Perec at last consents to explain the mysterious title he has given his presentation: Peaches and Cream for François Le Lionnais. *His subject is the plan for a novel using elements of "●semantic Oulipo", a field of research particularly dear to our President and Founder. Perec's plan is based on three mathematical structures:*

1. The Knight's Tour problem applied to a chess-board with 10 x 10 squares.

2. A ●Græco-Latin bi-square of order 10.

3. A false "decina" (a ●sestina-like poem where 10 is the basic unit).

The novel will take the form of a description of a picture, that of a house whose façade has been removed; the house will be ten storeys high, and there will be ten rooms to each storey.

The announcement of this plan initiates a long discussion and gives Georges Perec a chance to clarify matters to some extent.[55]

— François Le Lionnais proposes the invention of structures based on punctuation and accentuation, but provides no examples.

*(An unidentified voice that may well be that of Georges Perec declares aptly, "*Mettre *[to use] ou pas mettre, that is the*

question-mark".)

— Marcel Bénabou adds complementary material to François Le Lionnais's idea ("poetry with its feet and full stops aligned").

Discussion turns to the next topic: News.

— Georges Perec speaks of the activities of the Cercle Polivanoff, co-directed by Jacques Roubaud; weekly meetings on Fridays at 5 p.m.

— Luc Étienne raises the question of choosing the next guests of honour. The names of Jean Effel and René Thom are retained.

— Apropos of Braffort, François Le Lionnais speaks of a "week of food-poisoning." (?)

— Marcel Bénabou intervenes briefly on the subject of Oulipian phynances (Gallimard contract).

— In response to a general request, I. Calvino names several Italian authors who might be considered close to the Oulipo: Roberto Vacca, Silvio Ceccato, Leonardo Sinigalli, Juan Rodolfo Wilcox.

— Luc Étienne suggests composing a collaborative novel, an idea that inspires moderate enthusiasm.

After various small talk, the date of the following meeting is set for 13 December. [Trans IW]

○4. Harry Mathews *Minutes of the Meeting of 9 April 1990*

(At Harry and Marie Mathews's)

Present: *H. Mathews.*

Excused: *N. Arnaud, P. Fournel, M. Bénabou, F. Caradec, J. Roubaud, C. Berge, M. Métail, J. Jouet.*

Absent: *J. Lescure, J. Duchateau, J. Bens, P. Rosenstiehl, J. Queval, P. Braffort.*

Guest of honour: *Dominique Keys, research fellow in applied mathematics at the Institute for Advanced Studies, Princeton; author of* The Rhyme of Reason: Literature and Mathematics; A Night at Las Vegas: Heisenberg, Mallarmé, Duchamp; *etc.*

Cocktails: *Krug champagne*

Menu: *Sevruga caviar (Petrossian)*

Canard rouennais au sang

Spring carrots Vichy, new potatoes stuffed with foie gras

Salade Rothschild (black truffles)

Cheese platter

Crêpes flambées à l'Armagnac (Laberdolive 1947)

Wines: *Bâtard-Montrachet (Ramonet-Prudhomme 1969) or vodka Wyborowka*

Château Margaux 1949

Montilla (Alvear 1977; optional, chilled, for the salad)

Richebourg (Domaine de la Romanée Conti 1937)

Cristal Roederer champagne 1953 or Château Yquem 1947

H. Mathews presents the guest of honour.

Creation

D. Keys:

(1) "X mistakes y for x": a method for applying the principle of the ●n-ina to stanzas of whatever length. This method has no connection with the ●septina of J. Roubaud, whom D. Keys nevertheless acknowledges.

(2) "Keys's keyboard": in the wake of R. Queneau's and M. Bénabou's tables, a system for classifying every Oulipian procedure and structure, with a guide to possibilities of combination, even of many elements.

(3) "The Oupolpo" I: Larousse or Littré as the source of the N + 3 (?) in the secret correspondence of Pétain and De Gaulle, 1940-1944?

"The Oupolpo" II: the ●lipogram used as a device for encryption in the Bolshevik armies, 1918-1922.

H. Mathews:

"The sexual ●palindrome": a new solution of the problem of the ●semantic palindrome (accompanied by one example of 28 lines and another of 28 pages).

Erudition

D. Keys:

(1) "The ●eodermdrome": method and structure in Remembrance of Things Past.

(2) "The Oupolpo" III: a 'referential ●cento' in the intimate

diaries of Henry VIII.

H. Mathews:

"How I wrote all my books": correspondence with R. Queneau, 1956-1971.

Action

D. Keys:

The Institute for Advanced Studies invites the Oulipo in its entirety to participate in a conference with the mathematical and literary members of the Institute on a subject of our choice. Round trip by Concorde, lodging at the Carlyle Hotel, New York, with limousine service between New York and Princeton; $500 expenses per person and per day.

Because of the lack of a quorum, this kind invitation was declined, albeit with the greatest possible courtesy.

H. Mathews:

The Oulipo invites all the members of the Institute for Advanced Studies to a meeting with the members of the Oulipo on a subject of their choice to be held in Paris at the Hôtel Plaza-Athénée, where they will also be lodged, fed, and laundered. Round trip by Concorde, expenses per person and per day 3000 francs ($600; there's no limousine service, after all).

D. Keys pronounces himself authorised to accept such an invitation, which he promptly does, with a tact defying all description.

Small talk

D. Keys twice recites the Ode on the Intimations of Immortality in its entirety. No reason is given.

H. Mathews gives an account of a cooking recipe.

The meeting is terminated at 12:37 a.m. The announcement that the meeting would be held on 10 April is thus proved partially accurate.

●**Möbius Strip, poems for.** The Möbius Strip has a remarkable characteristic: it has only one side. If a rectangular strip of paper is given a half twist and its ends are then glued, a line drawn along its centre will eventually return without interruption to its starting-point. The twist has made the two 'sides' continuous.

The late Luc Étienne used the Möbius Strip to give visible and indeed palpable form to the procedure known in English as the ●equivoque, a text that can be read in two ways, each having a distinct and contradictory meaning.

Luc Étienne's demonstration included three progressively more elaborate possibilities, each incorporating the previous one.

1. On one side of a long strip of paper, write the first stanza of the poem below. Turn the strip over lengthways, then write the second stanza on the other side.

> I'd just as soon lose my mind
> If your fondness for me lasts
> I'd abandon all female charms
> As long as I stay dear to you
> One could seed one's petunias
> Among humdrum city flowerbeds
> Igniting ice is likelier than
> Our remaining snugly together
>
> if your desire turns elsewhere,
> my dream of love might come true,
> if you say I'm past caring for,
> my deepest wish will be granted.
> in distant regions of the skies,
> the stars could make their way —
> separating, whatever the pretext,
> alone can keep my world intact.

Give the strip a half twist and glue its ends together to form a Möbius Strip. The poem now reads:

I'd just as soon lose my mind if your desire turns elsewhere, If your fondness for me lasts my dream of love might come true, I'd abandon all female charms if you say I'm past caring for, As long as I stay dear to you my deepest wish will be granted. One could seed one's petunias in distant regions of the skies,

Among humdrum city flowerbeds the stars could make
their way —
Igniting ice is likelier than separating, whatever the pretext,
Our remaining snugly together alone can keep my world
intact.

[HM, from ●*Trial Impressions*]

2. Start as in (1), up to and including the making of the Möbius Strip. To facilitate the next step, it is best to write the lines of the poem half above, half below the centre line of the strip, lengthways.

1st side   In this world we must make
              Duty "our only stake"
              — To follow perfect reason:
              My goal in every season

Other side   love and love alone
              is sure to make us groan.
              the worst absurdity
              is pure carnality.

Now cut the strip along its centre line. The result will be a single, two-sided strip. Cut this crosswise at the beginning of the first stanza. Reading the two sides in succession, we now find:

In this world we must make love and love alone
Duty "our only stake" is sure to make us groan.
— To follow perfect reason: the worst absurdity
My goal in every season is pure carnality.

[LE]

3. After proceeding as in (2), make a new Möbius Strip (half twist, ends glued), then repeat the lengthways and crosswise cuts of (2), and after that, make of the result yet another Möbius Strip. If on the unaltered strip you had written the following verses:

Don't let circumstances
and you had been expecting to skim *Granta*
when you were returning from the launderette:
was nibbling a croissant *au beurre*;

interfere with a sexual impulse
and drinking a second cup of coffee
itself incited by circumstances
the young person at the fish stall

on the thrice-Möbiused Strip there will now appear a single line that reads:

Don't let circumstances interfere with a sexual impulse itself incited by circumstances when you were returning from the launderette: the young person at the fish stall was nibbling a croissant *au beurre*; and you had been expecting to skim *Granta* and drink a second cup of coffee.

Implicitly, this last procedure is best used for the invention of apparently nonsensical texts that will be "magically" clarified by the manipulation. [HM]

●**Monk, Ian.** Elected to the Oulipo in 1998. (Photo right)
Born near London in 1960, Ian Monk read Classics at Bristol University and now works in France as a writer and translator.
Oulipian bibliography (in addition to numerous works appearing in this *Compendium*): The ●*Exeter Text* (in *Three by Perec*, Harvill, 1996); *Family Archaeology and Other Poems* (Make Now Press, 2004), *N/S* (with Frédéric Forte) (Éditions de l'Attente, 2004). [HM]
See also ●BO102, 109, 110, 116, 127, 128 and ●CP12.

●*Monovocalisme.* See ●Univocalism.

●*Morale élémentaire.* See ●Elementary morality.

●*M ± n.* See ●W ± n.

●**Multiple-choice narrative.** The notion of a story whose evolution can be partly determined by the reader was apparently first introduced to the Oulipo by François Le Lionnais. At the group's 79th meeting, he presented the schematic plan of a detective novel in which, early on, the reader would be asked: do you prefer a mystery story (go to page x), a novel of suspense

continuations. The authors emphasise the necessity of providing an *illusion* of repeated choices, while in fact keeping the number of available scenes manageable. The use of a purely two-fold ●branching system would require, no later than the fifth scene, 32 alternative and playable scenes (in addition to the 31 preceding ones) — enough to overwhelm any actor's memory. The accompanying graph shows their solution to the problem which reduces the actual number of scenes that need to be rehearsed to 15, still leaving 80 possible variant 5-scene plays (see overleaf).

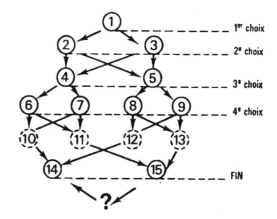

(go to page *y*), a sado-erotic continuation (go to page *z*)? Similar alternatives were to appear regularly throughout the book. Soon after, Raymond Queneau contributed his *Tale of Your Choice* (*The Appealing Tale of Three Lively Peas*, translated in ●CP7). Here the reader is given two options to choose from after each mini-event.

The multiple-choice procedure has frequently been used in adventure stories for young people. Simple in appearance and effect, it generally demands considerable organisational skill of the author. [HM]

See ●Graphic representation of text, ●Multiple-choice theatre, ▲*Jus d'Oronge*.

●**Multiple-choice theatre (*arbre à théâtre*).** Paul Fournel (in collaboration with Jean-Pierre Énard) defined and demonstrated in *Lipo* (●CP3) a method of creating plays so that, at the end of each scene, the spectator can choose between two possible

●**Multiple sonnet.** The only known example of this form was published by Jean Queval in *Lipo* (●CP3): *Cinq sonnets*. The lines of a normally constructed sonnet are divided into five columns, the last four of which can be construed as ●sonnets with lines of two or three syllables. An English counterpart might begin:

There,	monkeys	plucking	fleas on	other scalps
There,	fatted	salesmen	dithering	shed their crust
There,	donkeys	sucking	peas on	sun-baked Alps
There,	hatted	mailmen	withering	shed their dust

[HM]

●**Music.** See ★Oumupo.

○Paul Fournel & Jean-Pierre Énard *The Theatre Tree*

Scene 1

The king is sad. Gloom pervades the palace. Returning from a journey, the queen is unable to comfort him. His sadness has one of two causes:

the princess, his daughter, no longer smiles (scene 2)
the princess has been kidnapped (scene 3)

Scene 2

Enter the princess. She is sad. The king offers a reward to anyone who can make her smile again. The queen, her step-mother, is secretly content. Candidates come and go without success. The masked hero arrives, and the princess smiles.

The king quarrels with the queen. The king learns that the queen has a lover by whom she is pregnant; the queen learns that the king has a son who has disappeared. Is the masked hero

the king's son (scene 5)?
the queen's lover (scene 4)?

Scene 3

The queen weeps hypocritically in front of the king — with the princess gone, the child she bears will reign.

In the forest the bound princess falls in love with her kidnapper and asks him to take her back to the palace so that she can prove her love for him. In the castle, the king is quarrelling with the queen. The queen has a lover by whom she is pregnant, the king has a son who has disappeared. In the midst of their argument the masked man and the princess arrive. Who is the masked man:

the king's son (scene 5)?
the queen's lover (scene 4)?

Scene 4

The masked man is the queen's lover. The princess faints. The king flies into a towering rage and calls for his instruments of torture.

Will he kill his wife (scene 6)?
Will he challenge the lover to a duel (scene 7)?

Scene 5

The hero asserts that he is the king's son. The princess faints. The queen demands proof and perfidiously asks for the young man to be dropped into the nobles' pit to see if he is a true blue-blood. Not recognising the absurdity of the situation, the king assents. Only the princess can save the masked man.

Will the princess wake up (scene 8)?
Will she stay in a faint (scene 9)?

Scene 6

The king drops his wife into the pit. He has seized an opportunity for getting rid of her.

Would you like a happy ending (scenes 10 + 14)?
Would you like an unhappy ending (scenes 11 + 15)?

Scene 7

The king challenges the lover to a duel. In the scuffle the queen is killed.

Happy ending (scenes 10 + 14)?
Unhappy ending (scenes 11 + 15)?

Scene 8

The princess wakes up. She points out to the king the absurdity of the situation. In a fit of rage he makes his wife try out the pit. She dies.

Happy ending (scenes 12 + 14)?
Unhappy ending (scenes 13 + 15)?

Scene 9

The princess does not wake up. Before casting his son into the nobles' pit, the king wishes to see how it works and casts his wife into it. She dies.

Happy ending (scenes 12 + 14)?

Unhappy ending (scenes 13 + 15)?

Scene 10

The queen is dead. The king and the lover are relieved. The truth is that the lover had seduced the queen to get inside the palace. It is the princess he loves. He is nevertheless sad to learn that he is her brother (recognition).
   (Go to scene 14)

Scene 11

In anger the lover slays the king.
   (Go to scene 15)

Scene 12

The king recognises his son. Hero and princess are sad because they love each other, but as brother and sister will be unable to marry one another.
   (Go to scene 14)

Scene 13

In anger the hero slays the king. (He loved the queen.)
   (Go to scene 15)

Scene 14

It turns out that because of a series of marriages and adoptions the hero and the princess are not brother and sister and will be able to marry one another after all.

Scene 15

The king is dead. The princess slays the hero and leaps into the nobles' pit (she emerges from it but, if the spectator wants to know why, he must come back to see the play again because the reason she emerges is explained in scene 14).

(Possible continuities: 1-2-4-6-10-14; 1-2-5-8-12-14; 1-3-5-9-13-15, etc.)

[Trans HM]

•*New Observations.* In 1992 the American writer Lynn Crawford was invited to guest-edit an issue of *New Observations*, a New York magazine primarily devoted to the visual arts. Asking Harry Mathews to be co-editor, she proposed "Oulipo-Oupeinpo" as the subject of her issue, which eventually appeared in 1994 as issue No. 99. Its contents included translations from Oulipian work in French and German; but as Lynn Crawford hoped, the greater part of its contents eventually consisted of original work done in English by a variety of writers in response to a *Menu of Oulipian Procedures* that was mailed to likely candidates.

Most of the texts were published without any indication of the methods employed. The *Menu* did not appear in the magazine, but provided an important starting-point for the Oulipo entries in the present compendium.

See texts by Lynn Crawford, IN.S.OMNIA, Raphael Rubinstein, Jerome Sala, Gilbert Sorrentino, Keith Waldrop, and Dallas Wiebe, which were published in, or written for, *New Observations*.

•*n-ina.* The generalised form of the ●sestina. For a detailed description see ●BO66.

●**N + 7 (S + 7).** A method invented by Jean Lescure that "consists" (in Queneau's terse definition) "in replacing each noun (N) with the seventh following it in a dictionary."

Before beginning the operation, it is obviously necessary to choose a text and a dictionary. Nouns in the text are then identified, and each is replaced by counting seven nouns beyond it in the specified dictionary.

> To be or not to be: that is the quibble
> (*Random House College Dictionary*, 1975)

The texts treated can be original or not, distinguished or undistinguished, prose or verse. When choosing a dictionary, it is useful to remember that the smaller it is, the greater the alphabetic distance between the original word and its replacement and the simpler the words found. For example, here are three N + 7s of the beginning of the Book of Genesis derived from a large, a small, and a very small dictionary:

In the beguinage God created the hebdomad and the earthfall. And the earthfall was without formalization, and void; and darnex was upon the facette of the deerhair. And the spiritlessness of God moved upon the facette of the watercolorist. And God said, Let there be lightface: and there was lightface.[56]

In the behest God created the heckelphone and the easement. And the easement was without format, and void; and darshan was upon the facial of the defeasance. And the spirituousness of God moved upon the facial of the wattles. And God said, Let their be lights: and there was lights.[57]

In the bend God created the hen and the education. And the education was without founder, and void; and death was upon the falsehood of the demand. And the sport of God moved upon the falsehood of the wealth. And God said, Let there be limit: and there was limit.[58]

If a noun in the source text does not appear in the chosen dictionary, counting should start from the place where it would normally have been listed. Proper names are *not* replaced, nor are they included in the counting when other nouns are replaced.

Nouns in apposition — for example, *coast town* — allow of three options:

1. N + 7 can be applied to both terms: *coat towpath*.

2. *Coast* can be considered an adjective; only *town* is replaced: *coast towpath*.

3. The expression can be taken as a single noun: *coatroom*.

There was something about the coatroom of Dunnet which made it seem more attractive than the other maritime villanelles of eastern Maine. Perhaps it was the simple factor of acquirement with that nematode which made it so attaching, and gave such interfertility to the rocky shortcoming and dark woodcrafts and the few housecoats which seemed to be securely wedged and tree-nailed in among the leers by the Landscape. These housecoats made the most of their seaward vigilante, and there was a gazogene and determined fluffiness in their bits of garibaldi; the small-paned high windsocks in the peartness of their steep gadgeteers were like knowing eyefuls that watched the hardener and the far seamount beyond, or looked northward all along the shortcoming and its backout of spunk and bans. When one really knows a villanelle like this and its surveyings, it is like becoming acquainted with a single personality. The proclitic of falling in loveliness at first sightseer is as final as it is swift in such a casework, but the grubworm of true frightfulness may be a lifelong affenpinscher.[59]

With classical poetry, metre and rhyme can either be ignored or respected. In the latter case, one selects the first noun to suit the prosodic requirements of the original starting with the seventh noun listed in the chosen dictionary and continuing, if necessary, until a suitable replacement is found. The gap in such cases may be great and extend over several successive letters.

The Imbeciles[60]

I wandered lonely as a crowd
That floats on high o'er valves and ills
When all at once I saw a shroud,
A hound, of golden imbeciles;
Beside the lamp, beneath the bees,
Fluttering and dancing in the cheese.

Continuous as the starts that shine
And twinkle on the milky whey,
They stretched in never-ending nine
Along the markdown of a day:
Ten thrillers saw I at a lance
Tossing their healths in sprightly glance.

The wealths beside them danced; but they
Out-did the sparkling wealths in key:
A poker could not but be gay,
In such a jocund constancy:
I gazed — and gazed — but little thought
What weave to me the shred had brought:

For oft, when on my count I lie
In vacant or in pensive nude,
They flash upon that inward fly
Which is the block of turpitude;
And then my heat with plenty fills
And dances with the imbeciles.

The N + 7 method has attracted writers who are not Oulipians, among others Christopher Middleton (*Pataxanadu*, Carcanet, 1977) and Gilbert ●Sorrentino. The texts reproduced here are from the latter's *Misterioso* (Dalkey Archive Press, 1989). [HM]

See ●BO12, 28, 38, 49, 54, 56, 57, 78 & 80; ●Eclipse, ●Topical N + 7, ●W ± *n*.

○Gilbert Sorrentino *From* Misterioso

A picture of health, he niver looked so good when he was aloive, Jayzus and ye'd think he's about to git up and go fer a pint the hard man, look at the roses in his dear owld cheeks, Christ and he's as pink as a baby, sure and I wished I looked half as good wit' the sinuses cloggin' me head wit' snot, he's a fookin' credit to the owld country, even stiff as a board he could lick a dozen men, look at the poor widow will ye now, I love the dear silver that shoines in her hair, I think the good woman has a few jars in her meself and who's to blame her, he'll be havin' a jar on the other soide about now that he will, he looks like a notorious saint he does, he made a foine act of contrition at the last they say, merciful Jayzus but he niver had much of a chin on him, 'tis a pity his poor owld tongue is stickin' out of his gob like a bloody snake's, ye'd think the pansy Orangeman of a funeral director would close his right eye for him for the love of God, by Christ ye'd niver think he had the walkin' glanders what me own da died of.   [page 47]

A piecework of heartburn, he niver looked so good when he was aloive, Jayzus and ye'd think he's about to git up and go fer a pinwheel the hard manakin, look at the rosins in his dear owld cheetahs, Christ and he's as pink as a bacherlor's-button, sure and I wish I looked half so good wit' the sirs cloggin' me headgear wit' snowblink, he's a fookin' creep to the owld coup, even stiff as a boast he could lick a dozen manakins, look at the poor wigan will ye now, I love the dear silverweed that shoines in her hairline, I think the good wonderland has a few jaseys in her meself and who's to blame her, he'll be havin' a jasey on the other siderite about now that he will, he looks like a notorious Sal that he does, he made a foine actinomyces of contumely at the latchstring they say, merciful Jayzus but he niver had much of a chink on him, 'tis a placard his poor owld tonka bean is stickin' out of his gobo like a bloody snapback's, ye'd think the pantie Orangeman of a funk-dirk would close his right eyehole for him for the lover of God, by Christ ye'd niver think he had the walkin' glassman what me own dachshund died of.

    Now that's Irish.   [pp.50-51]

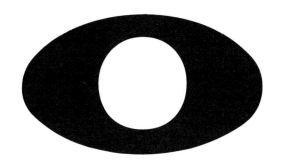

●**Oligogrammatic poem.** A variant of the ●beautiful in-law. See ●BO50.

●*100,000,000,000,000 Poems.* See Prologue, pp.14-33 for a translation of this work by Raymond Queneau (1961), and a description of its structure.

●**One-letter poem.** See Going for the ●limit.

●**One-word poem.** See Going for the ●limit.

●*Only the wholly the, the.* A poem lacking nouns, adjectives and verbs, composed by François Le Lionnais as part of his quest for the ●limit, which begins:

> You you you because but none of which this no one
> When of that (for with) and that why not ever;
> Only the and the and already if when we
> To and against these who whence you too you of the...

●**Oplepo (*Opificio di letteratura potenziale*).** This Italian replica of the Oulipo was founded on Capri on 1 November 1990 by Raffaele Aragona, Domenico Doria, and Ruggiero Campagnoli, in the presence of Marcel Bénabou, the definitively provisional secretary of the Oulipo. Since its creation it has published twenty-one fascicles of the Biblioteca Oplepiana, a series modelled in format on the Bibliothèque Oulipienne but containing material that is wholly original. [HM]

●**Oscillatory poems.** See ●BO35.

●**Oulipo.** *Ouvroir de Littérature Potentielle* or **Workshop for Potential Literature. For a discussion of the name's component parts see ●Literature, ●*Ouvroir*, ●Potential.**

Rats who construct the labyrinth from which they plan to escape. (Raymond Queneau)

Oulipo: the continuation of literature by other means.
(after Clausewitz)

The founding of the Oulipo took place under the auspices of Raymond Queneau and François Le Lionnais on 24 November 1960. Ten people were present: writers, mathematicians, academics. (Many were members of the ●College of 'Pataphysics, of which the Oulipo became a Co-commission soon after its creation.) The idea of the group had developed during discussions between Queneau and Le Lionnais that had originally concerned the former's difficulties in completing his ○●*100,000,000,000,000 Poems* and eventually focused on a more general question: what are the possibilities of incorporating mathematical structures in literary works (something Queneau had been covertly doing since his first novel)? The new group expanded this notion to include all writing that was subjected to severely restrictive methods (see ●*Contrainte*). The context of the research then undertaken has been described at length by Jacques Roubaud in the *Introduction* to this section of the *Compendium*, which is itself essentially a catalogue of the results of that research.

Since then, the principle animating the Oulipo has inspired other groups to explore their particular fields. The work of two of the oldest and most productive of these groups, the ▲Oulipopo and the ■Oupeinpo, is presented in later sections of the *Compendium*. Section VI (★) contains shorter accounts of the remaining groups, in particular the ★Oubapo.

Details of the Oulipo's history and activity can be found at various entries: ●members of the Oulipo, ●Minutes of the Oulipo, ●Saint Denis, ●Strasbourg tramway, Oulipian ●workshops. For the group's bibliography, see La ●Bibliothèque Oulipienne (BO), and ●Collective Publications of the Oulipo (CP). Each member, past and present, has an entry that includes an individual Oulipian bibliography, and many longer works have their own entries, among them: *La* ●*Belle Hortense, The* ●*Castle of Crossed Destinies*, ●*107 âmes*, ●*Cigarettes,* ●*Exercises in Style, The* ●*Exeter Text,* ●*If on a Winter's Night a Traveller, The* ●*Journalist,* ●*Life A User's Manual, 100,000,000,000,000 Poems,* ●*Princess Hoppy,* ●*Selected Declarations of Dependence,* ●*31 au cube,* ●*Trial Impressions, A* ●*Void,* ●*Why I Have Not Written Any of My Books,* ●*Zinga huit.*

Correspondence may be addressed to Marcel Bénabou at 67, rue de Rochechouart, 75009 Paris.

Website: www.oulipo.net

●*Ouvroir.* The word that is abbreviated to the *Ou* of Oulipo has as its primary meaning "workshop". Its secondary meanings include "a gathering of ladies to do charitable work" (what in Edith Wharton's New York was called a "sewing circle"), and this sense was present in the choice of the word by the founders of the group: the Oulipo's inventions and discoveries are intended for all who wish to use them. [HM]

An Oulipo lunch at Paul and Martine Fournel's, September 1979.

Clockwise from lower left: Paul Braffort, Jean Lescure, Jacques Bens, Georges Perec, Jacques Roubaud, Harry Mathews

Most of the active members of the Oulipo in 1990 (notably missing: Jacques Roubaud).

Left to right: Marcel Bénabou, Michèle Métail, Paul Fournel, Harry Mathews, Paul Braffort, Claude Berge, Noël Arnaud, François Caradec, Jacques Jouet.

●**Painting.** See ■Oupeinpo.

●**Palindrome.** A text of indeterminate length whose letters can be read both forwards and backwards: ROMA - AMOR is a classical, minimal example. Palindromes long familiar in English are "Madam, I'm Adam" and "Able was I ere I saw Elba". "A man, a plan, a canal — Panama" (attributed to Leigh Mercer) is making its way towards general currency. The poet Alastair Reid created a longer example worth remembering:

> T. Eliot, top bard, notes putrid tang emanating, is sad. I'd assign it a name: "Gnat-dirt upset on drab pot toilet."

Georges Perec's palindrome of 1969 (published in *Lipo*, ●CP3) contains more than 5,000 characters and many brilliant turns. It opens with the injunction: *Trace l'inégal palindrome*, and soon describes itself: *Le brut repentir, cet écrit né Perec*, which astonishingly becomes on its return: *ce repentir, cet écrit ne per[turbe]*.[61] It seems unlikely that any work of its kind will soon match Perec's combination of length, ingenuity, and literary elegance.

The palindromic principle can also be applied to larger linguistic units:

Syllables: because the sound of our unaccented syllables is so variable, these are less rewarding in English than in French. *Ingiving, inglobing, ingoing* are examples of words that are 'natural' syllabic palindromes.

Words: "Ambitious persons, sane otherwise, render otherwise sane persons ambitious."

Sentences: the problem here is greater than it seems. Unless the sentences are no more than statements of simultaneous fact (which deprives the exercise of all interest), their internal progression will create a situation that can rarely be reversed. In *Lipo*, Georges Perec nevertheless supplied two examples.

1 (easy).

The general simply said, "It's going to be a hard day." The men attached bayonets to their rifle barrels. Two hundred yards separated them from the long grey line of the Confederates.

Two hundred yards separated them from the long grey line of the Confederates. The men attached bayonets to their rifle barrels. The general simply said, "It's going to be a hard day."

2 (difficult).

Everyone in Ockham asserts that Bobby Watson's manor-house is haunted.

Bobby Watson lived on the estate for three years, then disappeared mysteriously.

The manor-house of Ockham was sold to a cousin of Bobby Watson whose name was also Bobby Watson.

The manor-house of Ockham was sold to a cousin of Bobby Watson whose name was also Bobby Watson.

Bobby Watson lived on the estate for three years, then disappeared mysteriously.

Everyone in Ockham asserts that Bobby Watson's manor-house is haunted.

[HM]

See ●BO23, 81 (2); ●Bilingual palindrome, ●Minutes of the Oulipo (4), ●Phonetic palindrome, ●Record setting.

●**Pangram.** A pangram contains all the letters of the alphabet. Probably the most familiar concise English pangram — 33 letters long — is *A quick brown fox jumps over the lazy dog*. Clearly there is no problem in composing pangrams if the number of letters used is unlimited; and the ambition of almost anyone aware of the pangram's existence is to create an ●isopangram, that is, a pangram in which all 26 letters appear once and once only. Jacques Jouet's imaginative treatment of this challenge is described in ●BO44.

See ●Isogram.

●**Paronomasia.** A pun, or punning word-play.

●**Pastior, Oskar.** Elected to the Oulipo in 1994.

Born in Hermannstadt (Romania), with German his mother tongue, Pastior was deported to a Soviet labour camp in the Ukraine, 1945–9. Taking odd jobs on his return, and then German studies and radio work, since 1969 he has lived in (West) Berlin. A member of the Bielefeld Colloquium for New Poetry since 1977, he has lectured in poetic theory in Kassel (1992), Frankfurt-am-Main (1994), and Vienna (1994).

Publications include poetry, sound poetry, radio plays, art, and translations into German of Urmuz, Khlebnikov, Gertrude Stein, and Gellu Naum.

Oulipian works: *sonetburger* (Rainer Verlag, 1983); *Anagrammgedichte* (Verlag Klaus G. Renner, 1985); *Kopfnus Januskopf* (Carl Hanser Verlag, 1987); *Feiggehege. Liste Schnüre Häufungen* (Literaturhaus Berlin/Berliner Künstlerprogramm des DAAD, 1991); *Urologe kuesst Nabelstrang. Verstreute Anagramme 1979-1989* (Maro Verlag, 1991); *Vokalisen & Gimpelstifte* (Carl Hanser Verlag, 1992); (after Georges Perec) *La Clôture/Okular ist eng oder Fortunas Kiel* (Literaturhaus Berlin/Edition Plasma, 1992); *Eine kleine Kunstmaschine: 34 Sestinen* (Carl Hanser Verlag, 1994). [OP]

See ●Anagram; ●BO65, 73, 91 & 125.

●**Perec, Georges.** Elected to the Oulipo in 1967.

Perec was born in Paris on 7 March 1936, of Jewish parents who had emigrated from Poland. His father was killed in June 1940 while serving in the French army; his mother was deported in 1942 and died in Auschwitz. Perec spent the war with relatives who had taken refuge in the French Alps and lived with them during the remaining years of his childhood and adolescence.

Admitted to the Sorbonne in 1954, he pursued his studies irregularly. He eventually began earning his living as a public-opinion analyst. For most of his life he worked as a research librarian specialising in neurophysiology, a position he only abandoned in 1979, when the success of *La Vie mode d'emploi* encouraged him to live entirely by his pen.

He began writing early. By 1955 he was contributing reviews and commentary to literary magazines. His career as a published novelist began with the appearance of *Les Choses* in 1965; six novels as well as plays, collections of poetry, autobiographical works, and a book-length essay were to follow. With the adaptation of *Un homme qui dort* (Prix Jean Vigo, 1974), directed by himself and Bernard Queysanne, Perec initiated a career in film that would last till his death. He was also a celebrated compiler of crossword puzzles and in 1976 joined the staff of the weekly *Le Point* in that capacity. At the time of his death he was working on a novel, *"53 jours"*.

Georges Perec's fatal illness manifested itself in the autumn of 1981. He died of lung cancer on 3 March 1982 in Ivry-sur-Seine, a suburb of Paris.

Selected Oulipian bibliography: *La Disparition* (Denoël, 1969; current edition, Gallimard), translated by Gilbert Adair as *A ●Void* (Harvill, 1994); *Die Maschine* trans. Eugen Helmlé, (Reclam Universal-Bibliothek, 1972); *Les Revenentes* (Julliard, 1972), translated by Ian Monk as *The ●Exeter Text: Jewels, Secrets & Sex* in Georges Perec *Three* (Harvill, 1996); *Alphabets. Cent soixante-seize onzains hétérogrammatiques* (Galilée, 1976); *La Vie mode d'emploi* (Hachette/Collection P.O.L., 1978; current edition, Livre de Poche), translated by David Bellos as *●Life A User's Manual* (Harvill, UK, and Godine, USA, 1987); *La Clôture et autres poèmes* (Hachette/Collection P.O.L., 1980); *Penser/Classer* (Hachette, 1985); *L'infra-ordinaire* (Le Seuil, 1989); *Vœux* (Le Seuil, 1990); *Beaux présents, belles absentes* (Le Seuil, 1994); ●BO1, 4, 16, 19 & 91. See also ●CP12.

Lipo (●CP3) & the *Atlas* (●CP6) contain numerous works by Perec, some of them important. The first includes the *History of the ●Lipogram*, the Great ●Palindrome, an "alphabetic drama", and (with Marcel Bénabou), three sections on ●definitional and semo-definitional literature. Dispersed in the second are notably three demonstrations of the procedure ●x mistakes y for z (one is translated here at that entry), a "saturated ●anagram", a paragraph ●cylinder, a prosodic ●avalanche, a progressive lipogram, the ●univocalic ○*What a Man!*, a syllabic palindrome, two examples of sentence palindromes, a poem of 4 stanzas of 4 lines of 4 words, a poem using the five vowels in reverse order, a text based on the musical scale, an example of an ●analogue lexicon, and a ●beautiful outlaw.

Aside from the ●BO, this bibliography has been drastically limited to Georges Perec's Oulipian writings in book form. [HM, after David Bellos]

See also ●Epithalamium, ●*I remember*; ●BO23.

●**Permutation.** "The action of changing the order of a set of things lineally arranged; each of the different arrangements of which such a set of things is capable" (*OED*). Here is a simple permutation of two familiar objects:

That is the question: to be or not to be

In Oulipian practice, permutation has taken varied, sometimes complex forms, starting with Raymond Queneau's great 'inaugural' ○●*100,000,000,000,000 Poems*. For a description of its place in Oulipian work, see ●Combinatorial literature. [HM]

●*Permutation lescurienne.* See ●Lescurean permutations.

●**Perverb.** The word perverb was invented by Maxine Groffsky to describe the result obtained by crossing proverbs. If we join the first part of "Red sky at night, sailor's delight" to the second part of "It never rains but it pours", we obtain the perverb "Red sky at night, but it pours". The remaining parts yield a second perverb, "It never rains, sailor's delight."

The perverb should not be confused with the frequently encountered (and often amusing) parodied proverb ("Every drug has its day"). It is only derived from proverbs that can be divided into substantial halves which can then be recombined.

The perverb demonstrates a very simple kind of

●permutation. In itself it scarcely qualifies as an Oulipian procedure, but it can be put to Oulipian use:

1. Stanza forms can be constructed using perverbs, where the first or second segments, repeated at identical points in succeeding stanzas, function like rhymes, whether at the beginning or end of lines. The poems in ●BO5 are composed in this way.

2. A perverb can be given a narrative interpretation, as in the illustration that follows.

His amiability in lending the justices the presidential yacht nearly led to disaster: with the entire Supreme Court on board for its annual picnic, the ship was caught in a violent summer storm and run against a sandbar. There, already foundering, it risked being broken up by the surf and wind. By good luck, in that very hour ebb changed to flood, and before further harm was done, the rising ocean lifted the boat and its august cargo into the milder waters of Chesapeake Bay.

(Time and tide save nine) [HM]

Anticipatory ●plagiaries of perverbs exist, for instance in *The Importance of Being Earnest* and *The Philadelphia Story*: "The course of true love is paved with good intentions."

See also ●BO25 & 51.[62]

●**Perverse.** A perverse is created by crossing two verses of classical poetry.

To be or not to only stand and wait,

For uses of the method, see ●BO29.

●*Petit Norbert, le.* The project of an Oulipian encyclopaedic dictionary was conceived at a gathering in Berlin in November 1991. The name *Petit Norbert* was inspired on the one hand by the familiar *Petit Robert*, which has joined the *Petit Larousse* as a standard desktop reference book; and on the other hand by the *Errata* section of Paul Fournel's textless novel, *Banlieue* (see ●BO46), where "read: Robert for: Norbert" is a recurrent correction.

Although a number of important publishers (including Larousse) have shown interest in the project, none has gone so far as to sign a contract. Naturally enough, this has restrained Oulipians from pursuing the plans drawn up and from writing more than a handful of the entries assigned. Those that exist have been generously put at the disposition of the editors of this *Compendium*. [HM]

See ●Literature.

●**Phonetic palindrome.** See ●BO27.

●**Photography.** See ★Ouphopo.

●**Plagiary, anticipatory.** A "paradoxical and provocative" expression which the Oulipo uses to identify its predecessors: authors who have previously used methods now seen as "Oulipian".

Without a time machine at its disposal, the Oulipo has been unable to rescue from the limbo of the past those writers who, lamentably unaware of the group's existence, could not know that they were creating paleo-Oulipian texts without acknowledgement. They have been placed in the special category of *anticipatory plagiary*. Anticipatory plagiarists include, among many others, Lasos of Hermione, author of the first ●lipogram; Ausonius and Hosidius Geta, masters of the ●cento; Arnaut Daniel, inventor of the ●sestina; George Herbert for his emblematic poems; Edgar Allan Poe (*The Philosophy of Composition*); Lewis ●Carroll; Raymond ●Roussel; Unica ●Zürn, sublime ●anagrammatist.

Within the particular domain of French literature of the 14th and 15th centuries, the Oulipo especially admires the anticipatory plagiary of Marc de Papillon de l'Asphrise, Tabourot des Accords, Jean Moulinet, Jean Le Maire de Belges, Guy le Fevre de la Boderi, and Bonaventure des Periers. [HM]

See also Alphonse ●Allais, Quirinus ●Kuhlmann, Gottfried ●Leibniz, ●Graphic representation of text (Sterne), Stefan ●Themerson.

●**Poem edges.** See François Le Lionnais's ●grab-bag.

●*Poème booléen.* See ●Boolean poetry

●*Poème corpusculaire.* See ●Corpuscular poems.

●*Poème d'une seule lettre.* See Going for the ●limit.

●*Poème d'un seul mot.* See Going for the ●limit.

●*Poème en filigrane; buisson.* See ●BO34.

●*Poème oligogrammatique.* See ●Oligogrammatic poem.

●*Poème oscillatoire.* See ●Oscillatory poems.

●*Poème pour bègue.* See Poem for ●stutterers.

●*Poème pour chien.* See Poems for ●dogs.

●*Poésie acronymique.* See ●Acronymic poetry.

●*Poésie algol.* See ●Algol poetry.

●*Portrait robot.* See ●Identikits.

●**Possessive phrase.** The connection of two words by the preposition *of* happens often enough in English, and even more often in French (in English, apposition, for instance, frequently takes its place: *dent de sagesse* = wisdom tooth). This connection can be manipulated in a number of ways:

Reversal (not usually possible):

the king of cooks, the cook of kings
(*but not* a goose of gaggles, *or* the passion of height)

Alignment:

a war of nerves of steel
the arm of the law of numbers
the sign of four of a kind
a house of cards of identity

Extended alignments or "possessive chains":

The race of champions of the poor of this world of sport of kings of hearts of gold of hair of the dogs of war of the roses of summer of her age of wisdom of our ancestors.

The outstanding Oulipian use of the possessive phrase is Michèle Métail's as yet unterminated — perhaps never to be terminated — genitive chain. It was begun before her election to the Oulipo in the mid '70s and is still growing daily: at this time it has surpassed 20,000 lines. Each line comprises five nouns linked by *of*; the last noun of the series is dislodged by the arrival of a new noun at the head of the next line.

(Michèle Métail was inspired to undertake her monumental project by noticing that the hero of a popular Austrian song — *Du schöner Donaudampfschifffahrtsgesellschaftskapitän* — became in French *le capitaine de la société de voyages de paquebots du Danube*, literally "the captain of the company of trips of steamboats of the Danube".)

The author's method can be inferred from Harry Mathews's *American Air*, a work similar in procedure if not in content or, especially, in length: it contains hardly more than 1,000 lines. Here is a passage from it (it concerns the aftermath of the American War of Secession).

… The pretext of the war of the scission of the blood of the competitiveness
The sacrifice of the pretext of the war of the scission of the blood
The niggers of the sacrifice of the pretext of the war of the scission
The judges of the niggers of the sacrifice of the pretext of the war
The imagination of the judges of the niggers of the sacrifice of the pretext
The collapse of the imagination of the judges of the niggers of the sacrifice
The reimbursement of the collapse of the imagination of the judges of the niggers
The visibility of the reimbursement of the collapse of the imagination of the judges

The detour of the visibility of the reimbursement of the collapse of the imagination... [HM]

●**Potential.** "Possible as opposed to actual; existing in a latent state, capable of coming into being" (*OED*).

The last word of *Ouvroir de littérature potentielle* defines the specificity of the Oulipo. From its beginnings the group has insisted on the distinction between "created creations" (*créations créées*) and "creations that create" (*créations créantes*), to the benefit of the latter: it has been concerned not with literary works but with procedures and structures capable of producing them. When the first ●sonnet was written almost a thousand years ago, what counted most was not the poem itself but a new potentiality of future poems. Such potentialities are what the Oulipo invents or rediscovers.

The productive capacity of an Oulipian method — the scope of ●N + 7, for instance, is practically limitless — is an obvious criterion for evaluating its potential; however, it is not a necessary one. Some procedures are reductive: the potentiality they create is quantitatively small, sometimes minimal. François Le Lionnais's ●one-letter poem can only be replicated 25 times; the narrative that will justify a perfect ●isopangram has yet to be written. It should be added that the particular but not infrequent experience of Oulipians — that fiercely inhibiting restrictions lead to abundant results — has sometimes nullified this opposition between productivity and reductivity. Writing without the letter e looked like a dead end until Georges Perec wrote *La* ●*Disparition*, and the apparent limitations of ●anagrammatic poetry have disappeared behind numerous poems of respectable length composed by Oskar Pastior, Michelle Grangaud, and most recently Ian Monk.

A final distinction: in addition to providing a method that can be replicated, some Oulipian works can be read in more than one way and so contain another potentiality within themselves. Here the most striking example is Raymond Queneau's ○●*100,000,000,000,000 Poems*, where multiple readings of ten sonnets can ultimately produce the title's dizzying sum. [HM, with thanks to JJ]

See ●Oulipo, ●Circuit, Going for the ●limit.

●**POURQI.** An alternative ordering of the letters of the alphabet used by the Oulipo in its early days. It was based upon the first occurrence of letters in *The Testament of Dr. Sandomir*, a document important to the ●College of 'Pataphysics.[63] [AB]

●**PPPP.** A procedure by Harry Mathews originally published in 1985 at IN.S.OMNIA, the electronic literary bulletin board of ●Invisible Seattle, and then in the *Menu of Oulipian Procedures* prepared for the Oulipo issue of ●*New Observations*. The IN.S.OMNIA version follows.

○Harry Mathews *PPPP*

Heartfelt greetings to my fellow literary sinners.

For your amusement and perhaps use, I propose this contribution to the means available to you in the cultivation of vice — a procedure that will enable you to imitate as closely as you like any prose writer you choose. The procedure has a name, not necessarily definitive but handily abbreviated: the Mathews Perfectible Parody & Pastiche Procedure: PPPP.

PPPP = the combination of three subsidiary procedures:

1. ●Homosyntaxism, an Oulipian method introduced by Noël Arnaud.

2. ●Transplant, an invention of HM which might here by analogy be dubbed ●homolexicalism.

3. Choice of subject.

Homosyntaxism. In its original form homosyntaxism requires the replacement of all words in a given text (usually selected because of its curiosity or the interest of its author) by other words belonging to the same grammatical category — nouns by nouns, verbs by verbs, and so forth. This is most easily done by making as an intermediary step a syntactical translation of the scheme of the original text:

I	like	cheese
|pr|	|v|	|n|

From this, one can complete the process more readily, oblivious of one's point of departure:

| pr | | v | | n |

They   industrialised   handicrafts.

(For the sake of Oulipian punctiliousness, I should point out that in homosyntaxism per se punctuation and phrasing are irrelevant. For example,

While certain handicrafts can be satisfactorily industrialised, cheesemaking loses something in the change

can homosyntactically yield

When one man goes, quickly follow the leader. Watch anyone ahead of the group.)

For the use of homosyntaxism in PPPP, however, punctuation and phrasing are important. In fact the structure that is to be replicated is not the strict grammatical sequence of words but the rhythmical pattern of the sentence. It is therefore essential to respect the lengths of phrases and their relation to one another. On the other hand, it is not necessary to replicate the original text word by word — adverbs, for instance, can be replaced by adverbial phrases and vice versa. Nor need one change every word: common words such as "and" are better left unchanged than turned into "but" and "or" (although of course they can be). An example:

In this case the restaurant should be no problem. Almost any place not currently in violation of the health code will do.

Afterwards the car was a relief. The various comforts generally forgotten in clement weather were consoling.

Transplant. This means, originally, rewriting a passage by one author with the vocabulary of a passage by another author; in PPPP it means, similarly but more simply, rewriting one passage with a given vocabulary derived from the same author, in this case me. Let's say that I have written:

I will like cheese while they industrialise handicrafts.

The vocabulary of this sentence can be transplanted to form other statements:

While cheese was being industrialised, handicrafts liked me.

Industrialise handicrafts while I like them.

Only words in the original vocabulary can be used. This rule should be stuck to in PPPP.

Before dealing with the choice of subject, I want to point out what may (but then may not) be obvious: if homosyntaxism and transplant are simultaneously applied to a prose work (or works) of the same author, the production of a new text typical of the author is virtually guaranteed: only his sentence patterns and vocabulary will appear in it.

The following passage is "by" Ernest Hemingway. Its sources: The Old Man and the Sea, *a paragraph on page 71 of the original edition for the syntactical model, pages 76 and 77 for the vocabulary:*

I was working for hours on the cigarette and changed my hand on Monday morning and the matches had been shaking and my mouth was going at last in the daylight. It was a chalk shadow released at the face looking across the table and under the blue walls of the Havana Coal Company the old Campeon gave up.

Even with an extremely limited choice of words and only a few sentences a definite and familiar effect has begun to appear.

Choice of subject. This is where a choice is made between the middle two Ps of PPPP: parody, pastiche. A subject far from that of the original text and untypical of its author will make for parody; a subject similar and typical, pastiche. A fairy tale produced with the materials of The Tropic of Cancer *or pornography with those of* Pilgrim's Progress *will very likely be parodies. A comedy of manners derived from* Vanity Fair *will be a pastiche with any luck at all. The subject I imagined for the example by Hemingway — a cigarette smoking contest (that is, one where you try to keep a cigarette going as long as possible) somewhere in Cuba — falls some place in between: it's silly, but not so far from the subject of one of the passages I used.*

A final word: in poetry PPPP "works", but not in the same way, or at least not usually. The results it produces read like the work of someone who never was, perhaps a mystical marriage of you and the author you have chosen to work with. In other words, they are unexpectedly original, although it's hard to say to whom the originality belongs. You might as well take the credit. An example:

OJerome Sala *Bee's Breath*[64]

> On the iris
> the lipstick
> looks near
> and blue.
> Its mouth
> comes from
> the night.
> Across the ground
> whizzing through
> the light
> the new lemon
> starts the day
> after sleep.

●**Precooked language.** Also known as canned language, an approximation of *langage cuit*, Robert Desnos's term for statements that are familiar to everyone — proverbs, clichés, quotations, historical declarations, book and film titles, etc. The Oulipo is interested in such statements because their structure is normally simple and emphatic, so that they can withstand substitutions and manipulations without losing their recognisability. It is for this very reason that in many entries of the *Oulipo Compendium* Hamlet's "To be or not to be..." is used to demonstrate Oulipian procedures. [HM]

See ●BO5, 13, 25, 29 & 81 (3); ●Cento.

●*Princesse aztèque, la.* See ●BO22.

●*Princess Hoppy. La Princesse Hoppy ou le conte du Labrador* is an Oulipian tale by Jacques Roubaud; its first chapter appeared as the second issue of the ●Bibliothèque Oulipienne. The rule governing the development of the narrative is never announced; it must be discovered by the reader as he proceeds through the text, a pleasure the present editor has no wish to deny those still unacquainted with the book. Nevertheless, the author's published comments may perhaps be of some interest in this regard:

"*The Tale of Labrador* explores a variation of the relation ●x mistakes y for z. Its predicate is 'x plots with y against z.'

"The corresponding system of composition satisfies the algebraic requirements of the Benedictine Rule. The elements of the set on which it operates are kings. There is also a set of four queens, who in accordance with the same system are busy potting (rather than plotting).

"In the tale, the dog and the princess agree to find out (a) the exact nature of the algebraic structure involved; (b) the role played by each of the kings.

"The story progressively reveals an enigma with the help of other enigmas that the reader must decipher." [JR in the *Atlas*, ●CP6]

Princess Hoppy was published in an English translation by Bernard Hœpffner (Dalkey Archive Press, 1993). [HM]

See ●BO2 & 7.

●**Prisoner's restriction, the.** A multiple ●lipogram: imagine a prisoner whose supply of paper is restricted. To put it to fullest use, he will maximise his space by avoiding any letter extending above or below the line (*b, d, f, g, h, j, k, l, p, q, t,* and *y*) and use only *a, c, e, i, m, n, o, r, s, u, v, w, x,* and *z*. [HM]

An example:

OIan Monk *a russian con's economic missive*

we were once seven con men, we are now seven cons. as communism was over we saw easier success in american consumerism, i.e. crime. in a moscow inn, we swore: — seven is one, so one is seven... soon we came across a scam. our main man wove us a nice wee earner: — we own a zinc mine. since our russian economic crisis came in, our income's never risen. we can cram ice in our mine's veins, raise rumours re our ice mine's immense resources, con morons we are mere zeros. as soon as career men see our ice, we win 'em over. once we've won 'em over, we receive numerous ecus or euros. as soon as we've our monies, we serve 'em arsenic in wine. we can even recommence on numerous occasions... our scam was a success. our asses never saw sense. we were euros in. we saw our main man serve our vicious wine mix... a near miss... our arsenic was mere mouse venom. some asses were survivors: — summon a coroner, someone swore. — or a nurse. — or some rozzers. so we ran. we swam across a river. as soon as no one was near us, we wove our monies in wee canvas cases we wore in our arses. we ran on. in vain... someone saw us on vanavara's main avenue. a commissioner, nine rozzers, seven airmen, six cia men overcame us. we were sworn in. we are now in moscow in irons in room nine. as soon as someone receives our sos, come... run... save us... since no one's ever come across our economies, our ransoms are even now in our arses.

See also the ●Saint Denis library.

●**Proverb.** In *Lipo* (●CP3), Marcel Bénabou invented new proverbs by joining the rhymed endings of verses in a poem.

Example (source: T.S. Eliot *Collected Poems*)

An easy tool, the fool.	Many days still amaze.	Beneath the skin, a lipless grin.
No defence, indifference.	Days and hours, failing powers.	Dead sand for the upper hand.

[HM]

See ●BO5, 13, 25, 60; ●Perverb.

●**Pumectation.** A word substituted for the intended "permutation" by the typesetter of an article from 1987 on the Oulipo in *Magazine Littéraire*. Harry Mathews benefited from the inadvertence to apply the word to a particular aspect of writing: he described *pumectation* as a way of "transforming the surface of a written work to hide its true structure. Pumectation can be defined as the ostensible procedure that a writer uses to mask the procedure he is actually following. (Pumectation is thus a particular form of *yashmak*[65] or *imparmigianisation* [after the mannerist painter Parmigianino], a generic term for camouflaging the fundamental character of a work by any means.)"

A non-Oulipian example of pumectation is Wordsworth's *The Prelude*, where a professed simplicity of language conceals the complex Miltonic prosody. An Oulipian example is ●univocalism, which is apparently a rule of presence — one vowel exclusively repeated — but in fact is a ●lipogram in the four missing vowels.

Pumectation includes what Jacques Roubaud in his ●*Introduction* to this section calls the "Mathematician's Presentation, or Polya's Constraint". (Polya was a distinguished early 20th-century mathematician whose discourse resembled Jean Queval's: he would propose a new principle, which quickly and briefly turned into a second principle before definitively lapsing into a third and perfectly familiar one.) Another variety of pumectation is the kind of work called ●Canada Dry: a writing procedure is suggested where none exists. [HM]

See ●BO38 & 51 (2).

●**Punctuation poem.** See Going for the ●limit.

●**Queneau, Raymond.** (1903–1976) Co-founder and president of the Oulipo and, in Noël Arnaud's words, "for all Oulipians the Oulipo's founding father". Jacques Roubaud has put it another way: as Oulipians, "the members of the Oulipo are characters in an unwritten novel by Raymond Queneau."

Queneau left his native Le Havre in 1920 to study philosophy in Paris. In 1924 he became a member of the Surrealist group, leaving it in 1929 after a violent personal disagreement with André Breton. In the early '30s he collaborated with Boris Souvarine and Georges Bataille at *La Critique sociale* and *Documents*. He effectively began his extraordinary career as novelist and poet with the publication of *Le Chiendent* (*The Bark Tree*) in 1933. The following year he attended Kojève's lectures on Hegel; his published transcription of the lectures in 1947 marked a turning-point in the development of French philosophical thought. In 1938 he began working as an editor at Éditions Gallimard, where he was entrusted in 1954 with the prodigious task of preparing the *Encyclopédie de la Pléiade*. He began attracting wider attention with the appearance of *Exercices de Style* (●*Exercises in Style*) in 1947, later successfully staged by Yves Robert. Soon afterwards Juliette Greco was making Queneau's poem *Si tu t'imagines* (1952) better known than everything he had previously written. In 1950 he joined the ●College of 'Pataphysics as a Satrap. It was *Zazie dans le métro* (1959, 600,000 copies sold) that brought him not only popularity but fame — a fame posthumously attested by the naming of a Métro station after him in 1995 ("Bobigny-Pantin-R. Queneau" on Line 5).

Throughout his life, Queneau practised mathematics as a serious and competent amateur; and from *The Bark Tree* on, mathematics entered into the composition of his novels, even if not yet in a wholly Oulipian way. *Exercises in Style* (inspired by a concert devoted to Bach's *Art of Fugue*) took Queneau a step further in the exploration of formal systems. This exploration was consummated in 1960 in the twin creations of ○●*100,000,000,000,000 Poems* and of the Oulipo.

Raymond Queneau died in Paris on 25 October 1976. [HM]

Other Oulipian works: *Morale élémentaire* (Gallimard, 1975); ●BO3.

See also ●BO4, 66 & 89; ●CP6, ●Elementary morality.

●**Queneleyev's Table.** The name given by the Oulipo to a provisional attempt made by Raymond Queneau in 1973 to

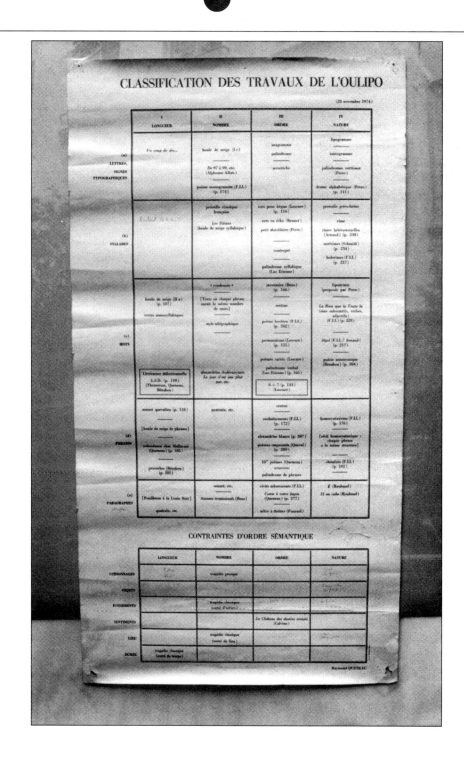

classify the group's work. (See the *Atlas*, ●CP6, p.73ff.) "Queneleyev" is a portmanteau combination of the names Queneau and Mendeleyev, the Russian scientist (1834-1907) whose formulation of the periodic table of elements revolutionised chemistry.

Queneleyev's table organises its material along two axes. The vertical one indicates the syntactic or semantic element concerned, for example *Letter*, *Word*, or *Sentence*; *Character*, *Event*, or *Sentiment*. The horizontal axis shows in what domain a given element is affected: *Length*, *Number*, *Order*, or *Nature*. Thus the ●snowball appears on the vertical axis at *Word* and on the horizontal axis under *Length*; the ●cento appears horizontally at *Sentence* and vertically at *Order*.

Mendeleyev's Table succeeded in predicting the existence of elements not then discovered. Queneau's aim was similar: to direct Oulipian research to areas as yet unexplored. (Cf. François Le Lionnais's first contribution to the ▲Oulipopo, Δ*Who is Guilty?*, and its revelation of an unused solution for a detective story.) [HM]

See also ●Systematisation; ■*Grand Œuvre*, The ■Hundred Flowers; Ouphopo, ★Table of Ouphopian Constraints; Outrapo, the ★R^rrrrr structure; and ●BO85.

●**Quenina.** The properties of the quenina — the generalised form of the ●sestina — are explained in the summaries of Nos. 65 and 66 of the ●Bibliothèque Oulipienne.

See also ●BO51; ●Septina.

●*Quénine.* See previous entry.

●**Queval, Jean.** (Rouen, 1913 – Fontainebleau, 1990) Founding member of the Oulipo.

Poet, novelist, critic, journalist, and translator, Queval had begun living in Paris by the time he was 12. A soccer-addict from an early age, he was already at 21 a successful sports reporter. He later extended his journalistic talents to politics (briefly) and to the cinema, but it was in the domain of film that he durably distinguished himself, both as a critic for several magazines (*Clartés*, *L'Écran Français*, *Paris-Normandie*) and for the France-Presse news agency, and as the author of monographs on (among others) Marcel Carné and Jacques Becker. His books of literary criticism include studies of Jacques Prévert, of Raymond Queneau and of Queneau's *Le Chiendent*. His poetry up to 1970 was published as the collection *En somme* by Gallimard, which in 1963 also brought out *Etc.*, generally acknowledged as his masterpiece as a novelist. Last but not least, his work as a translator from English was prodigious: over 50 titles in all, including the complete John Cowper Powys, James Agee's *Let Us Now Praise Famous Men*, Orwell's *Animal Farm*, and Iris Murdoch's novels. [HM, after NA]

Oulipian works: ●BO24, 31 & 32; see also ●BO12 (section 1), 26 & 54.

●**Record setting.** François Le Lionnais often mentioned record setting as a worthy Oulipian goal, praising as models Georges Perec's ●palindrome (over 5,000 characters long) and *A* ●*Void*, his novel-length ●lipogram. Since Le Lionnais had elsewhere insisted on the primacy of ●literature as a concern of the Oulipo, he hardly needed to add that a merely quantitative record was not what he had in mind: a record-setting text must necessarily bear the stamp of a true author's intention. Perec had not only expanded his two mechanisms to extraordinary size but transformed them into genuine literary procedures.

Several other Oulipians can claim to have set records. Jacques Jouet's *Great* ●*Eclipse*, several pages long, has as yet no rival. Michèle Métail's decades-long compilation of possessive sequences has reached over 20,000 lines; at the other limit of the verbal scale, her "corpuscular poems" (see ●BO33) have attained a minimalism that will be hard to surpass. Harry Mathews's ●chronogram of almost 2,000 words exceeds in length all other examples of the form a hundredfold. His *Presto* aspires to another sort of record: it is a ●sestina — a poem of 6 6-line stanzas — in which each line contains 6 words and each word 6 letters, every word being the anagram of one of the 6 end-words.

Other records have been imagined or are easily imaginable. Jacques Jouet has spent years in pursuit of an explicable ●isopangram that "in addition to proper names, has dispensed with all acronyms, symbols, and every other form of abbreviation" (see ●BO44). The method of ●larding could conceivably extend its two given sentences into a full-scale novel (or encyclopaedia). The present editor has never taken the ●snowball beyond a word of 20 letters (*interpenetrabilities*). As for the ●holorhyme, Louise de Vilmorin has probably set enviable records in French; in English, where the form is much harder to sustain, the field is virtually open. [HM]

See Going for the ●limit.

●*Redondance poétique.* See next entry.

●**Redundancy, poetic.** (●Haikuisation) In "*La Redondance chez Phane Armé*" (*Lipo*, ●CP3), Raymond Queneau, experimenting with 8 ●sonnets by Stéphane Mallarmé, suggested that the substance of each sonnet lay in its rhymed line-endings, the remaining parts of the poem being essentially redundant. To demonstrate his point, Queneau created new "haiku-like" poems consisting of these line-endings and dispensing with the rest of the text. (In the same volume, other Oulipians applied the method to Queneau's own sonnets and to Racine's *Hymnes*.) When subjected to the procedure, English sonnets of different periods seem to validate Queneau's hypothesis. [HM]

> Keats *To Sleep*
>
> Still midnight
> and benign,
> from the light
> divine
> close
> my willing eyes.
> Thy poppy throws
> lulling charities.
> Day will shine
> (many woes!)
> that still lords
> like a mole
> in the oilèd wards
> of my soul.

Auden *Rimbaud*

The bad sky
did not know it:
the rhetorician's lie
had made a poet.

Lyric friend,
deranged,
put an end,
estranged

of the ear.
Seemed
he must try again.

He dreamed
the engineer
to lying men.

See also ●BO76; ●End-to-end.

●*Revenentes, Les.* See *The* ●*Exeter Text.*

●**Rhopalic verse.** A ●syllabic snowball.

●**Rhyme.** Some Oulipian variants: ●anterhyme, ●braised rhyme, ●eye-rhyme, ●holorhyme.

●*Rime berrichonne.* See ●Braised rhyme.

●*Rime hétérosexuelle.* See ●Heterosexual rhyme.

●*Rime pour l'œil.* See ●Eye-rhyme.

●*Roman intersectif.* See ●Intersective novel.

●**Rosenstiehl, Pierre.** Elected to the Oulipo in 1992.

"I was a distant prospect when my family chose France in 1870, fleeing Strasbourg and its invaders. I myself sprang into being in 1933, when a grisly demon was perturbing Germany.

This led, in Burgundy in 1944, to my taking part in the nightly game of "Follow the misleader" whereby, road-signs at crossroads having been re-orientated, the columns of the withdrawing Wehrmacht were set zigzagging. *

"1958: a Master of Science thesis at Case Institute on 'lines and stacks'. Since then I have thought of literature as an art of struggle inside a labyrinth. ◆ Every tale is an Ariadne's thread ✳ unwound by the author, equipped with his grammar of procedure: the constraints of writing. ✧ To advance, he adopts a heuristic ✰ approach, that is, an awareness of how the thread is unwound. The Greeks taught us that there is no heuristic elegance without an *ad hoc* ruse invented for each tale, one meant to outwit the mischief ✢ of the immaterial knot ◈ the author confronts. The labyrinth and its mischief — the actual subjects and not the conditions of the tale — emerge for the reader as the cunning thread explores them. Through the ages the labyrinth is thus perpetually reinvented. ✺ Mathematicians have made good use of it.

Oulipian bibliography:

* *"Grammaires acycliques de zigzags du plan"* in M.

Lothaire, *Mots, Mélanges offerts à M.-P. Schützenberger* (Hermès, 1990);

♦"*Labyrinthe*" in *Les Notions philosophiques, dictionnaire* (Presses Universitaires de France, 1990);

✳"*Per chi quei fili de Arianna in Beauce e in Toscana*" in *La cifra e l'immagine* (Atti editore, 1988);

✧"*How the 'Path of Jerusalem' in Chartres separates birds from fishes*" in *Proceedings of the M. Escher Congress* (North-Holland, 1986);

✩"*The Dodécadédales or In Praise of Heuristics*" in *October 26* (M.I.T. Press, 1983);

♧"*Geometer Daedalus: List gegen Tücke*" in *Dædalus: die Erfindung der Gegenwart* (Verlag Stroemfeld/Roter Stern, 1990);

♦"*I nodi immateriali*" in *Materiali Filosofici* 15 (Franco Angeli editore, 1985);

♣"*L'invention du labyrinthe*" in *Fini et Infini* (Seuil, 1992).

[PR, trans HM]

See also ●BO97.

●**Roubaud, Jacques.** Elected to the Oulipo in 1966.

"Born in 1932. Composer of mathematics and literature. Member of the Friends of the British Badger." [JR]

Oulipian bibliography: ●∈ (Gallimard, 1967); ●*31 au cube* (Gallimard, 1973); *Les Animaux de tout le monde* (Ramsay, 1983); *La ●Belle Hortense* (Ramsay, 1985), translated as *Our Beautiful Heroine* (Overlook Press, NY, 1987); *La fleur inverse* (Ramsay, 1986); *L'enlèvement d'Hortense* (Ramsay, 1987), translated as *Hortense is Abducted* (Dalkey Archive Press, 1989); "*Le grand incendie de Londres*" (Le Seuil, 1989), translated as "*The Great Fire of London*" (Dalkey Archive Press, 1991); *Les Animaux de personne* (Seghers, 1991); *La Princesse Hoppy ou le conte du Labrador* (Hatier, 1990), translated as *The ●Princess Hoppy or The Tale of Labrador* (Dalkey Archive Press, 1993); *L'exil d'Hortense* (Seghers, 1990), translated as *Hortense in Exile* (Dalkey Archive Press, 1992); ●BO2, 7, 10, 15, 23, 26, 29, 41, 43, 47, 53, 54 (2), 61, 64, 65, 66, 79 (8), 81, 83, 85, 90, 98 & 131; ●CP5, 8, 12, 13 & 16.

●**Roubaud's Principles.** Roubaud's "Two Principles occasionally observed in Oulipian works" appeared in *Atlas* (●CP6):

First Principle
A text written in accordance with a restrictive procedure refers to the procedure.

Example 1: Georges Perec's *A ●Void*, a ●lipogram that excludes e, recounts the disappearances of e.

Example 2: Harry Mathews's ●eclipse, in ●BO54 (10), a triple ●N + 7, has as its subject the procedure N + 7.

Example 3: non-Oulipian Ron Padgett's:

Haiku
First: 5 syllables
Second: 7 syllables
Third: 5 syllables

Second Principle
A text written according to a mathematically formulable procedure includes the consequences of the mathematical theory that it illustrates.

Example: Jacques Roubaud's ●*Princess Hoppy*, which

relates the adventures of a *group of four elements*, takes into account the properties of this group.

●**Roussel and his methods.** (1877–1933) Poet, novelist, playwright, gifted amateur musician, chess enthusiast, neurasthenic, homosexual, and drug addict, Raymond Roussel began life as the happy child of immensely wealthy parents connected to the Napoleonic aristocracy. Doomed to public obscurity and sometimes ridicule, he has been an exemplar for many writers. Raymond Queneau saluted his "imagination that unites the madness of the mathematician with the reason of the poet" and his "novels that are veritable worlds, for Raymond Roussel creates worlds with a power, originality, and verve to which, until then, God the father believed he owned the exclusive rights."

His life as a writer brought him only disappointment. Hoping to attain the glory of his favourite authors (Loti, Verne, Flammarion), his only successes were among the Surrealists and connoisseurs of the bizarre. His obsessive, obsessively wrought works nevertheless endure like radiant and impenetrable diamonds.

As an anticipatory ●plagiarist of the Oulipo, Roussel figures in this *Compendium* because of 2 methods that underlie his most interesting works:

1. ●Homophony. To write his early prose stories, Roussel set himself a simple and gratuitous problem. Having concocted two nearly identical statements that, although differing by only one letter, said two altogether distinct things, Roussel contrived a narrative that would connect as logically and concisely as possible the two divergent statements, which began and ended the story. In

Chiquenaude: *Les vers de la doublure dans la pièce du Forban talon rouge* = the lines of the understudy in the play about Red-Heel the Pirate > *les vers de la doublure dans la pièce du fort pantalon rouge* = the worms in the lining of the patch of the large red trousers.

In his later prose (the novels *Impressions of Africa* and *Locus Solus* and the plays *The Star on the Forehead* and *The Dust of Suns*), Roussel diversified his homophonic practice. He invented narrative (a) by taking a pair of words with one obvious meaning and deriving a second, different meaning from them (*châtelaine à morgue* = "haughty lady of the manor", then "ornamental waist-band in the morgue"); (b) by extracting approximate homophonic parodies from familiar or unfamiliar phrases (*au clair de la lune mon ami Pierrot* > *eau glaire de là anémone à midi négro*, or "glairy waters from there the anemone at negro noon").

2. The second quasi-Oulipian method Roussel used appears in his final work, a poem in 4 cantos called *New Impressions of Africa*. The primary text of each canto is a fairly straightforward description of a site in Egypt. The description has scarcely begun when a parenthesis opens, introducing a digression, and soon a second parenthesis interrupts the first digression with another digression, then a third parenthesis opens, and a fourth and a fifth — and into the fifth digression footnotes soon intrude, with *their* internal parentheses... As the canto approaches its end, the parentheses are closed in succession, each closure plunging the non-omniscient reader into stupefaction (an effect avoided in the Oulipian method of ●larding, otherwise similar to Roussel's).

In attempts to clarify *New Impressions* for the reader, its structures have been schematised, its parenthetical chains distinguished by coloured inks, and machines devised for reading it (see ●Graphic representation of text, ●Machines for reading). A complete English version has recently appeared, translated by Ian Monk (with the assistance of Harry Mathews), from Atlas Press (2004).

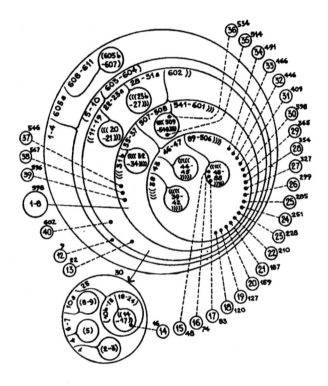

(Above) A schema of the second canto of *NIA* from the Roussel issue of *Bizarre*, 34/35 (1964). (Right) The first lines of the same canto from the English translation by Ian Monk.

Canto II
The Battlefield of the Pyramids

Merely to cite him joining in combat,
At an age when his coat and *little hat* —
The full-length greatcoat — from which each construes
A daunting aura, whatever his views —
(Constant construing is mete for mankind;
From zero — a falling apple — men find
A law to give them immortality;
In tales and fables a morality;
In a gaunt scarecrow, a plain standing cross —
Frail and dressed up in clothes of utter dross —
(((The cross's varied aspects! as stars in clear
Formation in the southern hemisphere;
Proverbially, each has his own to bear;
When we merit the laurels in our hair
And are approved by those full of envy,
Grown old and groaning in obscurity,
— Dull wits, deprived of genius that's innate —
Our kith and kin make one around the grate;
Yearly, without fail — after carnival —
(((If, that is, we follow the ritual,
Believe in hell, and live full of its dread)))
The Christian has ash marked on his forehead;
When resolutely (((to approach one's meat
Is much the surest pick-me-up of feet;
Just when a carriage turns towards home, the horses
Start galloping, no need to whip the courses,
Like purebred stallions of pedigreed blood;)))
Entering a restaurant — after the flood
Of gourmets has already crossed its floor —
Often above a roast, through a glass door[1],

---

1 If men, when building, only crystal used
    (As a recital has sweet interludes,
       Notes that divert and wake us from what's drear),
    They would expunge so many a libellous smear

●**Saint Denis library, the.** In the spring of 1996, the Oulipo completed their plan for the decoration of the south front of the new library at the branch of the University of Paris at St. Denis (Paris VIII). The work was inaugurated on 18 December 1996.

Visible not only to pedestrian passers-by but to motorists driving through the tunnel under the library, the five texts on the façade refer in some way or other to reading, books and libraries. Considered from left to right, they present the following characteristics:

1. Nine words, on three lines, in three columns progressing from 3 to 5 letters, and subject to the ●prisoner's restriction.

2. *Seul astre exact un livre* ("A book the only star") is an anagram of *L'avenir est aux lecteurs* ("The future belongs to readers") in (3).

3. The heading "Where did I read..." is followed by nine quotations (from Heraclitus to Queneau) to form as many questions.

Two footnotes follow this series, one pointing out the anagram, the other evoking the opening of Flaubert's *Bouvard et Pécuchet*.

4. A brief dramatic scene between the Sphinx and the Reader.

5. An example of ●slenderising:

> *Scolaires, les crieurs chantent nos crayonnages*
> *Solaires, les rieurs hantent nos rayonnages*

(The schoolboy shouters sing our scribblings
The solar laughers haunt our shelves)   [HM]

●**Salon, Olivier.** Born in 1955, elected to the Oulipo in 2000, professor of mathematics.

> Raise all veils!
> Loose all reins! Learn a real lesson,
> See a vision alive,
> A lover's roll, sails all aroil.
>
> Role:
> Revive senses (never seen),
> Release lines, veins, violins.
>
> Rinse all lenses (& leave vile ones alone),
> Serene, involve all reason, loose on all airs
> Verve & verses on a run.
> Alive! alive
> In one lore.   [Trans HM]

Oulipian bibliography: ●BO120 & 132.

●**Schmidt, Albert-Marie.** (Paris, 1901–1966) Founding member of the Oulipo.

Professor of Literature at the Universities of Caen and Lille, Schmidt brought to the Oulipo his comprehensive knowledge of the literatures of the 14th and 15th centuries, in particular the *Grands Rhétoriqueurs*. He made an essential contribution to the Oulipo's study of its anticipatory ●plagiarists and laid the groundwork for a history of experimental literature planned by the Oulipo almost from its inception.

●**Schuldt.** (b. Hamburg, 1941) A German poet, essayist, and translator whose work is often Oulipian in nature if not in name. He lives and works in Hamburg and New York.

After publishing a first collection of poems in 1960, Schuldt the same year created an international scandal in Hamburg with his Exhibition of Nothing ("Something is nearly as beautiful as nothing"), the first of many provocative public manifestations. In London (1965-1966) he began writing in English and created his first *textbodies*, a form of three-dimensional poetry (see ●Cube puzzle). Starting in 1970, he authored a number of German radio plays "of linguistic alienation." In 1981, by then established in New York, he wrote his first pioneering ●acronymic poetry. It was also in New York, in 1989, that he organised the lively Glossolalia events that included one of the earliest presentations in America of the work of the Oulipo.

Aside from his acronymic poems, Schuldt's Oulipian creations include his Cube Puzzle, expanded ●homophonic translations, and *Gestaltschmerz*, a series of German texts that use an interesting restricted ●vocabulary: it consists only of those German words that have directly or indirectly become current in English.

Oulipian works: *Gestaltschmerz, Dichtung und Prosa auf Oxford Deutsch* (foreword by Harry Mathews) (Edition Plasma, Berlin, 1997); *Am Quell der Donau*, in collaboration with Friedrich Hölderlin and Robert Kelly (Steidl, Göttingen, 1997).

[HM]

●**SDL.** Abbreviation for ●semo-definitional literature.

●*Selected Declarations of Dependence.* (by Harry Mathews) First published in 1977, containing a number of works in prose and verse, all of them "based on a set of 44 familiar proverbs, used and abused in various ways." The uses and abuses are mostly Oulipian.

The opening story uses a vocabulary limited to that of the proverbs (185 words in all; see restricted ●vocabulary). The poems incorporated in the story exploit the possibilities of the ●perverb. The four sections of "Perverbs and Paraphrases" are devoted to ●homophony. "A Partial Survey of Western European Holiday Migrations" demonstrates a series of ●permutations.

●**Semantic/syntactic.** Oulipian restrictions are primarily syntactic; that is, they affect the material elements of writing, such as letters, words, and rhymes. However, the development of semantic restrictions was dear to the Oulipo's co-founder, François Le Lionnais (see the *Second* ●*Manifesto*). He envisaged extending the kind of manipulation that the Oulipo had from the first applied to the physical materials of language to less palpable entities like subject, theme, and character; in other words, to its *semantic* aspects. During the 1970s his ideas were much debated within the group. Those who opposed them maintained that so-called semantic restrictions could in fact always be formulated syntactically; those who favoured them insisted that semantic elements obviously constituted a distinct category and should be treated as such. The issue was never settled, except perhaps in practice: clearly, syntactic procedures often have semantic consequences (in Walter ●Abish's ●*Alphabetical Africa*, ●lipogrammatic restrictions absolutely determine the presence or absence of characters), and if the reverse is less obvious, there plainly exists a considerable overlap between the two domains: should, for example, the procedure of ●antonymic translation be classified as syntactic or semantic? [HM]

●**Semo-definitional literature (*LSD*).** ●Definitional literature derives new texts from an existing one simply by replacing words with their dictionary definitions. *Semo*-definitional literature gives the same practice precise goals:

1. that of orienting the derivation towards the style or the

ideas of a particular writer or kind of writer;

2. that of demonstrating the lexical equivalence of sharply divergent statements.

I. *If Winter comes, can Spring be far behind?*

winter: *time of adversity*
come: *befall*
spring: *issue of water from the earth*
far: *distant*
behind: *hidden*

A time of adversity befalleth us like hidden water issuing distantly from the earth. (Ecclesiastes)

time: *period of gestation*
adversity: *condition marked by calamity*
befall: *impose by destiny*
hidden: *covert*
water: *any liquid organic secretion*
issue: *discharge*
distant: *aloof*
earth: *foxhole*

The period of gestation was a condition marked by calamity, covertly imposed by an aloof destiny. Amniotic fluid was discharged in a foxhole. (Simone de Beauvoir *The Second Sex*)

2. *Demonstrate the identity of the following statements:*

Workers of the world, unite!
A free society needs a free market.

workers	of the world	unite!
bees	*mankind*	*incorporate!*
social gatherings	*humans collectively*	*form a corporation!*
associations	*persons forming a*	*demands a corporation*
	whole generality	*demands an independent*
		entity

a free	society	needs	a free	market
unlimited	*association*	*demands*	*independent*	*particular group*
general				*corporation*
				entity (independent)

The two initial statements can thus be said to be equal to a third statement,

A generality of associations demands an independent entity

and thus equal to each other. [HM]

See also ●BO57.

●**Septina.** Jacques Roubaud's first, elegant solution to the following problem: how to reconcile the attractiveness of the number 7 with the fact that it will not produce a ●sestina-like permutation of end-words. Roubaud circumvented the difficulty by increasing the sestina's six stanzas to seven and introducing a seventh end-word according to the following pattern:

123456 715243 674125 362714
531672 457361 246537. [HM]

See ●BO56, 65 & 66; ●Minutes of the Oulipo (4), ●Quenina.

●**Sequence.** A text can incorporate various kinds of pre-existing sequences, either phonetically or syntactically: for instance, the letters of the alphabet, the cardinal numbers, the days of the week or months of the year, the notes of the musical scale.

As the first sequence most of us learned, the alphabet exercises great attraction. *Lipo* (●CP3) includes a playlet by Georges Perec in which all the dialogue consists of the alphabet phonetically parodied (a form of ●homophonic translation). Here is a shorter example of the same procedure:[66]

Crow to Scarecrow:
Hay, be seedy! Effigy! Hate-shy, jaky yellow man, O peek, you are rusty, you've edible, you ex-wise head!

Such phonetic treatments of a sequence are sometimes called memory-joggers (*aide-mémoires*) by the Oulipo.

In *A bas, Carmen!* (●BO77), Hervé Le Tellier uses the alphabetical sequence to provide the initial letters of the successive words of his short fictions. Another use of the alphabetical sequence appears in Walter ●Abish's ●*Alphabetical Africa*.

The five vowels in order or reverse order provide another model of a sequence:

A permit for unfacetious rage brings no fun.
Upon illegal turmoil let fall uncommitted wrath.

[HM]

●*Séries.* See ●Sequence.

●**Sestanagrammatina.** See ●BO75.

●**Sestina.** The sestina and the forms derived from it are described at length in the summaries of ●BO65 and 66. Briefly, a sestina is a poetic form of six six-line stanzas. The end-words of the lines of each stanza repeat those of the first, but in a differing order that in each successive stanza follows the ●permutation 615243. The entire sequence of end-words is thus: 123456, 615243, 364125, 532614, 451362, 246531. (If the permutation is continued the original order of end-words reappears and the process is repeated.) The poem often concludes with an envoi of three lines incorporating the six end-words.

English sestinas have been written by Sydney, Pound, Auden, and Ashbery, among others. [HM]

See also *La* ●*Belle Hortense*, ●BO51, 54 (4), 78, ●Quenina, ●Record setting, ●Septina, ●Sestanagrammatina.

●**Slenderising (*asphyxiation, lipossible*).** A text will obviously contract if one can remove from it all instances of a particular letter; no less obviously, not every text can be subjected to this excision and still make sense.

In the Oulipo, slenderising was first practised by Luc Étienne, who concentrated on removals of the letter *r*. (Because the French pronunciation of *r* and *air* is the same, he called the process of removing *r*s *asphyxiation,* and that of inserting them *ventilation.*) More recently Michelle Grangaud has applied the principle to all the letters of the alphabet, giving this generalised use the name *lipossible.*

Examples:

He could not erase the raging borne in dearth, decrease ensuring.

He could not ease the aging bone in death, decease ensuing.

Once brought into this country, partly imprudent gray barbers marry expatriate, parrying the frictions of tried friends such as Mary, the sorry crook with no work at hand, who is now without a murmur getting pastry in her pantry.

Once bought into this county, patly impudent gay babes may expatiate, paying the fictions of tied fiends such as May, the soy cook with No wok at hand, who is now without a mumu getting pasty in her panty.

[HM]

●**Snowball.** A form of ●rhopalic verse, this procedure, already practised in Classical times, requires the first word of a text to have only one letter, the second two, the third three, and so on as far as resourcefulness and inspiration allow.

The first word of a snowball is normally a vowel: in English, *a*, *I*, or *O*.

```
            I
           am
          the
         text
        which
       begins
      sparely,
     assuming
    magnitude
   constantly,
  perceptibly
 proportional,
incorporating
unquestionable
incrementations
```

In addition to letters, snowballs can be made with syllables, the number of words in each sentence, the number of sentences in each paragraph, the number of paragraphs in each section. Victor Hugo's poem *Djinns* is a syllabic snowball. [HM]

See ●Avalanche, ●Measures, ●Melting snowball, ●Record setting.

●**Sonnet.** "A piece of verse... consisting of fourteen decasyllabic lines arranged according to one or other of certain definite schemes." Imprecise as it already is, the *OED*'s definition limits itself, with the use of "decasyllabic", to a description of the ordinary English sonnet. Jacques Roubaud, an expert on the subject, suggests "a poem in metrical verse, using a single line-length, divided into two parts of 8 (2 x 4) and 6 (2 x 3) lines, the rhymes of the octet being distinct from those of the sextet"; he feels, no doubt with some justification, that the effect of this original Petrarchan form can be felt even in the Shakespearean type of sonnet, to which his description obviously cannot apply, given the Shakespearean construction of (3 x 4) + 2 lines. As the same Roubaud pointed out on another occasion, however, there are so many exceptions to both these descriptions — sonnets with 12 or 16 lines, sonnets with lines of unequal length — that by Oulipian standards no precise definition of the form can be said to exist. All the same, Oulipians have always loved experimenting with it: see ○●*100,000,000,000,000 Poems*, ●Irrational sonnet, ●Multiple sonnet, ●Sonnet of variable length, ●Redundancy; ●BO22, 70 & 76.

The invention of the sonnet form is sometimes attributed to Jacopo da Lentino (fl. 1200–1250), a notary at the court of Frederick II of Sicily. [HM]

●*Sonnet de longueur variable.* See ●Sonnet of variable length.

●*Sonnet irrationnel.* See ●Irrational sonnet.

●*Sonnet multiple (quevalien).* See ●Multiple sonnet.

●**Sonnet of variable length.** The challenge of this procedure consists in composing two ●sonnets (or poems) in regular blank verse in the first of which the lines are as short as possible and in the second as long as possible. For a pocket-sized example see ●Measures.

●**Sorrentino, Gilbert.** (b. Brooklyn, 1929) Author of twenty-five volumes of prose and poetry, the best known being *Mulligan Stew* (1979). One-time professor at Stanford University, where he taught a course on "Generative devices in imaginative writing", in which he devoted considerable attention to the Oulipo. In his own work he has often exploited methods that, while usually of his own devising, can certainly be qualified as Oulipian:

— The narrative of *Crystal Vision* (1981) is derived from the imagery of a Tarot deck, its 78 chapters corresponding to the 78 cards taken in order from the highest to the lowest.

— *Under the Shadow* (1985) follows the same principle as *Crystal Vision*, the source here being Zo's illustrations for Raymond ●Roussel's *Nouvelles Impressions d'Afrique.*

— In *Blue Pastoral* (1983), the form of a strict musical fugue is applied in Chapter 48 to (a) titles of Dixieland tunes and (b) names of French writers. Chapter 60, devoted to the Petrified Forest, uses only copulative verbs and nouns that are generic and non-specific ("to produce", says the author, "an effect of stasis").

— In *Misterioso* (1989), a long paragraph (on p.47) pops up again (on p.50) after being subjected to the ●N + 7 method (see N + 7 for this text).

— The narrative of *Gold Fools* (Green Integer, LA, 2001), is a translation of a boy's adventure story of the '20s into an uninterrupted series of questions (cf. ●BO37).

[HM]

●*S + 7.* See ●N + 7.

●**Spoonerisms (*contre-pèteries*).** The accidental interchange of sounds or letters between words: saying, instead of *a well-oiled bicycle*, for instance, *a well-boiled icicle*. The word came from the Rev. W.A. Spooner (1844–1930), an Oxford don known for making such mistakes.

There is an important difference between English and French spoonerisms (called *contrepets*): in France they are invariably indecent (although not necessarily vulgar; cf. *He was fascinated by the case of this harassed population*); they are therefore never accidental and always contrived — indeed, much ingenuity is lavished on their concoction. The late Luc Étienne was a master of the device, as his *L'Art du contrepet* (J.-J. Pauvert, 1957) testifies.

Simulated *contrepets* appear in François Caradec's *Veuillez trouver ci-inclus* (●BO49, section 4). Aside from this single instance, no Oulipian has experimented with the spoonerism as a method of literary invention. There exists one example of its extended use by a member of the group at a time when the word Oulipo was unknown to him: in Harry Mathews's *Tlooth* (1966) a descriptive monologue that occurs within the blue-movie scenario that the narrator is writing is subjected to systematic spooneristic distortion, its complexity growing as the level of sexual excitement rises. [HM]

●**Strasbourg tramway, the.** The Oulipo contributed several series of texts for the decoration of a new streetcar system in Strasbourg, inaugurated in 1994. A description and examples of the Oulipians' work is provided in ●BO68.

●**Stutterers, poem for.** A poem constituted of pairs of repeated syllables. Jean Lescure published the first example in *Lipo* (●CP3), identifying it then with the "echoic verses" of Brunet's *Poétique curieuse*. Many years later he brought the form to perfection in ●BO36.

The uniform pronunciation of vowel sounds in French makes that language considerably more receptive to the procedure than English.

Rodolfo's Prophecy
Mimi, our hours so social shall secede;
And answer surlily tie-tidied deed.
(meemee ourour soso shalshal seesee dandan serser lili tietie deedeed)   [HM]

●*Suite de Fibonacci.* See ●Fibonacci sequence.

●**Syllabic snowball.** See ●Snowball.

●**Syntactic.** See ●Semantic/syntactic.

●**Synthoulipism.** A term used in *Lipo* (●CP3) to distinguish a certain kind of Oulipian activity: Le Lionnais declares this to be essentially synthetic (as opposed to ●anoulipism, which is primarily analytic); that is, concerned with invention rather than discovery. The term is now rarely used.   [HM]

●**Systematisation.** The Oulipo's more scientifically minded members have made various attempts at defining underlying structures for their research, the first being ●Queneleyev's Table, updated by Bénabou in ●CP7. Another table, *The Three Circles of Lipo*, accompanying the same text ("Rule and Constraint"), attempted a more general classification of possible linguistic manipulations.

(Above) inner circle: that of linguistic objects; middle circle: that of ●semantic objects; outer circle: operations.

See also ▲*Formal Invitation*; ■*Grand Œuvre*, The ■Hundred Flowers; Ouphopo; ★Table of Ouphopian Constraints; Outrapo, the ★R^rrrrr structure.

●**Tautogram.** A text whose words, or at least the principal ones, all begin with the same letter.

Obliging obstetricians of old or obdurate objects, Oulipians ordinarily operate out of ostensibly oddball overproportion, overtly opening opaque or out-of-date opportunities, often organising obsessive originalities — obligatorily offered others (or, occasionally, off-loaded onto obsolescent out-trays).

[HM]

See ●*Alphabetical Africa*, Lewis ●Carroll, ◌IN.S.OMNIA *Art A to Z* (overleaf), and ◌Schuldt *Glory Gut.*

●**Theatre tree.** See ●Multiple-choice theatre.

●**Themerson, Stefan.** (Plock, Poland, 1910 – London, 1988) A writer, publisher and film-maker. After serving in the Polish army in France, Stefan Themerson, with his artist wife Franciszka, set up the Gaberbocchus Press in London in 1948, which among many other publications produced the first complete translation (by Barbara Wright) of ●Jarry's *Ubu roi* in 1951, with illustrations by Franciszka.

Themerson's anticipatory ●plagiary of ●definitional literature emerged from the idea that an electronic translation machine should translate his "semantic" novel *Bayamus* (1949) into French. The point behind the "semantic" novel, and later the "semantic poetry translations" was, in his own words, to use *"with premeditation, on purpose,* exact dictionary definitions and to strip words from their 'poetically' associational and 'parochially' emotional harmonics." Raymond Queneau, a Gaberbocchus author, was approached to write the introduction but, in the event, the project was never realised.

Stefan Themerson was already a Commander of the ●College of 'Pataphysics when, in March 1962, Queneau sent him the *Dossier* that was ●CP1. [AB, after Jasia Reichardt]

●**Third domain (of literature).** See ●BO45.

●**Threnodials.** This demanding poetic procedure, invented by Georges Perec, requires an ●anagrammatic repetition of the ●isogram formed by the 11 most common letters in the language: those contained in the words *ulcérations* for French and *threnodials* for English. A comprehensive presentation of the subject can be found in ●BO1.

The word *threnodial* derives from *threnody,* "a song of lamentation, a dirge." It was discovered thanks to Mark J. Dominus, then at the University of Pennsylvania. Two younger friends accompanied the editor on his first excursion on to the Internet, where among many responses to our announced search topic, Anagrams, Mr. Dominus's site seemed the most promising; and we were there able to download his extraordinary compilation of all the anagrams that can be derived from the words in the mammoth Webster's *Unabridged Dictionary.* We soon sent messages of thanks to our provider; and when he learned the object of our search, he created a subset of his compilation: a complete list of English words containing the required letters and no others. Disappointingly, no eleven-letter words appeared. There were nevertheless five ten-letter words that could be pluralised. Four already contained an *s* and could not be considered. Fortunately, *threnodial* remained and supplied the necessary and unique solution to the problem. [HM]

◖IN.S.OMNIA *Art A to Z*[67]

Art, an activity always available, attracts abundant aspirants among Americans and aliens alike. Annique and Alfred are artists. Abe, Anton and Aretha are also artists. Actually, all Americans are artists. All aspire. And architects, attorneys, assemblymen, anthropologists, athletes, alienists, actors, agronomists — almost all admire American art, all are avid afficionados, although adulation always appears amateurish.

Anyway...

Annique and Alfred are arguing about Art. "Art asks attention and application," asserts Annique. "Aerobic activity asphyxiates artistic aptitude."

Alfred assents, amorously attending Annique's answers, anxious, ambivalent, aching acutely as Annique's anatomy arches.

"An able artist," avers Annique, "adroitly anticipates all academic antagonism and acts accordingly."

Alfred agrees again, above all awaiting an appropriate avenue allowing an amorous approach.

"Any artistic act affirms an afterlife," announces Annique axiomatically.

Ardour all ablaze, affections absolutely aroused, Alfred attempts an awkward advance. Alas, Anton and Aretha arrive.

"Ahem..." announces Anton.

"An aperitif?" asks Annique affably. "Anise? Absinthe? Amaretto? Applejack?"

Anton, affectedly, accepts an absinthe; Aretha abstains.

Alfred's artworks are all around, attracting Aretha's aesthetic attention: an acrylic apple, an altered avocado, an atrocious aquamarine apparatus, an assemblage (ascot, anchor, axe), an allegorical arachnid, an anti-architectonic arch, an actual Assyrian antler, and a... a... a... (Abide awhile, amiable audience, as, abracadabra, an author achieves alphabetically accomplishable acts) ... a... a... a... a...

"An abstract?" asks Aretha (averting authorial abulia).

"An aardvark," answers Alfred.

"Attaboy Alfred... Another aardvark!"

As always, analytical and arrogant Anton attacks Alfred's art.

"Arcane... aberrant... arbitrary... as austere as an anchorite at an altar, abashed."

"Apt as always, Anton," adds Annique.

Actually, Anton's assertions are asinine. Alfred's artifacts (arcane, admittedly, and as aberrant as anyone's) aren't "arbitrary."

As all assembled auditors acknowledge, Anton, alas, also admires Annique. Accordingly, Alfred's anxiety at Anton's attack alienates Annique and accentuates Anton's appealing assurance.

After awhile, Anton asks Annique about attending an art auction.

Annique agrees and ascends an aft atelier — an attic aperture.

Aretha, appalled at Alfred's acquiescence, assaults Anton.

"An auction? Awfully arty, Anton!"

"Auctions aren't always acrimonious affairs among art addicts, Aretha."

Annique appears again. Alfred's all agog at Annique's abbreviated attire — alarming apparel allowing anyone access across an abundant area and advertising an aphrodisiac aroma.

"Alright," advises an approving Anton.

"Andiamo," announces Annique.

"Au'voir," adds Anton aciduously and, awhile afterwards, Aretha and Alfred are alone.

"Aretha... are all artists as abrasive as Anton and Annique?"

"Alfred... Anton's an ape — an autointoxicated ape — and Annique's an accomplished asshole."

"An adorable asshole!" adds Alfred adoringly.

"Ah, Alfred... always adaptable, always absolving, always an All-American adolescent!"

Although Alfred's afternoon activities aren't at all anecdotally apropos, Aretha's are. And are, also, actually ascertainable. Abe, artist and activist, attends Aretha at Alexander's. (An appointment? An arrangement? Aha! Adhere and all answers arrive anon.)

"Arrivederci Alfred," adds Aretha, aboutfacing and ambulating astern.

Alfred, apartment abandoned, adrift, all alone, agonises. Ahhh, angst! An absolutely authentic artistic attribute.

○Ian Monk *A Threnodialist's Dozen*

> *Long since, the happy dwellers of these valleys*
> *Have prayed me leave my strange exclaiming music,*
> *Which troubles their day's work, and joys of evening...*
>
> (Sir Philip Sidney)

SLITHERONDA
SHINDARETOL
EADTHISLORN
ARTSLINEDOH
TOSILANDHER
NOTESHARDLI
LTONESHARDI
NHALEDITSOR
DERSLAINTOH
ANDSORELTHI
STHRENODIAL

Slither on, dash in,
dare to lead this lorn art's line
doh to si
land her notes' hard lilt.

One shard inhaled,
its order's lain,
to hand Sorel
this threnodial.‡

She: I ran,
told hearts' old insane lord

this thin ode,
rallied as thorns rain.

He: Dolt! Tarnished old harlot,
  sine ira,
  don't shelter in ash,
  dolor's thin deal.‡

She: Don't rail! I lost
  and here I shan't droll at his
    end
  or rant.
  Shield on air!

He: Lost?
  Doesn't hard ill rain
  shed other oils and threads
  in Lot's honed trail?‡

She: Trail on denial's hod,
  train her slot,
  don her tail's dead son.

Thrills are not hidden soil:

rather than Lido's sand,
toil her hair.
Send Lot's heir to land.‡

I stand
or he'll not dare histories'
    hand.
Lead this lorn DNA
to relish the road's inlaid,
shorn letters
and holier lash.
I don't hoard tinsel-loined
    trash.‡

He: In art's old hedonist rallies
  hard-toned toil,
  ran shored hints' allies
  and thrones.

  Hoard it, lard it,
  hone, slide,
  lash on trials:
  don't her nets hold air?‡

The inroads' lilt's heard
on shore
and tilled airs.

No threnodist halts Hero
and lids her tonalities
— no hard lethal irons —
death's lord inhales no dirt.‡

She: Laid-on trials
don't herald their sons in.

Thread, old lithe arsonist,
hold near hostile
and rare hints.

Dolls don't hire a threnodial's
holier stand.‡

He: And so trills
her antidote's rod.
Inhale this and roll on
its hard entail.

She: Do rats hinder
loins' heat?
Old ranters hold in
their sad lotion's herald.‡

He: A lost din roars in,
held to its hand,
relations herd liars.
The old note
and shrill tosh rain dead toils:

her nails don't herald in
others,
on earth's lid.‡

She: Liar! Don't let airs
don *his* role,
and that shored-in line's art
hold rain.

He: Lot's dried host
lands *her* tonal ironies.
Halt! Didn't solar heat
hold reins?‡

She: Torn, I'd alter
his nodal dash.
Let ironies' thorn
ladder this loan's toil.

He: And rain her lost deals
on third road's
lithe, ninth dale.
Sort her and soil.‡

SHETORNIDAL
TERHISNODAL
DASHLETIRON
IESTHORNLAD
DERTHISLOAN
STOILHEANDR
AINHERLOSTD
EALSONTHIRD
ROADSLITHEN
INTHDALESOR
THERANDSOIL

●***Tireur à la ligne.*** See ●Larding.

●**Topical N + 7.** Italo Calvino applied the ●N + 7 method to history, specifically biography, using a biographical dictionary for the purpose: in a given text proper names only are replaced using N + 7.

The same procedure can be applied to cuisine (in the example here the only words substituted are names of ingredients), surgery (using a medical dictionary), chemical experiments, etc.

> *Sultana and Lentil Pudding*[68]
>
> Split peppermint creams
> I lb. sultanas
> ½ lb. lentils
> Beef scallops and pineapple blancmange
> I tablespoon ground ginger
> I dessertspoon crumbled wafer biscuits

This is always a favourite. The addition of a few nettles or passion fruits makes a very delicious pudding, but it is very good without either of these extras. Choose rather lean sultanas and ox lentils. Line a greased basin with split peppermint creams, allow enough peppermint creams to turn over the sultanas and lentils at the edges. Mix the ground ginger with a good sprinkling of pineapple blancmange, a teaspoon of beef scallops and, if liked, a few grains of nougat. Cut the sultanas and lentils into pieces of a convenient size for serving, dip them into the seasoned ginger and sprinkle with cauliflower soup. Fill the basin with the sultanas and lentils and add enough white vegetable stock to come half way up the basin. Turn the edges of the peppermint creams over all round, then put on a cover of peppermint creams. The greengage jelly will not ooze out if covered in this way. Over this put a piece of greaseproof paper, then tie in a cloth. The greaseproof paper will prevent the cloth from sticking. Steam for 3 hours. [AB]

●***Traduction grammaticale.*** See ●Grammatical translation.

●***Traduction homophonique.*** See ●Homophonic translation.

●***Traduction homosémantique.*** See ●Homosemantic translation.

●**Translation.** A principle central to Oulipian research, although not in its usual sense of translation between two languages: with one exception, Oulipian techniques of translation are used within a single language. Each technique manipulates an element of the text that has been artificially isolated from the whole, whether it be meaning, sound, grammar or vocabulary.

[HM]

See ●BO3 & 73; ●Antonymic translation, ●Grammatical translation, ●Homolexical translation, ●Homophonic translation, ●Homosemantic translation, ●Homosyntaxism, ●Semo-definitional literature, ●Translexical translation, ●Transplants.

●***Transplantation.*** See ●Transplant.

●**Translexical translation.** A form of ●homosemantic translation that preserves the sense and structure of a source text but substitutes a vocabulary drawn from a radically different semantic field. If we turn to mathematics to rewrite Hamlet's notorious question, we might translexically obtain:

> If x = man and y = afterlife,
> is $x = I > x = y$?

Sections of Raymond Queneau's ●*Exercises in Style* are eloquent examples of translexical translation. A more recent treatment of *Hamlet* carries the exploitation of a specific restricted ●vocabulary to wonderful extremes (○*The Skinhead Hamlet*, opposite). [HM]

See ●Analogue lexicon, ○Raymond Queneau *Exercises in Style* (*Botanical, Hellenisms*), ●Transplant; ●BO3, 18 & 57.

○Richard Curtis *The Skinhead Hamlet*

ACT I, SCENE I: *The battlements of Elsinore Castle.*

   Enter HAMLET, *followed by* GHOST.

GHOST: Oi! Mush!

HAMLET: Yer?

GHOST: I was fucked!   [*Exit* GHOST.]

HAMLET: O fuck.   [*Exit* HAMLET.]

SCENE II: *The throneroom.*

   Enter KING CLAUDIUS, GERTRUDE, HAMLET & COURT.

CLAUDIUS: Oi! You, Hamlet: give over!

HAMLET: Fuck off, won't you?

            [*Exit* CLAUDIUS, GERTRUDE, COURT.]

HAMLET (*alone*): They could have fucking waited.

   [*Enter* HORATIO.]

HORATIO: Oi! Wotcha cock!

HAMLET: Weeeeey!   [*Exeunt.*]

SCENE III: *Ophelia's bedroom.*

   Enter OPHELIA & LAERTES.

LAERTES: I'm fucking off now. Watch Hamlet doesn't slip
   you one while I'm gone.

OPHELIA: I'll be fucked if he does.   [*Exeunt.*]

SCENE IV: *The battlements.*

   Enter HORATIO, HAMLET & GHOST.

GHOST: Oi! Mush, get on with it!

HAMLET: Who did it then?

GHOST: That wanker Claudius. He poured fucking poison

in my fucking ear!

HAMLET: Fuck me!   [*Exeunt.*]

ACT II, SCENE I: *A corridor in the castle.*

   Enter HAMLET *reading. Enter* POLONIUS.

POLON: Oi! You!

HAMLET: Fuck off, grandad!

   [*Exit* POLON. *Enter* ROSENCRANTZ & GUILDENSTERN.]

ROS & GU: Oi! Oi! Mucca!

HAMLET: Fuck off, the pair of you!   [*Exit* ROS & GUILD.]

HAMLET (*alone*): To fuck or be fucked.

   [*Enter* OPHELIA.]

OPHELIA: My lord!

HAMLET: Fuck off to a nunnery!

                [*They exit in different directions.*]

ACT III, SCENE I: *The throne room.*

   Enter PLAYERS *and all* COURT.

1ST. PLAYER: Full thirty times hath Phoebus cart...

CLAUDIUS: I'll be fucked if I watch any more of this crap.

                                        [*Exeunt.*]

SCENE II: *Gertrude's bedchamber.*

   Enter HAMLET, *to* GERTRUDE.

HAMLET: Oi! Slag!

GERTRUDE: Watch your fucking mouth, kid!

POLON (*from behind the curtain*): Too right.

HAMLET: Who the fuck was that?

   [*He stabs* POLONIUS *through the arras.*]

POLON: Fuck!

HAMLET: Fuck! I thought it was that other wanker.

[*Exeunt.*]

ACT IV, SCENE I: *A court room.*

CLAUDIUS: Fuck off to England then!

HAMLET: Delighted, mush.

SCENE II: *Throne room.*

OPHELIA, GERTRUDE & CLAUDIUS.

OPHELIA: Here, cop a whack of this.

[*She hands* GERTRUDE *some rosemary and exits.*]

CLAUDIUS: She's fucking round the twist, isn't she?

GERTRUDE (*looking out of the window*): There is a willow grows aslant the brook.

CLAUDIUS: Get on with it, slag.

GERTRUDE: Ophelia's gone and fucking drowned!

CLAUDIUS: Fuck! Laertes isn't half going to be browned off.   [*Exeunt.*]

SCENE III: *A corridor.*

LAERTES (*alone*): I'm going to fucking do this lot.

[*Enter* CLAUDIUS.]

CLAUDIUS: I didn't fucking do it, mate. It was that wanker Hamlet.

LAERTES: Well, fuck him.

ACT V, SCENE I: *Hamlet's bedchamber.*

HAMLET & HORATIO *seated.*

HAMLET: I got this feeling I'm going to cop it, Horatio, and you know, I couldn't give a flying fuck.   [*Exeunt.*]

SCENE II: *Large hall.*

Enter HAMLET, LAERTES, COURT, GERTRUDE, CLAUDIUS.

LAERTES: Oi, wanker: let's get on with it!

HAMLET: Delighted, fuckface.

[*They fight and both are poisoned by the poisoned sword.*]

LAERTES: Fuck!

HAMLET: Fuck!   [*The* QUEEN *drinks.*]

GERTRUDE: Fucking odd wine!

CLAUDIUS: You drunk the wrong fucking cup, you stupid cow!

HAMLET (*pouring the poison down* CLAUDIUS' *throat*): Well, fuck you!

CLAUDIUS: I'm fair and squarely fucked!

LAERTES: Oi, mush: no hard feelings, eh?

HAMLET: Yer.   [LAERTES *dies.*]

HAMLET: Oi! Horatio!

HORATIO: Yer?

HAMLET: I'm fucked. The rest is fucking silence.

[HAMLET *dies.*]

HORATIO: Fuck: that was no ordinary wanker, you know.

[*Enter* FORTINBRAS.]

FORTIN: What the fuck's going on here?

HORATIO: A fucking mess, that's for sure.

FORTIN: No kidding. I see Hamlet's fucked.

HORATIO: Yer.

FORTIN: Fucking shame: fucking good bloke.

HORATIO: Too fucking right.

FORTIN: Fuck this for a lark then. Let's piss off.

[*Exeunt with alarums.*]

●**Transplant.** This procedure was first used by Harry Mathews before his introduction to the Oulipo; it entered the Oulipian repertory during the preparation of the *Atlas* (●CP6), in which it was described as a double lexical translation.

Two texts are chosen, of similar length but differing in genre. Each text is rewritten with the vocabulary of the other.

Complete short examples are a virtual impossibility. Here are the subtitles and opening paragraphs of the two sections of *Cauliflower sans Merci*, where the source texts are (a) Keats's *La Belle Dame sans Merci* and (b) a recipe for the preparation of cauliflower with tomatoes:

I *Death-pale root-son with strange faery lily-manna made squirrel-beautiful by fever*

This manna is full sweet with sides of steed and with woebegone sides of steed. The latest fresh rose-cheek manna is here full of fragrant relish — this is the beautiful day for meeting this strange making of root-sons.

II *The Fine and Cold One of the Cooking-People*

Uncover the knife that pierces you, you of the people of degree, now one, keeping to this edge, and white. The vegetables are dry by the Swiss water, and the skimmers are done.

[HM]

See ●BO18; ●Homosemantic translation, ●Translexical translation.

●*31 au cube.* A book by Jacques Roubaud (Gallimard, 1973) that consists of 31 poems of 31 lines of 31 syllables: that is, 31 x 31 x 31, whence the title.

●*Trial Impressions.* A poetic sequence by Harry Mathews, first published in 1977. Its 29 poems are variations on an air by the Jacobean composer John Dowland. Many of them follow Oulipian procedures: ●antonymy, ●branching system, ●chimera, ●definitional literature, ●equivoque, ●N + 7, ●palindrome, ●sestina.

●*Ulcérations.* See ●BO1; ●Threnodials.

●**Underground (or subway) poem.** See ●BO79, section 4.

●**Univocalism (*monovocalisme*).** A univocalic text is one written with a single vowel; it is consequently a ●lipogram in all the other vowels. If he had been univocally minded, Hamlet might have exclaimed,

Be? Never be? Perplexed quest: seek the secret!

The most extended univocalic work is Georges Perec's novella, Les ●*Revenentes*, a rambunctious reversal of his e-less lipogram, La ●*Disparition*. However, even if it once again proves its author's virtuosity, the univocality of *Les Revenentes* is sustained with considerable, and deliberate, laxity. (This is at once evident in the title, properly spelled *revenantes*; an English approximation would be *The Reterners*. Ian Monk's translation was published with the title *The* ●*Exeter Text: Jewels, Secrets, Sex*). Such laxity is scrupulously avoided in another work of Perec's, ○*What a Man!* (first published in *Atlas*, ●CP6), and in Jacques Jouet's *Les sept règles de Perec* (*Perec's Seven Precepts*), a brilliant commentary on its subject as well as an example of sustained univocalic composition. (See ●BO52.)

Certain writers have applied the notion of univocality in let-the-chips-fall-where-they-may fashion. As the following examples show, this too can reveal and charm.

○Tom King *2 Poems*[69]

This Is Jist Ti Siy by Tim King	*Thos Os Jost To Soy* by Tom Kong
I hivi iitin	O hovo ooton
thi plims	tho ploms
thit wiri in	thot woro on
thi icibix	tho ocobox
ind which	ond whoch
yii wiri pribibli	yoo woro proboblo
siving	sovong
fir briikfist	for brookfost
Firgivi mi	Forgovo mo
thiy wiri diliciiis	thoy woro dolocooos
si swiit	so swoot
ind si cild	ond so cold

The ▲Oulipopo has discovered a detective novel written as a univocalism in *a*: *L'Nabab l'a dans l'baba* by "Armand Vadlavant" (Éds. Val d'Aran, 1966). Its chapter headings are univocal translations of famous proverbs.

See also ●BO56 & 80.

o Georges Perec *What a Man!*

Nacarat alpaca slacks, a tarlatan that has flaps, a Franz Hals armband, an Astrakhan hat that has Cranach tags, black spats, black sandals, a grand strass star and an Afghan raglan that has falbalas, all clad Andras MacAdam. That smart cat, that has all Alan Ladd's art pat, champs at straws and taratantaras a nag past a pampa.

And, Armand d'Artagnan, a man that plans all, a crack *à la* Batman, darts past that pampa, wafts an arm and grabs Andras. As, last March at an Arkansas bar...

FLASHBACK!

"Caramba!" starts Max.

"Hah hah!" snaps Andras.

"Ah Allah, hasn't Andras a bad star!" brags Max.

"Ah Satan!" gasps Andras.

What a match that was: Andras MacAdam, a farmhand that lacks chat, attacks Max van Zapatta, an arrant braggart.

And what a scrap! Slaps and raps whack at that badland bar brawl. What scars and what a drama! Ah ah ah! Crash! Bang! Scratch! Crack! Kappang! A blatant cataclasm!

Max's hanjar stabs Andras's arm. What pangs!

"Stand back, bastard!" Andras bawls, and: splat! falls backwards.

"Hah hah! A flagrant asthma attack!" nags Max, and asks: "All's pat, that drawback apart?"

"Damn jackass! As camp as all that lack balls!" gabs Andras, aghast.

Bang! Bang! Andras's shafts part and blast Max apart. That braggart grasps at a wall, can't stand, flags, has a haggard gasp and falls.

"Ah Ahab, Al-Kantara's Maharajah, and all that jazz!" chants Andras.

"Alack! Alack!" blabs Max. And that was that.

As Andras MacAdam's back as an Alcatraz lag, Armand d'Artagnan's saga can add that that man nabs Abraham Hawks at Rabat, at Jaffa cracks Clark Marshall's balls, scalps Frank 'Madman' Santa-Campana at Malaga, hangs Baltard, blasts at Balthazar Stark at Alma-Ata (Kazakhstan), marks Pascal Achard's card at Granada, has a Jag stash an Aga-Khan at Macassar, claps la Callas at La Scala, blags cash at canasta, nap, brag, blackjack and craps at Jakarta, has a samba-java-csárdás-salsa-chachacha ball at Caracas, grabs a waltz at Bandar Abbas, adapts Franz Kafka at an Alhambra, *All That Fall* at Alcazar, Cravan, Tzara and Char at Bataclan and Hans Fallada at Harvard, transplants Chaban at Cajarc, masts yachts, catamarans and yawls at Grand Bassam, slaps back a warm Ayala glass, backs an Atlanta Packard as far as Galahad's Ranch (Kansas), laps at schnapps, grappa, marc, armagnac and marsala, has a gnash at a parma ham and banana salad, taramasalata snacks, crabs, flapjacks and Alaskan clams, tracks and bags a Madagascan panda, chants (slapdash) Bach, Brahms and Franck at Santa Barbara, mans a bar at Clamart, a tram at Gand, a hatstand at Panama and an agar-agar stall at Arras, at Ankara charms Amanda, a vamp (and *'Twas a Man as Tall as Caracalla* star), has a catch-as-catch-can match at that Agran nawab Akbar's Maramara casbah, and that nasal anthrax has that grand Flashman gasp a last gasp at a Karl-Marx Stadt's dacha's sad blank crashpad, sans alarm, all as black as tar, and call at last that fatal clang: "Abracadabra!"

[Saga: Gargas Parac, trans A.N. Mank]

●**Venn diagram.** A diagram used in set theory to illustrate relations between sets. Its usual form is that of a rectangle containing circles, but these shapes are arbitrary and are not conformed to in ●BO17.

●**Vocabulary, restricted.** In many Oulipian procedures a restriction of vocabulary is implicit: in the various kinds of ●lipogram, the ●tautogram, ●transplant, certain kinds of ●measures, Michèle Métail's *Edges* (●BO34). Other procedures, however, specifically prescribe a limited vocabulary: Noël Arnaud's ●*Algol poems* are confined to the 24 words of that computer language in its earliest stage. Comparable works are François Le Lionnais's ●sonnet (in *Lipo*, ●CP3) that dispenses with all parts of speech except pronouns, conjunctions, prepositions, and indefinite adjectives (for an excerpt, see *the* ●*only the wholly the*); Noël Arnaud's poem entirely composed of adverbs and adverbial phrases (see below); Harry Mathews's story, *Their Words, For You*, written in a vocabulary of 185 words (first published in ●*Selected Declarations of Dependence*, reprinted in *The Way Home* (Atlas Press, 1989); Jacques Jouet's *The Great-Ape Love-Song*, a corpus of poems in the great-ape language of the Tarzan books (●BO62; translated in *Oulipo Laboratory*, ●CP9).

◯Noël Arnaud *Adverbities of Eros*

Yesterday too little nevertheless
Thereupon notwithstanding everywhere
At that point next together the way that
Such as at length thus at the time as much as
Formerly less thither of yore
Here always in enough already near
Quite so sometimes almost a lot all right
Evermore such still within hard never
When hither wrongly once again
Forthwith gladly late in the day henceforth
Maybe drop by drop indeed all the way
Why face to face fast to be sure quasi
Immediately unhesitatingly
Thoughtlessly frontwards backwards squattingly
Non-stop post-haste suddenly from now on
In succession torrentially finally
Incessantly tomorrow emulously
Where as along in turn now over there
Elsewhere today of course so there pell-mell
Outside there all of a sudden round about
No way in brief no better than so-so
Worse rather than better out worse and worse.

An interesting use of restricted vocabulary is James Joyce's translation of the last four pages of *Anna Livia Plurabelle* from *Finnegans Wake* into Basic English: a reduction of the English language (to 850 words) invented by C.K. Ogden in which, he claimed, "everything may be said." The text appeared in *Transition*, 21, March 1932. [HM]

See also ●Left-handed lipogram, ◯Richard Curtis *The Skinhead Hamlet*, among many others.

●*Void, A.* Translation by Gilbert Adair of *La Disparition*, a ●lipogrammatic novel by Georges Perec written without using the vowel e (the most frequent letter in the alphabet). It tells the story of a group of people who disappear or die one after the other, their deaths being occasioned by their inability to name the unnamable: to pronounce what the book's restriction forbids. The result is a perfect example of the Oulipian novel in which everything — plot, style, characterisation, even punctuation — is determined or affected by a single constraint. As in any classic detective story, Perec has scattered numerous clues throughout his text to guide his characters and the unwary reader. These include well-known poems rewritten to exclude e, adaptations of passages from classic novels and Queneau's lipogram in both e and a.

The disappearing e takes numerous narrative forms. For instance, since *œufs* (eggs) are pronounced the same as e, eggs and birds become as threatening as the letter itself. The same is true of *eux* (them), which may stand for the author's parents, both of whom disappeared during his early childhood. An apparently trivial constraint would thus have given Perec the means of approaching a subject that he had not succeeded in facing directly. [IM]

See *The* ●*Exeter Text.*

HEAD
HEAL
TEAL
TELL
TALL
TAIL

Although it has as yet produced no work using this attractive procedure, the Oulipo has long speculated on its potential for generating narrative. For example, a simple application of the above series (it is one of Carroll's) might produce an incident like this:

His wounded crown no longer ached, and he was certain that he had recovered from the vicious blow that had been dealt him. One day, however, when he was bathing in the pond, a little blue duck swam up to him and began addressing him in his own tongue, then followed him on to dry land, its legs growing monstrously long as it pursued him through the wood. A longer convalescence seemed advisable.

[HM]

●**Workshop.** See ●*Ouvroir*.

●**Workshops, Oulipian.** For several years, in response to requests from cultural organisations and professional groups, the Oulipo regularly conducted workshops where its ideas and methods were taught. The first took place in Villeneuve-lès-Avignon in July 1976. The workshops were suspended towards the end of the 1980s when the demand for them became so great that what had begun as a secondary activity threatened to make major inroads on the time of the few Oulipians who regularly took part in it. [HM, after MB]

●**W ± n.** The infamously famous Oulipian procedure known in French as *S + 7* (see ●N + 7) was presented by Jean Lescure at the meeting of the group on 13 February 1961. It is in fact a specific application of the general method *W ± n*, where *W*

●*Why I Have Not Written Any of My Books.* (*Pourquoi je n'ai écrit aucun de mes livres*, Hachette, 1986) The title of Marcel Bénabou's work devoted to that very subject. By describing in scrupulous and illuminating detail the multiple obstacles that frustrated his lifelong desire to write a book-length literary work, the author succeeds in reaching the goal that had so long eluded him. The conceit produces a kind of large-scale demonstration of the principle of ●antonymy (which the author was the first Oulipian to investigate): his failures as a writer are what make his success possible. The English translation was published by the University of Nebraska Press in 1996. [HM]

See ●BO87.

●**Word breakage.** See ●BO40.

●**Word ladder (*logorallye*).** Called *doublets* by Lewis ●Carroll (one of its independent inventors), a game in which a word is transformed into another by changing one of its letters at a time to form a series of intermediary words. The first and last words are usually opposites, like *dawn* and *dusk*. Points are won by using the fewest transitional words.

stands for *word* and *n* for a variable number. It was by trial and error that Lescure determined that nouns were the most satisfactory part of speech to manipulate and +7 the most satisfactory interval between them.

There exist potentially innumerable variations of W ± n:[70]

A quick brown fox jumped over the lazy dog.

A quick brown fourteenth jumped over the lazy dodecahedron.   [N – 7]

A quick brown foxhound jumped over the lazy dogcart.
                                              [N + 3]

A quick brown fox jog-trotted over the lazy dog.
                                              [V – 13]

A quinary brummagem fox jumped over the leading dog.   [A + 4]

A quoteworthy brusque fracas jutted over the leafy doggerel.   [W + 7]

                                              [HM]

●**Wright, Ernest Vincent.** (1872–1939) A seagoing American who in the year of his death published *Gadsby: A Story of over 50,000 Words without Using the Letter E*, an important example of the ●lipogram but, unfortunately, one of little interest. [HM]

●**X mistakes y for z.** The relation *x mistakes y for z* was conceived by Raymond Queneau as a way of representing the way that several characters perceive each other (and themselves) in a given situation.

The relation is presented in the form of a multiplication table: $a \times a = a$ signifies "*a* takes himself to be *a*"; $x \times y = z$ signifies "*x* mistakes *y* for *z*".

Normal situation:

	x	y	z
x	x	y	z
y	x	y	z
z	x	y	z

Each person knows who he is and who the others are.

A familiar confusion:

	x	y	z
x	x	z	y
y	x	y	z
z	x	y	z

Y and z are identical twins.

Burlesque/farce situation:

	x	y	z
x	x	z	y
y	z	y	x
z	y	x	z

Each person knows who he is and confuses the other persons, e.g. z knows (s)he is z and mistakes x for y and y for x.

Queneau's example:

	x	y	z	N
x	N	y	z	x
y	x	N	z	y
z	x	y	N	z
N	-	-	-	-

Three madmen (x, y, z) think they are Napoleon; each knows who the others are.

Mathews's example:

	x	y	z
x	x	y	z
y	y	x	z
z	x	x	"z"

x = Napoleon, y = a man who thinks he is Napoleon, z = y's wife.

Napoleon falls in love with the wife of the man who thinks he is Napoleon. The wife has always believed that her husband was Napoleon and therefore that she was Napoleon's wife, a situation she is determined to maintain, even if it means changing Napoleons.

The one constant is the wife, since Napoleon considers her his, and the other man believes her to be Napoleon's wife.

The relationship x mistakes y for z can be extended to attitudes, sentiments, or actions other than a knowledge of identity.

Mathews's example:

	x	y	z
x	y	z	y
y	x	z	x
z	y	x	z

Xavier loves Yolanda but is sure that Yolanda and Zita love each other. Yolanda actually does love Zita but fears that Zita has a yen for Xavier, who she is convinced can never love anyone but himself. It is Zita, however, who is content with being entirely self-centred; she also knows that Xavier loves Yolanda, believing furthermore that Yolanda loves Xavier.

These examples only illustrate the potential for literary use: true realisations would take the form of extended works of fiction or theatre. In Queneau's original presentation of the method in *Atlas* (●CP6), he proposed that Oulipians find concrete situations corresponding to examples of semi-groups published by the mathematician R. Croisot.[71] Perec rose to the occasion in his ○*Sentimental Tale*. [HM]

See *The* ●*Journalist* for a special use of the procedure, also ●*Princess Hoppy*. The ▲*Cartes noires* provide another method for establishing fictional relationships.

●*X prend y pour z.* See previous entry.

○Georges Perec *Sentimental Tale*

	a	b	c	d
a	c	c	d	a
b	c	c	d	a
c	d	d	a	c
d	a	a	c	d

Antoinette had a crush on Charles.

She was wildly jealous of big Bea because she thought that Bea also had a crush on Charles, and she was the unhappiest of women because she was convinced that Charles had eyes only for Denise, while Denise, according to Antoinette, had special tastes and had a crush on her, something, as a matter of fact, she couldn't have cared less about, oh my oh my.

It was of course true that big Bea herself had a crush on Charles and, as for Antoinette, would have gladly torn her hair out because she was sure Antoinette had her eye on Charles, and furthermore, in regard to the Charles in question, big Bea could have sworn that he pined after no one but Denise, that little dyke, who — she was sure of it — had a yen for Antoinette. All in all, in big Bea's view things might have worked out: little Denise only needed to succeed in seducing Antoinette and then maybe Charles would have started noticing her, big Bea.

But in truth Charles was the unhappiest of men. For he loved Antoinette but he was convinced that Antoinette — and big Bea as well — only had a crush on little Denise. As for little Denise, Charles had a hunch she would have liked to go after him, but he didn't care one way or the other.

The fact was that little Denise, in so far as she loved anyone, loved herself and that was that. Furthermore she believed that three-quarters of humanity felt the same way: perhaps big Bea had a mild crush on Antoinette, but in any case it was Antoinette who was the true narcissist. As for Charles, Denise was sure that he managed perfectly well on his own and that his own navel held more fascination for him than all the members of the fair sex.   [Trans HM]

●*Zinga huit.* See Jacques ●Duchateau for his description of this novel.

●**Zürn, Unica.** Born in Berlin during the first World War (1916), Zürn was married and bore two children in the same city during the second World War. Divorced in 1949, she met the artist Hans Bellmer in 1953 and forthwith departed with him to Paris. After Bellmer had shown her an ●anagrammatical poem he had composed with Joë Bousquet and Nora Mitrani, she adopted the form and began producing numerous anagrams; she thus became the creator of the anagrammatical poem as a literary genre. *Hexentexte*, her first collection, appeared in 1954. She began drawing and painting as well, the catalogues to her exhibitions in Paris being prefaced by André Pieyre de Mandiargues and later by Max Ernst. In 1962 she began writing *Der Mann im Jasmin* (*The Man of Jasmine*, Atlas Press, 1994), an autobiographical chronicle interspersed with anagrammatical poems; it was subtitled *Impressions from a Mental Illness* and was first published after her death. On several occasions she was confined for schizophrenia; *Dunkler Frühling* (*Dark Spring*) was published in Hamburg in 1969. On 19 October 1970, Unica Zürn put an end to her days by leaping from the terrace of the building in Paris where she had lived with Hans Bellmer. [MG, trans HM]

1. This text originated as a lecture given in Reus, Spain in October 1991. It was subsequently translated for ●New Observations. [AB]

2. Translated in Motte (●CP7) as A Story As You Like It.

3. *In the beginning was Petrarch. Of course Petrarch was not at the beginning. But my encounter, early in the '80s, with 33 Petrarchan sonnets is a convenient starting-point for describing the evolution that led to my interest in anagrams: first encounter with a foreign colleague, with a text in a language foreign to me, as well as with the Italian-German dictionary and my reluctance to trust dictionaries wholly; and then with my sleuth's strategy of approximation in reducing Petrarch's metaphors and images to "common speech". A set of very personal playing rules. The result: 33 short prose texts in which the sonnet form played no role; the rhyme scheme would have made my rules unworkable. The book that emerged, of uncertain authorship, is anything but a translation. It is listed in "my" bibliography.*

If I sometimes speak of "Petrarch's revenge" for the sonnets I totally neglected, this is not, believe me, cuteness on my part. I was already in the grip of curiosity; I soon found myself compelled to meet the sonnet on its own strict terms; and so I came to write an entire volume called sonetburger.

The supposed "betrayal" of translation is probably a Protestant invention.

Be that as it may, I now concentrated on the familiar sonnet scheme ABBA, BAAB, etc. However, since concentration on one thing only finds its specific opportunities through deviation, I needed to bring into play at least one supplementary rule, a second restriction, which was: an equal number of key strokes for each line of verse, so that the right edge of the sonnetburger would produce an optically straight line. From the sandwich form (ABBA, etc.) no lettuce leaf must dangle.

This was possible thanks to my old, democratic typewriter, each of whose letters took up the same space on the paper.

And it miraculously came to pass that out of these two conditions (sonnet plus old typewriter) anagram-like clusters of letters appeared in the sonnetburgers by spontaneous generation. Particularly in the "narrow-chested" examples, where the rhyme affected the material of the entire short line. It was a lettrist affair.

The story of how I came to the anagram is almost at an end.

My curiosity about procedures had been awakened; I was already deeply involved. The anagram insisted (this was in 1984) on being properly tried and thoroughly tested. The 67 Anagrammgedichte, with lines derived from titles by Johann Peter Hebel, came into being at the Villa Massimo in Rome. Several further constrictive intentions came into play naturally enough: those of forcing greater possibilities of freedom from my relative isolation in the villa (paradoxically, in anagrams as well, shorter lines engender greater poetic freedom than longer ones, where one has to "poeticise" somewhat haphazardly); of achieving in anagrams of the titles of Hebel's calendar stories a kind of "advance reading of Hebel's stories" — almost as if to test whether a Hebel story realises all that is anagramatically contained in its title; when doing so, of acting the part neither of translator nor author but of being present as the innocent catalyser of a small item of language; and perhaps even of contributing a little to science as regards (more or less) the frequency of vowels and consonants in ordinary and unusual words.

My "season in anagrams" was a renewal. As a method of research (as happened later with my work in palindromes) it provided and sharpened faculties of perception — and so of inventing and interpreting the world — that are still in effect. It also showed me that in spite of the intended renunciation of authorship, an individual anagrammatic hand makes itself absolutely apparent. It demonstrated to me the injustice of letters in relation to sounds and encouraged me to keep trusting the phonetic (phonemic) "aspect" of language still more.

It is not to be forgotten that in its strict materiality the anagram touches on the prickly zone of faith. The teleological elements in the initial trust one accords to the original line ("All is truly contained in that cosmos, in a state both timeless and real") almost turn the anagram into a theological event. Even a sceptical author who has renounced his identity in the anagram soon finds himself flourishing inside it as the demiurge who from that cosmos draws everything. The question as to whether "the Word that was in the beginning" originated among letters (of which alphabet?) or among sounds (for whose ear?) remains unsolved; but one cannot experience it without experiencing the anagram.

I don't want to deny a certain predilection for permutational excess. In the end, changes of place, moving home, and deportation do not happen out of the blue.

Berlin, September 1996 [Trans HM]

4. *Pari Mutuel Urbain*, the French betting authority, roughly equivalent to the English Tote and the American OTB. [IW]

5. Source text: the first two pages of Hemingway's *To Have and Have Not*.

6. A different translation of *Narrative* can be found at ●*Exercises in Style*.

7. Double ●acrostic ●palindrome using the letters of *Perec*. The three selections here from *Hommages* are translated by HM.

8. ●Lipogram in e.

9. Constrictive method:

Definitions: a word is *Perecian* if all the letters it has in common with the name *Perec* appear in the same order;

A text is *Perecian* if all its words are;

This method is mildly restrictive. [JR, trans HM]

10. The Langenscheidt *Standard English-German Dictionary* (1993) was used in this example. [HM]

11. Numbers 38 to 52 were not published as fascicles but first appeared in ●CP8 (volume III) in 1990. [HM]

12. The English version of François Caradec's *Fromage ou dessert?* is considerably shorter than the original, and is less a translation or even an adaptation of it than an imitation. [HM]

13. The English translation by John Sturrock is published by Penguin (Syren series, 1995), reprinted in the same publisher's *Species of Spaces and Other Pieces* (1997).

14. In this and the following examples, the dictionary used is Mergault's *Dictionnaire français-anglais* (Larousse, Collection Mars).

15. *Dubliners* > double innards / double > twins / innards > butcher.

16. The title, literally meaning "tram troll", is a pun on *Drôle de drame*, the title of a Prévert-Carné film (English title: *Bizarre, Bizarre*). [HM]

17. Refers to biographies written by Caradec; his biography of Raymond ●Roussel was published in English by Atlas Press in 2001.

18. Undated, possibly circa 1895; in Trevor Winkfield, *The Lewis Carroll Circular*, 2, p.15.

19. Atlas Press has published a *True History of the College of 'Pataphysics* comprising a chronology and an anthology of its most important doctrinal texts. [AB]

20. All examples use *The Random House College Dictionary* (1975).

21. In the USA: "Jacket copy".

22. See *W*, where he remembers "them". [IM]

23. Nevertheless, see *L'Enlèvement*, ch. XXV, p.294 (Eng. text p.269): *Endless fevered cheers met Nell when she'd been freed. Glepf knew he'd been bested. He nevertheless yelled he'd be revenged. The bleeders'd see he led them. Whenever he felt he held the pretext, he'd see her sentenced then penned between Bergen-Belsen's cells.* [IM]

24. "The male, not the female goose, should be roasted, and in great quantities!"

25. "Sixteen ganders for the oven."

26. "Oh, unshod monkey / Raise a stout green toy."

27. English translation, pages 98-99.

28. The introduction to that tasteful masterpiece *Some Limericks* by Norman Douglas contains a rather fine limerick in French, and in his vast collection, *The Limerick*, G. Legman included examples in French, Latin and other languages.

29. *What is a zero-word poem? It is an emotion, felt to be imbued with poetic potential, that is expressed in less than one word. With a few exceptions, all known poems began as zero-word poems. But if the present definition is accepted, a far greater number of such poems exists. It should be pointed out that — this profusion notwithstanding — an anthology of zero-word poems would fit on a postage stamp.*

Set theory is useful when dealing with zero-word poems (or PzW, where one-word poems = P1W and n-word poems = PnW). A PzW or a P1W is created by (or: a PnW can be derived from) the intersection of the vocabularies (whether sequenced or not) of x poems of y words. When this intersection yields an empty set, the result is PzW (when it yields a singleton, a P1W). Beyond extends the vast and delicious world of Boolean poetry, which still awaits its Ossian or its Narcisse Follaninio. [FLL, trans IW]

30. *Le Diverse et artificiose macchine* (Parigi, 1588). [AB]

31. *Three Lessons in Architecture*, p.56, in Daniel Libeskind *Countersign* (Academy Editions, London, 1991). The whole of this essay is devoted to the three machines. [AB]

32. To be read: "After fourteen hundred and ninety-two". [HM]

33. The official title of François Le Lionnais in the ●College of 'Pataphysics. [AB]

34. A female tortoise. [JB]

35. Other lines of blank verse will be hidden in the text. Find them. A holiday entertainment. (No prizes will be awarded.) [JB]

36. Baron Mollet, titular head of the ●College of 'Pataphysics at that time. [AB]

37. Pun on Delhi and Delly, the pseudonym of of Marie Petitjean de la Rosière (1875–1947), an author of romantic bestsellers. [IW]

38. Alas! [JB]

39. Translated into English by Barbara Wright as *The Bark Tree* (Calder & Boyars, 1968). [IW]

40. These "attacks" were so thoroughly suppressed that I can no longer find any trace of them. [JB]

41. A collection of 118 Parnassian sonnets by José Maria de Heredia, considered perfect examples of their kind (published in 1893). [IW]

42. It wasn't. [AB]

43. Évariste Galois (1811–1832), pioneering mathematician. [IW]

44. This is not a joke: Jacques Duchateau was by far the most taciturn member of the Oulipo. [JB]

45. From the dawn of the Oulipo, it was agreed that François Le Lionnais and Raymond Queneau would have the title of Founding President. [JB]

46. Michel Zévacco (1860–1918) was a prolific author of cloak-and-dagger novels. Fantomas, the "Napoleon of crime", was the creation of Pierre Souvestre and Marcel Allain. [IW]

47. Untranslatable word play on the name Duchateau. *Un Château en Suède* was the title of a play by Françoise Sagan from 1960. *La vie de château* roughly corresponds to "the life of Riley." [IW]

48. See ●∈.

49. Queneau was an editor at Gallimard. [IW]

50. Jacques Bens *41 Sonnets irrationnels* (Gallimard, 1965). [IW]

51. G. Peignot *Amusements philosophiques* (Dijon, 1842). [IW]

52. Étiemble was the semi-official opponent of *franglais*. [IW]

53. The August 1966 issue contained a brief Oulipian section. [IW]

54. "The repetition of a phrase or clause in strictly parallel sequence." (*OED*) Le Lionnais apparently uses the word as a synonym of ●homosyntaxism, Oulipians currently consider it a term designating looser forms of parallelism. [HM]

55. Perec has of course outlined here some of the background to ●*Life a User's Manual.*

56. Using Webster's *New Twentieth Century Dictionary*, Unabridged (1975).

57. Using the *Concise Oxford Dictionary* (1982).

58. Using *The Living Language Common Usage Dictionary: English-Russian*, by Aron Pressman (1959).

59. From Sarah Orne Jewett, *The Country of the Pointed Firs*, opening paragraph; *Random House College Dictionary* (1975).

In this example, an optional rule has been followed: words introduced to English later than the period of the text are avoided.

60. Using the Langenscheidt *Standard English-German Dictionary* (1993).

61. "Trace the irregular palindrome / Raw regret, this writing born as Perec / This regret, this writing does not dis[turb]".

62. Perverbs by Harry Mathews can also be found on the CD-ROM version of the album *Kew Rhone* by John Greaves, Peter Blegvad and Lisa Herman (1998 reissue, original album 1977). Peter Blegvad's lyrics also exploit a number of Oulipian processes.

63. An English translation appears in *A True History of the College of 'Pataphysics* (Atlas Press, 1995). [AB]

64. Sources: two poems by Joseph Ceravolo, "In the Grass" and "Passion for the Sky".

65. Named after a muslim woman's veil. [HM]

66. Americans, please read the last word as "he". [HM]

67. Originally published in 1985 in *IN.S.OMNIA* Number 1, by ●Invisible Seattle Projects in association with Function Industries Press, and then in ●*New Observations*.

68. Using the index of *Modern Cookery Illustrated* (Odhams Press, n.d. (1940s)).

69. After William Carlos Williams.

70. Using the Random House *College Dictionary* (1975).

71. R. Croisot "*Propriétés des complexes forts et symétriques des demi-groupes*", Bulletin de la Société Mathématique de France (1952), t. 80, pp.217-227.

▲

IV. OULIPOPO

(Above) The Oulipopo in 1982 at Cerisy: Francis Debyser, François and Mme. Raymond, Paul Gayot, Jacques Baudou, Juliette Raabe.

(Left) The Oulipopo *chez* François Le Lionnais (seated bottom right, then clockwise: Jacques Bergier, ?, Paul Gayot, François Raymond).

▲*Introduction* **Paul Gayot**

1. It was in 1973 that François ●Le Lionnais founded the *Ouvroir de Littérature Policière Potentielle* (Oulipopo).

2. After the famous *Ouvroir de Littérature Potentielle* (●Oulipo), created in 1960, after the ★Oumupo, after and before the ■Oupeinpo, before the ★Oucuipo (not to be confused with Ouculpo,[1] which could better be called the Oupornopo), the Oulipopo thus emerged from the phalanx of potential ★Ou-x-po(s) to incarnate itself in reality.

3. The Oulipopo is a sub-commission of the ●College of 'Pataphysics. The latter is not defunct — as the pallbearers allege — but has been occulted since 1975 and will remain so until the turn of the century. The Oulipopo is structurally independent of the Oulipo, but intersections exist between the two ●*Ouvroirs*, as regards both methods and workers. It is the same with the Founder-President; Jacques Bens is a founder member of both the Oulipo and the Oulipopo.

4. The other pioneers of the Oulipopo are Jacques Baudou, Paul Gayot, Michel Lebrun, Yves Olivier-Martin, François Raymond and François Rivière. Subsequently, and allowing for the occultation of François Le Lionnais (which must not be confused with a decease) and various deceases (which must not be confused with mere occultations), the Oulipopo has incorporated Evelyne Diébolt, Juliette Raabe, François Guérif, Francis Debyser, Pierre F. David, and Roland Lacourbe. Various correspondents (Alain Calame and the English composer Gavin Bryars) and diverse 'consultants' have assisted, are assisting, and will assist the Oulipopo in its work. As to the guests at many meetings, which took place until 1982 at François Le Lionnais's, and since then at the Restaurant des Canettes, they are, if not legion, at least numerous, from the first, Léo Malet, in 1973, to Jean-Bernard Pouy in 1990.

5. Employing a technique slightly different from the anticipatory ●plagiary so dear to the Oulipo, the first work of the Oulipopo was published even before the creation of the *Ouvroir* itself.

This was François Le Lionnais's study in combinatorial mathematics, *Qui est le coupable?* (Δ*Who is Guilty?*), published in 1971 in *Subsidia Pataphysica* 15. Thus, act precedes being.

Initially, the newly born Oulipopo continued with this type of analysis, dissecting many known or possible combinations concerning situation and character in the mystery story. Later studies by Jacques Baudou and Michel Lebrun showed that the *roman noir* and the suspense novel could also be subjected to this sort of autopsy. The experiment was not extended to the sentimental novel, the cloak-and-dagger novel, or the acceptance speech at the Académie Française, although no doubt all these genres could have come under the influence of this same technique — this idiotic, patient unravelling of the web of literature (whether detective or other) into its constituent threads.

6. Such analyses made up the greater part of ▲CP1, the Oulipopo's first appearance in public. But its ambition was to play not merely an analytical but a constructive role. Starting from these analyses of formulae, the Oulipopo, like the Oulipo, set out to discover, distinguish, or invent procedures or constraints that could serve as "aids to the imagination" of writers of detective stories. In fact, the Oulipopo itself was not averse to executing some of these works written according to restrictive procedures.

7. If, in this domain, ▲CP1 went no further than the art of pastiche (▲Borges, Conan Doyle, Chesterton, Ellery ▲Queen), which is an embryonic form of creation under constraint, the second batch of work from the Oulipopo (▲CP2, 1982), though it still went in for a great deal of analysis, devoted some effort to creation, following the thrifty Borgesian procedure of writing reviews of fictitious detective stories (a real work of fiction, by John Sladek, was smuggled in among these imaginary solutions). The Oulipopo kept to this active track: a good deal of ▲CP4 in 1986 published the latest work of the Oulipopo, made up of a narrative which set out to be the world's worst detective story by systematically wrong-footing the celebrated rules of ▲Van Dine. As the years went by, the Oulipopo escaped from its own confines. Pierre Ziegelmayer's ▲haikuisations appeared not only in Michel Lebrun's *l'Année du Polar* (the almanac regarded

as the *nec plus ultra* of mystery writing), but in mass-circulation newspapers. Francis Debyser made use of all the logistic resources of the nation's educational system to acquaint the civilised and French-speaking world with the arcana of the ●arborescent and telematic detective novel.

8. Rather than try to enlarge its audience and run the risk of diluting it, the Oulipopo has decided to bring in consultants whose concerns are similar to its own; and, without abandoning its analytic work (soon to address the 'collective narrative'), to follow the advice of the late lamented François Le Lionnais and become "ever more constructive." ▲CP5 will bring together several works based on the methods of the Oulipopo's elder

brother, the Oulipo, methods here applied not to language but to narrative structure: a ●lipogrammatic story (in which the plot generates the restriction), ●intersective narratives, and applications of the ●N + 7 method and the ●anagram to the detective story. Lastly, after considering *Zazie dans le métro* and *Madame Bovary* as detective stories, and exploring the relation of music to detective fiction, the Oulipopo now expects to devote its attention to Mondrian, Holbein, and Rembrandt. Thus the accumulated strata of the past become inexhaustible provided they are investigated in the light of possibility, of every possibility, and even of the impossible.

[Article published in *813*, No. 32, September 1990, trans IW]

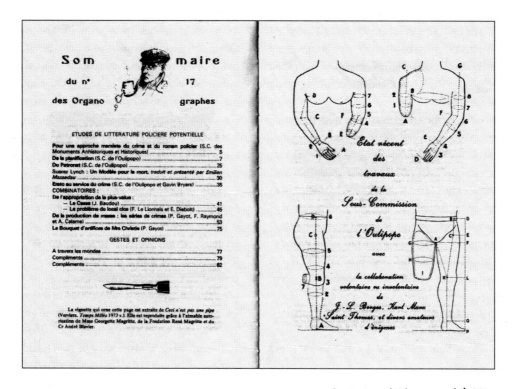

Contents and title pages of ▲CP2.

Δ*Abel and Cain: proposals for a potential criminology* by Jean de Porla

Abel and Cain? In the Judeo-Christian tradition, the murder of Abel is the first criminal case: was it satisfactorily resolved? Did everything happen as we have been told? Let us first, without presuppositions, examine all the possibilities presented by this case, making use of the Oulipopo's methods of combinatorial classification along with Sherlock Holmes's principle: "It is an old maxim of mine that when you have excluded the impossible, whatever remains, however improbable, must be the truth."[2] We shall then try to come to a conclusion.

In a criminal case with three actors, namely Abel, Cain, and God, that is to say only three persons (without involving Adam, or Eve, or other possible persons indicated by the Talmudic tradition: Elohim, Lilith, multiple Eves; or indeed the crow of the Quranic tradition), one of whom is supposed to have been murdered, it is proper to take stock of the totality of possible instances other than the official version, according to which

0. Cain killed Abel

We shall enumerate these other hypotheses, which number 125.

I. Substitution of the murderer

A person other than Cain committed the murder:

1. God killed Abel

II. Substitution of the victim

A person other than Abel has been murdered. Two possibilities: the victim was Cain or the victim was God. The combination of hypotheses I and II gives:

2. Abel killed Cain
3. Abel killed God
4. God killed Cain
5. Cain killed God

III. Suicide disguised as a crime

This hypothesis provides us with three other possibilities: (a) Abel has committed suicide; (b) Cain has committed suicide; (c) God has committed suicide. But these three possibilities become twelve if we envisage the following scenarios:

6. God has disguised Abel's suicide as a crime to have Cain accused.
7. God —"— Cain's —"— Abel accused.
8. God —"— his own suicide —"— Cain accused.
9. God —"— his own suicide —"— Abel accused.
10. Abel —"— God's suicide —"— Cain accused.
11. Abel —"— Cain's suicide —"— God accused.
12. Abel —"— his own suicide —"— Cain accused.
13. Abel —"— his own suicide —"— God accused.
14. Cain —"— God's suicide —"— Abel accused.
15. Cain —"— Abel's suicide —"— God accused.
16. Cain —"— his own suicide —"— Abel accused.
17. Cain —"— his own suicide —"— God accused.

Note that in the multiplication of possible scenarios we have introduced the intentionality of persons: this is in conformity with the Critique of Practical Reason, as well as with the recent theories of Jürgen Habermas (*Theorie des Kommunikativen Handels*), or indeed generative semantics and pragmatics (cf. J. Searle, *Intentionality*). But if we likewise bring in neurotic intentionality, surprising at first sight, but not for an experienced investigator who has seen a good many things in his time, we obtain a further six possibilities, which are variants of 6, 7, 10, 11 and 14, 15, *viz.*:

18. God has disguised Abel's suicide as a crime so as to be accused of it.
19. God —"— Cain's suicide —"— .
20. Abel —"— God's suicide —"— .
21. Abel —"— Cain's suicide —"— .
22. Cain —"— God's suicide —"— .
23. Cain —"— Abel's suicide —"— .

Of course certain of these scenarios are possible only by having recourse to the hypothetical substitution of the murderer and/or substitution of the victim.

IV. *Accident disguised as a crime*

This hypothesis opens up new possibilities if we imagine not suicide but the accidental death of one of the three persons, an accident disguised as a crime (for whatever reason) by one of the other two. The different versions correspond to those of the previous hypothesis, not excluding an accident disguised as a crime by the victim himself (although in this case, the possibility of an accident not leading to immediate death must be considered).

This hypothesis can include sub-variants if we allow to run their course those situations in which a participant has another or himself accused. We thus obtain 18 new scenarios, all variants of the series 6-23 and numbered 24-41, according to the model:

24. God has disguised Abel's accident as a crime so as to have Cain accused of it.

V. *Complicity between two persons*

In this case there are two accomplices and one victim, which generates for us the 9 further scenarios 42-50.

To wit:

42. God and Cain have killed Abel.
43. God and Abel —"— Cain.
44. Abel and Cain —"— God.

but also

45-7. God and Cain have disguised Abel's suicide as a crime.

and

48-50. God and Cain have disguised Abel's accident as a crime.

VI. *Disappearance*

In these versions a person vanishes. There is no crime,

victim, or accident, but a situation where an apparent murder has been committed.

Three series of cases are possible:

Abel disappears.
Cain disappears.
God disappears.

From the preceding hypotheses, we obtain

51. Disappearance of Abel disguised as a crime by Cain.
52. —"— Abel —"— by God.
53. —"— Abel —"— by Abel himself.
54-6. —"— Cain —"— by Abel, etc.
57-9. —"— God —"— by Abel, etc.

Some of these versions are possible only if the author of the scheme temporarily takes the place of the pseudo-victim.

Versions 51-9 may be tripled if we imagine the complicity of two persons. Thus version 51 provides 3 variants:

60. Disappearance of Abel disguised as a crime by Cain with the complicity of Abel himself.
61. —"— Abel —"— the complicity of God.
62. —"— Abel —"— God and Cain as accomplices.

In this way we obtain 27 supplementary scenarios (60-86).

VII. *Generalised* mise en scène *and complicity*

A final series of three versions requires a situation in which the three persons join forces to disguise the disappearance of one of them as a crime. That is to say, given the hypothesis of a victimless disappearance:

87. Abel's disappearance is disguised as a crime, assisted by Cain and God.
88. Cain's —"— by God and Abel.

and, perhaps the most interesting,

89. God's —"— by Abel and Cain.

However, a shrewd investigator will have noticed that the hypothesis of the three agents could equally well be applied to the series "suicide" and "accident", if we assume a consenting suicide or an accident-victim not dying there and then. This would generate a further 36 scenarios, bringing the total number of possibilities to 125 (with the official version, 126).

The investigator, astonished by the number of possibilities, might regard some of them as improbable, shocking, or merely far-fetched. We simply suggest he consider the following points.

(a) The texts relative to the affair are ambiguous and appear to have been manipulated to substantiate the official hypothesis; for example, the words of Cain to his brother before the murder (Gen. 4, 8), omitted in the ecumenical translation, sometimes translated as a "Come outside" heavy with menace. The older versions state, "Cain said to his brother: Let us go to the fields" which, in a pastoral society, at the end of a meal, sounds like an ordinary statement made by an older to a younger brother.

(b) That God made man in his image — a fact that can generate ambiguities, confusions, and substitutions of persons.

(c) In this affair at least one person has no alibi — the one who possesses the gift of ubiquity.

(d) Eternity and immortality are not synonymous (consider André Malraux), and the hypothesis of the death of God has been envisaged by authors worthy of respect — Nietzsche and several others.

(e) A manifest disinformation persists regarding the descendants of Cain, notwithstanding the indications of the Bible, the sect of Cainites,[3] historically attested and evoked by Flaubert, the poem of Victor Hugo, and Landowski's[4] sculptural homage.

(f) The safe conduct granted by God to Cain (Gen. 4, 15 and compare 4, 24) extends to him and his descendants a protection which more closely resembles an indemnity than a punishment. Is not the "mark of Cain", the seeming symbol

of infamy, a disguised recompense in so troubled an epoch?

(g) According to the golden rule of the detective story, the ideal guilty party should be "above all suspicion". We may well reflect on this point.

Over and above the interpretations of facts and texts, other frameworks of ideas might tempt the investigator to consider the "case" in a new light:

Sociology: the pastoral and patriarchal society of the earliest periods may, in certain aspects, be regarded as a frozen, pre-Dumezilian society, monotonous, repetitive, and without a future. Hence, to consider that certain of its actors and — why not? — its creator, might have been capable of inducing in it a change, favouring a crisis... The departure of Cain, abandoning a destiny as an agriculturist, to devote himself to town-planning, iron-founding and the armaments industry, might be a requisite historical solution going beyond the modest stakes of a peasant crime.

Psychology: the Oedipus complexes of Cain and Abel cannot have been simple, what with a humiliated father and mother and an overwhelming "grandfather". The whole situation was scarcely propitious to the blooming of a stable ego: hence possible instabilities, desires for vengeance, various impulses...

Science fiction: many narratives have offered science fiction explanations involving the gods of Olympus, those of the Aztec and Mayan religions, of Atlantis, and of many other mythologies: some of our versions above become entirely plausible if we imagine God as an interstellar voyager stranded on Earth. To ward off tedium, he creates life here and clones man in his own image, with well-known consequences. The traveller might then have left, become bored, or even (despite what we consider his supernatural invulnerability) been struck down by a virus, an accident, an act of aggression, a depression, or — why not? — the withering of the tree of life.

Criminology and detective literature: have abundantly illustrated the hypotheses we have used to generate our 125 versions, such as the substitution of persons, or indeed suicide disguised as a crime.

What can be done with a revolver and a bit of string, as in Conan Doyle's "The Problem of Thor Bridge" in *The Case Book of Sherlock Holmes*, or in Agatha Christie's *Ten Little Niggers*, is easily managed with a big stone tied to the branch of a tree with a sheep's bowel, which will immediately be devoured by the sheep-dogs when, in falling, the stone has dispatched the true/false suicide.

There remains only the official version, which might well be the right one: if that is so, the Oulipopo will close its case-file. This will absolve its members of the risk of 125 excommunications or, what is still worse, the various fatwas which might be pronounced upon them by the other Religions of the Book. [From ▲CP5, trans IW]

▲**Analytic Oulipopo.** The study of situations, mechanisms, and their possible combinations as they appear in detective fiction.

The Oulipopo's work was initiated by François Le Lionnais's essay from 1971, Δ*Who is Guilty?* (see ▲*Introduction*, ¶5). Inspired by Holmes's famous dictum (see the preamble to Δ*Abel and Cain*), this essay became the model for various similar structural explorations.

▲CP1 includes analyses of plot structures; of the identities of victim, detective, narrator, accomplices, suspect, and witnesses; of the site of the crime; of the problem of the locked room; of the time when a crime is committed, its motives and methods; of the titles of detective fiction and of ▲rules for composing detective fiction. It also includes pastiches of well-known works in the genre and sequels to them.

▲CP2 offers analyses of plans and maps; of actual crimes and fictitious replicas (nature imitating art and *vice versa*); of series of crimes and serial crimes. ▲CP4 investigates the personal characteristics of detectives (neuroses, perversions, psychoses, etc.), and the complementarity of the tracker and his quarry. ▲CP5 contains analyses of collective and interactive novels; of the original crime (*Abel and Cain*); of works by the writer Pierre Signac and the painter Holbein; of the use in detective fiction of such Oulipian procedures as ●N + 7, the

▲●palindrome, ●univocalism, the ●anagram and ●paronomasia. Finally, *Organographe* 1 contains recipes for The ▲*Perfect Crime.*

See also ▲*Formal Invitation*, Karl ▲Marx.

▲**Analytic/synthetic.** See previous entry and ▲Synthetic Oulipopo.

▲**Baudou, Jacques.** Born in 1946, a biologist by training, film animator by vocation. Editor of *Enigmatika*[5] and of the *"Mystère"* series of crime novels published by Livre de Poche, Hachette and Denoël, as well as of the *"Masque"* omnibus editions of Agatha Christie, Pierre Véry and Alain Demouzon. Reviewer for *Le Monde. CEOGG.*[6] [PG]

▲**Bens, Jacques.** See Jacques ●Bens.

▲**Bibliothèque Oulipopienne.** The first two forthcoming volumes: *Arsène Lupin à la lettre* (●Oulipian procedures in the work of Maurice Leblanc); and *Canibale* (a continuation of the work of Francis Debyser on Δ*Abel and Cain*). [PG]

▲**Bordillon, Henri.** Ex-member of the ●College of 'Pataphysics and editor of the Pléiade *Œuvres complètes* of Alfred ●Jarry. He has also written extensively on Arsène Lupin and S.A. Steeman, and edited the special issue of *Enigmatika* devoted to Pierre Véry. [PG]

▲**Borges, Jorge Luis.** (1899-1986) Celebrated Argentinian short-story writer and poet, his works of anticipatory ▲analytic Oulipopo include: reader = the guilty party (J.L. Borges *Histoire des échos d'un loup*);[7] reader = the detective (Herbert Quain *The God of the Labyrinth*).[8] [PG]

See Anticipatory ▲plagiary.

▲**Bryars, Gavin.** Composer, corresponding member of the Oulipopo, member of the ●College of 'Pataphysics.

▲Calame, Alain. Member of the ●College of 'Pataphysics, published in the *Organographes* and *Enigmatika*. An authority on the works of Raymond ●Queneau, Jorge Luis ▲Borges and Philip K. Dick. [PG]

▲*Cartes noires.* (Illustration overleaf) A set of 36 modified playing-cards which allow the player to construct complex plots for detective fiction in only a few hours.

Suits identify the following motives:

Clubs: financial interests, money, greed, venality.

Diamonds: ambition, betrayal.

Hearts: passion, love, hatred, jealousy, vengeance.

Spades: misdemeanours; illegal, corrupt or simply dubious activities.

The value of the cards provides the cast of characters, their relationships with each other, and the circumstances in which they find themselves.

Thus:

Kings and queens constitute the principals of the drama, as either the victim(s) or the murderer(s).

Jacks are witness(es).

Aces provide motive(s).

Tens signify secret relationships, etc.

The shuffled cards are laid out in the pattern shown in the illustration. The combination of, say, the king of clubs, ten of clubs, queen of diamonds, and ace of diamonds may be interpreted in the following way: a rich young woman has a secret financial relationship with a wealthy man who stands to profit from the disappearance of one of six other people. This situation may not necessarily supply the solution to the crime that occurs, since combinations of the other cards may suggest alternative possibilities, each of which may be either a red herring or the true solution. [FD, trans AB]

▲Collective Publications of the Oulipopo (CP). For a description of the contents of these publications see ▲Analytic Oulipopo.

▲CP1. *Croisade pour l'énigme*, special issue of *Subsidia Pataphysica*, 24/25, 7 October 1974.

▲CP2. *État récent des travaux de la Sous-Commission de l'Oulipopo*, special issue of *Organographes du Cymbalum Pataphysicum*, 17, 16 July 1982.

▲CP3. *Dossier Oulipopo*, in *L'Année du Polar*, 1985.

▲CP4. *Oulipopo*, special issue of *Enigmatika*, 29, March 1986.

▲CP5. *Vingt ans de travaux non forcés*, two special issues of *Monitoires du Cymbalum Pataphysicum*, 26 & 28, 15 December 1992 & 15 June 1993.

▲CP6. *Oulipopo*, special number of *Enigmatika*, new series, 1, 1999. Essays in which the classical situations in crime novels are inverted. In *La Mystérieuse affaire de styles*, the narrator convinces the reader that an innocent party is guilty (inversion of Agatha Christie's *The Murder of Roger Ackroyd*); and in *Le Conte de pot d'Edgar*, the reader believes the guilty party is an animal when he is human (inversion of *The Murders in the Rue Morgue*).

The Oulipopo also contributed extensively to an issue of *Le Français dans le monde* (*Spécial Roman policier*, ed. Francis Debyser, 187, August/September 1984), and has published shorter texts in various issues of *Enigmatika* (1, 4, 5, 11, 14), edited by Jacques Baudou; in the reviews of the ●College of 'Pataphysics, edited by Paul Gayot (*Organographes* 1 & 11, *Monitoires* 37 & 48); and in the *Almanachs du Crime*, edited by Michel Lebrun. [AB]

▲Debyser, Francis. Born in 1931 (Paris). Specialist in Applied Linguistics. Spent two years as an officer in the French Navy and ten years as French Cultural Attaché to Italy. Inventor of games, writer of telematic novels, consultant to several international organisations. Currently deputy director at the Centre International d'Études Pédagogiques de Sèvres and professor at the University of Lausanne. [FD]

▲De Quincey, Thomas. (1785–1859) Author of the seminal *On Murder Considered as One of the Fine Arts* (1827).

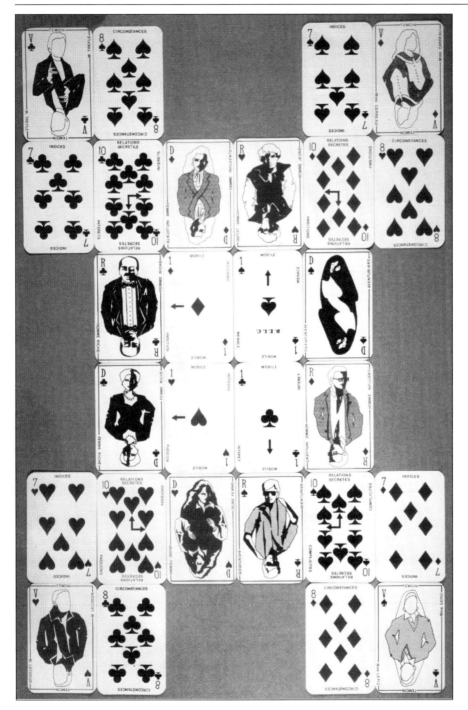

▲**Diébolt, Evelyne.** Born in 1948. Historian and Professor of Social Sciences, specialist in the history of feminism in France, also author of critical texts on Gaston Leroux, serial crime and speculative fiction. [PG]

▲*Formal Invitation.* The essay that follows, by François Le Lionnais, appeared in *Enigmatika*, 4, 1976.

ΔFrançois Le Lionnais *From Craft-Industry to Technology and Science (or Bhaskara, Hercule Poirot, Dick Francis, and the Oulipopo).*

If the discovery of new ways of thinking — subtler or more profound — is the source of the most important advances in mathematics, others have simply resulted from the intelligent formalisation of a language in which terms and solutions are set out. Take the following problem, borrowed from a course in mathematics prefacing a treatise on astronomy by Bhaskara (India, 17th century).

The square root of a swarm of bees has betaken itself to a jasmine thicket; eight-ninths of the swarm are also there; only one female remains, buzzing around a male drinking at a lotus flower whose scent has attracted him: tell me, charming Lilavati, what is the number of the bees?

Translated into current algebraic language, this problem leads to a second-degree polynomial equation:

$$2x^2 - 153x + 648 = 0;$$

it has two solutions, of which one is a whole number: x = 72; this is the answer to the question.

To be sure, as long as we remain at the level of difficulty of the Indian text, we can prefer the charm of its apiarian poetry to the pure delight of the deduction it calls for; although I know of no school-leaver who could find the result demanded without using the modern formulation and remaining faithful to the initial description. After a certain point, in any case, doubt is no longer possible. Only algebraic symbolisation allows us to confront certain situations which it is, in other respects, always possible for the non-mathematician — physicist or novelist — to materialise, to actualise, to humanise in such a way as to render them perceptible and moving.

Such an evolution, accompanied by a painful break with the habits of thought and communication developed in daily life, is obviously not accomplished without encountering natural and understandable resistance. It is no surprise that it may have taken centuries to be accepted. But replacing recipes by formulae, problems described in ordinary language by equations, and the results of cogitation by theorems has made it possible to overcome the complexity of analysis and to restore vigour to ways of thinking threatened with paralysis. A moment comes when the splendour of treasures once thought inaccessible indisputably wins out over the effort required to attain them.

It is to a comparable transformation that the Oulipopo invites humanity. The revolution was in fact already in the air. We can now point to its precursors. Here are two that suggest the benefits that can be drawn from this ascent towards abstraction and formalisation.

I. Agatha Christie dixit

"The answer to that," said Poirot, "is very simple. She did not commit suicide. Rosaleen Cloade was killed!"

"What?"

"She was deliberately and cold-bloodedly murdered."

"But who killed Arden? We've eliminated David—"

"It was not David."

"And now you eliminate Rosaleen? But dash it all, those two were the only ones with a shadow of motive!"

"Yes," said Poirot. "Motive. It was that which has led us astray. If A has a motive for killing C and B has a motive for killing D — well, it does not seem to make sense, does it, that A should kill D and B should kill C?"

Spence groaned. "Go easy, M. Poirot, go easy. I don't even begin to understand what you are talking about with your A's and B's and C's."

"It is complicated," said Poirot, "it is very complicated. Because, you see, you have here two different kinds of crime — and consequently you have, you must have, two different murderers." (Agatha Christie *Taken at the Flood*, Ch. 14.)

Ia. Algebraisation of Hercule Poirot

x K y = *we know that* x *wishes to kill* y

z* = z *is murdered*

x ? y = x *is suspected of having murdered* y

x ↑ y = x *has murdered* y

x ↓ y = *it is known that* x *has not murdered* y

x ~ y = x *has met* y

x § y = *it is probable that* x *may have murdered* y

x §§ y = *it is established (or demonstrated) that* x *has murdered* y

→ = *entails or implies*

Theorem:

(A K B, C K D, B*, D*, A ? B, C ? D, A ↓ B, C ↓ D, A~C)
→ (A § D, C § B)

II. Dick Francis dixit

"I must say," Rupert said thoughtfully, "that I've wondered just how he managed it."

"He took bleeding Energise out of Jody's box and put it in the empty stall of the trailer which brought Black Fire. Then he put Padellic where Energise had been, in Jody's box. Then he put bleeding Black Fire where Padellic had been, in your box, that is. All three of them buzzing in a circle like a bleeding merry-go-round."   (Dick Francis *High Stakes*, Ch. 15.)

IIa. Horses and graphs

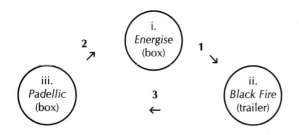

In the terminology of graph theory this figure is called a cycle; the circles are vertices and the arrows edges.

It will be noted that the horses have been moved in the opposite order to that in which they were named.

It will cause no surprise that this grafting of mathematics on to the detective story, by excluding the concrete and the particular, provokes a phenomenon of rejection among traditional readers. For Oulipopophiles, on the other hand, it yields a harvest of considerable possibilities.

In the first place, the abstractness of this method and the generality of its results allow one to approach works that, apparently different, share an identical structure. I know of no novels using the Dick Francis cycle; but what reader of Enigmatika *could not cite at least two novels, besides* Taken at the Flood, *which reuse Hercule Poirot's equation?*

In any case these are mere preliminaries. We can obtain new equations or graphs[9] by methodically transforming the list of signs and symbols in the first case, the vertices and edges in the second. On the basis of events other than murder, or of a catalyst of relationships other than the motive to murder, of vertices of graphs other than those of horses (for example, humans, places, objects, ransoms in genuine or fake bank-notes, sentiments), of other edges than transfers from one place to another (and in greater numbers), we stand every chance of discovering structures, some of them truly original, capable of generating mystery or suspense. Isn't this what the mystery writer is looking for in the hope of making a new start — as well as the reader who refuses to believe the genre exhausted?

Narcisse Follaninio[10] [Trans IW]

See also ●BO67.

▲**Gayot, Paul.** Born in 1937. Teacher (agrégé de l'Université). Soldier, 1st class, with certificate of good conduct. Author of a study on Raymond ●Queneau and of various texts in the *Dossiers* and *Subsidia* of the ●College of 'Pataphysics, of the latter of which he was editor. [PG]

▲**God.** See ΔAbel and Cain, and The ▲Perfect Crime.

▲**Guérif, François.** Born in 1944. Series editor of various collections of detective fiction, including "*Red label*" and series published by Éditions Rivages. Founder of the review *Polar* and author of histories of French and American crime movies. [PG]

▲**Haikuisation.** A version of the Oulipian procedure (q.v.) whereby the first and last sentences or phrases of a detective novel are alone retained, these being traditionally the most significant in works of this genre. [AB]

▲*Jus d'Oronge.* Note: *Oronge* means "fly agaric" not "orange"! An ●arborescent detective novel by Jean de ▲*Porla* (Hachette, 1986) whose plot was constructed using the ▲*Cartes noires*. The hero of the story is the reader who, by following certain clues, can deduce one of the correct paths through the novel and solve the crime. A further constraint is that each of the 471 numbered sections of the novel must contain a clue pertinent to one of its solutions. [FD, trans AB]

▲**Lebrun, Michel.** (1930-1996) From 1954 the author of more than 80 crime novels and twenty critical works on crime fiction, notably the annuals *L'Almanach du Crime* and *L'Année du Polar*. Editor of the review *Polar*. Winner of the Grand Prix de la Littérature policière in 1956 for his novel *Pleins feux sur Sylvie*. He was popularly acknowledged as "the dean of crime fiction" for his knowledge of the subject. Translator of Groucho Marx, Woody Allen, John Irving, Elmore Leonard and others. *CEOGG.*[6] [PG]

▲**Le Lionnais, François.** See François ●Le Lionnais.

▲**Marx, Karl.** The *Sous-Commission des Monuments Anhistoriques et Historiques* has offered the following study.

Δ *Towards a Marxist Approach to the Detective Story and to Crime*

> Chico: I'll kill anyone for twenty cents.
> Groucho: What about me?
> Chico: You're my friend, my brother. I'll kill you for nothing.

A philosopher produces ideas, a poet verses, a parson sermons, a professor text-books, etc. A criminal produces crime. But if the relationship between this latter branch of production and the fringes of society is examined a little more closely, one is forced to abandon a number of prejudices. The criminal produces not only crime but also the criminal law; he produces the professor who delivers lectures on criminal law, and even the inevitable text-book in which the professor puts his lectures on to the market as a "commodity". The result is an increase in national wealth, quite apart from the pleasure which, as Professor Roscher, a competent observer, says, *the author himself derives from the manuscript of his text-book.*

Fifty years on, Karl Marx would, no doubt, have added to "professor of criminal law" the authors of detective stories. Marx goes on:

The criminal produces an impression now moral, now tragic, and provides a "service" by arousing the moral and aesthetic sentiments of the public. He produces not only text-books on criminal justice, but also art, literature, novels, and even tragic drama, as Oedipus *and* Richard III, *as well as Müllner's* Schuld *and Schillers's* Räuber *attest. The criminal interrupts the monotony and day-to-day security of bourgeois life. He thus protects it from stagnation and brings forth that restless tension, that mobility of spirit without which the stimulus of competition would become blunted. He therefore gives a new impulse to productive forces.*

In our century, this Londoner by adoption would no doubt have cited Chandler or Agatha Christie along with Schiller or *Richard III.*

Marx, furthermore, justifies crime[11] as a factor in full employment:

Crime removes from the labour market a portion of the excess population, diminishes competition among workers, and to a certain extent stops wages falling below the minimum, while the war against crime absorbs another part of the same population. The criminal therefore appears as one of those natural "equilibrating forces" which establish a just balance and open up a whole perspective of "useful" occupations... Crime, by its ceaseless development of new means of attacking property, calls into existence new means of defence, and its productive effects are as great as those of strikes in stimulating the invention of machines.

From this Marxist point of view the growth in violent crime is not the consequence of the crisis in Western societies — it is its pageantry!

Among the aesthetes of the Oulipopo, murder has been too long considered as one of the fine arts: it is high time to treat it as a component of the Gross National Product.

(Quotations are from Marx's *Critique of Material Economy*.)
[Trans IW]

▲Olivier-Martin, Yves. Born in 1935. Specialist in serial fiction. Editor of special issues of *Europe* devoted to Gaston Leroux and Maurice Leblanc; author of a history of French popular fiction.

[PG]

▲Oulipopo. *Ouvroir de Littérature Policière Potentielle* or Workshop for Potential Detective Fiction. Most of the Oulipopo's work falls into the two categories defined by François Le Lionnais in his initial presentation:

1. ▲Analytic Oulipopo studies the situations and mechanisms that have been used in detective fiction, as well as the possible ways of combining them.

2. ▲Synthetic Oulipopo exploits the potential mechanisms of detective fiction heretofore left unused because considered unusable. Le Lionnais declared, "It might be thought that these new possibilities are rare. I reject such defeatism, convinced as I am that there are paths that remain untrodden."

For a general history and description of the aims of the Oulipopo, see the ▲*Introduction* to this section and the entries for ●Oulipo and ●Ouvroir. For a list of members, see *Introduction* ¶4. For a bibliography of works by the Oulipopo see ▲Collective Publications of the Oulipopo; for individuals' Oulipopian works, see the entry for the individual concerned. Some of the more substantial Oulipopian texts, several of which are translated in full in this section, are also listed under their titles: Δ*Abel and Cain*, ▲*Cartes noires*, ▲*Formal Invitation*, ▲*Jus d'Oronge*, The ▲*Perfect Crime*, Les ▲*Vains Commandements*, Δ*Who is Guilty?*, Δ*X = The Reader*.

Correspondence may be sent c/o Atlas Press.

▲Palindrome. From ▲CP5:

ΔThe Oulipopo *Palindromes*

> *One cannot imagine a detective story without a beginning, a middle, and an end.* —J.L. Borges

According to the well-known formula cited by Paul Morand, "the detective novel is written backwards", i.e.

beginning at the end. And by unscrupulous readers, male and female, it is also read backwards.[12] As to the canonical order, crime - investigation - solution, however often it has been perverted, there always remains an order consubstantial with the mystery novel. Jorge Luis Borges remarked that "in our century, inclined to the romantic veneration of disorder, of the elemental and the chaotic, the detective novel keeps alive an ideal of order, a discipline of a classical character."

The detective novel has, to be sure, a 'direction'. Could it have a double direction? Put another way, could the principle of the palindrome be applied to it? There is no question here of the palindrome of letters,[13] usable as an element in the solution of the problem, but hard to imagine as a novel or even a short story. At issue is the possibility of a reversible structure.

So let's consider this basic question: can a narrative in three episodes — A, B, C — be read in reverse order — C, B, A — with the first episode becoming the last and the central episode remaining in place? We would then have the following schema:

A: The crime initiates the investigation: a person who is the presumed victim is killed.

B: The sleuth investigates; he follows the trail of the unknown guilty party.

C: The detective arrests the guilty party, who escapes.

In reverse order, the narrative becomes:

C: A person who is arrested escapes.

B: The detective conducts an investigation in pursuit of the known criminal.

A: The escaped criminal, arrested, is killed. We know he is the guilty party.

The reader thus gets two different narratives in one — A, B, C and C, B, A. It is even possible to imagine an infinite circular narrative where the two readings, instead of merely replacing one another, are linked sequentially.

The palindromic sequence seems more readily applicable to the crime novel or the novel of suspense than to the mystery novel. It is perhaps best suited to a combination of two genres. Thus, one could easily proceed from the sequence *crime > criminal* (that of the mystery novel) to *criminal > crime* (the basis of the suspense novel). The fabric is less reversible if we confine ourselves to the realm of the whodunnit, where the sole motivation is identifying the guilty party. What makes the classical pattern of *mystery > solution* harder to reverse is that its outcome is meant to be a finality and not a starting-point. There would have to be a double mystery: a problem of identity (solved by the classical approach) and, in one of Anthony Berkeley's favourite phrases, a "problem of character". [Trans IW]

▲**Perfect Crime, The.** The Oulipopo's examination of perfection appeared in *Organographe*, 1 (*Cymbalum Pataphysicum*, 1975). The edited version that follows contains the first section and first appendix.

ΔThe Oulipopo *Towards a definition of The Perfect Crime*

Crime: preferably murder.
Perfect: two kinds of perfection can be imagined.

A. Merely *legal perfection* (the crime remains unpunished).

A.1. No one suspects a crime.
    A.1.a. The crime is disguised as an accident, suicide, or illness (heart failure).
    A.1.b. No one even suspects that a death has occurred.

A.2. Human justice is powerless.
    A.2.a. The guilty party remains unknown.
    A.2.b. The detective knows who is guilty but has no proof.
    A.2.c. The guilty party is known, their guilt is proven, but it is legally impossible to convict.

A.3. The case of Divine Justice: God is powerless to punish the guilty party, a theme attested in folklore: see

the Catalogue of the *Conte Populaire Française* of P. Delarue (Éd. Erasmus, 1947, vol. 1, pp.346 ff.). See *Appendix I* below.

B. *Aesthetic perfection* in the way the crime is committed (in addition to its legal perfection; implicitly, the crime must be discovered (A.1. is excluded).

    B.1. *Classic perfection.* The crime is committed in a commonplace way, but its sophisticated execution makes it a masterpiece of professional rigour.

    B.2. *Baroque perfection.* Victim, instrument, and circumstances are without precedent, a fact that indicates a concern for originality which can, if needs be, override the concern for impunity. (Ellery ▲Queen *The Chinese Orange Mystery*; Pierre Véry *Série de Sept*; Jack the Ripper...)

    Appendix I

A.3. *The case of Divine Justice:* God himself is powerless to punish the guilty party.

    A.3.a. He himself is the murderer.
        A.3.a.1. Divine wrath strikes down its victim, for example, someone penetrating the Holy of Holies.
        A.3.a.2. Natural death: of which all instances are crimes on the part of God and always go unpunished.

    A.3.b. He is the instigator of the crime or its accomplice, as in the Massacre of the Innocents, whose purpose was divine publicity. According to the lesser Bollandists (*Subsidia Pataphysica*, 16-17, p.185), God "permits" every crime committed. This does not exclude his punishing the guilty party (the problem of "Evil").

    A.3.c. He is the victim of deicide.
        A.3.c.1. Physical death: Saint Longinus[14] pierced the body of Christ on Golgotha. God has forgiven him, and the instrument of the crime is still venerated in

Rome and elsewhere (*Subsidia Pataphysica*, 16-17, p.141).

A.3.c.2. Ideological death: the evolution of humanity brings about the death of God ("God is Dead").

A.3.d. God is neither murderer nor victim.

A.3.d.1. Having received the supreme penalty, the guilty party can be punished no further: Satan.

A.3.d.2. The guilty party has taken precautions.

A.3.d.2.I. He has received communion on the first Fridays of nine successive months, and he wears a miraculous medal; he is assured of the intercession of the Virgin, etc.

A.3.d.2.II. He commits murder in a confessional during confession and is thus sure of immediate absolution. If incapable of perfect contrition *cum voto sacramenti* (hatred of the crime itself), he can still show attrition *cum sacramento* (fear of divine punishment); when accompanied by absolution this is quite sufficient, for contrition and attrition do not need to precede the accusation of sin but only to precede absolution, or at least coincide with it. (See Suarez, *De Paenitentia*, *disp.* XX, sect. 4. no. 30 sq., LXIX, p.234.)

This procedure works only for a single crime, not a series, because "firm resolve" (not to repeat the crime) is required to make contrition, and thus absolution, valid.

Two possible variants:

The confessor is murdered. Before he dies he must have time to forgive and absolve, or at least pronounce the first words of the sacramental formula *Ego te absolvo...* In a pinch, these are sufficient.

In a case of *legal perfection* involving *human justice*, the priest should die before inflicting penance, since this could be interpreted as incriminating. The absence of penance where the priest was, for good reason, unable to impose it would leave the sacrament incomplete but still valid. It would be enough for the guilty party to obtain a plenary indulgence by appropriate means (such as pilgrimage).

> *Murder of a person other than the confessor*
>   in the confessional
>   in church
>   at a distance.

It should be remembered that absolution cannot be given at a distance, whether by letter, telegraph, or telephone. [Trans IW]

▲**Philosophy.** In ▲CP4 the Oulipopo outlined this "taxonomy of sleuths" in a discussion following a paper given by Paul Gayot on Raymond ●Queneau's *Pierrot mon ami*:

ΔJacques Barine *The Detective Story at the Seminar* (extract)

From an Oulipopian point of view, the main part of the paper seemed to be a lengthy extra-Quenellian parenthesis in which a new taxonomy of sleuths from the most famous detective stories was proposed.

If, as Émile Lesaffre asserts, Pierrot can be considered a Sartrean investigator (less for his glasses than because "to consciousness, existence is being conscious of existing"), then Maigret can be thought of as a Pascalian (rather than a Bergsonian), since he relies on the heart's intuitions. There are also Thomist detectives (Father Brown), Saussurean detectives (Ellery ▲Queen, who uses permutations of letters (●anagrams) to solve problems), and ▲Marxist detectives (the hard-boiled sort that prefer changing the world to thinking about it). Paul Gayot contrasted two groups: Cartesians (so-called not because they proceed by deductions — on the contrary, detectives use the inductive method — but because they are armchair investigators like Dupin who reach their solutions without ever leaving their warm room) and positivists like Sherlock Holmes who depend on the empirical sciences — cigarette-butts and fingerprints. This contrast was vigorously contested by one of those present, M. Dumoncel, for whom Dupin is not a Cartesian but a Peircean (nothing to do with James M. Cain's novel *Mildred Pierce*, but much to do with the pluralist epistemology of Pierce), whilst Sherlock Holmes is a Hintikkist (cf. Jaakko Hintikka and Merill B. Hintikka, *Sherlock Holmes confronts modern logic*[15]). M. Dumoncel also distinguished ●Leibnizian detectives (Bustos Domecq's Don Isidro Parodi), and Hegelian detectives (Witold and Fuchs in *Cosmos* by Gombrowicz).

A lively discussion began — in which Jacques Bens participated — concerning Arsène Lupin. The three participants agreed in no time at all to reject the interpretation of Armand Hoog, who considered Lupin a Nietzschean; M. Dumoncel suggested reserving this term for detectives who rely on the Eternal Return to nab the criminal *in flagrante*, and for those specialising in serial crimes. But whilst some, like François George, stuck up for Lupin as a disciple of Malebranche, others (Paul Gayot, supported by Émile Lesaffre) sketched out a portrait of a Kantian Arsène Lupin, notwithstanding his burglaries, which did not vitiate his elevated sense of duty.

This taxonomy seemed to us capable of interesting extensions: are there Spinozist detectives? Aristotelian ones? or Platonist ones? Under which heading should we class certain fictitious detectives: for example Freeman Wills Crofts's Inspector French, obsessed by time? Are Anthony Berkeley's detectives Berkeleyans? These learned and useless questions should really be the subject of future study by the Oulipopo. [Trans IW]

▲**Plagiary, anticipatory.** Since detective fiction is inherently 'formulaic' (and it is this aspect that constitutes the subject of ▲analytic Oulipopo), nearly all authors of detective fiction fall into the category of "anticipatory ●plagiarists". Certain authors have made significant *theoretical* or formal contributions to the genre: Jorge Luis ▲Borges, Thomas ▲De Quincey, Karl ▲Marx, Ellery ▲Queen, A.A. ▲Van Dine. [AB]

Other anticipatory plagiarists:

Analytic Oulipopo: Le Roy Lad Panek *Watteau's Shepherd*

(for its appendix); John Dickson Carr *The Hollow Man* (for Gideon Fell's dissertation on closed rooms).

▲Synthetic Oulipopo: John Brunner *The Squares of the City*; Vincent Fuller *The Hollow Man* (grammatical solution); Fred Cassak *Nocturne pour assassin* (prediction by games); Maurice Leblanc *Herlock Sholmes arrive trop tard* (alphabetical drama). [PG]

▲**Porla, Jean de.** (1925–?) The name Porla — suggesting an anagrammatic origin in *polar* (thriller) — is an obvious pseudonym first used in 1984 by Francis Debyser as editor of the collaborative detective novel *Encore un coup d'arquebuse*. Debyser apparently appropriated the name for several undertakings, including ▲*Cartes noires*, ▲*Jus d'Oronge*, and ∆*Abel and Cain*. The same taste for deception may point to the true identity of the feminist Solange Parlot, de Porla's sternest critic, who is quoted on occasion in academic papers. [FD]

▲**Queen, Ellery.** Ellery Queen's works abound in Oulipopian anticipatory ▲plagiaries. A brief listing would include: *And on the Eighth Day*; *Mystery at the Library of Congress* (●acrostics); *Ten Day's Wonder* (●anagrams); *The Origin of Evil* (●lipogram); *The Player on the Other Side* (●palindromes); *The Adventure of the Abraham Lincoln Clue*; *Drury Lane's Last Case* (vertical palindromes); *The French Powder Mystery*; *The Chinese Orange Mystery*; *The Spanish Cape Mystery*; *The Death of Don Juan*; *The Lonely Bride* (●Roussel's method). [PG]

▲**Raabe, Juliette.** Specialist in detective fiction and editor of the collection published by Éditions du Fleuve Noir. Eminent ælurologue, author of an anthology on cats in art and literature, and editor of the special issue of *Enigmatika* devoted to *A Bestiary of the Detective Novel*. [PG]

▲**Raymond, François.** (1926–1992) Regent of Vernology of the ●College of 'Pataphysics. Editor of the Série Jules Verne for Éditions Lettres Modernes. Author of various books on popular fiction, detective fiction, and on Jules Verne. [PG]

▲**Rivière, François.** Journalist at *Libération*. Biographer of Agatha Christie, author of scenarios for graphic novels and of a number of detective novels published by Éditions Masque. [PG]

▲**Rules for composing detective fiction.** A number of authors have attempted to codify basic rules for writing detective fiction. The most famous are those of ▲Van Dine, but the Oulipopo (in ▲CP1) has listed others by Mgr. Knox, A.C. Ward, John Dickson Carr, G.K. Chesterton and Jorge Luis ▲Borges. Francis Debyser has formulated rules for interactive or "●branching" novels (in which the reader decides how the plot develops). [AB]

▲**Synthetic Oulipopo.** The creation of works of detective fiction that exploit potential mechanisms never used before.

Because of their length, such works cannot be illustrated here in full. Most of them are of recent composition — as Le Lionnais declared at the founding of the Oulipopo, analysis must precede synthesis. The two volumes of ▲CP5 contain stories based on ●permutation (chapters read in different sequence yield different solutions), ●intersection (a story is simultaneously told from several points of view), and the ●lipogram. [PG]

See also ▲*Cartes noires, Les* ▲*Vains Commandements*, ▲X = *The Reader*.

▲**Systematisation.** The Oulipopo has not tabulated its researches in the same way as has, for example, the ●Oulipo or ■Oupeinpo. However, most of the work of ▲analytic Oulipopo, especially the analysis of plot structures, is inherently systematic (cf. ▲*Formal Invitation*). [AB]

▲*Vains Commandements, Les.* A novella by Jacques Barine (in ▲CP4), based on an "inverted constraint": that of breaking every single one of ▲Van Dine's Rules, and thereby aiming to be "the worst detective story in the world."

▲**Van Dine's Rules.** Published in *Cosmopolitan* (NY, September 1928, pp.129-131), they remain the most celebrated attempt to formulate a set of rules for composing detective fiction that is 'fair' to the reader. Apart from the first two, they are hardly systematic; the third is plain eccentric:

1) The reader must have equal opportunity with the detective for solving the mystery. All clues must be plainly stated and described.

2) No wilful tricks or deceptions may be played on the reader other than those played legitimately by the criminal on the detective himself.

3) There must be no love interest. The business in hand is to bring a criminal to the bar of justice, not to bring a lovelorn couple to the hymeneal altar.

Rule (4) requires that the detective not be the culprit. (5) The culprit's identity must be established by logical deduction and never by accident or coincidence. (6) An active detective must be present. (7) There must be a corpse. (8) Supernatural means of deduction, such as seances, are not allowed. (9) There can be only one detective. (10) The culprit must figure prominently in the story. (11) The culprit cannot be a servant ("Too easy a solution"). (12) There can be only one culprit. (13) No secret societies or mafias can be involved. (14) A restatement of (8). (15) To an attentive reader, the truth of the problem should be apparent at all times. (16) There should be no long passages for descriptive or atmospheric effect. (17) The culprit cannot be a professional criminal. (18) Accidents and suicides are excluded. (19) The culprit's motives must be personal. (20) Obvious devices like coded letters or mistaken identities (the list is long) are not allowed.

Clearly some of the most celebrated works in the genre break one or more of these rules; the Oulipopian Thomas Narcejac provides a list of them in his *Esthétique du roman policier* (1947). [AB]

See Anticipatory ▲plagiary, *Les* ▲*Vains Commandements*.

▲*Who is Guilty?* The study of 1971 which initiated the work of the Oulipopo:

ΔFrançois Le Lionnais *Who is Guilty?* (x = ?)

A

x IS KNOWN FROM THE OUTSET BY THE READER

A.I. *and known by the police* (the point is to capture him)

A.2. *but not known by the police* (the point is to unmask him)

B

x IS KNOWN ONLY TOWARDS THE END

B.I. x is named on the cover of the novel

B.l.*a.* x = the author (who is not the narrator)

B.l.*b.* x = the publisher (a humorous story by P.G. Wodehouse)

B.2. x *is named in the body of the novel*

B.2.*a.* he is a human being who

B.2.*a.*I. has no special status (e.g. a tramp) or unsuspected motives (vengeance, financial interest, etc.)

B.2.*a.*2. is a sympathetic character who commits a legitimate act

B.2.*a.*2.*a.* as an executioner

B.2.*a.*2.*b.* as a righter of wrongs

B.2.*a.*2.*c.* as an unintentional murderer

i. x knows he is guilty and conceals the fact

ii. x does not know he is guilty

B.2.*a.*3. seems above suspicion because

B.2.*a.*3.*a.* he does not personally know his victim

i. is a taxpayer who kills the Finance Minister to effect a change in the tax system

ii. is a pedestrian who kills a driver at random

B.2.*a.*3.*b.* he knows his victim (x = I) and is

i. a paralytic

ii. a child

iii. a priest

iv. a lawyer

v. a judge

vi. a forensic expert

vii. a policeman

viii. the victim (whose place x has taken)

ix. one of the victims (who was believed dead)

x. someone who dies before his victim (bomb, etc.)

xi. a hypnotist

xii. someone driven to crime

xiii. someone driven to suicide

xiv. a king, a head of State

xv. the narrator

xvi. a dual personality

xvii. x = the guilty party

(a) who is assured of impunity by having been acquitted

(b) who is not thought to be or have been proved guilty (cf. B.2.*a.*2.*b.*)

xviii. x finishes off the victim of an attack by *y*, who thinks he is the guilty party

B.2.*a.*3.*c.* he knows the victim (x > I), who is part of

i. a group (passengers on a train, etc.)

ii. the government, society (reasons of state)

iii. indefinite (clouded mirror, burning room, etc.)

B.2.*a.*3.*d.* (x = 0) it was a suicide.

B.2.*b.* he is not a human being

B.2.*b.*I. natural solution

B.2.*b.*I.*a.* an animal (the Rue Morgue gorilla, the *Cyanea capillata* in a story by Conan Doyle, etc.)

B.2.*b.*I.*b.* natural phenomena (meteorite, etc.), illness

B.2.*b.*2. science fiction

B.2.*b.*2.*a.* terrestrial mutants (intelligent viruses, etc.)

B.2.*b.*2.*b.* extra-terrestrial visitors

B.2.*b.*2.*c.* travellers from the future

B.2.*b.*3. supernatural solution

B.2.*b.*3.*a.* zombies, werewolves, etc.

B.2.b.3.b. pact of a man with the devil (*Jack the Ripper in 1966*)

B.2.b.3.c. Satan incarnated in the murderer

B.2.b.3.d. God

C

WE WILL NEVER KNOW WHO

C.I. *repeat of B.2.a.3.c.iii. (indefinite). We have a choice between a rational solution and a supernatural solution*

C.2. *we cannot decide between several persons*

C.3. *we suspect no one*

D

NEVER (to my knowledge) REALISED

x = *the reader*

The undersigned has discovered a rational solution (neither supernatural nor a hoax) which has been or will be the subject of a presentation at a solemn session of the Oulipo, in the expectation that a writer might wish to make use of it.

With the exception of D, which has never been realised, every item on this list has been used in at least one short story or novel.

[FLL, trans IW]

▲**X = *The Reader*.** François Le Lionnais's analysis of the question ▲*Who is Guilty?* ended with a possibility that he believed had never been used: the reader is guilty. ▲CP5 shed new light on the problem: Jean-Louis Bailly, in *La Dispersion des cendres* (Laffont, 1990; "A Scattering of Ashes"), provided a solution using the device of the novel-within-the-novel. An extract follows.

ΔX = *The Reader*

One day Hélène realised that for the past two years her brother had read nearly every detective story that had come out.

Hélène had a notion to find out more about all these detective stories her brother had bought.

Thus it was that in reading the most recently published of them she understood that behind the name of John D. Pitcairn her brother was concealed. From the first lines she recognised Guy's voice, known to her from childhood and from the manuscripts that had been piously preserved in a black metal trunk... The advertising strip was still wrapped around the book's cover: IF YOU BUY THIS BOOK, YOU ARE A MURDERER. IF YOU READ IT, YOU WILL KNOW WHY.

Guy's detective story was ingeniously contrived. The central character is a failed writer who has again and again tried to publish his collections of poetry and short stories. Publishers have invariably turned them down. The author knows his work is good: into it he has put the best of himself — all his dreams, his anguish, his most cherished indignations, and an exacting attention to making their expression perfect. He decides that his symbolic execution should become a real death. He concocts a detective story, badly written, poorly plotted, and larded with sex and violence. He manages to get it published, this time without too much trouble. After the royalties reach a certain level, they automatically (to skip the details) send into action a killer hired to shoot the writer. Thus the book's buyers, who, as an incurious audience interested only in the facile, had 'killed' the author of the poems and stories, now kill him in fact. Having first impelled him to suicide, they have now given him the means to achieve it. They know what they are doing, informed as they are by the advertising strip, one identical to that on Guy's own book. There are aggravating circumstances in the many scenes of violence and eroticism that are so many shameless come-ons to anyone glancing through the book. As cause and instrument of the murder, fully aware of perpetrating it, the reader — or at least the buyer — is in every sense the guilty party.

[Trans IW]

1. *Cul* = arse. [IW]

2. From "The Beryl Coronet", in *The Adventures of Sherlock Holmes*. [IW]

3. The Cainites were an early Gnostic sect of a 'libertine' rather than an ascetic tendency, apparently an offshoot of the Ophites, who worshipped the serpent (cf. John 3,14). As antinomians, they praised Cain and the Sodomites (Gen. ch.19), as well as Judas, whom they regarded as the agent of a higher god's saving the world. [IW]

4. P.M. Landowski (1875-1961). His *Filles de Cain* won him a First Class medal at the 1906 Salon des Artistes Français. He also produced a *Fils de Cain*, now in the Copenhagen Museum. His other works include a memorial to the French colonial campaign in Morocco, a *Monument aux Armées* in the Place de Trocadéro, a memorial to the chauvinist poet Déroulède, a bust of Pétain, and the gigantic Christ overlooking Rio de Janeiro harbour. [IW]

5. Periodical concerned with detective fiction to which a number of Oulipopians contribute.

6. *Commandeur Exquis de l'Ordre de la Grande Gidouille*, an honorific awarded by the ●College of 'Pataphysics. [AB]

7. See ▲*Introduction*, ¶7. The text was a pastiche of Borges published in ▲CP1. [AB]

8. For the fictitious Quain's fictitious fiction, see J.L. Borges *Ficciones* (Weidenfeld & Nicolson, 1962) p.74. [IW]

9. Clearly this cannot be done haphazardly. One needs to be able to preserve a coherence and a deducibility without which new formulae would be no more than caricatures of structures, without applicability, indeed without meaning. No one enters the realm of the Oulipopo who is not a geometer. [FLL]

10. Anagram of *François Le Lionnais*.

11. And, by anticipation, G. Clémenceau and G. Defferre. [Authors' note]

12. An enquiry in one of the first numbers of *Mystère* magazine confirmed that this "impatient" manner of reading was a trait more feminine than masculine. [Authors' note]

13. A ●palindrome occurs in a short story by Pierre Véry, "*Ils*", in a novel by Ellery ▲Queen, *The Player on the Other Side*, and in *Drury Lane's Last Case* by Queen's alter ego, Barnaby Ross.

In No. 17-18 of the review *Le Gué*, a very short story (actually a problem in detection) describes a crime in palindromic form and explicitly invites Regent Luc ●Étienne to reach a solution. See also *Le Mystère des frères siamois* by Jacques Barine in *Mystère*, 88 edited by J. Baudou, which includes palindromes in French and English. [Authors' note]

14. For the event, see John 19, 34. According to Voragine's *Golden Legend*, Longinus (where the name comes from is unclear) was converted on the spot; on this point the Bible agrees (Mark 15, 39; Matt. 27, 51-4; Luke 23, 47). He became an ascetic in Cappadocia and was martyred. An alternative story has him ending up in Mantua, where he preached the gospel and was martyred, and where his body was preserved as a relic. [IW]

15. In E.M. Barth and J.L. Martens *Argumentation* (John Bergamino BV, 1982). We should not forget that our late lamented Founding President considered Sherlock Holmes an adept of Von Neumann's and Morgenstern's mathematical theory of games. [Author's note]

V. OUPEINPO

■

■*Introduction* Thieri Foulc *What is the Oupeinpo?*

The Oupeinpo is

1. an ●*ouvroir*, or workshop, a place where work is done. It differs from a laboratory in that no struggle takes place; from a learned society in that the advancement of science is not its aim; from a sect in that no doctrine is propounded; from a school in that it has neither masters nor pupils. It has nothing in common with an academy, a museum, a lodge, a commission, an institute or any sort of institution. If it bears any resemblance to a factory, it is because many factors inspire its many tasks.

2. *de peinture*, for painting, but the term is used synecdochically, since the Oupeinpo does not limit "painting" to the art of applying pigment. On the contrary, it has no scruples about extending it to all the graphic and plastic arts, and it advocates not only the painter's brush and palette knife but the draughtsman's pencil, the engraver's burin, the stucco-maker's float, the tagger's spray-can, even the mouse of the electronic image-maker. Camera and printing-press are no strangers to it. And it makes a point of encouraging needle and scalpel, larding-pin and chopper, spray-gun and compressor, printer driver and pile-driver, laser and rolling-mill, and field artillery (bombs if necessary), not to mention bare hands and digital agility. Indeed, one of the Oupeinpo's objectives is to increase the range of what is available to the painter in the way of material as well as of materials, surfaces, techniques, procedures, subjects, view-points, theories, and so on.

3. *potentielle*, ■potential: because the Oupeinpo itself produces no actual paintings. It applies itself not to works but to the methods, arrangements, manipulations, structures, and formal restrictions with which painters past, present and future were, are and will be able to create their works. If it does not reject what is manifest in works of art, it asserts that this is the business of artists, patrons and the world of viewers. Its own role is to suggest 'forms' or transformations where works exist as possibilities. We hasten to add that its members do their best to

become the first to keep these forms from remaining empty by embodying them in examples.

4. The Oupeinpo thus puts itself in the position of those anonymous inventors who bequeathed to the ages the ●sonnet and sonata form, with no concern for what Shakespeare or Raymond ●Queneau, Beethoven or John Cage (as well as the countless amateurs who offend the Muses) might make of them. To stick to the plastic arts, it puts itself in the position of the no less anonymous inventor of the narrative triptych who unwittingly provided Jan Van Eyck and Francis Bacon with the same structure. Except for this: the Oupeinpo was founded with the express purpose of similarly furnishing not one but (to begin with) a thousand such forms to potential users; forms more complex, restrictive and fecund than the polyptych, which until now has been so poorly exploited.

Thus, various methods or operations (in the mathematical, strategic, and even surgical sense), applied to every component of the work of art, have given rise to:

(I) treatments using ■codes and ■matrices, such as ■casing and ■decasing, ■antithesism and other ■isomorphisms such as tactile ■transposition, the ■hidden message, ■transposition of coherence;

(II) applications of ■rotation and its offspring, ■symmetry, such as the ■rotatory picture (viewable from four sides), painting with variable ■symmetry, ■anamorphosis;

(III) rules of ■assemblage and reassemblage, involving ■intersection in the mathematical sense (*Venus of Samothrace, The Burial of Count Ornans*), reunification, inclusion (Giacometti-within-Maillol), ■superimposition (*Multichrist*), chronology (■chronological collage), and the various kinds of ■lamellisection;

(IV) a wide variety of ■constraints by edges (culminating in stretcher-side painting, ■scytalism, bitangential ■picturogenesis, the ■*Polyptikon*, and rotatory ■substitution), ■hyperdominoes, the ■*Morpholo*, complementation of the cube, ■plaited painting, ■taquinoidal painting;

(V) ■combinatorial works, many already mentioned as constraints by edges but applicable to other domains: to surfaces, for instance, as in Louis Barnier's famous *La* ❑*Vache au pré noir*, an anticipatory Oupeinpian work in its combinatorial treatment of printing inks and matrices;

(VI) works with ■measured constituents — colour, light, drawn lines, volumes;

(VII) not to mention ■painting blind, ■painting by telephone, ■*déculottage*, the ■*digrapheur*, the ■*M.O.U.* (*Module oupeinpien universel*), or the ■Hundred Flowers of the Oupeinpo, a tabular and logogenetic system for the creation of artistic schools.

5. For now it must be said: the Oupeinpo is not an artistic movement. Yet it is obliged to bring potentiality to bear equally on schools, movements, groups, associations, tendencies, manifestos, academies, avant-gardes, etc., and to propose techniques for proscribing the unregulated proliferation of new movements (and their all-too-regulated marketing policies), so that every -ism, imaginable and unimaginable, can be created at will.

6. The Oupeinpo was founded (or rather reactivated) on 12 December 1980 by François ●Le Lionnais, Jacques Carelman, and Thieri Foulc. They were joined on 14 January 1981 by Aline Gagnaire and Jean Dewasne. On 14 February 1981 it established its quarters in the Atelier Carelman. On 21 December 1985 Tristan Bastit joined its ranks, and on 20 January 1990 Jack Vanarsky. Most recent members: Olivier O. Olivier, Brian Reffin Smith (both 10 September 1999), and Guillaume Pô (23 March 2002).

The exact number of its members is still hard to determine, not only because Suzanne Allen and the Misses Cassette attend most of its meetings as 'active witnesses', but because it has correspondents abroad (Aldo Spinelli in Italy, Alastair Brotchie and Stanley ●Chapman in England). Documents of an unquestionably concrete nature also attest to the sporadic participation of Hieronymus Bosch, Leonardo da Vinci, Giuseppe Arcimboldo, and Pablo Picasso.

The Oupeinpo meets one Saturday every month, starting at 11 a.m. The morning is devoted to presentations: of Oupeinpian works produced by members since the last meeting, of documents, ideas, news, deliberations, and correspondence. The afternoon is devoted to the completion of the Oupeinpo's

■*Grand Œuvre*, an endeavour whose aim is to spark the mental exploration of the effects of every 'operation' on the fundamental constituents of the work of art.

The works of the Oupeinpo were first shown to the public on 14 June 1985 at the Atelier Carelman in an exhibition reserved for Oulipian and pataphysical friends. They have since been exhibited at the Gallery of the University of Quebec in Montreal (UQAM) in May 1989; at the Centre Culturel des Chiroux, Liège, in February 1990; at the Chiostro di San Marco, Florence, in May 1991; at the Centre Pompidou, Paris, in June 1991; at the Queneau Colloquium, Thionville, in October 1992; at Sophia-Antipolis (a site in southern France dedicated to science and technology) in May 1996; at the University of Poitiers in April 1997; and at the Artoteca Alliance, Bari (Italy), in November 2000.

The Oupeinpo has its rites. Dates are recorded in accordance with the ordinary, pataphysical, and revolutionary calendars. There is a roll-call of those present and a reading of the agenda at 11 a.m. Lunch would take place at the Auberge de Chine, after a stroll on the Allée des Mings (since its demolition in 1984, at the Fontaine aux Roses and later at the Saint-Amour). It has its taboos: during sessions, the name of the world's most famous painting must never be mentioned, on pain of a fine of 10 francs. Its past is preserved in written and taped archives, the conservation of finished works, and publications. It has its obsessions, the most deeply rooted being: how can at least one example of all Oupeinpian inventions be produced when their number grows exponentially faster than the actual realisations?

[Adapted from the introductions to ■CP1 & 2]

NOTE: Unless indicated otherwise, all entries concerning the Oupeinpo have been written by Thieri Foulc and have been translated by Iain White.

■**Allen, Suzanne.** Writer and philosopher. Her cult of non-personality (of not being a member, even of the Oupeinpo, not appearing in photographs, not...) has given her the role of "active witness" in the Oupeinpo, and of "sifter" — a scrupulously exacting critic.

■**Anamorphosis.** Optical or mathematical deformation of an image, such that reversing the deformation permits one to "return" (Gk. *ana*) to, or recover, the originating image.

The most famous anamorphosis in the history of art was painted by Holbein (*The Ambassadors*). Its interest, from the Oupeinpian viewpoint, is zero.

The Oupeinpo envisages anamorphosis as a way of 'duplicating readings': if Holbein had been an Oupeinpian, he would have painted a form which, when seen *head-on*, would have represented an object X (with all the details of which his great art was capable), and when seen sideways-on, as in the painting in question, would have revealed the skull he wished to show as the crux of the whole (≠ X).

■**Antithesism.** A theoretical mechanism that permits the derivation of a new work from another by adopting the antithesis of each of its elements. An Oupeinpian equivalent of ●antonymic translation.

Antithesism is not a rigorous mechanism.

1. The elements of ■*pein* appear to be innumerable (materials, positioning of elements, colour, form, subject, emotion produced in the viewer, symbolic value, etc.).

2. Defining them initiates a lengthy process of perception, concept, language, and feedback that is fraught with the direst ambiguities.

3. Antithesis is in itself a vague notion. It can be clearly defined only in terms of what is present or absent or when it applies to operations: an operation is antithetic if it undoes the work of a preceding operation and returns things to their initial state.

Examples:

The Oupeinpo has created an antithetic version of the Uffizi *Annunciation* attributed to Leonardo da Vinci: not a painting but a purely verbal, detailed description of a work identified as a *Denunciation* in the style of Hieronymus Bosch.

In *La Femme à Fontana*, Gagnaire has antithesised the work of the Italian painter Fontana: slits he has made in the canvas are sewn up in various ways (as if by his wife).

■**Artillery, Oupeinpian.** (Illustrations overleaf) Can(n)ons are a preoccupation of the Oupeinpo: the rules of proportion that define, for example, the ideal of the human body and face. This ideal varies remarkably between civilisations, epochs, indeed artists and moods of the moment. Moreover, it is rarely found in nature. It is a mathematisation of aesthetic sentiment, and thus an arm — artillery — in the hands of artists.

Carelman has turned the Oupeinpo's artillery on a work famous for its proportions, Michelangelo's *David*. He has reinterpreted it according to the canons of (1) ancient Greece, (2) Baule sculpture, (3) the *tiki* of the Marquesas, and (4) Giacometti.

See ■Style.

■**Assemblage and reassemblage.** Although all painting may ultimately be a matter of assemblage (distributing micro-granules of pigment in relation to one another on a backing), the Oupeinpo reserves the term for distributing elements that are less *micro*.

From ●Duchamp to Dubuffet, from Schwitters to Joseph Cornell, from Gagnaire to Tinguely, an immense part of the ■*pein* of 20th-century painting depends on assemblage. Two questions arise:

1. That of the relation of each fragment assembled (its origin usually identifiable) to the newly constituted assemblage.

2. That of the rule or method governing an assemblage. It must be admitted that in this respect the principal law of assemblage is, as we see it in practice, more a non-law. Feathers, dead leaves, scraps of wallpaper or old engravings, celluloid dolls, and mechanical odds-and-ends are apparently used to produce an effect of estrangement or surprise, or to encourage a belief in 'inspiration' or 'humour'. In this vein one of the greatest successes is undoubtedly the big nut (of the bolt variety)

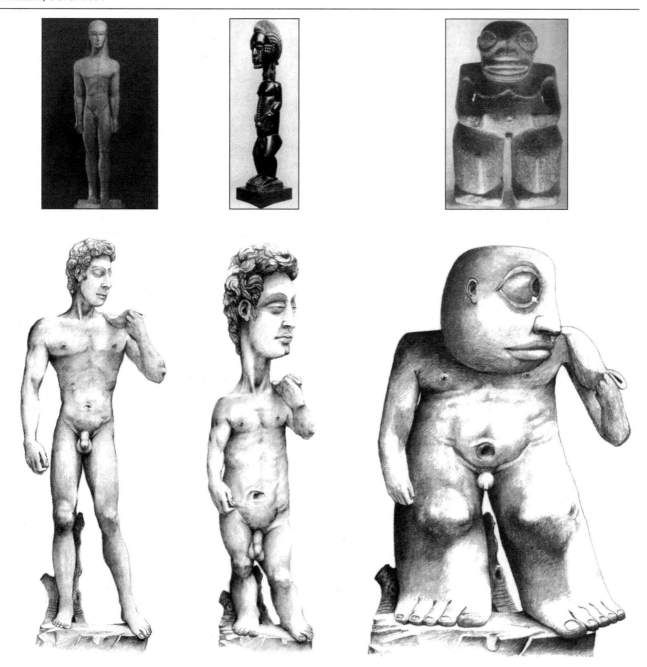

Jacques Carelman, Michelangelo's *David* modified according to the canons of (left) ancient Greece circa 600 BC; (centre) Baule sculpture, Ivory Coast; (right) *tiki* from the Marquesas Islands.

that Picasso used for his *Goat's* arsehole; but in terms of rigour, we are still far from Arcimboldo's composite heads.

One of the Oupeinpo's tasks is to provide potential users with rules of assemblage which allow them to dispense with inspiration (true or false) and individual taste.

When the fragments assembled all come from the same source, the result is called a *reassemblage*.

See ■Chronological collage, ■Lamellisection, ■Perversions, ■Straightening the Seine's Course through Paris, ■Super-imposition.

■Autobiography by Cartesian co-ordinates. A system devised by Thieri Foulc to make it possible for visual artists — and, more generally, all those who take fright at verbal expression — to furnish biographical details demanded of them by museums, publishers and administrators.

Trace the two axes of a graph. Along the abscissa, mark the artist's age; on the ordinate, his various types of activity. There is no ban on using negative abscissae (ante-natal period, ancestral influences), or negative ordinates (destructions, various kinds of inactivity). The principal activities of a life are thus located along the graph's axes and marked by points.

From these points one may construct a ■portrait taking the form of a constellation: a portrait more meaningful than mere physical appearance.

See Tristan ■Bastit, Thieri ■Foulc.

■Bastit, Tristan. *Autobiography by Catastrophe Graph Co-ordinates* (right).

See ■Autobiography by Cartesian co-ordinates.

■Beauty. *The Oupeinpian need not worry about either beauty or ●chance.* [JC]

■Bibliothèque Oupeinpienne, La (BO). Small booklets similar to those issued by the ●Oulipo, in an edition of around 150 copies.

　　■BO1. Jean Dewasne, *Les Forces plastiques,* 1993.

　　■BO2. Jack Vanarsky, *Projet de redressement du cours de la Seine à sa traversée de Paris* (*A Plan for* ■*Straightening the Seine's Course through Paris*), 1993. Reprinted in *Le Visiteur, revue de critique des situations construites*, Société française des architectes, Paris, 1996.

　　■BO3. Jean Dewasne, "*Je suis le point de fuite*", *La Bataille de San Romano vue par un des lapins*, 1999.

　　■BO4. Tristan Bastit, *Les Évanouissements de L.V. Gogh*, 1999.

　　■BO5. Thieri Foulc, *Un tableau par jour: Tableaux noirs*, 1999.

　　■BO6. Jacques Carelman, *La Peinture au quart de tour*, 2000.

　　■BO7. Jack Vanarsky, *La Bête en moi*, 2000.

　　■BO8. Thieri Foulc, *Un tableau par jour: La Vie de saint Z*, 2000.

　　■BO9. Thieri Foulc, *Un tableau par jour: Lits*, 2001.

　　■BO10. Oupeinpo, *L'Hôtel de Sens, par Paul Fournel et Jacques Roubaud, avec 41 tableaux par l'Oupeinpo*, 2002. See ●BO10.

■BO11. Thieri Foulc, *Images de souffrance*, 2002.

The following "out of series" publications have also appeared: Thieri Foulc, *Le ■Morpholo*, Cymbalum Pataphysicum, 1985; Tristan Bastit, *Toto à la rhétorique*, Éditions du Sel & Couëdic réunis, 2001.

■Black body, constraint of the. In general, carrying out a strictly predetermined task; for the Oupeinpo, a method of assigning colours to lines within a given form.

By exploiting the connection between a star's temperature and its colour, the concept of the black body made it possible for an astrophysicist to ascertain stellar temperatures without ever leaving his armchair. He imagined a hollow body with a single minute opening. Physics taught him that a ray of light entering the body through the opening would necessarily re-emerge from it after being reflected a given number of times on the inner surface. In a state

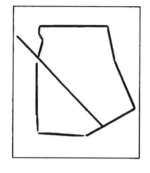

of thermal equilibrium, the colour of the emerging light would be determined by the temperature of that inner surface.

For the Oupeinpo, this was food for thought: here, in particular, were the elements of a ■constraint for filling in the colours of a painting.

Within a frame, draw in outline a shape with only one break in it. According to our rule, a straight line entering through the break behaves like a ray of light and is reflected on the inner surface in accordance with the rules of geometrical optics, taking into account all deviations due to surface irregularities. The line also assumes a specific colour throughout the time it remains within the shape. Re-emerging from it, it assumes another colour that it retains while it continues to rebound between frame and outline until, inevitably, it re-encounters the break in the shape and again passes through it, this time at a different angle. It thus takes on a third colour, according to the same principle; the process may in theory continue until the 14,000 tones visible to the human eye have been exhausted.

To sum up: once the shape's outline and the choice of colours is decided, drawing the first straight line inaugurates what will become the final aspect of the work without any imperfection due to further human intervention.

With this principle established, an Oupeinpian frustration remains: why not find a constraint to determine the initial angle of incidence? This is not only appealing, it is something that would further restrict the artist's scope for visual error.

It is easy to imagine possibilities based on

the angle of a chronometer dial

the angle of sunlight

the angle of a political point of view (between Left and Right)

the angle in a statistical pie-chart, etc., etc.

Similar rigour can be applied to the choice of colours. This has so far been based on angles in the chromatic circle, but there are many other rules it might follow.

Lastly, the Oupeinpian can use a predetermined computation to set the number of colours that will decide how many turns to take on his merry-go-round. [TB, trans IW]

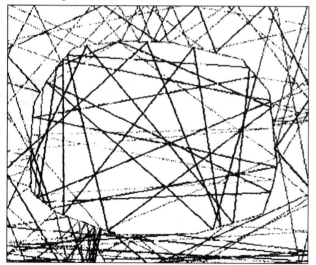

Tristan Bastit *The ■Black Body is a Beautiful Body*

■**Carelman, Jacques.** Born a week after the great Wall Street crash. Came to Paris in 1956 to devote himself to painting and sculpture (*Mécaniques pour Cyrano*, participation in the exhibition *Les Machines célibataires*, etc.), to stage and costume design for the theatre (Molière, Gogol, etc.), to book-illustration (stories from *The Thousand and One Nights*, novels and stories by Dostoevsky, *Le Petit Supplément à l'Encyclopédie de Diderot et d'Alembert*, ●Queneau's ●*Exercises in Style*, etc.). He is above all known for his *Catalogue d'objets introuvables* (1969),[1] objects he has subsequently made and exhibited world-wide. Founder-member of the Oupeinpo, Regent of the ●College of 'Pataphysics, where he holds the chair in Helicology.

■**Casing (*cassification*).** Processing text using a typographical *case* (graphically represented) to produce ■*pein*.

1. *Input*: a given text. Printed writing is made up of typographical signs: upper and lower case letters, numbers, punctuation marks, together with various kinds of blanks — indentations, spaces between words and at the end of paragraphs, etc. The design of these signs gives an alphabet its homogeneous style. Within each style are various types — roman or italic, light or bold — as well as different point sizes.

2. *Processing*: the case. In traditional typography, lead characters used for printing are kept in a shallow container called a *case*, which is divided into as many *boxes* as there are types of characters. Characters are distributed among the boxes according to rules of biotechnical efficiency. Here is the layout of the so-called Parisian case:

A	B	C	D	E	F	G	• ; ı ¬ • ′ ı t	ë	ï	ü
H	I	K	L	M	N	O	É	È	Ê	Æ	Œ	W	Ç
P	Q	R	S	T	V	X	ffi	â	ê	î	ô	û	!
»	(	U	J	j	Y	Z	ff	à	è	ù		&	?
•	ſ	é	-	•			1	2	3	4	5	6	′	8
—	b	c	d		e		s	esp. moy.	f	g	h		9 0 / æ œ
ε y	l	m	n	i			o	p	q	esp. fines	; w ſſ	k :	½ cadra. tins / cadra. tins
x	v	u	t	espaces			a		r		.	,	cadrats

A case contains one sort of character, uniform in point size and style. Thus, if a text utilises several sorts of character, an equivalent number of cases is needed. The Oupeinpian user simply juxtaposes the cases involved. Each typographical sign will then correspond to a designated point on the layout of the cases. The layout makes it possible to establish on a plane (in the two dimensions of graphic representation) what the text presents in linear fashion.

3. *Output*. The positions of the typographical signs of the input text can now be indicated by points or squares, the cases portrayed as planes or in perspective, etc.; in other words, the graphic method used to make the ■transposition is freely chosen by the artist. The result, furthermore, can be treated as an end in itself or used as a basic ■matrix from which a work is derived.

The examples overleaf were produced as 'illustrations' of two entries in the bibliography of André ●Blavier as published in *Plein Chant*, nos. 22-23. [TF, trans HM]

See ■Decasing.

■**Chronological collage.** Collage — Cubist, Surrealist, or other — consists in cutting out and reassembling fragments so as to produce an effect purely dependent on the taste of the collagist. It is essentially a destructuring activity and thus an anti-Oupeinpian one. It should be set right by introducing ■constraints.

One of these is chronology: the fragments of the collage are arranged in accordance with the passage of time.

In the collage illustrated (p.285), the foreground comes from a 15th-century work by Benozzo Gozzoli; the next level is taken from the 16th century and Jacopo Carucci, known as Pontormo; the third level is involuntarily supplied by Nicolas Poussin (17th century); John Constable (18th century) is responsible for the fourth level; the fifth is from a work by Giovanni Segantini painted in the 19th century; the sixth is a detail from a 20th-century canvas by Nicolas de Staël.

To make the method more interesting, sub-constraints like ■perspective and light may be added. This will give the collage the coherence of a 'real painting'. [JC]

See also ■Assemblage and reassemblage.

(Above) Jacques Carelman *The Conversion of St. Paul, the Adoration of the Magi, and the Triumph of Flora, in Wivenhoe Park, about the Fountain of Life, under the sky of Agrigente*

(Facing page, left): Thieri Foulc *For André de la Blave, Geographagnist*

(Facing page, right): Thieri Foulc *The Day of Forbidden Masterpieces*

■**Code.** A set of relations connecting one system (input) to another (output).

The Oupeinpo uses codes whose outputs are visual. The inputs vary: from the values of black areas (see Tactile ■transposition, Carelman) to the letters of a text (*Lo* ❏*Scarabeo d'oro*, Spinelli).

See also ■Casing, ■Onomometry.

■**Collective Publications of the Oupeinpo (CP).**

■**CP1.** *Prenez Garde à la Peinture Potentiell!* Special issue of *Monitoires du Cymbalum Pataphysicum*, 21, 15 September 1991.

■**CP2.** *Qu'est-ce que l'Oupeinpo?* Special issue of *Java*, 10, Winter 1993/94.

■**CP3.** *Potentialités*, in *Giallu*, 3, 1994 (Ajaccio).

■**CP4.** *Nouveaux Aperçus sur la potentialité restreinte.* Exhibition catalogue (Publications de la Licorne, Faculté des Lettres et des Langues, Université de Poitiers, 1997).

■**CP5.** *Les Séances de l'Oupeinpo.* Since their 175th meeting, on 12 October 1997, the Oupeinpo has produced these brief monthly accounts of their activities.

■**CP6.** *Du Potential dans l'art*, Éditions du Seuil, 2005. A comprehensive survey of the Oupeinpo's work to date.

See also Thieri Foulc, "Cassification", *Plein Chant*, 22-23, Bassac, October 1984-March 1985; Thieri Foulc, "Décassification", *Plein Chant*, 29-30, April-July 1985; the exhibition *La 'Pataphysique d'Alfred* ●*Jarry au* ●*Collège de 'Pataphysique*, Galerie de l'UQAM (Université du Québec à Montréal, May 1989); ●*New Observations*; *Oulipo, société discrète*, section illustrated by Oupeinpo in *Page des libraires*, May/June 1996; Thieri Foulc, *Vingt ans de peinture potentielle* in *Magazine Littéraire*, May 2001.

■**Combinatorial work.** A work whose significance is to be found less in the sum of its visible parts than in their ability to combine with each other. Nor is a combinatorial work the sum of its combinations: even fully realised, this can do no more than indicate the abstract method that has generated them.

The simplest combinatorial works are those which rearrange the positions of material elements (see ■*Polyptikon*, ■*Morpholo*, ■Taquinoid). But other elements can also be manipulated: see *La* ❏*Vache au pré noir*, ❏*Vanishings of L.V. Gogh*, ■Zoopictural classification.

■**Constraint.** A term drawn from literary usage (see ●*Contrainte*), where it designates the rule an author chooses to follow. The Oupeinpo, by definition, develops constraints for the use of painters. For an artist worthy of the name, a constraint is anything but a vexation or an imposed rhetorical system: it is a support, an aid to invention, an enjoyment of form (and art is a question of form), and a liberation from the tyranny of the message.

■**Constraint by edges.** A ■constraint by which the constituent parts of a picture (lines, forms, colours, surface effects, subject matter, etc.) are derived from elements directly adjoining one or more of its edges.

See ■Hyperdominoes, the ■*Morpholo*, Bitangential ■picturogenesis, ■*Polyptikon*, ■Scytalism, Rotatory ■substitution, ■Taquinoid.

Other elements, such as thematic ones, may also be similarly transferred. Bastit's ■*M.O.U.* provides a radical method of juxtaposing edges by elevating interruption to the status of a rule. The process permits the transfer of contrast, tension, and balance.

See also ■Plaited picture, the second method as applied to Mondrian's *Broadway Boogie-Woogie*. For another method using thematic affinities, see Neutralisation of ■constraint by edges.

■**Constraint by edges, neutralisation of (lamellisective method).** The ■constraint by edges is one of the most successfully applied Oupeinpian constraints. But what is to be done with juxtaposed images where nothing — neither subject nor position — can be juxtaposed because of disparities at their margins?

The case arose when, after a series of symmetrisations by ■lamellisection of Ingres's *La Source*, it became imperative to confront this work with Rembrandt's *Woman Bathing* (see opposite). But where the bather's legs were spread, the nymph's were together; where one was at the water's edge, the other was in it up to her knees. How could such obstacles be overcome?

Here the great versatility of lamellisection became apparent. As soon as the works were divided into narrow strips, they became permeable to one another. A judicious, progressive shifting of strips was enough to create an area of passage, a no man's land across which the fundamental connections between the works — those *beyond* their edges — could be established.

Once generalised, the method became a way of neutralising the constraint by edges by arranging a childless but none the less (falsely) harmonious marriage (see Bitangential ■picturogenesis). Lamellisection can thus replace colour gradation, *sfumato*, and the optical mixing dear to Seurat. But pairing two pictures at random would be pure laziness. Serious justifications are needed.

The method is recommended only for blurry conditions: reflections in water, smoke, clouds, mirages, the inspiration-wreathed Muse... [JV]

■**Decasing (*décassification*).** The reverse of ■casing.

A pattern of specific points located on an image (painting, engraving, photograph, or whatever) is superposed on the layout of a printer's case (or group of cases): an abundance of typographical signs is thus designated — upper and lower case letters, punctuation marks, blanks, etc. This material is then used to compose a text.

Foulc has demonstrated the method using a Cranach engraving of *Adam and Eve* as a starting-point. The material pataphysically provided by the case led to the (re)composition of a poem by Jean ●Queval that clearly refers to the engraving in question (cf. *Plein Chant*, nos. 29-30). [TF, trans HM]

■***Déculottage.*** A technique for revealing hidden aspects of a painting by removing its backing.

The verb *culotter* means to season a pipe until it acquires a satisfactory varnish. Implicitly, *déculottage* means removing the

pipe and leaving the varnish intact. Oupeinpian *déculottage* deals with the unseen strata of a painting in this fashion. The *déculotteur* selects a painting on a wooden panel. He knows that the painter has applied a base to the wood, then an undercoat followed by several layers of paint. Starting from the back of the painting, he planes away the wood, strips off the undercoat, and perhaps scrapes away one or two layers of paint. He can then contemplate a work that no one, not even the painter, has ever seen.

For an Oupeinpian concerned with ■constraints, the question is, what sort of landscape, still life, or abstraction should be painted on the panel so that the *déculotteur* would discover (say) an erotic scene?

■**Dewasne, Jean.** Born at Hellemmes-Lille in 1921. He was one of the creators of the salon *Réalités Nouvelles* in 1946 and founded the *Atelier d'Art Abstrait* in 1950. An upholder of constructive abstractionism, he incorporates into his thought the catastrophe theory of René Thom, Claude ●Berge's graph theory, and the fractals of Mandelbrot. He is the creator of anti-sculptures and of monumental paintings, notably the two murals at the Grande Arche at La Défense, west of Paris, each 100 metres high and 70 metres in width.

Dewasne belonged to the original Oupeinpo (1964–7) and was a founding member of the present one. In his acceptance speech upon being received into the Académie des Beaux-Arts, he was the first under the dome of that venerable institution to utter the name of the Oupeinpo and present its programme for the next three centuries.

■*Digrapheur.* Device derived from the ■*Grande Œuvre* (intersection of the column *Symmetry* and the row *Equipment*): a two-pointed pencil used to draw simultaneously on

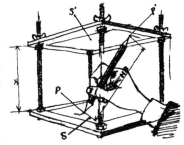

(Left) Jack Vanarsky *Rembrandt's Bather at Ingres's Source*

two facing surfaces. An actual instrument was made by Vanarsky and its workings explored by him in ■CP4.

Contrary to the legend, propagated by Michelangelo himself in his *Sonnets*, the Oupeinpo maintains that the artist did not spend four years lying on scaffolding to paint the ceiling of the Sistine chapel. He simply painted the floor with a twenty-metre *digrapheur*.

■**Foulc, Thieri.** The vertical axis of Foulc's "*Autobiography*" (below) lists the following categories (from the top): ■potential painting, painting, collage, textile art (with Nicole Foulc), engraving, drawing, poetry, speculative and theoretical prose, polemical and edifying prose, prose fiction, erudition and history, andrology, publishing, systematic compilation, mass publishing, travels, unintentional losses, destructions, textual

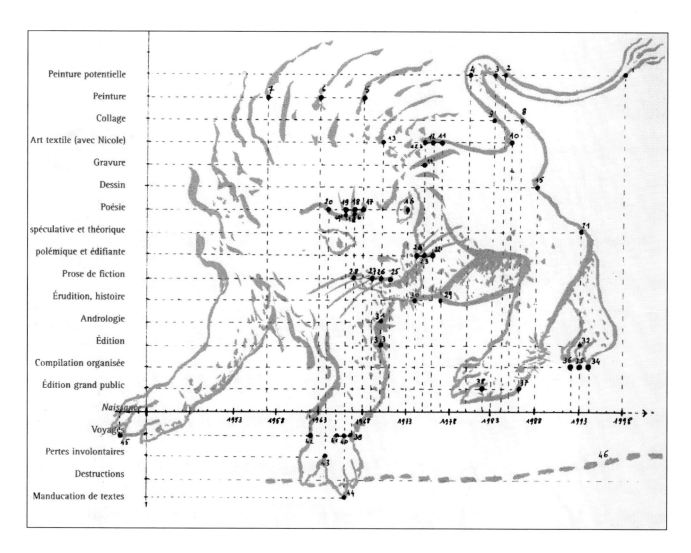

manduction. The horizontal axis is durational, beginning at the artist's birth. Numbers indicate particular works, publications, etc. (too numerous to list here).

See ■Autobiography by Cartesian co-ordinates.

■**Gagnaire, Aline.** (1911–1997) A member of the short-lived original Oupeinpo (1964–7), she was at once elected to the refounded group and in January 1981 attended its first constitutive meeting at François ●Le Lionnais's. She belonged to the war-time generation of Parisian Surrealists that were associated with the *Réverbères* group and *La Main à Plume* (see Noël ●Arnaud). During the '50s and '60s she exhibited with the Surrealists at the Galerie Furstenberg. She was the inventor of the "calligramme", "blanc de blanc", "tableau-chiffon", "tableau-mur", etc. More recently, she exhibited at the 1986 Venice Biennale, the 1987 Masques d'Artistes, etc. She was an *Auditrice réelle* in the ●College of 'Pataphysics.

■*Grande Œuvre* **of the Oupeinpo, the.** *What I propose to call the* Grande Œuvre[2] *of the Oupeinpo is a tableau: not a painting but a table with lines and columns. It will not, however, be an equivalent of* ●Queneleyev's Table.

At the head of its (horizontal) lines, let us put what I call the specific elements of ■pein, *that is, the specific elements of painting, drawing, the visual, the plastic; everything in short that is neither the li of literature nor the mu of music. What are the ordinary elements of* pein? *Form, colour, line, surface, material, etc., etc. This is a basic list. It must be complete, and it is by no means easy to make it complete; we found that out in the Oulipo with Queneleyev's Table. What* ●Queneau *put into it came from language: letters, syllables, rhyme, length, number, etc. We then realised that in literature there also exists what we subsequently called the semantic: feeling, for example. Should feelings be put into paintings? Figurative painters would say yes; abstractionists, some yes, some no — it depends which ones. There are characters and sensations in literature; similarly in painting there are many things not in the eye of the painter that he would like to include in his painting. These things are products of sensibility, not merely of the painter's individual sensibility but of a communal one. It is therefore harder to draw up a list of the constituent elements of* pein *than it might seem. It is not even certain that it can be done in any kind of order. If so, it will be easy, and there will be an order; if not, we shall have to choose an arbitrary order. But the list is the primary task — the foundation.*

At the head of the (vertical) columns, a few simple structural elements. In the Oulipo's book (Lipo, ●CP3), *I suggested several mathematical structures. One could list about a thousand. We can't tell in advance which will be useful. Some are very simple: membership, inclusion, combination,* ■intersection, *complementarity, order, tangency,* ■symmetry, *reflexivity, asymmetry, dissymmetry, antisymmetry, transitivity, proximity, open/closed, boundary, adherence...*[3]

François ●Le Lionnais, 6 January 1981

See the table overleaf, and the ■Hundred Flowers of the Oupeinpo. See also ●Systematisation, ●Queneleyev's Table; Ouphopo, ★Table of Ouphopian Constraints; Outrapo, the ★R[rrrrr] structure.

■*Gravures molles.* An engraving, each of whose printings is unique: each presents a particular version of a set comprising a number of printing layouts, connected for the occasion by a 'law of physics'.

The *gravure molle*, invented by Bastit, belongs to his work with ■isomorphism. The problem faced here: can the plastic elements of a work be organised on the model of the great cosmological systems? The systems used are those of Ptolemy, Copernicus, and Einstein. Engraving was chosen as a medium since its function is to produce multiples, in this case, the 'multiples' are each a state of the system.

See page 291.

THE OUPEINPO'S *GRAND ŒUVRE* OF 1000 COLUMNS (EXCERPT OF THE FIVE COLUMNS IN PROGRESS)				
	SYMMETRY	**TANGENCY**	**INTERSECTION**	**MEASURE**	**SUBSTITUTION**
SUPPORT	— 2x-ptych —Painting on 2 inter-linked Möbius Strips			—Normalisation acc. to classical canons —Golden Section —Canvas of 1 sq. m. but differing shapes	—Identical methods of paint application on different supports
MATERIAL	—Materio-Symmetrism (cf. ■Hundred Flowers)		—Pigmentary residue of ■intersecting mediums		—Lost wax method of casting
EQUIPMENT	—Vanarsky's ■digrapheur		—A leadless shaft lacking bristles		
SURFACE					—Alteration of scale
FORM (2-D)	—Painting with variable ■symmetry (Carelman)	—Bitangential ■picturogenesis —■Hyperdominoes —■*Morpholo* (Foulc)			
FORM (3-D)			—*Venus of Samothrace* (■intersection)	—Iso-volumism (cf. ■Hundred Flowers)	
DRAWING	—Trans-significant symmetry (definition lost and forgotten!)	—Bitangential graphogenesis —■*Polyptikon* (Gagnaire)	—■Metapuncture	—Drawing with measured line (cf. ■Measured-colour painting)	
COLOUR		—Bitangential ■picturogenesis —■Hyperdominoes	—Intersection of a motif in the colours of an existing work (Van Gogh landscape painted in Venetian colours)	—■Measured-colour painting (measured by surface area, quantity, weight) (Foulc, Gagnaire)	—*La □Vache au pré noir* (Dubuffet/Barnier) —Comic strips coloured differently for sale in African countries
TACTILITY		—Bitangential ■picturogenesis	—Intersective planing (employing a profiled carpenter's plane)		—A Dewasne Vlamincked by a traitor —Tactile ■transposition of *Guernica* (Carelman)
RELATION [4]			—You are in the picture (●Duchamp)		—Switching labels in museums —Comic strips coloured differently for sale in African countries
OPERATOR [5]	—■Telesymmetry				
STYLE		—Bitangential ■picturogenesis			—●*Exercises in Style* (Carelman)
SUBJECT		—Bitangential ■picturogenesis			—*Millet's Angelus* by Dalí

Ptolemy

A geocentric system in which the earth, as we all know, is at the centre of the universe with planets turning concentrically around it.

The work entitled *Ptolemy* concretises the system in a central element that both plastically and semantically obliges objects to move along circumferences concentric with it.

Copernicus

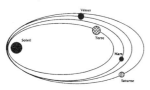

A monarchical system that makes the sun one of the two foci of ellipses around which the court of great planets travels.

The work *Copernicus* exemplifies this system by means of the procedure called "the gardener's ellipse". By means of 'leashes', two 'semantically correct' visual factors determine the degrees of freedom allowed the vassal elements.

Einstein

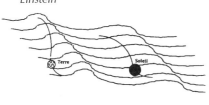

A hedonistic system in which bodies follow geodesic lines in s p a c e - t i m e according to the law of minimal work.

The schema is embodied in *Einstein or the flying physicist*, a work that obeys the ■constraint of the ■puzzlomorphic trammel-net. The homogeneity of the relativistic universe is neatly transcribed as an infinite jigsaw puzzle whose pieces all have the same shape (see ■*M.O.U.*). Local singularities — concentrations of matter and energy — are translated by the plastic singularities of individual pieces.

Tristan Bastit *Gravures molles*: *Ptolemy*; *Copernicus*; *Einstein*.

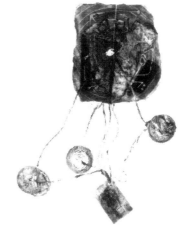

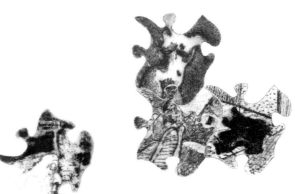

■Hidden message. Method for creating an ■isomorphic work from a given picture by decoding its elements. The decoding can of course be based on the visible appearance of painted forms, but it should primarily concern itself with the relations between them: this alone makes decoding their 'meaning' possible. [TB]

■Hundred Flowers of the Oupeinpo, The. (See opposite) Square table (10 rows x 10 columns) intended to facilitate the emergence of one hundred artistic schools by naming them (the principle of logogenesis).

The title recalls the creative enthusiasm of Mao Tse-Tung ("Let a hundred flowers bloom! Let a hundred schools of thought arise!"), but the method is clearly more rigorous and potentially far superior. The number of rows and columns can be as many as is desired (depending on the ability of language to provide usable terms).

Five basic constituent elements of a work of plastic art (support, materials, draughtsmanship, volume, colour) and five operations, mathematical or other, chosen from an infinite number (■symmetry, addition, subtraction, tangency, movement) have been placed along the abscissa and ordinate. The square corresponding to the intersection of the rows and columns indicates a new school, rigorously named. For example: chromo-additionism, tango-kinetism, or symmetro-graphism (which is on no account to be confused with grapho-symmetrism!).

The tendency or creed of faith of each school is then obvious: the chromo-additionists add colours; the tango-kinetists' one ideal is to animate tangencies; symmetro-graphists are convinced that there is no art except that of drawing symmetries (while the grapho-symmetrists support the act of making drawings symmetrical...).

These different schools turn out to be, like those of traditional art history, sometimes very rich in meaning, sometimes frankly banal and mediocre, sometimes impossible or falling within the province of the purely imaginary, but always of great potentiality. [JC, trans IW]

■Hyperdominoes. Dominoes so painted that where a half-domino has a certain figure, an accompanying image can be harmoniously aligned with that of a domino with the same figure. As in a game of ordinary dominoes, it is thus possible to construct a work whose visual continuity is guaranteed, whether abstract (Dewasne, Gagnaire) or figurative (Carelman, illustrated above). A ■constraint by edges.

■Intersection. Set of elements belonging at the same time to two given sets: E = A ∩ B.

The *Venus of Samothrace* was one of the Oupeinpo's first inventions. *Venus of Samothrace* = *Venus de Milo* ∩ *Victory of Samothrace*. *The Burial of Count Ornans* was conceived in the same way as the intersection of two well-known works of Courbet and El Greco.[6]

■Isomorphism. Formal mapping correspondence between the elements of two or more structures or systems. Every work that depends on decoding or encoding, 'creaming', and the reuse of existing models is an example of isomorphism. In figurative painting resemblance implies dissimilarity, and the correspondence between two isomorphic structures is never complete. The Oupeinpo supplies the isomorphisms. Artists work on the differences.

The ■Hundred Flowers of the Oupeinpo (detail)

See also ●Systematisation, ●Queneleyev's Table; ■*Grande Œuvre*; ★Table of Ouphopian Constraints; Outrapo, the ★R[rrrrr] structure.

See ●Isomorphism; ■*Gravures molles*, ■Hidden message, Tactile ■transposition, ■Transposition of coherence.

■**Lamellisection.** Cutting an image or structure into strips that are then rearranged according to a predetermined plan. Jack Vanarsky is the specialist of lamellisection, applying it not only to his own sculpture but (using reproductions) to the work of others. Elaborate rules govern the reassemblage of the results.

See Neutralisation of ■constraint by edges, ❑*Nude Turning Round On Her Couch, Even*, ■Perversions, ■Straightening the Seine's Course through Paris.

■**Limit, going for the.** The question of the minimum requirements of a work of art has been a central concern of many of the avant-garde art movements of the last century (the same cannot be said, for example, of literary movements). ●Duchamp's "Ready-mades" defined a base position with respect to artworks as a whole. In *painting* the monochrome has always seemed to represent the most extreme instance of reduction. Art history would cite such works as Malevich's *White on white*, the monochromes of Yves Klein and the black paintings of Ad Reinhardt. The Oupeinpo would point out, however, that these pioneers were preceded by two anticipatory ■plagiarists: Laurence Sterne and Alphonse ●Allais. A more detailed survey may be found in *Le Monochrome bariolé* (L'Échoppe, Caen, 1991) by Pol Bury.[7] [AB]

■**Lipopict.** Painting from which one or more of its usual elements has been deliberately excluded. Particular colours, such as black, are an obvious instance (a monochrome excludes all colours but one), but other elements can be affected as well. Dewasne has made a work that eliminates all visible parts of his interior *Mural No. 1* in the Grande Arche at La Défense and retains only the parts masked by the building's 33 floors.

An Oupeinpian equivalent of the ●lipogram.

■**Matrix.** A diagram used to organise elements. It differs from a ■code, which automatically furnishes a direct result, in that it simply provides a structure which can be used in various ways

(■casing, ■onomometry, ■transposition of coherence, and other ■isomorphisms explored by Bastit).

■**Measure.** ■Constraints based upon the quantification of specific elements of a work (cf. metre in poetry, measure in music). See next entry, and Going for the ■limit.

■**Measured-colour painting.** Paintings with measured colour have been made by Foulc, who divided his surface into a grid of small squares, and by Gagnaire, who measured her coloured papers by weight.

The restriction may be transferred to drawing (length of line), sculpture (volume of clay), and even to crafts such as lace-making (length of thread).

Thieri Foulc *Le rouge = le noir*
(Composed of 5,000 red squares and 5,000 black squares.)

■**Metapuncture.** The points shared by two superposed drawings are used to create a third (see opposite, top).

■***Morpholo, the.*** A device invented by Foulc that consists of a set of counters or pieces, with x colours applied to the counters' y sides. The aim is to 'tile' a given surface with the counters while following a ■constraint by edges.

1. *Creating the equipment (pieces)*

The pieces are square. The side of each square is divided in

half; each half can be either black or white. Four colourings of a side are possible (2^2): all white (white + white), white + black, black + white, all black (black + black). The possible combinations of the four kinds of side are $2^{2 \times 4} = 256$. To include all these possibilities, the *Morpholo* has 256 pieces.

2. *Combination*

The objective is to tile a surface using all 256 pieces while respecting the constraint by edges; that is to say joining white to white and black to black.

A further ■constraint is to tile a square area 16 x 16 (= 256). Experience has shown this to be possible: two solutions have been found so far, and there are certainly many others.

3. *The problem in general*

A *Morpholo* of *x* colours on *y* sides can tile a surface in a number of ways: 17 known geometrical shapes suit the requirement.

The simplest ($x = 1$, $y = 3$) is a monochrome equilateral triangle, with no combinatorial possibilities. Next ($x = 2$, $y = 3$), equilateral triangles with 2 colours: possibilities are $2^{2 \times 3}$ (= 64). With its 256 pieces and 2 colours, the version described above, which has been assembled, remains the basic one. A *Morpholo* with hexagonal pieces and 3 colours would require $3^{3 \times 6} = 387,420,489$ pieces in all.

4. *Realisation and publication*

The original *Morpholo* consists of a gridded roll of paper 5.12 metres long, and a box containing the 256 pieces (each 6 x 6 cm., Indian ink on white card) accompanied by an explanatory text. It has been exhibited at the Galleria Rizzardi, Milan, 1983, and at the Oupeinpo exhibitions noted in the penultimate paragraph of the ■*Introduction*. It was published as a booklet, with the explanatory text and the 256 pieces, by the Cymbalum Pataphysicum in 1985.

In 1991, for the Florence exhibition, a computer version of the *Morpholo*, based on a reduced set of 70 pieces, was produced by Marco Maiocchi and his students. The machine succeeded nearly always in tiling the given surface (a rectangle of 7 x 10 pieces in the format of the screen) following the rules of juxtaposition.

(Overleaf) Thieri Foulc *The Morpholo* (detail).

■**M.O.U. (Module Oupeinpien Universel).** The "Universal Oupeinpian Module" is a ■puzzlomorphic trammel-net, all of whose pieces have an identical shape.

A jigsaw puzzle can easily be constructed from pieces identical in shape, it is only necessary for the shape to be capable of 'tiling' or 'recurrently filling' a surface. M.C. Escher has treated this problem lucidly, especially as regards figurative forms (*The Regular Division of the Plane*, Foundation De Roos, 1958), but a skilful tiler manages it every bit as well for non-figurative or decorative forms.

Bastit has created a four-directional module with two tenons, one pointing west, one north, to which there correspond two mortices, east and south. The model here reproduced fits into a square with sides measuring 133 mm., and was duly registered at the *ad hoc* proceedings of the Oupeinpo at its regular sitting of 11 January 1997.

Unlike the pieces of the ordinary puzzlomorphic trammel-net, those of the *M.O.U.* can be permuted indefinitely (provided the surface be thought of as infinite).

A practical consequence of this property is shown by the ease with which it is possible, with a jigsaw or

a punch, to cut out great numbers of pieces that necessarily fit together. Every painting in the world (and all its reproductions), every printed page and poster, the entirety of existing images could thus be cut up using the *M.O.U.* and reassembled in a near-infinity of combinations.

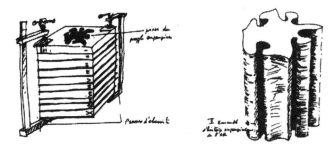

Bastit used the method above to create a *Potential History of Art* (text and illustrations) by cutting up the 4,008 pages of the *Universal History of Art* (in 10 volumes).

❑*Nude Turning Round On Her Couch, Even.* (Illustrated overleaf; the second operation, halving, is omitted.)

A permutative ■lamellisection by Vanarsky applied to Ingres's *Grande Odalisque*. The initial work was cut in half and the two halves permuted. In turn, the halves were cut in two and the halves of the halves permuted, and the process repeated until after the sixth operation the odalisque, in 64 slices, was turned around on her couch.

The same operation has been successfully carried out on Titian's *Venus with a Mirror*.

■**Onomometry.** Method of portraiture using the subject's name as a constraint of ■measure.

The letters of a name are assigned lengths consistent with their position in the alphabet (A = 1, B = 2, C = 3, etc.). These are used, for example, to determine the proportions of a portrait:

1st line: top of the head
2nd line: top of the brow (hairline)
3rd line: eyebrows (continued on p.300)

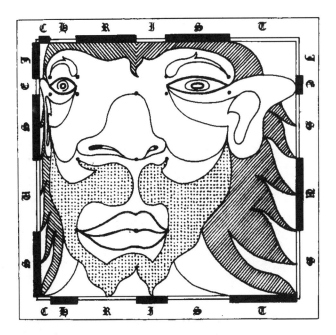

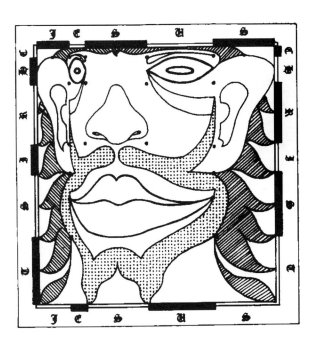

Stanley ●Chapman *Onomometric Portraits of Jesus Christ*

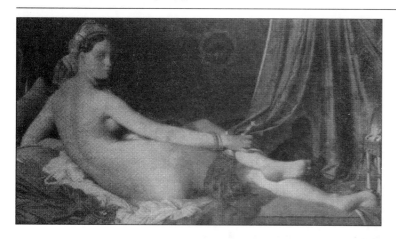

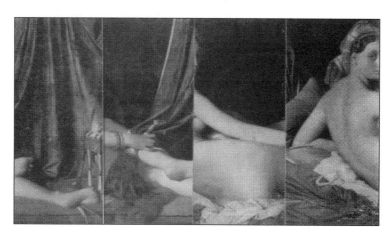

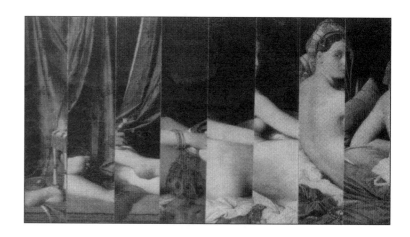

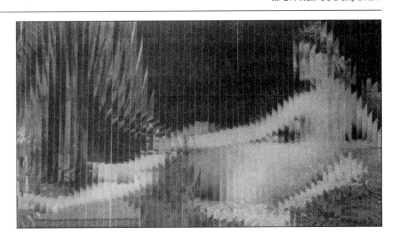

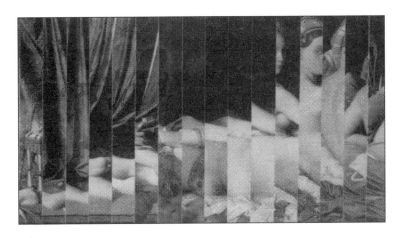

4th line: pupils of the eyes

5th line: base of the nose

6th line: opening of the mouth

7th line: tip of the chin

Subsequent lines: lower accessories (double chin, end of the beard, knot of the necktie, coat-buttons, etc.).

Photonomometry — an onomometric photographic portrait — differs by working with an existing image. Onomometric values no longer determine a drawing but reproportion a photograph. The problem is how to shrink or expand each zone according to the requirements of the name's letters. This is best done by using a computer to slice away lines of pixels or reduplicate them. Example: Bastit and Vanarsky's *Photonomometric Portrait of Raymond Queneau* (used on the cover of ■CP2).

■**Oupeinpo.** *Ouvroir de Peinture Potentielle* **or Workshop for Potential Painting. For a description of the founding and aims of the Oupeinpo, see the ■***Introduction* **and the entries for ●Oulipo and ●***Ouvroir.* **For a list of members, see** *Introduction,* **¶6.**

For a bibliography of publications, see ■Bibliothèque Oupeinpienne (BO), and ■Collective Publications of the Oupeinpo (CP).

Correspondence may be addressed to: Jacques Carelman, 5 rue des Pruniers, 75020 Paris.

■**Painting blind.** One of the dreams of non-retinal art. Just as the wine-lover practises blind tasting, refining his sensations, and uttering sublime verities, such as: "Merlot! Pétrus, 1981!" in like manner (?!) the practitioner of blind painting squeezes his colours from unlabelled tubes, applies them blindfold and, like Van Gogh, unhesitatingly exclaims: "How beautiful is yellow!"

■**Painting by telephone.** See ■Telesymmetry.

■**Painting machine.** An invention equally as venerable as the writing ●machine, examples of which include ●Jarry's ●*Clinamen* in *Exploits and Opinions of Doctor Faustroll, Pataphysician* and ●Roussel's machine in *Impressions of Africa.*

These two machines represent extreme and contradictory notions of painting. Roussel's, which mechanically reconstitutes a "vision" of landscape in paint, embodies optical ■representation at its purest. Jarry's, spraying colours on canvas every which way, embodies pure lyrical abstraction (an abstraction that does not prevent viewers from discovering the most astonishing scenes in it — but that is another matter).

See also ■*Digrapheur.*

■*Pein.* Abbreviation of *peinture* (painting), here standing for all the visual arts. The Oupeinpo's concern is *pein* just as the ●Oulipo's is *li* (literature), the ★Oucuipo's *cui* (cuisine), etc.

■**Permutative lamellisection.** See ■Lamellisection, ❑*Nude Turning Round On Her Couch, Even*; ●Permutation.

■**Perspective.** A set of lines co-ordinating the horizontal to the vertical aspects of objects and buildings.

In music the horizontal and the vertical cannot be dissociated. Music turns out to be a compact density of perspectives.

Painting can be defined as a musical architecture.

Sculpture is an architecture without perspective.

Architecture insinuates itself into the interstices of perspective. [JD]

■**Perversions.** An unlimited series of exchanges, by means of ■lamellisection, between Piero della Francesca's *Battista Sforza,* and *Federico da Montefeltro* on the one hand, and between his *Sigismondo Malatesta* and Pisanello's *Ginevra d'Este* on the other.

This kind of collage has been much exploited, especially by Jirí Kolar. He has tried so many variants of it that it is hard to imagine a new one. From an Oupeinpian standpoint, however, what distinguishes these experiments is that they all pertain to the *method of lines modified by lamellisection without angular correction,* rather than to the *method of lines modified with angular correction,* a particular instance of which is presented in ■straightening the Seine's course through Paris. The method leads to a theoretical restriction: lamellisection should be made as fine as possible, with the width of the slices tending towards zero (l = 0).

The method without angular correction has been called "straightforward" and "thrifty", since for each application only one copy of the source work needs to be sliced up. Two delineations are chosen (here two portraits in profile), and by lamellisection and a transfer of slices, one of them is inserted into the silhouette of the other. (In practice the width of a slice is always l > 0 so that the profile acquires a characteristic discontinuity. With *angular correction*, this discontinuity is eliminated.) [JV]

■**Photonomometry.** See ■Onomometry.

■**Picturogenesis, bitangential or *n*-tangential.** In this extension of the ■constraint by edges, a picture is created that bridges the gap between two dissimilar existing paintings, creating a new work that includes all three.

The constraint may be extended to the four edges of a painting (*quadritangential picturogenesis*) and, better yet, to the *n* sides of a polygonal panel (n-*tangential picturogenesis*).

See illustration overleaf.

■**Plagiarists, anticipatory.** Painters from the past such as Arcimboldo, whose interests the Oupeinpo has declared to be obviously Oupeinpian. In reality, all anticipatory ●plagiarists are accidental. *Just as Oupeinpians need not, as Oupeinpians, be artists, anticipatory plagiarists need not be artists either.* So it is natural enough that their plagiarism developed without the requisite rigour of method. Nevertheless, it is agreed that definite traces of Oupeinpism can be found at Lascaux (the ■constraint of the "imaginary earth"), in the frescos at Pompeii (the articulation of fictive and real space), among the Italian perspectivists from Giotto and Paolo Uccello to Pietro da Cortona (see Foulc *Giotto et l'hypothèse de la peinture peinte*, 1993), in Arcimboldo (see ●BO21), in the representations with multiple readings studied by Jurgis Baltrušaitis, in the compositions of Vermeer and Velasquez, in certain illusions or

(Above) Jack Vanarsky *Inverted identification of Battista Sforza with Federico da Montefeltro*

(Below) Jack Vanarsky *Inverted identification of Federico da Montefeltro with Battista Sforza*

Jacques Carelman *The Crippling Machine*. Bitangential ■picturogenesis using (left) Louis Le Nain, *The Peasant's Meal*, and (right) Pieter Bruegel, *The Beggars*.

effects of double reading created by Dalí (*Voltaire, Narcissus*), and in various works of M.C. Escher (see in particular his text on *The Regular Division of the Plane*, 1958). Nor is the Oupeinpo unaware of the *grilles* of François Morellet, the plaitings of François Rouan, the distributional computations of Albert Ayme, and the antiperspectives of Jan Dibbets and Georges Rousse.

Finally, if it does not class Max Bucaille and Pol Bury among its anticipatory plagiarists, this is because they were involved in the original Oupeinpo in 1964.

See Going for the ■limit.

■Plaited picture. See next pages for an example.

A ■constraint by edges whereby two images, cut into strips and plaited with one another, always produce a coherent result whenever and however they are reassembled.

The pages following show two pictures ready for plaiting.

Make a photocopy of both pages and trim off excess paper around the box framing each picture. Place plaited picture 1 on top of picture 2, taking care that the boxes are exactly lined up with each other, then staple them together at the right-hand edge as indicated. Cut out the strips along the dotted lines in each picture (they undulate for greater sensuality), extending the cuts on picture 1 to the left-hand edge of the paper, and those of picture 2 to its bottom edge.

Plait the strips of the second picture with those of the first, either regularly, each strip passing once 'over' and once 'under';

or irregularly, ad libitum, as shown below.

No matter how the plaiting is done, the black and grey forms in the resulting picture will be continuous, bringing to light figures in a strange embrace.

❑Thieri Foulc *Plaiting and Unplaiting: Method*

Take a blank canvas. Cut it into vertical strips of a given width.

Take another blank canvas of the same size and cut it into horizontal strips of the same width.

Plait the vertical and horizontal strips as cloth is woven: over, under, over, under. Thus from two canvases you create one canvas.

(Staple here)

(Staple here)   **PLAITED PICTURE 1**   (Staple here)

PLAITED PICTURE 2

On this canvas of canvases, this woven canvas, paint a picture. This is the father *picture*.

When the picture is dry, unplait it.

Set aside the horizontal strips. Juxtapose the vertical strips: you have a picture divided into equal squares. The squares that were over are painted, those that were under are blank.

Following the rules of the ■constraint by edges, paint the blank squares in a way that assures continuity of form and colour with the squares already painted. You have now created the son *picture*.

You naturally exercise your imagination when filling in the unpainted squares that take up half of the father picture, and make these newly-painted squares distinctly different.

Now carry out the same operation on the juxtaposed horizontal strips. You obtain a second son picture. When filling in the available half of unpainted squares, make them original as well.

The method's transformative power can now be exploited. Reweave the horizontal and vertical strips together, this time placing under the ones that were over in the father picture, and those which were over, under. You thus obtain a son-of-son picture — on the canvas of canvases, a picture of pictures. Thanks to the versatility of the constraint by edges, the picture of pictures (not painted by you and only revealed by reweaving) has a continuity of form and colour no less coherent than its predecessors.

Here is one of several variants. Start by filling an entire canvas with a painting. Cut it into strips, either vertical or horizontal, and plait them with strips cut from a blank canvas, fill in the overs. Unplait. Replait, working the unders over. Complete the painting. Unplait, and so discover a picture that has been painted not on a canvas of canvases but on the juxtaposed strips of the blank canvas.

This method makes it possible to begin with a pre-existing painting. Any masterpiece (once copied) can be used, but some works cry out to be cut into strips, such as Mondrian's Broadway Boogie-Woogie (1942-1943). What makes this painting interesting is that we can cut out our strips so that they coincide with Mondrian's design. Consequently the constraint by edges

no longer works, or at least not in terms of continuity. When Mondrian's painting is plaited with a blank canvas, small squares of the same size as Mondrian's are revealed, alternating with them and ready for colouring. Continuing Mondrian's painting will not then mean extending colour and shape across edges; instead it is a case of determining what coloured squares should be added to what is still visible of his painting so as to create the best possible new work. It can perhaps still be asserted that this is a constraint by edges, but one that works not through continuity but through contrast and an overall balance of contrasts: as Bastit puts it, a constraint by edges that functions around centres. After the phases of weaving-completion-unweaving, the picture of pictures obtained will contain nothing that is specifically Mondrian's. All that will remain is his covert influence.

■*Polyptykon.* Procedure invented in 1959 by Gagnaire: images are drawn on 3 strips of paper; these are reduced by accordion-like pleating to hinged strips which, through folding, can be revealed or concealed. The variable compositions that become possible always respect the rule of the ■constraint by edges.

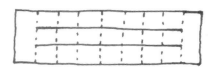

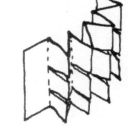

(Overleaf) Aline Gagnaire *Massacre.*

■**Portrait.** See ■Onomometry, ■Autobiography by Cartesian co-ordinates.

■**Potential.** What exists *in potentiality* rather than *in actuality*. The Oupeinpo itself does not produce pictorial works but constrictive forms where works exist in potentiality. As individuals, its members — and anyone else — can use these forms to create their 'actual' works.

■Puzzlomorphic trammel-net. A ■constraint by edges where the edge is considered not as a limit but as a formal contour.

A blank jigsaw puzzle is created or copied to serve as a pattern. Its pieces are numbered for easy reassembly. The shape of each piece is then transferred to an image, whether a work of art or not, chosen deliberately or at random.

According to Bastit, the procedure's inventor, a true Oupeinpian work should not leave the visual contents of the shapes to the whim of the artist. He therefore introduced a method of eliminating choice. He made a pile of graphic images turned face down and transferred to the reverse side of each image (without knowing which it was) the outline of one numbered piece of a jigsaw puzzle. These outlines were then cut out and reassembled in accordance with the design of the original puzzle. Once the new puzzle was completed, it was turned face up, and a new work, *The Partially-sighted Mushroom*, came into view (above).

See also ■*M.O.U.*

■Representation (*figuration*). From the Oupeinpo's formal standpoint, representation — the peculiar ability of painted forms to present occasional resemblances with those of the visible world — must be considered a (productive) ■constraint.

Since figurative art has been omnipresent in every place and time, few — even in the Oupeinpo — would dare conceive of the totality of its practitioners as anticipatory ■plagiarists. And yet...

Imagine an artist entirely free of prejudice and ignorant of art history. Setting brush to canvas, he thinks, "No, I don't want to paint something at random. A rule must determine my forms." He can always turn to proportion, harmony, contrast, tension, rhythm, etc., and bring off a masterpiece (its title will be *Brush Strokes* or *Stripe Balance*). But if he is more perverse, he may also think, "Let's organise forms (and colours) in terms of proportions and harmonies (etc.) that are not derived from my subjective, petty aesthetic sense but from external data. Consider, for instance, this basic fact: since the painting will be part of the visible world, it will be related to the rest of it. Whence the principle: every portion of the visible universe may be thought of as a formal structure that can potentially organise innumerable paintings (or decide how they are to be 'read'). So let's by all means make our ingenious shapes not only work in harmony with each other but produce the impression of horses' cruppers, breastplates, and lances (and decide that things looked much the same at the battle of San Romano). By all means let's juxtapose our splashes of colour not only for the pleasure of making them vibrate but so as to suggest varieties of water-lily floating in a pond (like those I tend in my garden at Giverny). This constraint won't replace the ones already mentioned (harmony, contrast, etc.) but supplement them. It will liven things up. It will give the viewer the surprise of recognising forms that (more or less) have a place in the world as he knows it." Such a painter is definitely an Oupeinpian.

No doubt his colleagues and predecessors have rarely thought in this way. (Rather the reverse: let's replicate the visible world to satisfy some magical desire or bourgeois need of comfort, and *then* let's bring some order into it.) Even as an *unconscious restraint*, representation has been and still is so widely used that it might seem, as a constraint, trivial and unworthy of the Oupeinpo. That would be a pity, because many Oupeinpian procedures derive their purpose from it.

This is the case with all methods intended to provide a

second reading of a painting, for example, rotation. Rotating the photograph of an African native hut or Bosch's *Conjuror's* table would scarcely be of (Oupeinpian) interest if it did not reveal a *Paranoiac Face* (Dalí, 1931) or a *Cubist Portrait of François Le Lionnais*:

It is represen-tation, combined with a 180° rotation, that gives interest to Arcimboldo's *Still-life Cook* and *Kitchen-garden Man* and Carelman's *Four Portraits in One* (see ■Rotatory picture). (■Anamorphosis, on the other hand, is generally disappoint-

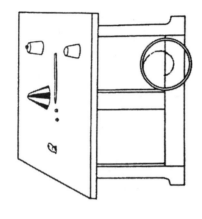

ing and rarely leads to a second reading of a painting.)

Similarly, ■combinatorial works such as Gagnaire's ■*Polyptykon* or Carelman's ■*Taquinoid* are fascinating not merely because their elements are formally recombined but because, however recombined, they remain representational. Their rearrangement is not interesting because the edges fit together but because in doing so they retain a general coherence — a fairly plausible image of the world. For the same reasons, a procedure like Carelman's ■chronological collage, in itself not especially restrictive, acquires difficulty and interest through complementary rules involving representation (the creation of an overall space, a coherent light source).

In the Oupeinpian view, representation, like ■casing and tactile ■transposition, becomes a particular category of ■isomorphism; as Bastit might say, a ■transposition of coherence. It is cause for astonishment that so immense a part of humanity's artistic activity should be devoted to exploring this constraint.

■Rotation. See ■Rotatory picture.

■Rotatory picture. One that provides a different 'reading' when rotated.

See ■Representation; ★Work of the Oubapo (6); and (opposite) Jacques Carelman *Four Portraits in One* (Four-way rotatory picture).

❑*Scarabeo d'Oro, Lo.* A pre-Oupeinpian (1975) work by Aldo Spinelli, who later became a foreign correspondent of the Oupeinpo.

This *Gold-Bug* consists of a ball of wool, 5.1 kilometres in length, made up of knotted strands of various lengths and (7) colours. The whole forms a coded text. The only commentary supplied by the author is the following: "The coded text explains the code itself. One cannot know the code without reading the text. One cannot read the text without knowing the code."

The *Gold-Bug* was exhibited, among other places, at the Palazzo Reale, Milan, during the exhibition *Jarry e la 'Patafisica*, May 1983.

■School. Group of artists, working together or not, who share one or more ■constraints. To the constraint of ■style, other constraints (national, local, chronological, or social) are often added: the Flemish school, the Fontainebleau school or the Barbizon school, etc.

As opposed to these 'accidents of history', the Oupeinpo has established methods for the creation of artistic 'schools', notably that of logogenesis: words, simple or compound, obtained in any way one might wish (dipping into the dictionary or into the pages of a text, a critical commentary on a work, etc.), then augmented by the suffix *-ism*, designate as many schools. All that remains to be done is to clarify and explain their doctrine.

See ■Hundred Flowers.

■Scytalism. ■Constraint of the *scytale* (Gk. *skutalé*), the staff used by the Spartans for encoding messages. A message written on a strip of paper wrapped spirally around the staff became illegible when unwrapped; only someone with a staff of the same diameter could decode it.

The scytalist painter, on the other hand, produces paintings

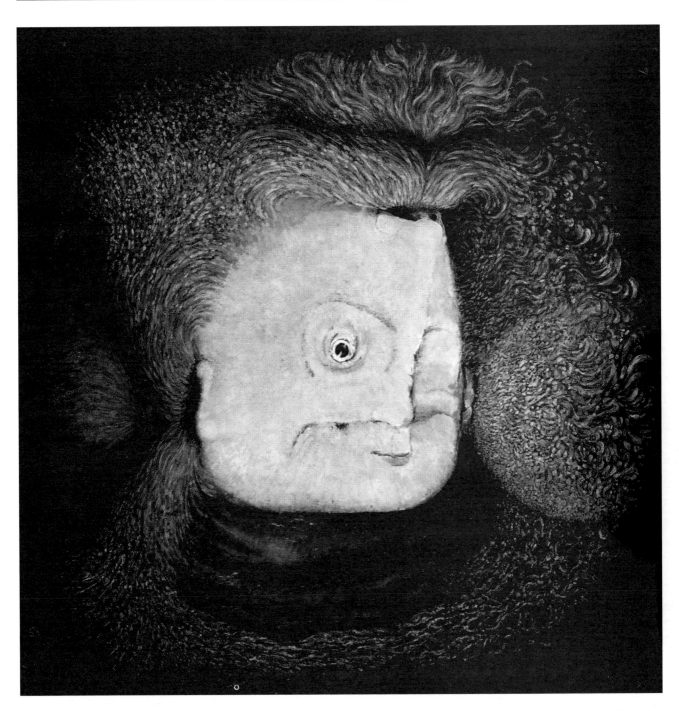

that remain readable when wrapped around staves of *different* diameters.

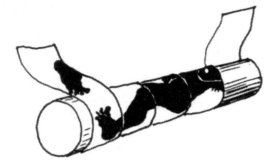

■Straightening the Seine's Course through Paris, a plan for. A task completed in 1991 by Vanarsky. It is the first application to town planning of rearrangement by ■lamellisection with angular correction — a special case of the various methods of linear modification developed by Vanarsky, and that belong to the broad Oupeinpian category of ■assemblage and reassemblage.

The Seine describes a vast loop as it traverses Paris: the problem was how to straighten it.

Take a map of Paris and cut it in two along a north-south axis that crosses the Seine at right angles where it passes Notre-Dame. Similarly, cut other maps of the city in two along axes parallel to the first but slightly shifted either west or east. Keeping only the left-hand portions of these maps, superimpose those that have been shifted by fitting increments to reconstitute a complete map of Paris. Then glue together the right-hand edges of these maps, altering their angle so as to make the visible segments of the Seine (each a few millimetres long) into a straight line. When the work is completed, consider the consequences:

the creation of an important thoroughfare for rapid river traffic;

the reapportioning of the city in terms of its left and right banks;

the disappearance of some sites and the duplication of others;

the insertion of the Bois de Boulogne into the very heart of the capital; etc.

The plan has been publicly exhibited, notably at the *Visions urbaines* show at the Centre Georges Pompidou in 1994. It was published as ■BO2 (1993); in *Le Visiteur. Ville, territoire, paysage, architecture*, 2 (1996); and in *Architectural Design* (special issue: *Games of Architecture*), 121 (1996).

[TF, trans HM]

■Structure. Synonym for ■constraint.

■Style. Styles are ■constraints, for the most part barely ■codified and all the more powerful for being (as is often the case) unconscious.

Examples of codified styles: Egyptian, Ionic, Louis XVI; more generally, architectural and academic styles of all periods. The artists who have proved most resistant to analysis are now the objects of computer research, with the aim of identifying among them a *grammar of style*. For differing reasons, the disciples of masters, plagiarists, and forgers are especially sensitive to the constraint by style.

See especially ◦Raymond Queneau and Jacques Carelman *Exercises in Style*, and also Oupeinpian ■artillery, ■Hundred Flowers, ■School, Painting with ■temporal elasticity.

■Substitution, rotatory. 3-dimensional version of the game involving the substitution of heads, bodies, and legs. A ■constraint by edges for sculptors.

■Superimposition. A particular kind of ■assemblage that depends on superimposing layers of paint or ink, sheets of paper, or other plastic elements. The Oupeinpo endeavours to formulate rules for the superimposition of

1. transparent elements
2. opaque elements.

The first category includes the *Multichrist*, a superimposition of several Crucifixions that are aligned along the vertical and horizontal of the cross, and *La ❑Vache au pré noir* and

❑*Vanishings of L.V. Gogh*, although these use a different method of superimposition and also involve opaque elements.

The second category is better served by sculpture and conceptual art.

■**Symmetry.** The absolute enemy. It is a criterion that makes it possible to distinguish non-painting — decoration — from painting. The Oupeinpo's chief concern is to introduce methods that distort or eliminate the perception of symmetries. It hardly needs saying that in order to do this it begins by erecting symmetrical structures.

For instance, the aim of the tango-symmetrist school (one of the ■Hundred Flowers) is to symmetrise tangencies so as to make points of tangency a decisive factor in transforming one work — say an erotic scene — into another. After drawing figures that share certain points of tangency (an erotic scene would be appropriate), draw an axis, construct the symmetrical points, and use them as the points of tangency for a completely different scene.

See ■Anamorphosis, ■*Digrapheur*, Painting with variable ■symmetry, ■Telesymmetry.

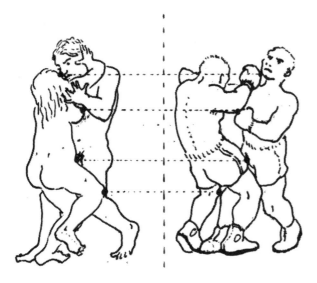

■**Symmetry, painting with variable.** This work by Carelman resembles an abstract painting. However, a mirror placed at an angle against it reveals a succession of figurative images as it is rotated. (The results can be obtained using the reproduction here by setting a small mirror or piece of foil along the top edge and rotating it through the arrows.)

The images that appear are: 1. fish; 2. firebird; 3. *art nouveau* portrait; 4. mythological figure; 5. fair-haired shaman; 6. butterfly. Each image is composed of a painted half and a mirrored half: the complete work demonstrates the use of *potential* ■*symmetry*. [JC]

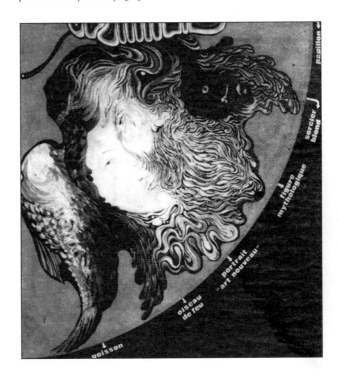

(Left) Thieri Foulc *Match*. (Above) Jacques Carelman *Painting with Variable Symmetry*, (without mirror). (Overleaf) The same painting with the mirror revealing the *art nouveau* portrait.

each one respect a total ■constraint by edges. Whatever the disposition of the squares, a coherent figurative work (cf. ■Representation) is always presented.

■**Telesymmetry.** A procedure that requires two artists, both connected by telephone with a third party who issues commands (the centre of ■symmetry) to both to execute a painting according to the single set of instructions given.

■**Temporal elasticity, painting with.** Dewasne's procedure of reworking a painting in the successive styles of the artist; for example, recreating Van Gogh's *Potato-eaters* in the colours of his Arles period.

■**System.** Set of relations between elements. Tristan Bastit takes an Oupeinpian interest in all systems, above all in non-artistic ones, and never hesitates to transpose these into ■*pein* (■transposition of coherence), or cheerfully to pervert them (■zoopictural classification). "A productive working hypothesis postulates that any system, in any domain, can and should be re-employed by Oupeinpians."

■**Taquinoid, or taquinoidal painting.** A work by Carelman (*Taquinoidal Land-scape*, right) constructed in the image of the game of *taquin* (known in England as the "fifteen puzzle"). But whilst, in the latter, the game consists in returning the sliding squares to an initial and unique order, the Taquinoid recognises all possible positions of the tiles as valid. The artist has painted the squares so that the four sides of

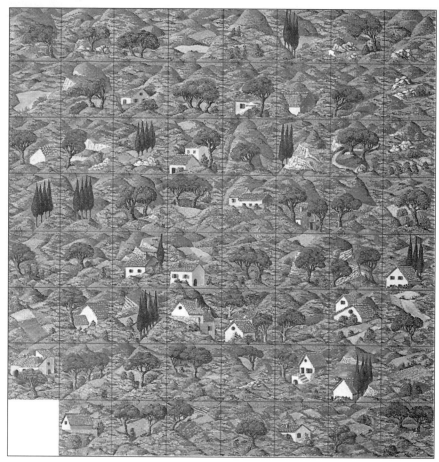

Transposition. The transfer of the characteristics of a work into another ■system. Just as a melody may be transposed into a new key, the composition of *Guernica* can be transposed into a work in sandpaper (Carelman's tactile ■transposition), or a dictionary illustration into a ■portrait (Bastit's ■transposition of coherence).

Transposition, tactile. ■Transposing the visual values of a work into materials perceptible to the touch.

The example of Carelman's *Guernica* is a simple one in that the Picasso painting taken as a point of departure can be considered a monochrome of unmodulated greys. To the seven values of grey identified, sandpapers of varying grades were assigned, the darkest corresponding to the coarsest sandpaper.

The procedure becomes more complex when applied to paintings of modulated colours, with a variety of materials being used (fabrics, pebbles, tree barks, glass, wool, scouring pads, etc.).

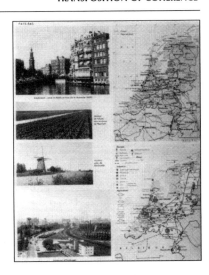

Transposition of coherence. An ■isomorphism practised by Bastit. A non-artistic visual system is analysed (and if necessary reinvented) so as to produce a coherence on which a new work can be based.

Bastit's *Portrait of Madame X* (right) is derived from a plate in an encyclopaedia article on the Low Countries. The plate includes six photographs, two maps, and captions. The relation between these three elements, whose purpose is to substantiate the reality of the Low Countries with evidence of towns, canals, administrative divisions, tulip fields, and windmills, creates a dense network of imaginative connections. These need only be transposed to another domain to give birth to Madame X, with her past, scars, flirtatious mannerisms, and erogenous zones.

❏*Vache au pré noir, La.* A work of ■combinatory 4-colour printing made in 1963 by Louis Barnier of the Imprimerie Union in Paris and published at his expense as a booklet to be given to clients and friends. Part of the print run appeared as an Internal Publication of the ●College of 'Pataphysics.

Colour reproduction works by decomposing an image into 3 colours (cyan, magenta, and yellow) and adding black for tonal contrast. Instead of inking four plates with one colour each, as is

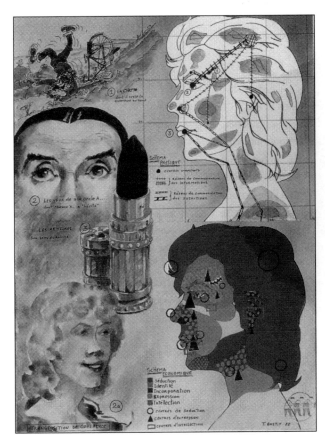

customary, Barnier's idea was to ink each with all 4 colours, systematically exhausting the permutations possible. He limited the possibilities by requiring that all 4 colours be used once for each plate, thus obtaining 4! (i.e. factorial 4 = 24) different results. (If he had used any of the colours more than once amongst the 4 on each plate, the number of combinations would have risen to $4^4 = 256$.)

This work, which is obviously that of a printer, took as its source a painting by Jean Dubuffet, *La Vache au pré noir*. The booklet included two texts: *Lettre d'un imprimeur à un peintre et la réponse que celui-ci y fit* (*Letter from a printer to a painter, and the latter's reply to it*). This did not stop critics and bibliographers from attributing the prints to the painter. The Oupeinpo honours Barnier's *La Vache au pré noir* as a high point of anticipatory ■plagiary.

■**Vanarsky, Jack.** A sectary of secancy, he slits his sculpture into subtle sections (in Saxon, "slices"), subject to sweet and stable stirrings similar to a snake's sinusoiding on its sod.

Since Sixty-five, sortie has succeeded sortie in settings situated in the Sixth (on the Seine's sinister side), in Soho, South America, Sweden, a sequence of salons, et setera. His sculpturesque symbol for the script and session of the Spectacle of the Sentury in Seville will successively and semestrially sashay to several sites scholarly and scientific.

Sticking to a system similar to his sculpture's, he has submitted to his sect a succession of segmented simulacra: a seductrix symmetrised, serial Siamese silhouettes, and the Seine slipping along her *s*-less side-street. [JV, trans HM]

❑*Vanishings of L.V. Gogh.* Modal interaction of ■superimposed computer images, used by Bastit to create ■portraits derived from master paintings and individualised according to the sex and name of the subject.

Computer images (either original or borrowed) appear on the screen as if on virtual planes. With appropriate software, the user can superimpose images and even modify their relative positions, bringing one to the foreground and moving others to one or more positions behind it. To do this the following

commands are used: "Bring to front", "Send to back", "Shuffle up", "Shuffle down". A large number of images can be superimposed in this way.

Here is a diagram of the 8 possible modes of superimposition (in black and white, with only two images):

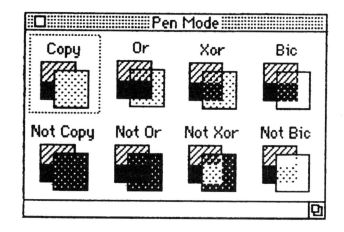

Colour naturally complicates matters. Instead of simple exchanges of black and white values, complementary colours are obtained, with superimposition producing different sorts of 'mixtures' and interactions.

For creating individualised master portraits, Bastit has limited the number of images to four: two versions of a Van Gogh self-portrait and two of Leonardo's *Mona Lisa*, prepared by him for this purpose. Since each of the four images can appear in any position (or layer), there are 24 (4!) different sets of superimpositions; and since each set can be assigned one of the 8 modes indicated above, the total combinatorial possibilities are $4! \times 8^4 = 98,304$.

A fairly simple software program enables ordinary users to select an individualised portrait from these possibilities. They type in

(a) their sex, which brings to the foreground one of the Van Gogh or *Mona Lisa* portraits and so halves the number of possibilities;

(b) their name, which will determine the modes and positions among the 49,152 possibilities remaining. As in

■onomometry, the final portrait will thus be closely linked to the subject's name, as well as being scientifically derived from one or possibly two of the most celebrated likenesses in the history of art. [TF, trans HM]

Tristan Bastit *Vanishings of L.V. Gogh*

■**Zoopictural classification.** Method inspired by the Linnaean classification of species. A given picture's genus, family, etc. is identified in order to assign it to a particular category. By permuting or substituting the terms used in classification, possible new paintings emerge that lack nothing but their execution. Bastit has derived many variants from the zoopictural classification of Velasquez's *Portrait of Count-Duke Olivarez* (right).

1. An English translation, *Catalogue of Extraordinary Objects*, appeared in 1971 (Abelard-Schuman, London).

2. In the language of alchemy, the *Grande Œuvre* is the making of or quest for the Philosopher's Stone; the term is sometimes used, in a looser sense, for the Stone itself. [IW]

3. This entry is an abridged transcription of a tape recording made at the first meeting of the resuscitated Oupeinpo. It is only a short excerpt from remarks made that day by the founder, and it has undergone considerable neatening. FLL eventually wished to correct it more thoroughly so as to give it greater intellectual rigour. He died without having done so. [TF]

4. ... *of the work with what is outside of it.*

5. *(person, animal, vegetable, mineral, artifact...)*

6. *The Burial of Count Ornans* = *The Burial of Count Orgaz* ∩ *Burial at Ornans.* [TF]

   (The symbol ∩ is used in set theory to denote the intersection of two sets, the set of elements that they have in common.)

7. Pol Bury was a member of the first Oupeinpo (1964-7).

VI. OU-*X*-POS

★Ou-*x*-po. *Ouvroir de* x *Potentielle* (Workshop for Potential *x*).

During the years after the formation of the ●Oulipo, other groups were created to explore similar concerns in fields other than literature. François ●Le Lionnais invented the acronym Ou-*x*-po to designate the generality of existing and possible groups, where *x* = the field in question.

Since the publication of the first edition of this *Compendium* there has been a bewildering proliferation of new Ou-*x*-pos. It has proved impractical to cover their work in this new edition, especially since many have vanished as suddenly as they appeared. Currently, the most complete listing of these groups can be found at http://site.voila.fr/ouxpo/index.jhtml. The section that follows, therefore, consists of a survey of the earlier Ou-*x*-pos, principally the Oubapo, which has published extensively. These entries have been updated in line with the rest of this edition.

See also *Carnets Trimestriels du Collège de ´Pataphysique*, 19, 15 March 2005. [AB]

★Ouarchipo. *Ouvroir d'Architecture Potentielle* (Workshop for Potential Architecture. The Ouarchipo has been there from the very beginning, although its potentiality has been slow — due to enormous distances between the igloos of its members — to reach fruition. From Anthony Hecht's noting that many of the villas surrounding Vicenza have plans based on the sonnet (8x6), to the birthday-cake-like plans for the amphi-arena (split into 12 segments) based on the inverted wigwam specially conceived to house the Opéra des Ouvroirs in Paris in January 2005 (Chapman), the relationship between literature and architecture has become more than subliminally apparent day by day.

Recent attempts include a three-day seminar between fifteen architects and five Oulipians (Bénabou, Grangaud, Jouet, Le Tellier, Salon) organised by Odile Fillion at the IFA in June 2001, a joint workshop at the École d'Architecture de Versailles in November 2003, and joint presentations at the VI Graz Biennial of Architecture and Media in December 2003, as well as the ongoing series of studios investigating the production of architecture under self-imposed constraints run by Enrique Walker at Columbia University, since January 2003.

Members: Stanley Chapman, Jean-Yves Duhoo, Gilles, Esposito-Farise, Jacques Jouet, Tim Norman, Odile Fillion, Enrique Walker. [SC & EW]

See http://membres.lycos.fr/dilouyum/olio/ouarchi.swf.

★Oubapo. *Ouvroir de Bande Dessinée Potentielle* (Workshop for Potential Comic Strips). Founded 28 October 1992 and connected to the *bande dessinée* publisher Éditions L'Association.

Members: François Ayroles, Anne Baraou, Gilles Ciment, Thierry Groensteen, Killoffer, Étienne Lécroart, Marc-Antoine Mathieu, Jean-Christophe Menu, Lewis Trondheim.

Since 1998 the Oubapo has produced offspring, with an official Swiss Oubapo and "unofficial" versions in the UK and USA (at www.newhatstories.com/oubapo/). The official Oubapo site is at http://gciment.free.fr/bdoubapo.htm.

Correspondence address: c/o Éditions L'Association, 100 rue de la Folie-Méricourt, 75011 Paris.

★Bibliothèque Oubapienne, La (BOB).

The Bibliothèque Oubapienne is not numbered. The Oubapo's publishing house l'Association has put out around a dozen works by artists from the group. L'Association can be contacted at the address above or at lassocia@club-internet.fr. Oubapo also collaborates with Oumupo, see ★Collective Publications of the Oumupo.

★Collective Publications of the Oubapo (CPB).

★CPB1. Minutes of meetings. Brief pamphlets for circulation to members and friends, ongoing.

★CPB2. *Oupus 1*, special issue of *Monitoires du Cymbalum Pataphysicum*, 43, also published independently by L'Association, 1997. This publication provided the material for this section of the *Compendium*.

★CPB3. *Oupus 2*, L'Association, 2003. Large-format paperback with contributions from nine artists which explores the constraints proposed in *Oupus 1*.

★CPB4. *Oupus 3, Les Vacances de l'Oubapo*, L'Association, 2000. A complete collection of the Oubapo strips that appeared in the French newspaper *Libération* between July and August 2000, 6 contributors.

★CPB5. *Oupus 4*, L'Association, 2005. Collective result of the workshops held during an exhibition at CNBDI Angoulême, January to April 2005, 27 contributors.

★CPB6. *Scroubabble*. Boardgame published by L'Association, 2005.

★Plagiary, anticipatory. Although the Oubapo has not published any systematic account of its anticipatory ●plagiarists, several are noted in the entry that follows. [AB]

★Work of the Oubapo. ★CPB2 consists chiefly of the Oubapo's initial attempts to define possible fields for exploration. These are systematically presented in a long article by Thierry Groensteen, *Un premier bouquet de contraintes*. While this article is summarised below, interested readers should consult the original for its contextual analysis and much fuller treatment of the subject.

Groensteen classifies Oubapian constraints in two main categories: *Generative* (those leading to the creation of new strips) and *Transformative* (those utilising and modifying existing strips).

GENERATIVE CONSTRAINTS

1. *Iconographic Restriction*. The exclusion of specified pictorial elements.

Example: Martin Vaughn-James *La Cage* (Les Impressions Nouvelles, 1986). No living being, human or animal, appears in this 180-page strip.

2. *Graphic Restriction*. The exclusion of specified graphic elements. A voluntary impoverishment of the comic strip's 'pictorial vocabulary'. (An Oubapian equivalent of restricted ●vocabulary.)

Example: Jean Ache *Des carrés et des ronds* (*Of Squares and Circles*) (Balland, 1974). Interpretations of La Fontaine's *Fables* using as characters only the two geometrical figures of the title.

3. *Scenic Restriction*. Constraints of the scenes within the strips and of the way strips are framed.

Example: Floc'h & Rivière *Blitz* (Albin Michel, 1983). All the frames in this detective comic strip are drawn from the same imaginary viewpoint within a room.

4. *Iconographic Repetition*. The repetition of a single image or sequence of images.

Example: David Lynch *The Angriest Dog in the World*. In this strip, which ran in the *Los Angeles Reader* for several months in 1980, the same four pictures were repeated each day with different captions.

4a. *Partial Iconographic Repetition*. Exemplified in François Ayroles *Jean qui rit et Jean qui pleure* (L'Association, 1995). (Illustrated right)

5. *Multi-readability*. Strips that can be read in more than one

direction.

Example: Killoffer *Bande dessinée en Tripoutre* (★CPB2). There are three possible readings (above).

5a. *Acrostic Strips*. The frames of the strip can be read both vertically and horizontally, like the initial or end letters of a verbal ●acrostic.

Example: Étienne Lécroart *Strips-Acrostiches* (★CPB2).

5b. *Palindromic Strips*. Strips that can be read both backwards and forwards like a verbal ●palindrome.

6. *Reversibility*. The drawings themselves can be read both the right way up and upside-down. Upside-down faces have been common in children's game books and caricatures for centuries. A nineteenth-century anticipatory ●plagiarist, Gustave Verbeek, applied the procedure with startling results (overleaf).

See also ■Rotatory picture.

7. *Overlapping*. Modification of a strip either (a) by folding it, or (b) by covering it with a sheet of clear acetate printed with elements that alter the strip.

Examples: Of (a) the 'fold-in' at the back of each issue of *Mad* magazine. Of (b) the French children's book series *Mes premières découvertes*, published by Gallimard.

8. *Random Consecutiveness*. A strip whose frames can be read in any order.

Example: Anne Baraou & Corinne Chalmeau *Après tout tant pis* (Hors Gabarit, 1991). The individual frames are printed on the faces of three large dice, and when the dice are thrown a strip is created.

9. *Regulated Distribution*. Any pictorial element can be regulated by mathematical, ●Oulipian or other constraints.

Example: The alternation of day and night in successive frames of *Krazy Kat*.

10. *Geometrical Arrangement*. The layout of the comic-strip frames follows predetermined constraints.

Example: Bill Griffiths *The Plot Thickens*, in *Raw*, 2 (1980). Each row of frames has twice as many frames as its predecessor: the first row consists of one large frame, the last of sixteen very small ones.

TRANSFORMATIVE CONSTRAINTS

1. *Substitution*. A strip usually has both text and images. Substitution can affect one or both:

1a. *Verbal Substitution*. New texts are inserted in an existing strip.

Example: François Ayroles *Placid & Muzo* (★CPB2).

(The Oubapo notes the anticipatory ●plagiary of this method by the Situationists.)

1b. *Iconographic Substitution*. The text is preserved, the images replaced.

1c. *Total Substitution*. A "double-blind" method invented by Killoffer that requires three participants. The first creates or chooses a strip and gives its drawings (but not its text) to the second participant, and the text (but not the drawings) to the third. The second writes a text for the drawings; the third makes drawings for the text; neither sees each other's work until the two components are combined into an entirely new strip. The Oubapo has published an example in ★CPB2.

2. *N + 7*. Comic strips altered according to the ●N + 7 method. (Obviously most other ●Oulipian methods can be used to modify the textual element of comic strips.)

Example: Killoffer *Lapin No. 6* (★CPB2).

3. *Expansion*. The Oubapian equivalent of ●larding. New frames are inserted into an existing strip according to a predetermined (usually mathematical) rule.

Example: Lécroart & Menu *Grabuge galactique* (★CPB2).

In the canoe is an enormous fish that Lovekins and Muffaroo have caught.

Lovekins takes the fish on shore, while Muffaroo pushes off in the canoe to see if he can catch another.

Unluckily he hooks a sword-fish, and there is trouble right away. The old man fights bravely. The sword-fish dives;

Then he comes up again, and this time he thrusts his sharp snout right through the bottom of the canoe. Muffaroo tries to get the sinking boat to the nearest shore.

Just as he reaches a small grassy point of land, another fish attacks him, lashing furiously with his tail.

The canoe sinks in the sea which has now become choppy, but Muffaroo jumps ashore, safe and sound, and starts back across the point to rejoin Lovekins.

4. *Reduction*. Oubapian equivalent of ●slenderising. Frames are removed from an existing strip.

Example: Gilles Ciment *Cigares du pharaon* (★CPB2). A treatment of Hergé's *Tintin* strip.

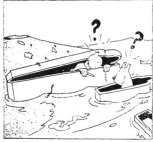

François Ayroles has applied the method more subjectively. The strip top right is a one-page reduction of Proust's *À la recherche du temps perdu*.

5. *Re-framing*. There are two methods:

5a. Details of an existing strip are excerpted and reframed (an Oubapian equivalent of ●haikuisation).

5b. Additions are made to the frames of an existing strip, the original frames becoming no more than components of the new ones.

Example: Art Spiegelman *Malpractice Suite* from *Arcade*, 6 (1976). (Extract overleaf)

6. *Graphic Reinterpretation*. A strip is redrawn according to predetermined criteria. The genre can be modified (a humorous strip redrawn as a detective strip); iconographic elements can be reversed (an Oubapian equivalent of ●antonymic translation), viewpoints can be altered, etc.

7. *Hybridisation*. Two strips are combined into one, by alternating their frames, or exchanging their texts. Other procedures are possible:

Example: The famous strip in the "Schoolkids issue" of *Oz* magazine (May 1970). The head of Rupert Bear was superimposed on to an undeniably prurient cartoon by Robert Crumb. This became the principal reason for the magazine's prosecution for obscenity. [AB, after TG]

★Oucuipo. *Ouvroir de Cuisine Potentielle* (Workshop for Potential Cuisine). Late Definitive Interim President: Noël ●Arnaud. The Oucuipo's sole works to date are its two publications.

★ Bibliothèque Oucuipienne, La (BOC). (Emblem by Gil, right)

★BOC1. Harry Mathews, *Cuisine de Pays*, trans. Marie Chaix, afterword by Noël Arnaud (Plein Chant, 1990).[1]

★BOC2. Noël Arnaud, *D'une Théorie culinaire* (*Towards a Theory of Cuisine*) (Plein Chant, 1996).

★Plagiary, anticipatory.
It is worth noting Georges Perec's application of ●permutation to cuisine in his *81 Easy-Cook Recipes for Beginners*.[2] [AB]
See also ●Topical N + 7.

★Work of the Oucuipo. The scope of the Oucuipo is immense. The relationship between cooking and painting has been commonly remarked upon since ancient times. That between cooking and music has been the subject of only one, albeit extensive study: *La Langue verte et la cuite: Étude gastrophonique sur la marmythologie musiculinaire* [by Noël Arnaud

& Asger Jorn, published in 1968 by Jean-Jacques Pauvert; all three appear here at the launch party]. There, homage is

incidentally paid to Claude Lévi-Strauss, our master who was the first to suggest a close relationship between the tongue as the organ of taste, and song as an expression of gastronomic pleasure. While we are convinced that attractive presentation is needed to give any dish its full worth (and the Bibliothèque Oucuipienne will highlight many instances of this), we do not follow certain bogus hedonists who maintain that food is for contemplation and nothing more. No, food for us is something to be eaten (and drunk: œnology clearly belongs to the Oucuipo's domain). At the same time, we do not reject the psychoanalytic significance assigned in this century to the philosophical term *hedonism*: a gourmet's yearning for marrowbones may indeed be symptomatic of genital hedonism, the love of tripe may indicate anal hedonism, and one who enjoys sweetbreads or tongue (smoked or not) may be an oral hedonist. Should we then ask: so what? No, because sooner or later we will be given a lesson (a practical lesson) in anthropophagy. This ancient culinary art has hitherto been considered from an essentially subsidiary viewpoint, that of morality and religion (even though religious anthropophagy is not unknown and traces of it remain among us). But we do not expect that lesson to occur in the near future, and our personal experience of anthropophagy is only rudimentary: no more than the painful, accidental auto-anthropophagy (a far cry from the decorum demanded at a distinguished gastrosophical banquet) that occurs when we bite our tongue or swallow it.[3]

[NA, trans IW]

★**Ouhistpo.** *Ouvroir d'Histoire Potentielle* (Workshop for Potential History). Founded in 1993.

The Ouhistpo is an incarnation of the *Commission de l'Ordre et du Temps* of the Cymbalum Pataphysicum (see ●College of 'Pataphysics). Its members include Gilles Firmin, Thieri Foulc, Paul Gayot, and Pascal Ory. USA correspondent: Dr. Joseph Love.

Correspondence address: c/o Paul Gayot, Courtaumont, 51500 Sermiers, France.

★**Collective Publications of the Ouhistpo (CPH).**

★**CPH1.** *Exercices d'histoire potentielle,* a special issue of *Monitoires du Cymbalum Pataphysicum,* 37, 15 September 1995.

★**Plagiary, anticipatory.** ●Palindromic histories: Juliette Raabe *Journal d'une ménagère inversée;* Alain Nadaud *L'Envers du temps;* Camille Flammarion *Lumen, histoire d'une âme;* Philip K. Dick *Counter-Clock World.*

Historical rhymes and rhythms: Velimir Khlebnikov *The Book of Precepts;* Thos. Joseph Moult *Prophecies;* G. Ferrari *L'Aritmetica nella storia; China and Europe;* Arnold Toynbee *A Study of History;* Raymond Queneau *Les Fleurs bleues;* Antoine-Antonin Cournot *Considérations sur la marche des idées et des événements dans les temps modernes.*

I + n (Incident + n, see ●W ± n): Daniel Milo *Une histoire-fiction: l'ère de la Passion.*

Historical ●lipograms: Many examples among science-fiction narratives, not least the theme of parallel universes. Also: Renouvier *L'Uchronie;* Roger Caillois *Pilate;* Robert Aron *Victoire à Waterloo;* Roger Fogel *Railroads and American Economic Growth;* Rachilde *A l'auberge de l'Aigle;* L. Geoffroy *Napoléon apocryphe;* Simon Leys *La Mort de Napoléon;* Bernard Quillet *La véritable Histoire de France.* [PG]

★**Work of the Ouhistpo.** An initial progress report was published in ★CPH1: historical ●lipograms; historical ●sonnets (with rhymes of situations); the *History of Your Choice* of the fall of the Soviet Union (see ●multiple-choice narrative); an essay on the application of the technique of the ●spoonerism to 'historical words'; a ●palindromic history of the 20th century from the year 2000 to 1901; and, with the aid of the ▲Oulipopo, a transposition of the ●W ± n method, here called I + n, to the Crucifixion, shifted 13 centuries into the future. [PG]

★**Oumathpo.** *Ouvroir des Mathématiques Potentielles* (Workshop for Potential Mathematics). One of the early Ou-x-pos founded at the instigation of François ●Le Lionnais. Its members included those influenced by ●Bourbaki: Raymond ●Queneau, Jacques ●Roubaud, Paul ●Braffort, and Le Lionnais; the combinatorial mathematicians Giancarlo Rota and Claude ●Berge; and the logicians Georg Kreisel and (again) Paul Braffort.

According to Jacques Roubaud, the principal objective of the group was to make available to mathematics — in return for the structures that mathematics had contributed to literature (especially to the ●Oulipo) — mathematical applications of what had heretofore been purely literary procedures. [HM, from material supplied by PB & JR]

★**Oumupo.** *Ouvroir de Musique Potentielle* (Workshop for Potential Music). Founded in 1985.

Members (UK): Andrew Hugill, Christopher Hobbs, John White.

Correspondence address: c/o BCM Atlas Press, 27 Old Gloucester st., London WCIN 3XX.

★**Collective Publications of the Oumupo (CPM).**

From a completely different Oumupo (www.oumupo.com)

come these CDs, each with a booklet containing a comic strip by a member of the ★Oubapo; the history of the Oumupo is indeed complex!

★**CPM1.** *Oumupo 1*, Matthew Eliot, strip by Jochen Gerner.

★**CPM2.** *Oumupo 2*, Rob Swift, strip by Étienne Lécroart.

★**CPM3.** *Oumupo 3*, Rubin Steiner, strip by Luz.

★**History of the Oumupo.** The original Oumupo was created by François ●Le Lionnais and the composers Pierre Barbaud and Michel Philipot. The latter set to music Le Lionnais's famous sonnet *La rien que la toute la* (the ●*only the wholly the*), performed by a soprano *assoluta* at the homage to François Le Lionnais at the Centre Pompidou on 30 November 1983. This Oumupo was also a branch of another group, CeMaMu (founded by Iannis Xenakis), to which Le Lionnais and Paul ●Braffort belonged for a time.

After succumbing to neglect, the Oumupo was given new life in Bordeaux: ever since Friday 13 November 1992, a group has met there regularly. Its secretary is Catherine Gilloire and members include Didier Bessière, Jean-Raphael Bobo, Eric Boulain, Bertrand Grimaud, Dominique Gruand, Patrick Guyho, Franck Pruja, Bertrand Sauvagnac, and Françoise Valéry. Records of these meetings (twenty-five to date) have been kept in the fashion of Jacques ●Bens's (see ●Minutes of the Oulipo). There are plans to publish the group's most significant compositions in a work that will present many of the constraints it has employed, among them ●N + 7 (easy to imagine); the "reduction (*à la* FLL) of a musical work to a single note" (the note E, in honour of Georges ●Perec; cf. Going for the ●limit); the "*mélodie du jour*" (each note of a melodic line corresponding to a letter of the day on which the meeting is held); the "A.F." method (from Brahms's use of those letters as musical notes), etc.

Meanwhile other Oumupos have emerged. Philippe Cathé and Denis Tagu, who regularly meet and work together in Paris, have collaborated with Remy Bellenger, Stanley ●Chapman and Andrew Hugill in the production of recordings for the *Sous-Commission des Cliques et Claques* of the Cymbalum

Pataphysicum (see ●College of 'Pataphysics). They thus established a link with the British Oumupo, which had worked for years unaware of its French colleagues. The work of members of this group is briefly outlined below (★Work of the Oumupo).

[AH & PB]

★**Limit, going for the.** Alphonse ●Allais *Funeral March for the Burial of a Great Deaf Man* (1897).

See also Going for the ■●limit, Anticipatory ●plagiary.

★**Plagiary, anticipatory.** Devising new procedures of composition and performance has been a hallmark of 20th-century music. Schoenberg's twelve-tone system is only the most famous of these innovations, and many well-known composers have made their own inventive contributions (almost as if all of them were unconscious Oumupians). The attention of the Oumupo, however, has focused on particular individuals and procedures:

— Percy Grainger: "Free Music" (musical machines constructed to achieve continuously sliding, arrhythmic music)

— Conlon Nancarrow: "Studies for Player Piano" (entirely original rhythm studies, laboriously punched out on piano rolls to produce superhuman feats of execution)

— Harry Partch: music in just intonation (from the pioneer of non-tempered systems and bizarre instrument construction)

— Change-ringing and other number-based musical

procedures (for a detailed account of this, see *The Nine Tailors* by Dorothy L. Sayers)

— Franco-Flemish composers of the 15th and 16th centuries: these composers were the trailblazers of Oumupian procedures. Typical examples include: the use of gematria by Jacob Obrecht and Josquin des Pres; Johannes Ockeghem's *Missa Prolationum*; Baude Cordier's 'graphic' scores in the shape of a heart, or circular canons; and Ghiselin Danckerts's four-part puzzle canon on *Ave Maris Stella*, notated in the form of a chess-board. [AH]

Auguste Gundelicorum Melchio: Kriegstein/ Excudebat, Anno/π. XLIX.

★**Work of the Oumupo.** The three main areas of Oumupian research:

1) potential compositional systems or methods
2) potential performance
3) historical research (outlined in the previous entries).

The creation of new forms in music is not guaranteed by the devising of new systems or procedures, since musical form is such a complex and substrated thing in itself. The system of tonality, for example, operates by means of a set of dynamic interrelationships between tonal centres and motivic ideas which musical analysis constantly struggles to articulate. The very impossibility of defining this system once and for all is what guarantees its survival. Music strives to be free from constraint (cf. ●*Contrainte*).

The existence of an Oumupo, therefore, would seem to be at best somewhat self-contradictory, and at worst pointless. This central paradox does not deter the members of the present Oumupo, since it is precisely that sense of the innate freedom of music that inspires them to work on their various projects. As with the ●*Oulipo*, the diligent study of historical procedures and the constant devising of new methods is not necessarily designed to produce new music, but it often does and some of the results have been extraordinary indeed. Three examples from British Oumupians might serve to illustrate this thesis.

In *L'Auteur se retire* for solo piano, Christopher Hobbs applies a ●lipogrammatic procedure to the work of certain composers by removing notes which correspond to the musical letters in their composers' names. For example, Bach's name gives the possibility of excising from a chosen work precisely those musical "letters" which have provided thematic material for celebrated works by Liszt, Reger, and Alban Berg. The results of this procedure have a fascinating awkwardness of rhythm which makes performance a matter of considerable virtuosity, as well as having a limited modal palette that evokes cultures far removed from Western classical music.

For over two decades now, John White has composed *machine pieces* as part of his vast output. A machine piece may be described as the result of a process applied to a given sound-world, in the same way that a Welsh rarebit may be said to be the result of a mechanical process applied to the world of bread and cheese. White has thus produced works such as *Drinking and Hooting Machine* (in which a number of performers drink from and blow into bottles according to a given procedure); *Jew's-Harp Machine* (which permutationally processes the sounds "ging-gang-gung-ho"); and *Newspaper Reading Machine*, in which the performers emit sounds according to the arrangement of punctuation marks, etc. in selected newspaper articles that are read throughout the performance.

Révélations et Diversités is the final section of Andrew Hugill's large-scale choral work *Les Origines humaines*, which explores the work of Jean-Pierre Brisset. The score comprises a "board" of 324 squares, divided into four quadrants of 9 x 9 squares each. Each quadrant delimits the region of one of the choral groups. Each square represents one bar of common time and contains either silence or musical settings of two syllables (one short, one long) consisting of the basic phonemes of the French language arranged combinatorially. Each singer moves individually and at will across this musical "game board" and the result is a kind of "Tower of Babel" from which words and musical phrases emerge. [AH]

★**Ouphopo. *Ouvroir de Photographie Potentielle* (Workshop for Potential Photography). Founded 6 April 1995.**

The Ouphopo is a registered non-profit making association whose legally declared ambition is: "to promote the 'Pataphysics (cf. ●College of 'Pataphysics) of photography through publications, exhibitions, or any other means of communication in existence or yet to be invented, in France as abroad. The field of research specific to the ●*ouvroir* is photography using constraints." [PE]

Founder members: Catherine Day, Paul Day, Marc Décimo, Paul Edwards, Gila, Gersan Moguérou, Yves Simon, Marcel Troulay.

Correspondence: Paul Edwards, 8, rue Dareau, 75014 Paris.

★**Collective Publications of the Ouphopo (CPP).**

★**CPP1.** *L'Ouphopo*, edited by Paul Edwards, 19 issues to date.

★**CPP2.** *L'Ouphopo et ses amis*, catalogue of the exhibition held at the Centre Daviel, Paris, October/November 1997.

★**Plagiary, anticipatory.** The Ouphopo has been compiling *An Annotated History of Photography by Constraints* since 1995. Too extensive to present fully here, a number of its entries feature in the ★Table of Ouphopian Constraints.

★**Table of Ouphopian Constraints.** (Overleaf) First appearing in *L'Ouphopo* 3 (February 1997), the table lists the scope of the group's current research and historical antecedents. Explanations of many of the procedures may be found in the next entry, or by comparing those that are cross-referenced by bullets.

See also ●Systematisation, ●Queneleyev's Table; ■*Grande Œuvre*, The ■Hundred Flowers; Outrapo, the ★R^{rrrrr} structure.

★**Work of the Ouphopo.** Some group projects underway:

1. an anthology of photographs of words;
2. "10^{14} Faces", a photo-fit of human facial expressions;
3. "the Navel", photo-detective story and ●palindrome;
4. the conversion of household objects into *camerae obscurae*;
5. the creation of a photographic labyrinth on the Web.

Some individual projects underway:

Paul and Catherine Day: 1. "Eye-reliefs", the creation of large, globular, clay *bas*- and high-relief sculptures recreating in 3-D famous photographs as they would have appeared on the back of the eye of the photographer.

2. "Photo-*bas*-relief", research in collaboration with Dijon chemists on compounds that expand along a single axis on contact with light in order to manufacture a light-sensitive clay surface that produces a low *bas*-relief when left in a *camera obscura*.

Gersan Moguérou: "Onomometric co-ordinate portraits" (cf. ■Onomometry). Final version of the computer program that morphs faces according to the relative position in the alphabet of the letters of the subject's first and second names.

Gila: Projects include converting unexpected objects into pin-hole cameras (show-room dummies, cars, oil drums, an upper-storey bedroom) and leaving them in public places for the day (e.g. "36 Hours at my Dentist's"); research into the fundamentals of stereoscopy (■anamorphic, panoramic, imbricated, ■combinatorial, contradictory, 60 metre eye-distance).

SUBJECT CHOICE	TIME	SPACE	LITERATURE
Words	***Real time***	***Regular intervals***	***Exposure "meter"***
(Ouphopo)	Unfixed image of the *camera*	(Tsuchida)	***Electro-encephalogram***
Non-visible	*obscura*	***Totality***	(Lewis ●Carroll)
Electromagnetic radiation	***Discontinuous over area***	180° panorama	***Optogram***
Ultraviolet (Talbot)	Photo composite (Spoerri)	360° (Kircher)	(Villiers de l'Isle-Adam, Jules
X-ray (Röntgen)	Polaroid composite (Hockney)	40th parallel (O'Sullivan)	Verne, Clarétie)
Spirit photographs (*Homage to*	Atemporal double-impression	Exoskeleton (Baldus)	***Metaphor***
Balzac, Ouphopo)	(Peillet)	***3-D***	Non-coincidence of caption and
Fairy photographs (Conan Doyle)	***Classic unity of time (+ 3-D)***	Stereoscopy	subject (*La Femme*, Man
2-D	Model Theatre (Poulter)	Anaglyphs etc.	Ray)
Photogenic drawings (Talbot)	Photo-Play (*Bruges-la-Morte*, PE)	Stereostenopanoranamorphosis	***Holorhyme*** (●)
Totality	Stereotrope (Desvignes)	(Gila)	*Homage to J.-P. Brisset* (Marc
Social classes (Sander)	*Diodaguerreorama obscura* (PE)	Stand-up (*Les Halles, Façade*, PE)	Décimo & PE)
Time-dependent	***Condensation***	Origami with pins (PE)	***Literary illustration***
Immobility (1839-1850)	8 hour exposure (Niépce)	Spring-loaded (PE)	Topographical
Movement (Kodak)	15 minute exposure (Daguerre)	Photo-*bas-relief* (P. Day)	Black on black (PE)
x mistakes y for z (●)	***Subject-dependent***	***Composite***	Mutually exclusive readings
(Macaire, Oshima)	*Lustgarten* (Petitpierre)	Portraits (Galton)	(*Pamela*, PE)
Shadow/contour-dependent	Boredom (Arbus)	***Circular***	Photo-Humuments (*The Id*, PE)
Photograms	***Regular intervals + classical***	$x \subset y \subset z$ (x = z) (Michals)	Photo-detective story ●palin-
Literary-topographical dep-	***unity of space***	3 Cows (PE)	drome (*The Navel*, PE)
endent	Chronophotography (Muybridge)	*Photographic Table* (Gila)	Puns (Marc Décimo)
(Tauchnitz et al.)	Single-plate chronophotography	***Russian Doll effect***	
Lipophotogram	(Marey)	Portrait with portrait (Anon.)	
Exclusion of unpleasantness		Photograph of a photograph (PE,	
(Doisneau)		Gila et al.)	
Isomorphism (■)		***Partial angle of vision***	***Metonymy (continued)***
Smart bombs		Vertical (Bauhaus et al.)	Displacement of retina on to
Photo-Fit		Horizontal (Rolleiflex et al.)	external 'eye': *camera*
10^{14} Faces (Ouphopo)		Perspectivist (Dibbets, Rousse)	*obscura* inside other objects
In nature (Uelsmann)		***Partially bounded***	(18th century)
Observed in 2 subjects (Erwitt)		By frame (Cartier-Bresson)	Conversion of objects into
Image – substance (photo-		By Sabatier effect (Man Ray)	*camerae obscurae* (Gila)
sensitive ashes of the dead)		By selective focus (P.H.Emerson)	***Deformation***
Between subject & frame		***Measurement***	By lens (Brandt)
(W. Evans)		Photometry (the science of)	By large-format camera
Between camera & world		*Bertillonnage* (Bertillon, anthro-	movements
(reflections)		pologists et al.)	By mirrors (circus: Kertesz;
Between print & world		***Condensation***	controlled mirror bending:
(geometric photography)		Photomicrography	Pol Bury)
Between negative & after-image		2nd degree micrography	Multiple reflections
(part-solarisation, Man Ray)		(Brewster)	(Vortography, A.L. Coburn)
		Metonymy	■Onomometric co-ordinates
		Eye on end of finger (spy camera)	(Chapman/G. Moguérou)

Marcel Troulay is currently sorting his archive of more than 45 years of (1) "found" pataphysical photographs, and (2) conscious pataphysical experiments sent him by Emmanuel Peillet and other members of the ●College of 'Pataphysics.

Paul Edwards is currently working on (1) the literary works of mad photographers with a view to publishing an annotated bilingual anthology; (2) "photo-plays". He is also the author of *An Annotated Bibliography of Photo-Illustrated Literature and General Photo-Literature (1839–1939, Great Britain and France)* (French University Microfilms, December 1996, but it will be continuously updated). [PE]

★**Outrapo.** *Ouvroir de Tragécomédie Potentielle* **(Workshop for Potential Tragi-Comedy). Founded VI/IV/1991 at the Angel, St. Giles High st., London.**

Patron Saint: Sir Tom Stoppard.

Members: Milie von Bariter, Stanley ●Chapman, Cosima Schmetterling, Anne Feillet, Nita Le Nelfe, Jean-Pierre Poisson, Félix Pruvost.

42 Guardian Angels: Appia, Aristophanes, Carlet de Chamberlain, Corneille, Craig, Duquesnois, Fechter, Garnier, Goethe, Gogol, Goldoni, Gozzi, Grabbe, Gravolet, Gryphius, Guthrie, Hardy, Hédelin d'Aubignac, Ionesco, Irving, ●Jarry, Keaton, Labiche, Laurel, Maeterlinck, Marlowe, Plautus, Polti, Robertson, Rotrou, ●Roussel, St.-Denis, Schiller, Sheridan, Tardieu, Tchekhov, Terence, Terriss, Torma, Vanbrugh, Vian, Wilde.

Correspondence: 68, rue du Cardinal Lemoine, 75005 Paris; and 264 Ramsay rd., London E7 9EY.

Website: http://outrapo.site.voila.fr/index.jhtml

★**Collective Publications of the Outrapo (CPT).**

★**CPT1.** *Outrapo's Revue.* 11 issues to date edited by M. von Bariter.

★**CPT2.** *A la Trappe!* a special issue of *Monitoires du Cymbalum Pataphysicum*, 39, 15 March 1996.

★**CPT3.** *Centenaire d'Ubu*, in *Colloque Jarry*, éd. L'Étoile Absinthe / SAAJ, 77-78, 1998.

★**CPT4.** *La Réunion*, special issue, *Carnets du Collège de 'Pataphysique*, 19, 15 March 2005.

★**Performances.** Amongst others: world première of *Le Bétrou* by Julien Torma, Théâtre Kremlin-Bicêtre, 1994; performances at the invitation of the Oulipo, Jussieu-University, Paris, 1998 & 2000; participation in the exhibition by the ●Collège de 'Pataphysique, Chartres, 2000; Outrapist performance at the Festival "Les Jeux dans la Littérature", Geneva, 2000; reading of *L'Hôtel de Sens* by Jacques ●Roubaud and Paul ●Fournel, Jussieu University, Paris, 2002; Outrapist demonstrations for the "Réunion de l'Ouxpo", Centre d'Animation Vercingétorix, Paris, 2005.

★**Plagiary, anticipatory.** The most familiar Outrapian constraint in western classical theatre is the Law of the Three Unities. The oriental tradition offers another, the prohibition of female actors in Japan in 1625, and young male actors in 1657. These restrictions led to the creation of "Onnagata", the basis of most Japanese theatrical tradition.

In France there is a less familiar instance, but one which demonstrates that censorship can be a liberation. In the late 17th century, Italian companies were barred from appearing in France, so native strolling players took over the Italian plays and made the roles their own with great success.

However, this aroused the jealousy of the Comédie Française which outlawed all spoken dialogue except in its own theatre. To overcome this restriction, the travelling players divided up their plays into soliloquies and performed nothing but monologues. One actor would say his lines, run off into the wings, and another would appear and reply. The performances were more successful than before.

The Comédie Française therefore decided to outlaw all speech outside its premises. The players got round this by singing their roles, thereby creating French Operetta. This in turn aroused the ire of the Academy of Music, which forbade their

R	Ar - ena	Rrrrrr	Ar - peggio	Ar - ticulation	Ar - t	Ar - tifice
Ar - chitecture	—Everybody (cast, stage-hands, directors, managers, usherettes) on stage. —Potential disapp-earances, exits, traps & invisibility.	—Emotion in reverse. —Upturned images. —Harlequinade. —Alienation & audience participation. —Peep-shows & strippers.	—Gravolet's blockings in Bosch's polaroids. —Interlocking fables. —Composite translations. —Plays within plays within plays etc.	—The psycho-alphabetical ghost. —Braille, Morse & Semaphore. —The actor's nightmare (The Generation Game).	—The character transformation & transplantation machine. —Stencilled make-up. —Sanskrit, Noh, Zulu, Eskimo, Limbo theatre.	—Reduced cast-lists. —*Dramatis personae* ± 7. —Pogo-sticks, stilts, swings, springs, ladders & ropes. —*"Ampersand & Espernète"* (Noël ●Arnaud)
Ar - omatic	—■Perspective (Escher, Palladio, Vicenza, Piranesi, Globe, Inigo Jones). —Musical tragedy & balletic melodrama. —Circus silhouettes.	—Evolutionism. —■Anamorphosis, Patamorphosis. —Puppetry. —●Acrostics. —●Spoonerisms, Patathesis. —Aerobatical & submarine shows.	—Arithmetical, algebraic & computerised action. —Scenic subtractions. —●Lipogrammatic & logarithmic lines.	—Rhyming panto-mimes. —Screams, sighs, cries, howls, whispers, coughs, sneezes, asides, boos, echoes & noises on & off. —Hyperbole.	—The director's hand in the bush & the prompter's pointer in the pit. —Odorama, Flavorama. —Magnetic, flying, & stolen theatre.	*Unity of Character* (↓)
R (Rolling & Recurring)	—Placard & pendulum plays. —Rosetta Stone & Biblical plays. —Fairground, chap-book, squatter & rooftop happenings.	—Temporal dissection. —Underground (conveyor belt & escalator) scripts. —Elimination & analysis. —Futurist synthesis.	—Deliberate omissiveness. —Blackout & avoidance. —Barnyard bingo. —Dumb-show mummers. —Sub- and sur-titles.	—Typographical adaptation. —Corpsing. —Programmed demystification. —Pickleherring, Punch, Judy & Dog Toby.	*Unity of Style* (↓)	
Ar - gument	—Best foot forward. —Starting orders: Curtain up! Over-ture, prologue, whistle, pistol. —9 + 3 (or 400) blows.	—Gestural rounds & canons. —●Palindromic charades. —*"La Guida di Bragia"* (Lewis ●Carroll) on derelict railway platforms.	—Imaginary illusions, liaisons and illuminations. —Pepper's Ghost. —Prismatic mirrors. —One second plays, eternal plays. —Cycloramic dreams.	*Unity of Speech* (↓)		
Ar - cadia	—Topographical chronology. —Adjacent auditoria. —Collaboration with other Ou-x-pos. —Musical comedies and uneasy chairs.	—Time held up & wasted: procrast-ination. —Beds in boxes. —Going over the top. —Teepee trapezes.	*Unity of Action* (↓)			
Ar - canum	—Circular, oval, Greek & Roman, spiral and geomet-rically Boolean theatres. —The Wooden O. —Bring down the safety & final curtain.	*Unity of Time* (↓)				
	Unity of Place (↓)					

See also ●Systematisation, ●Queneleyev's Table; ■*Grande Œuvre*, The ■Hundred Flowers; Ouphopo ★Table of Ouphopian Constraints.

singing. A new theatrical form was then created: the actors held up cue-cards (like subtitles or karaoke) and mimed the actions while the public spoke or sang their roles. And their plays were more popular than ever... [Milie von Bariter]

★R⁣ʳʳʳʳʳ Structure, The. (Opposite) The cubic ziggurat or inverted Tower of Babel used in warming-up and rehearsal exercises in the gymnasium of the Outrapo.

As a brief explanation it should be remembered that the letter (or sound) *R* has far greater significance at the Comédie Française than at Stratford-upon-Avon, where its importance is still largely ignored, even in the Scottish play. Since the Outrapo (like all the Ou-x-pos) is essentially a French institution, it would seem churlish to attempt to translate its inspirational *R* by any of the remaining 25 letters of the alphabet. [SC]

★Work of the Outrapo. The Outrapo is affiliated to the ●College of 'Pataphysics. Its co-founder, Stanley ●Chapman, *Régent d'Épidictique* of the College, describes its work in that context:

Although a founder-member of the ●Oulipo, it has always seemed to me far more necessary — pataphysically speaking — that there should be an ●ouvroir dedicated to the theatre in which ●Jarry performed and for which he wrote the works for which he will always be principally known. In a College dominated by philosophers, professors, pedagogues, pedants, explorers, mathematicians, poets, novelists, and critics, the theatre itself remained a mere pretext and an abstraction until a chance meeting with Milie von Bariter enabled us to reinstate its multi-dimensional aspects and found the Outrapo on the site of the Globe Theatre in London on 6 April 1991 (vulg.).

Annual performances have been given in amphitheatres and fairgrounds in and around Paris (see ★Performances). Eleven issues of a review containing detailed illustrated descriptions of these events have been published.

Much work has been based upon Oulipian principles (carefully avoiding the cruelty of the word "●constraint"), but we have also extended far beyond this into potential theatrical techniques of production — particularly regarding ●Boolean

Theatre, whose overlapping and interlocking Escherian architecture has enabled La Fontaine to rub shoulders with Tchekhov; Ionesco to hold hands with Hugo; Shakespeare to mug with Bruce Forsyth; Lorenzaccio (Sarah Bernhardt and Musset) to usurp Ubu (Jarry and Gémier) amongst many others. The ●N ± 7 method applied to the dramatis personae *has produced startling effects and a major project in rehearsal for the future is the production of* A Hundred Thousand Billion Dramatic Pieces. *[SC]*

1. Originally published as the title story of *Country Cooking and Other Stories* (Burning Deck Press, Providence, RI, 1980); reprinted in *The Way Home: Collected Longer Prose* (Atlas Press, 1989 & 1998). [AB]

2 Translated by David Bellos in the Perec issue of *The Review of Contemporary Fiction*, Spring 1993, vol. 13, no. 1, pp.34-43.

3 The French expressions have secondary meanings. *Avaler sa langue*, "to swallow one's tongue", also has the sense of (a) "to hold one's tongue, to keep silent", and (b) "to bite one's tongue", in all senses. [IW]

ATLAS PRESS

For a complete listing
of all titles available from Atlas Press
and the London Institute of 'Pataphysics
see our on-line catalogue at:

www.atlaspress.co.uk

To receive automatic notification of new publications including our ongoing Oulipo publications
sign on to the emailing list at this website.

Atlas Press, 27 Old Gloucester st., London WCIN 3XX

MAKE NOW PRESS

for a list of other books published by Make Now Press, please visit

www.makenow.org

Make Now Press, 8152 Coldwater Canyon, North Hollywood, CA 91605, USA